Gezi at Ten

Studies in Critical Social Sciences Book Series

Haymarket Books is proud to be working with Brill Academic Publishers (www.brill.nl) to republish the *Studies in Critical Social Sciences* book series in paperback editions. This peer-reviewed book series offers insights into our current reality by exploring the content and consequences of power relationships under capitalism, and by considering the spaces of opposition and resistance to these changes that have been defining our new age. Our full catalog of *SCSS* volumes can be viewed at https://www.haymarketbooks.org/series_collections/4-studies-in-critical-social-sciences.

Series Editor
David Fasenfest (York University, Canada)

Editorial Board
Eduardo Bonilla-Silva (Duke University)
Chris Chase-Dunn (University of California–Riverside)
William Carroll (University of Victoria)
Raewyn Connell (University of Sydney)
Kimberlé W. Crenshaw (University of California–LA and Columbia University)
Heidi Gottfried (Wayne State University)
Alfredo Saad-Filho (Queen's University, Belfast)
Chizuko Ueno (University of Tokyo)
Sylvia Walby (Lancaster University)
Raju Das (York University)

Gezi at Ten

Domination, Opposition
and Political Organization

Edited by
Ozan Siso
Ufuk Gürbüzdal
Eren Karaca

Haymarket Books
Chicago, IL

First published in 2024 by Brill Academic Publishers, The Netherlands
© 2024 Koninklijke Brill NV, Leiden, The Netherlands

Published in paperback in 2025 by
Haymarket Books
P.O. Box 180165
Chicago, IL 60618
773-583-7884
www.haymarketbooks.org

ISBN: 979-8-88890-350-6

Distributed to the trade in the US through Consortium Book Sales and Distribution (www.cbsd.com) and internationally through Ingram Publisher Services International (www.ingramcontent.com).

This book was published with the generous support of Lannan Foundation, Wallace Action Fund, and the Marguerite Casey Foundation.

Special discounts are available for bulk purchases by organizations and institutions. Please call 773-583-7884 or email info@haymarketbooks.org for more information.

Cover design by Jamie Kerry and Ragina Johnson.

Printed in the United States.

Library of Congress Cataloging-in-Publication data is available.

*to those we lost in Gezi
and to all those who have suffered injustice
ever since in Turkey and elsewhere*

Contents

Notes on Contributors   IX

1 Introduction
    Political Stagnation over the Past Decade   1
        Ufuk Gürbüzdal

PART 1
In the Footsteps of Gezi

2 The Gezi Popular Rebellion
    A Critical Evaluation   15
        Sungur Savran

3 The Gezi Resistance at the Edge of Populist Rupture   57
        Kürşad Ertuğrul and Aylin Topal

4 A Mirror to the Past, a Step to the Future
    Kernels of Organized Movement in the Gezi Uprising   74
        Gökhan Atılgan and Ezgi Kaya Hayatsever

PART 2
Two, Three, Many Gezis

5 Gezi and the Yellow Vests Protests
    "End of the World, End of the Month, Same Struggle?"   113
        Antoine Dolcerocca, Sebla Ayşe Kazancı and Arca Özçoban

6 Re-visiting the "Populist Moment"
    Geographies of Grassroots Movements and Left Populism in Greece, Spain and Turkey   131
        Athina Arampatzi

PART 3
Dissenting a Step Further beyond Gezi

7   Watchmen as AKP's "Brownshirts"?
    Regime Debate and Police Order in the Post-Gezi Period   161
      Selin Dingiloğlu and Çağlar Dölek

8   In Search of the Labor Movement in Turkey
    A Panoramic Review vis-à-vis the Gezi Uprising   189
      Ezgi Pınar and Adem Yeşilyurt

9   The Legacy of the Gezi Resistance and Its Effects on Turkey's Socialist Movements of the Past Decade   212
      Eren Karaca and Özgür Balkılıç

10 From Gezi to the New Regime
    How the AKP Continued Its Regime-Building after the Gezi Resistance   238
      Fatih Yaşlı

11 Concluding Remarks
    Ten Years of Contradictions and Possibilities   271
      Ufuk Gürbüzdal and Ozan Siso

    Index   279

Notes on Contributors

Athina Arampatzi
is an HFRI Postdoctoral Research Fellow (PI) at the Department of Spatial Planning and Development, Aristotle University of Thessaloniki. She received her PhD degree in Social Geography at the University of Leeds, UK and holds an MSc in Urban Sociology (University of Amsterdam) and an MA in Architecture (Aristotle University of Thessaloniki). Arampatzi's work engages with social innovation, urban governance and social movements, by employing action research and participatory engagement with activist groups. She has published in international academic journals, such as *European Urban and Regional Studies*, *Social Movement Studies* and *Urban Studies*.

Gökhan Atılgan
is a professor at Ankara University Faculty of Communication, Turkey. He is the author of the books *Kemalizm ile Marksizm Arasında Geleneksel Aydınlar: Yön-Devrim Hareketi* [Traditional Intellectuals in Between Kemalism and Marxism: Yön-Devrim Movement], *Behice Boran: Öğretim Üyesi, Siyasetçi, Kuramcı* [Behice Boran: A Scholar, Politician, Theorist]. He is also co-editor of the book *Siyaset Bilimi: Kavramlar, İdeolojiler, Disiplinler Arası İlişkiler* [Political Science: Concepts, Ideologies and Inter-disciplinary Relations] and *Osmanlıdan Günümüze Türkiye'de Siyasal Hayat* [Political Life in Turkey: From the Ottoman Period to the Present]. His research is concerned with Marxism, socialist thought in Turkey and Turkish politics.

Özgür Balkılıç
is an associated professor at Abdullah Gül University, Kayseri. Having received B. Sc. and M. A. degrees from the Middle East Technical University, Ankara, he was admitted to the doctoral program within Department of History at Wilfrid Laurier University, Ontario in 2010. He graduated from this university in 2015 with a thesis entitled as "For the Union Makes Strong: The İstanbul Metal Workers and Their Struggle for Unionization in Turkey, 1947–1970." His research primarily focuses on working class politics, social movements and various aspects of social history of the Turkish Republic during the 20th century. He has published in both national and international journals, including *Turkish Studies, Nationalities Papers, Mülkiye* and SBF. Balkılıç is the writer of two books: *Temiz ve Soylu Türküler Söyleyelim: Türkiye'de Milli Kimlik İnşasında Halk Müziği*, 2015 and *Ekmeğimiz ve Birliğimiz İçin: İstanbul Metal Sektöründe Sınıf Mücadeleleri, 1947–1970*, forthcoming. Moreover, he translated studies of

several prominent scholars, such as Max Weber, Michael Mann, Bernard Lewis, Ira Katznelson and Jeremy Popkin into Turkish. He currently investigates the transformation of âşık/Alevi music in modern urban spaces in Turkey during the 1960s and 1970s.

Selin Dingiloğlu
is an assistant professor in the Department of Political Science and International Relations at Üsküdar University, Istanbul, Turkey. Her primary area of study is political ideologies with an interdisciplinary research interest that spans political sociology, social history, and political philosophy. She is currently working on the lumpenism and radicalism debate across modern political thought as well as Turkish politics. She obtained her BA in Political Science and International Relations from Marmara University, and her MA in Modern Turkish History from Boğaziçi University. She received her PhD in Political Science from Istanbul University, with a dissertation entitled "The Aesthetic Ideology of Turkish Islamism". She is a board member of Social History Research Foundation of Turkey (TÜSTAV).

Antoine Dolcerocca
is Assistant Professor of Sociology at the Alma Mater Studiorum-Università di Bologna, Italy. His research focuses on political economy, environmental sociology, property rights and inequality, and land and natural resource management.

Çağlar Dölek
is an assistant professor in the Department of Sociology at California State Polytechnic University, Humboldt. He works through an interdisciplinary research agenda cross-cutting the fields of critical criminology, police science, political economy, and social history. His research problematizes the formation of state power with the advent of modern policing and its dialectical association with the contested processes of class formation and social marginalization. He is currently finalizing a book manuscript titled *Policing Slums in Turkey: Crime, Resistance, and the Republic on the Margin* that is under contract with the Edinburgh University Press. He serves on the editorial boards of the *Journal of Justice, Power and Resistance*, *Humboldt Journal of Social Relations*, and *Praksis*, a Turkey-based journal of social sciences that embraces the heterodox tradition of historical materialism.

Kürşad Ertuğrul

is a professor in the Department of Political Science and Public Administration at the Middle East Technical University in Ankara, Turkey. His fields of interest are Turkish politics, European studies, social and political theory, and social movements.

Ufuk Gürbüzdal

is an independent filmmaker and a Ph.D. student in the Department of Political Science and Public Administration at Middle East Technical University. Gürbüzdal completed his bachelor's and master's degrees at Bilkent University. He was employed as a research assistant in the Faculty of Communication at Hasan Kalyoncu University for about three years. His research interests include media and cultural studies and social movements.

Ezgi Kaya Hayatsever

is PhD candidate and Research Assistant in Ankara University Faculty of Communication, Turkey. Her ongoing PhD work focuses on the impact of digital labour on journalistic regimes.

Eren Karaca

received her PhD degree from the Department of Sociology at Binghamton University after attaining her BS and MS degrees from Middle East Technical University in Turkey. Currently, she works as an adjunct lecturer at TED University in Ankara. Her scholarly interests lie in the fields of social policy, health policies, political economy and state-capital relations.

Sebla Ayşe Kazancı

holds a master's degree in Human Rights from Sciences Po Paris. Her academic interests revolve around the intersection of social, economic, and cultural rights, particularly in the context of gender equality.

Arca Özçoban

holds a master's degree in Social Sciences from Humboldt University of Berlin. His academic interests include political sociology, political economy, and state-society relations in Turkey.

Ezgi Pınar

is a lecturer and researcher at the Faculty of Political Science at Istanbul University. She has conducted postdoctoral studies at Philipps-Universität Marburg, Freie Universität Berlin, Science-Po, and the University of Konstanz.

Her research interests include theories of the state and neoliberal restructuring, critical political economy, labour politics, and Turkish politics. Pınar has published on various topics, including the integration of Syrian migrant workers into the labour market in Turkey, labour force management, and state-capital relations in Turkey, with a particular focus on education policy. Her most recent publication explores social reproduction theory. Additionally, she is a member of the editorial board of *Praksis*.

Sungur Savran

received his BA in Politics at Brandeis University, Massachusetts, USA, and his PhD in Economics at Istanbul University, Turkey. He has taught at Istanbul University, Faculty of Economics, and (as a visiting professor) at several US colleges, including the Graduate Faculty of the New School for Social Research, New York. Savran currently teaches at Istanbul Okan University, Faculty of Humanities and Social Science. He has published articles in *Monthly Review*, *Capital and Class*, *Khamsin* and other journals, and has edited and written chapters for several books on Turkey and Marxist economic theory published in the US and Britain, as well as many books and articles in Turkish. Savran is currently preparing a book titled *General Theory of the Modern Age* to be published by Brill. He is on the editorial board of the journal of theory and politics *Devrimci Marksizm*, published quarterly in Turkish, and its English-language annual edition, *Revolutionary Marxism*. He has worked extensively as a trade union educator. Savran is actively engaged in internationalist Marxist politics within the Revolutionary Workers Party (DIP) of Turkey and the International Socialist Centre Christian Rakovsky.

Ozan Siso

is a researcher who specialises in international political economy, theories of state, and strategies of collective action. After attaining his dual Bachelor's degrees in Sociology and French and Francophone Studies from The Pennsylvania State University, Siso received his Master of Science degree in Equality Studies from the University College Dublin. He currently works as an editor for the *Marx and Philosophy Review of Books* located in the United Kingdom.

Aylin Topal

is an Associate Professor of the Department of Political Science and Public Administration at Middle East Technical University. She serves as the Chairperson of Latin and North American Studies at the same university. She holds a PhD in Political Science from the New School for Social Research in New York. Previously, she was a Visiting Scholar at Oxford, Harvard and Pittsburgh Universities. Topal's research interest lies in the political economy of development, social movements and agrarian change. Her articles have been published in high ranking SSCI journals such as *Journal of Urban Affairs*, *Critical Sociology*, *International Journal of Urban and Regional Research*, *Climate and Development*, and *Women's Studies International Forum*. She is the editor of the journals *Critical Sociology* and *Praksis*. Topal is one of the editorial board members of the Brill Political Economy book series. She is one of the founders of Global Sustainability University.

Fatih Yaşlı
is an assistant professor at Bolu Abant İzzet Baysal University in Turkey. He received his PhD from the Department of Public Administration and Political Science at Ankara University in 2008. Yaşlı is a scholar and writer known in Turkey for his books and columns. His studies particularly focus on Turkey's political history, nationalism, fascism, and Islamism. His published works include *Kinimiz Dinimizdir: Türkçü Faşizm Üzerine bir İnceleme* [Our Grudge Is Our Religion: A Study on Turkist Fascism], *Türkçü Faşizmden Türk-İslam Ülküsüne* [From Turkist Fascism to the Turkish-Islamic Ideal], *Antikomünizm, Ülkücü Hareket ve Türkeş* [Anticommunism, the Nationalist Movement, and Türkeş].

Adem Yeşilyurt
is a PhD candidate in Sociology at EHESS (Paris, France). His research interests include digital labour, future of work, coworking spaces, political economy of media, social movements, and everyday life. His doctoral research focuses on the spatiotemporal transformation of work in digital capitalism, particularly in the case of coworking spaces. He has been a founding member of the Kocaeli Academy for Solidarity, and editorial board member of *Praksis* (in Turkish) and *Journal of Class & Culture*. He is currently co-editing a book on geographies of everyday life.

CHAPTER 1

Introduction

Political Stagnation over the Past Decade

Ufuk Gürbüzdal

> The common and mistaken question of the state and the nature was:
> Where does Transoxiana flow?
> The only and correct reply from a raised hand in the farthest row:
> Into the heart of a pale insurrection by the people's children.[1]

∴

Penning an introduction for an edited volume on the Gezi Resistance is undoubtedly one of the most arduous tasks that I have ever faced. During the Gezi Resistance and since then, we have witnessed a great number of devastating developments; therefore, addressing a tumescent event like Gezi from an objective point of view today is admittedly a difficult task. Nevertheless, it is inevitable to breast this demanding task because it has for the last ten years been on the political agenda of the Justice and Development Party (Turkish: *Adalet ve Kalkınma Partisi*, AKP) leadership. The government's resentment towards Gezi is so implacable that members of professional chambers, writers, and intellectuals alike are to date criminally prosecuted in the infamous Gezi Trial and have been sentenced to lengthy prison terms simply because they participated in the Gezi protests. It is thus not only relevant but necessary to consider the socio-political reverberations of Gezi from a primarily self-reflexive perspective at its decennial.

İmre Azem's documentary *Ecumenopolis: City Without Limits* (2011) tackles the transformation of İstanbul by the neoliberal policies. By expressing the danger of İstanbul transforming into an ecumenopolis entirely made out of concrete, the documentary exposes the imminent threats to the city's habitable

---

1 This stanza, taken from Ece Ayhan's poem *Unknown Student's Monument* (Turkish: *Meçhul Öğrenci Anıtı*), was translated into English from its original by the author of this chapter.

environments and its nature by the capital's rampant gentrification and the constant effort to increase profits.² Taking place only two years after the documentary, Gezi emerged as a societal objection to the concrete ecumenopolis. Within this respect, Gezi was a collective request for the right to the city. The religious-conservative, and therefore intrinsically authoritarian, policies of the AKP governments since 2002 have constantly been aimed at eliminating the colourful diversity of manifold urban lifestyles. Those who did not meet the necessities of this religious-conservative political imaginary were among the people who took the streets during Gezi. On this note, Gezi was also a political demand for respect for different lifestyles, which was raised mainly by the educated urban youth of the Turkish working-class. Not least, Gezi was also the defence of labour in the face of the capital's incessant incursions. Indeed, Turkey's white-collars, who have been victims to the precarization of labour concretized by short-term contracts, endless working hours, and increased rates of unemployment, comprised an indispensable part of Gezi. The tents set up in Taksim Square, as well as the books and food circulated in the "Taksim Commune" for free, were tangible and prefigurative expressions of a utopian kernel that demanded a more humane life experience for the ordinary working people whose everyday lives were stuck in the vicious cycle of production and consumption in a neoliberal society.

At the decennial of Gezi, a reflection on what the political possibilities and barriers might be in front of left-wing politics in Turkey would be a reasonable point of departure to consider Turkey's contemporary socio-political climate from a critical perspective. One of the substantial emerging political opportunities is the withering away of religious and denominational distinctions among the younger generations of Turkey, which traditionally separated the Turkish working-class in cultural and political terms. This is not to say that religious ideologies have been replaced by a *pure* form of working-class culture or consciousness for the youth of Turkey. No social class experience is ever lived as a purely economic one without religious or cultural mediations. From this point of view, innumerable religious codes embodied in divergent social practices and political choices will obviously remain influential in Turkey's socio-political arena.

Nevertheless, newer generations in Turkey have witnessed in their early politicization processes that the one who gained political power by exploiting a discourse of religious and cultural victimization may itself be the authoritarian

---

2   Mücella Yapıcı, one of the interviewees in the documentary, was imprisoned in 2022 as one of the defendants in the aforementioned Gezi Trial.

perpetrator of intense socio-political oppression. I suppose that these generations will probably remain more vigilant against socio-political polarization by religious codes. A whole generation has beholden how religious discourse has been instrumentalized for economic and political ends, and, as it can be deduced from the declining number of young people who consider themselves as "religious" (KONDA, 2018a, 2018b), this will likely have socio-political outcomes in the immediate future of Turkish society. Those who think that this proposition is a product of naive optimism should look more carefully at the women wearing hijabs marching shoulder to shoulder with those in shorts in recent years' May Day parades in Turkey.

On the other hand, I am of the opinion that one of the most obvious obstacles in the way of left-wing politics in Turkey is the widespread mood of political dismay. A discussion of socio-political affairs on a relatively slippery ground that involves human emotions would not lead us to a dead-end of subjectivity, as feared by some, and, to the contrary, would rather help us better apprehend the socio-political reality of Turkey. The feelings of political dismay should be considered as a political obstacle rather than a tenable political opportunity. Ten years after the resistance, we are once again reminded by the continuing political passivity of a significant proportion of the Turkish population that sharpening socio-economic contradictions do not necessarily pave the way for a stronger left-wing political mobilization.

This is not to ignore several notable workers' strikes and student protests of the last years, nor is it to dismiss joint struggles to protect nature by local people and environmental organizations since 2013. In fact, there have since been many protests by professional chambers for their work conditions and the women's organizations have constantly battled for gender equality over the last decade. However, since 2013, the country has been in a stage of consecutive bombings, a military coup attempt, liquidation of left-wing and liberal academy, increased rates of violence, femicide and child abuse, everlasting political scandals, tremendous levels of nepotism, natural disasters, including an earthquake that adversely affected over ten million citizens, and an unending economic crisis. Since 2018, in particular, Turkey has had its share of socio-economic upheaval, with the government's repeated failed attempts at resolving its currency crisis and stabilizing inflation rates. As a result of the excessive emotional baggage that arose out of all the aforementioned, there is today a shared collective feeling of political desperation, reinforced by a state of social disintegration in the current political moment largely deprived of the influence of left-wing politics. We cannot turn our back on the concreteness of this socio-political deadlock that has gradually become more evident within the last ten years.

This pessimistic socio-political landscape should be considered the final phase of a far-reaching societal process since 2013 by which the people have gradually withdrawn from the political scene. In June 2013, Turkish society had a rehearsal of taking its political destiny into its own hands in the Gezi protests. In its aftermath, the collective political energy of the people on the streets was channelized to the *ordinary* political means of representative democracy. Except for a handful of socialist organizations, long-established social democratic political parties or left-wing political traditions of Turkish politics have pointed to ballot boxes as their primary political means. In this viewpoint, the General Election of June 7, 2015, was supposed to be one of the first steps that would return politics to its *ordinary* course.

However, the blood spilled by a bomb attack only two days before the General Elections of June 7 in the Diyarbakır rally of the Peoples' Democratic Party (Turkish: *Halkların Demokratik Partisi,* HDP) marked the beginnings of a climate of fear in Turkey, where collective distress and anxiety would be the *new ordinary* for the following two years. From the bomb explosion in the Diyarbakır rally of HDP to the terrorist attack near İstanbul Beşiktaş Vodafone Park Stadium in December 2016, metropolises and other big cities of Turkey were targeted with consecutive bomb attacks, which took the lives of hundreds. At the end of 2016, one of the main concerns about these attacks was whether the ordinary people of Turkey were becoming desensitized to the violent environment brought about by terrorism. After the explosion near Kızılay Square in the capital city of Ankara on March 13, 2016, only those whose workplaces were located in the area or those who had to commute to work via the Kızılay route passed through the square. With the violent political environment engendered by the military coup attempt on July 15, 2016, squares and streets of Turkey entirely ceased to host gatherings and demonstrations by political groups. With every individual bomb attack and mass shooting that took place from 2015 to 2017, freight and anxiety took over and impeded more and more people from going out on the streets and being in crowded places (KONDA, 2018c: 17).

As the working masses were drawn back from the squares and the streets, individual politicians have regained importance in the political arena of Turkish politics. President Recep Tayyip Erdoğan, who had already emerged victorious from the 2014 Presidential Election of Turkey, has concentrated significant central political authority in his hands following the 2017 Turkish Constitutional Referendum. In parallel to this, the political agenda of the Turkish political opposition parties has been narrowed down to finding a presidential candidate who could take over President Erdoğan, as well as other individual politicians who could win AKP-led municipalities. In due process, direct political actions of the working masses have gradually faded into oblivion. The Turkish political sphere has thus been left to the capricious competition of individual political figures once again.

The 2018 Turkish Presidential Election could be said to be the ultimate political moment when the remnants of the collective political energy of the people left over from Gezi were absorbed in the ballot boxes. A considerable number of the people who filled the squares and streets in Gezi waited for an official statement from the Republican People's Party's (Turkish: *Cumhuriyet Halk Partisi,* CHP) presidential candidate Muharrem İnce on the night of the election to no avail. CHP electorate's waiting for an official statement in front of the television had a symbolic significance as it signified the pullback of the people from the squares and streets. Five years after Gezi, which signified a revolt against social injustice and political irregularities, İnce's statement, which came one day later than the election, was normalising an alleged stealing of the votes by his political opponents based on his argument that the speculated amount of stolen votes were not enough to close the gap between İnce and Erdoğan.

The political repression, particularly in the form of police violence, has negatively impacted the presence of the popular political voice in the squares and streets. However, against rising costs of electricity and gas in 2021, it was not the government, nor was it the police, who impeded the socialist organizations from being present in the streets; it was instead the ordinary citizens with everyday lives who insisted on pulling back from streets and urged waiting for the next election. It has been a widespread belief among Turkish citizens that public demonstrations against the government's policies would politically benefit the government and should therefore be avoided. A significant proportion of the political dissidents in Turkey today consider street protests as a dangerous form of political action that may play into the hands of the government. The lower socio-economic strata of Turkish society patiently await the next elections despite the unbearable severity of the ongoing economic crisis.

This political mentality, which has confined popular political participation to competitions of individual politicians and their political parties, does not welcome any kind of political criticism of opposition candidates who are said to be the sole political solution. It is a consequence of this political mentality in part that the transportation price increase of CHP's İstanbul Metropolitan Municipality was unquestioningly considered a legitimate economic policy by a considerable proportion of the people, who support İstanbul Mayor Ekrem İmamoğlu and felt compelled to defend the price increase, which in fact would be an extra burden on their own wallet. It is true that impeding the possible revival of the revolutionary potential of Gezi has been AKP's principal political concern since 2013 and has ever since led AKP to pursue an openly counter-revolutionary path (Savran, 2022: 24–25). However, the popular pullback from what Gezi politically stood for should not be entirely reduced to the policies or hegemonic triumph of the AKP government. Likewise, the ideological triumph of *the Party of Order*, which could be contextualized in the contemporary Turkish setting as a bloc of capitalists and a great number of political parties from the left to the right should not be overlooked.

It is important to account for the socio-economic catastrophe that large segments of Turkish people have been facing today in order to fully contextualize the people's current political psychology. While the working-class is crushed under a serious economic crisis as a whole, a diverse range of social groups such as youth, women, children, ethnic and religious minorities, LGBTQI+ and certain occupational groups have all been facing peculiar problems that have gradually accrued over the last decade. In the wake of the retreat of popular movement from the streets and concomitant loss of economic security and political rights, these social groups now largely feel obligated to support alternative political candidates to those from AKP without distinguishing their political agendas. These disempowered social segments are in search of the shortest political path to an immediate political change. Even the discussion of long-established and uncompromising differences among the oppositional Nation Alliance's (Turkish: *Millet İttifakı*) constituent parties seems to be provisionally put on hold until a government changeover takes place. In such a political climate, any political criticism against individuals serving at the Nation Alliance, whether in the capacities of the parliament member, mayor, or prospective candidate for these positions, is unwarranted by a significant proportion of the above-mentioned disempowered segments of the society.

One such notable social group is the youth of Turkey, the majority of which have now for a long time sought to leave the country due to concerns about their own future or that of the country. According to the government-run Turkish Statistical Institute's (Turkish: *Türkiye İstatistik Kurumu*, TÜİK) statistics, those whose ages range from 25 to 29 constitute the largest demographic population who emigrated from Turkey in 2019 (TÜİK, 2020). Among prominent causes for the young people's pessimism about their future are nepotism, favoritism, and corruption rampant in Turkey. The reality of nepotism in contemporary Turkey is so bitter that, according to a questionnaire conducted in 2020 (MAK Danışmanlık, 2020), almost four fifth of the Turkish youth is of the opinion that an untalented young individual who receives preferential treatment may get ahead of their peers who are more talented. Furthermore, three fourth of the Turkish youth think that favoritism and preferential treatment are the essential factors of employment in the Turkish labor market, and only one-tenth of the Turkish youth believe that qualification and equal opportunity play an importance in finding a job (MAK Danışmanlık, 2020).

The young people who think that their efforts will not be rewarded in socio-economic terms have been facing a great crisis of meaning which drags them into a cynical attitude towards their formal education and intellectual development. Moreover, the severe devaluation of the Turkish Lira and the aggravating conditions of labor in Turkey have led well-educated people who graduated from the leading universities of Turkey to seek job positions abroad. Over the last five years alone, hundreds of thousands of highly educated people employed in pivotal industries such as the health sector and defense industry quit their jobs to be employed abroad (Independent Türkçe, 2019). The majority of young people who have recently graduated from prestigious Turkish universities prefer working in low-qualified jobs abroad to being employed in Turkey (T24, 2022).

Along with age, other variables such as lifestyle, political views, ethnolinguistic background, religious identity, gender, and socio-economic status seem to play an important role in the feelings of happiness, safety, and security in Turkey. The number of happy Turkish citizens drastically decreased over the last years (KONDA, 2018c: 5). In fact, Turkey ranked 112th out of 145 countries in the 2022 World Happiness Report, dropping 35 rows since 2013 (Duvar English, 2022; Country Economy, n.d.). While conservative people in Turkey describe themselves and the society in general as happy, those who self-describe as modern think otherwise (KONDA, 2018c: 5); as a matter of fact, the decline in happiness among those who support opposition parties since 2015 has been remarkable, while the depression in Kurdish and Alevi minority groups has risen above the average depression index of Turkish society (KONDA, 2018c: 12). Not surprisingly, it has also been determined that depression in low-income groups is more prevalent than for those with higher incomes (KONDA, 2018c: 4).

Women, LGBTQI+, children, and certain occupational groups, whose civil liberties and human rights have been systematically violated over the last ten years, are also continuously exposed to violent repression. In 2019, tens of thousands of children were officially reported to be victims of sexual abuse (Cumhuriyet, 2021). Between 2019 and 2021 alone, over a thousand women were murdered in Turkey. In 2018, almost half of the Turkish citizens stated that they were worried about going out and being in crowded places; this rate was higher for women (KONDA, 2018c: 18). Women's organizations have been fighting for the re-adoption of the İstanbul Convention (Turkish: *İstanbul Sözleşmesi*) that protected women from domestic violence in Turkey, where femicide has been on the agenda of political parties and non-governmental organizations (We Will End Femicide Platform, 2020).

Moreover, while all outdoor activities organized by LGBTQI+ were banned by governors without exception in 2021, eight hate murders were committed against LGBTQI+s in the same year (Kaos GL, 2022: 11, 26). As a result of the government's long-term populist rhetoric that aimed to turn the educated workforce into a hate figure in the eyes of the conservative strata of society, doctors and healthcare professionals have been assaulted both verbally and physically by patients and their relatives. According to the report published by Sağlık-Sen (2022), 57 healthcare workers were subjected to physical violence in the first month of 2022 alone. The premeditated annual murder of about a million animals in Turkey gives an idea about the tightening spiral of violence as well as the present social psyche and the associated uneasiness of ordinary people in Turkey.

The press and the academia, the two fundamental veins of freedom of speech, have also been adversely affected by the course of affairs in Turkey since 2013. In 2022, Turkey ranked 149th out of 180 countries in press freedom and was reported to have 90% of its national media under government control (Reporters Without Borders, n.d.). Television channels that are critical of government policies have come under penal investigations and have been imposed heavy sanctions by the High Council for Broadcasting (Turkish: *Radyo ve Televizyon Üst Kurulu,* RTÜK) (Reporters Without Borders, n.d.). According to the current data gathered by the Committee to Protect Journalists (2021), 18 journalists are imprisoned in Turkey. One symbolic moment for the repression of Turkish academia was the police manhandling and arresting scholars during a protest in 2017 against the liquidation of dissenting academics at Ankara University by presidential decrees (Diken, 2017). The attempts to suppress academic freedom and to accordingly change the very fabric of universities by the central government's appointment of faculty to these institutions have since only picked up speed. One example has been the 2021 appointment of a university rector by President Erdoğan to Boğaziçi University from outside the university, which met with nationwide criticism and trumpeted demonstrations by students and faculty for months.

After the bomb attacks that took place between 2015 and 2016, a considerable proportion of the people of Turkey have been dragged into a feeling of political despondency in the face of the social traumas of the last years' harsh socio-economic and political environment. As Kentel's study (2022: 152–154) also shows, in recent years of Turkish history, a series of social events that caused social outrage such as political repression, bomb attacks, the coup attempt, femicides, child abuse, and violence against animals have generated a sense of powerlessness in certain segments of the Turkish society. Regarding the incessant social traumas in Turkey, one participant in the study of Kentel

(2022: 154) gives the dramatic answer that they get used to something new every passing day. Turkish society is now worn out by social traumas. In the absence of powerful labor organizations, it is not unpredictable that this social state of despondency will maintain the political plane where working masses retreat and individual politicians who are recognized as saviors come to the forefront. There is a considerable amount of people who argue that a relatively freer political environment could only be generated by a political change brought about by individual politicians; according to those defending this viewpoint, such a change might allow the reorganization of powerful popular movements. We will wait and see together the socio-political outputs of this political tendency towards the individualization of politics in the Turkish political sphere. However, it should be underlined today that the people of Turkey, who have been dragged into a feeling of political despondency in the face of consequential social traumas, would also be dragged into a sense of powerlessness in the face of endless political scandals rising with the individualization of politics.

The last few years have reminded us that the political arena has become the site of political scandals, personal squabbles, and dirty bargains as the working masses are drawn back from the political arena. In recent years, Turkish politics has been turned into an arena of scandal politics. Political blackmail, illegally circulated CCTV footage and video clips of mayors, politicians, and businessmen exposed by intelligence officers, and scandalous statements by mob leaders about bureaucrats occupy almost every inch of the political agenda in Turkey. From radical allegations about state officials to the sex tapes of businessmen on Twitter, the public's collective political voice has been drowned in hideous deliriums of gutter politics. The struggle over wealth and power among the power groups is so limitless and greedy that the mud of the battle over *sharing* public wealth is now spreading everywhere. From the 1960s to the 1990s, Turkey's political agenda was already familiar with political scandals, political blackmailing, and dirty bargains. On the other hand, as we have witnessed in June 2013, gutter politics loses its sheer influence when the collective political voice of the people manifests itself. It is today more than necessary to remember and remind this fact with a tireless effort.

The more politics becomes the arena of competition for individual figures rather than a field of the direct political actions of working-masses, the more the public becomes a passive consumer of the agenda of gutter politics. The people should take their own political destiny into their own hands again, so that the individuals and groups, who are accustomed to a new trauma with each passing day, would not have to retreat into their corner with a greater amount of pessimism in the face of gutter politics. The dirty field of gutter politics should be rejected, and the public should remember the potential of its own political power because humanity is stronger than bombs, scandals, and dirty bargains.

The book you hold in your hands does not only examine the Gezi resistance at its decennial but also sheds light on multifaceted social, political, and ideological developments that have taken place over the last decade and the current possibilities. In colloquial terms, this book stands as an attempt at where we were then, where we are now, and what we could do in the near future. From the outset, I would like to express my intimate gratitude to the editors and authors of this volume who try to ponder on these pivotal questions with their precious contributions.

Bibliography

Committee to Protect Journalists (2021) *302 Journalists Imprisoned*. Available (consulted April 21 2023) at: https://cpj.org/data/imprisoned/2021/?status=Imprisoned&start_year=2021&end_year=2021&group_by=location.

Country Economy (n.d.) *Turkey – World Happiness Index*. Available (consulted March 9 2023) at: https://countryeconomy.com/demography/world-happiness-index/turkey.

Cumhuriyet (2021) *Dünyada Çocuk İstismarı Verileri!* Available (consulted March 9 2023) at: https://www.cumhuriyet.com.tr/haber/dunyada-cocuk-istismari-verileri-1849245#:~:text=T%C3%BCrkiye%20%C4%B0statistik%20Kurumu%27nun%20(T%C3%9C%C4%B0K,2%27si%20cinsel%20istismar%20kurban%C4%B1yd%C4%B1.

Diken (2017) *Ankara Üniversitesi Ablukada: Polis Gaz ve Mermiyle Saldırdı, 12 Gözaltı*. Available (consulted March 9 2023) at: https://www.diken.com.tr/ankara-universitesi-ablukada-akademisyenler-gozaltina-alindi-polis-gaz-ve-suyla-saldirdi/.

Duvar English (2022) *Turkey Regresses in World Happiness Report by Eight Rows, Ranks 112th*. Available (consulted March 9 2023) at: https://www.duvarenglish.com/turkey-regresses-in-world-happiness-report-2022-by-eight-rows-ranks-112th-news-60668.

Independent Türkçe (2019) *Mühendisler Neden Gidiyor? ASELSAN'dan Açıklama: Geçen Yıl 100–200 Kişi Ayrıldı*. Available (consulted March 9 2023) at: https://www.indyturk.com/node/11101/haber/m%C3%BChendisler-neden-gidiyor-aselsandan-a%C3%A7%C4%B1klama-ge%C3%A7en-y%C4%B1l-100-200-ki%C5%9Fi-ayr%C4%B1ld%C4%B1.

Kaos GL (2022) *Her Şeye Rağmen! LGBTİ+'ların İnsan Hakları 2021 Yılı Raporu*. Available (consulted April 21 2023) at: https://kaosgldernegi.org/images/library/lgbti-larin-insan-haklari-raporu-2021-web.pdf.

Kentel F (2022) *Türkiye'de Bir Arada Yaşarız Araştırması*. İzmir: Bayetav Yayınları.

KONDA (2018a) *10 Yılda Gençlerde Ne Değişti?* Available (consulted April 21 2023) at: https://interaktif.konda.com.tr/gencler-2018.

KONDA (2018b) *10 Yılda Ne Değişti?* Available (consulted April 21 2023) at: https://interaktif.konda.com.tr/hayat-tarzlari-2018.

KONDA (2018c) *Konda Barometresi, Temalar: Toplumun Ruh Hali*. Available (consulted April 21 2023) at: https://konda.com.tr/rapor/15/toplumun-ruh-hali.

MAK Danışmanlık (2020) *Türkiye Geneli Gençlik Araştırması*.

Reporters Without Borders (n.d.) *Türkiye Index 2022* (2022). Available (consulted April 21 2023) at: https://rsf.org/en/country-t%C3%BCrkiye.

Sağlık-Sen (2022) *Sağlık-Sen Ocak Ayı Sağlıkta Şiddet Raporu / 2022*. Available (consulted April 21 2023) at: http://www.sagliksen.org.tr/haber/12308/saglik-sen-2022-yili-saglikta-siddet-raporu.

Savran S (2022) *Türkiye'de Sınıf Mücadeleleri-1*. İstanbul: Yordam Kitap.

T24 (2022) *Marmara Hukuk Mezunu Dublin'de Kuryelik Yapan Tuğçe: 15 Bin Maaşla Dahi Türkiye'ye Dönmem*. Available (consulted March 9 2023) at: https://t24.com.tr/video/marmara-hukuk-mezunu-dublin-de-kuryelik-yapan-tugce-15-bin-maasla-dahi-turkiye-ye-donmem,46821.

TÜİK (2020) *Uluslararası Göç İstatistikleri, 2019*. Available (consulted April 21 2023) at:https://data.tuik.gov.tr/Bulten/Index?p=Uluslararasi-Goc-Istatistikleri-2019-33709#:~:text=T%C3%BCrkiye%27den%20yurt%20d%C4%B1%C5%9F%C4%B1na%20g%C3%B6%C3%A7,ise%20yabanc%C4%B1%20uyruklu%20n%C3%BCfus%20olu%C5%9Fturdu.

We Will End Femicide Platform (2020) *2020 Annual Report*. Available (consulted April 21 2023) at: https://kadincinayetlerinidurduracagiz.net/veriler/2949/2020-report-of-we-will-end-femicide-platform.

PART 1

In the Footsteps of Gezi

∴

CHAPTER 2

The Gezi Popular Rebellion
A Critical Evaluation

Sungur Savran

> Proletarian revolutions, like those of the nineteenth century, constantly criticize themselves, constantly interrupt themselves in their own course, return to the apparently accomplished, in order to begin anew; they deride with cruel thoroughness the half-measures, weaknesses, and paltriness of their first attempts, seem to throw down their opponents only so the latter may draw new strength from the earth and rise before them again more gigantic than ever, recoil constantly from the indefinite enormousness of their own goals – until a situation is created which makes all turning back impossible, and the conditions themselves call out: *Hic Rhodus, hic salta!*
>
> KARL MARX, *The Eighteenth Brumaire of Louis Bonaparte*

∴

Too many hagiographies have been written of the Gezi Park incident of 2013 in Turkey. This chapter aims to be an unrelentingly critical Marxist evaluation of that event. Gezi is no doubt of great importance for the history and the present-day political state of the country and was, in its day, a wonderful, ebullient, joyful experience for those who, such as the author of this chapter, shared the elating atmosphere of a communal understanding of social life. But enough of the self-justificatory celebrations of a political event that went astray despite its magnificent promise. Ten years on, an entire people who boldly stepped onto the stage of history to storm the heavens now need to "criticize themselves, constantly interrupt themselves in their own course, return to the apparently accomplished, in order to begin anew … until a situation is created which makes all turning back impossible" (Marx, 1972: 245–246). Only thus will we succeed in overcoming the evil forces that reproduce and exacerbate the exploitation, oppression and misery of the working people.

However, let us start out by recognizing the significance of Gezi and give it what is due to it before we delve into a critical appreciation.

1 The Achievements of Gezi

To our mind, the most significant aspect of Gezi is that it was the embodiment of the *mass method* of fighting against the reactionary Justice and Development Party (Turkish: *Adalet ve Kalkınma Partisi*, AKP) government that had already been in power for a decade, since late 2002. This was a people's rebellion, by no means restricted, as depicted in the international rendering of the event, to Gezi Park in Taksim Square in İstanbul and created a powerful tremor throughout the entire territory of the country, barely short of a full-scale revolution.

Up until that moment, two main ideological currents had dominated the political orientation of the left to this government (Savran, 2015: 43–45). One of these currents, one we have called left-liberalism ("liberalism" being used in the European and not the American sense), did not even oppose this reactionary government, but on the contrary supported it on the basis of the extremely tenuous theory that the Muslim-Oriental opposition in Turkey, dubbed "the periphery," was really the engine of the advance of democracy as against the so-called "center," the epitome of which was the army constantly holding the entire society under its tutelage and stifling democracy, "civil society" and even the development of capitalism. The Marxists warned this current regarding the suicidal risks that this kind of politics threatened, but were not heeded, given the atmosphere of worldwide disillusionment in Marxism flowing from the collapse of the 20th century experience in the construction of socialism.

The other main current of the left, still under the spell of the very strong influence of Kemalism, the founding ideology of the republic in the first half of the twentieth century, held the diametrically opposite political position of supporting a prospective military coup against Recep Tayyip Erdoğanand the AKP. As previous moves of the army to stop the rise of Islamism had been successful, albeit only briefly and only superficially in some cases, it was believed that this had to be the method of dealing with the AKP, still another variant of Islamism.

Both orientations failed dismally. The left-liberal chimera of an Islamist-led democratization turned out to be one of the most shameful cases of self-deception in the history of the international left. The putschism of the opposite wing of the leftwas proved to be a useless relic of the past in the context of the new balance of forces.

The Gezi popular rebellion offered the masses a new vision and a new method for social and political change by way of the self-activity of the exploited and oppressed masses independent of the different wings of the ruling classes. This was its most important aspect for the political climate of contemporary Turkey. Whether the popular revolt was successful in leaving behind a solid legacy in this direction is a question that is more debatable and will be dealt with later on.

Irrespective of the answer to this latter question, the people's rebellion formed a *watershed in Erdoğan's ruleover the country*. Up until the people's revolt, the AKPhad established a hegemony over large swathes of society, enjoying almost unlimited support from the imperialist countries and increasing its electoral clout on every new occasion to finally reach 58 per cent of approval for its far-reaching constitutional revisions in 2010, no doubt thanks also to the support of liberals, right and left.This gave Erdoğan the possibility of overcoming the interventions of the military in an unexpectedly resilient manner, unprecedented up until then. But with the earthquake created by Gezi, Erdoğan lost many allies at home and abroad, which forced him to look for new allies that had been hostile to him up until then, making his rule incomparably shakier. Hence from 2013 on AKP rulebecame much more of a rodeo ride. That Erdoğan was able to survive the many traps and hurdles that have emerged since then does not alter the fact that the riding became extremely rough after the Gezi rebellion. For the difficulties thus raised required of him a lot of deviation into side alleys and *led him to veer off of his strategic trajectory*. Thus, Gezi divides the two decades of Erdoğan's rule neatly into two different periods.

To put it in a nutshell, then, the military, the judiciary, universities, and other bourgeois custodian institutions established to safeguard the secular republic and Turkey's ties to Western institutions could not budge Erdoğan's government for a whole decade, but the popular rebellion that started in Gezi Park shook it to its very bones.

The people's rebellion also opened the floodgates to a series of struggles which, as we shall see, dominated the political scene up until the middle of 2015. Indeed, one of our main contentions in this chapter is that the Gezi events can only be properly understood if situated in the context of a cycle of uprisings and revolts that covered the entire period 2013–2015 (of which more below).

The people's rebellion was obviously also a testing ground for political and social forces: the working class and unions, the Kurdish movement, the various socialist parties and movements, the main opposition party, the Republican People's Party (Turkish: *Cumhuriyet Halk Partisi*, CHP), member of the misnamed Socialist International, and, of course, the entire spectrum of other social classes. In a certain sense it was a *dress rehearsal for future uprisings and mass eruptions*, full of lessons for socialist strategy and tactics. In order to draw lessons from this popular revolt, one certainly needs to understand the class nature of the uprising. No facile generalization will do in this area so the present chapter will devote a rather detailed and cool-headed analysis to this issue in order to shed light on possible future developments.

Itself the trigger for a new series of revolts domestically, the Gezi rebellion was surely also a *reply to the call of the Arab revolutions*. It undoubtedly had an internationally determined character, borrowing heavily from the experience of the revolutions and rebellions that preceded it, from Tahrir in Egypt all the way to the Occupy movement in the United States and itself gave an impetus to the Brazilian revolt that extended to 600 towns and cities in the space of a few days, a movement that started a dozen days after Gezi and adopted the slogan "The love affair is over, this is now Turkey", the "love affair" referring to the trust the Brazilian masses had invested in the successive governments of the left-wing Workers' Party (Brazilian Portuguese: *Partido dos Trabalhadores*, PT) and its historic leader Lula. We call all these diverse uprisings and insurrections the Third Wave of World Revolution and consider the people's rebellion called Gezi an inseparable part of that process. We will return to this aspect below.

Considered from a more historical angle, the popular rebellion triggered by Gezi stands out as the broadest-based uprising in the history of republican Turkey and the period immediately preceding the foundation of the republic (Savran and Ülker, 2018). Turkey experienced two bourgeois revolutions in the first quarter of the twentieth century and one proletarian insurrection in the second half of the century. Additionally, there were abortive attempts at setting up armed guerrilla uprisings. Finally, from 1984 on the country has been gripped by a powerful guerrilla war waged by the Kurdistan Workers Party (Kurdish: *Partiya Karkerên Kurdistanê*, PKK), which has gone through various phases without losing its elan since 1984.

Of these, the first bourgeois revolution of 1908 was the combination of several guerrilla movements in the Balkan peninsula and a truly mass movement all around the Anatolian heartland of the Ottoman Empire. This is the only revolutionary episode that can compete with the Gezi rebellion in terms of geographical expanse and mass character. However, although shorter-lived in comparison to the 1908 revolutionary process, the Gezi rebellion was more explosive in terms of the spontaneous self-activity of the masses than that episode.

The second bourgeois revolution, the one that resulted in the abolition of the Sultanate and the Caliphate and the establishment of the republic, developed in the form of a war that excluded, even suppressed, the independent activity of the popular classes. It was really a revolution without mass participation, surely an upheaval of the most radical kind in terms of the changes it brought about, but without making the masses a part and an agent of that radical upheaval (Savran, 2023).

The events of 15–16 June 1970 were, to put it succinctly, the opening of the age of proletarian revolutions in Turkey (Savran, 2020a). 150 thousand industrial workers conquered İstanbul as well as the neighbouring industrial zone extending from Gebze to Izmit, in direct collision with police and gendarmerie. It would be no exaggeration to conclude that a well-organized revolutionary party could have turned this insurrection into a successful proletarian revolution. This was the most massive class challenge to the capitalist order in the history of the country, but remained limited to a single region due to the precocious nature of the proletarian uprising.

The Kurdish revolt became a truly mass movement and has been supported, at least in its parliamentary extension, by millions of Kurds, but is naturally restricted regionally to those geographical areas where the Kurds are a majority, although due to heavy migration Turkey's metropolises also receive their share of the struggle.

Hence the Gezi rebellion stands out as an earth-shaking mass movement in the history of the country.

2 Defying Conventional Wisdom

Thus, the Gezi popular rebellion is an invaluable experience for all who stand on the side of the exploited and the oppressed. It is totally another thing, though, how Gezi was understood, analysed and presented to the rest of the world. In a situation in which the left had already been inundated ideologically for decades by a mixture of liberalism and postmodernist identity politics, the image of the uprising that became conventional wisdom on the left was extremely deformed.

Some characterizations are too fantastic to omit quotation. For instance, Ali Akay, a foremost spokesperson of postmodernism in Turkey, depicts Gezi in the following manner: "What came about is the micropolitics of desire as opposed to the macropolitics of political parties. The activists therefore wish for greater love, greater sexuality, greater freedom, a more experimental life" (Akay, cited in İnal, 2013: 27).[1] This was no doubt true for a minority of people

---

1 Ali Akay's article from *Radikal*, a Turkish newspaper that ceased digital broadcasting in 2016, is being cited through a secondary source due to the unavailability of *Radikal*'s archive.

in Gezi Park. The problem is that Akay simply generalizes on the basis of an observation of the people around him. Nilüfer Göle (cited in İnal, 2013: 28), a liberal sociologist of some fame, puts forth the following characterization: "In fact, the youth are experiencing, in a manner reminiscent of the Woodstock rock festival, an emblem of the peace and counter culture movements of the 60s, a sort of communal life on the square with music, ecology, politics, flowers, and beer."

A warning is in order for the international audience at this point. Whenever an event of some importance occurs in a certain country, say the revolution of Sudan in 2018–2019 end even beyond or the interrupted one of Chile of 2019, the mass movement is always, almost by definition, heterogeneous: participants come from very different backgrounds, from intellectuals and artists who may have been educated abroad, in most cases Western countries, and who usually speak fluent English, the *lingua franca* of the times, all the way to the indigent analphabets of the poor shantytowns that surround most cities in the Third World. It is always through the eyes of the same type of person that the international audience receives the news about the events occurring, the sophisticated polyglot who almost speaks the language of the international intelligentsia rather than the idiom of his or her people and who interprets everything through the lens of liberalism and its accoutrements. The image of Gezi that has been inscribed in the mind's eye of the international audience is fatally marred by this almost universal affliction of international communication on sociopolitical events, especially those that occur in the poorer countries.

Let us then proceed to dissect some aspects of the received opinion of the left-liberal *cum* postmodernist picture painted for the international audience. Two other caveats, though, at the outset. First, nine people have recently been sent to jail and are now serving time for long terms of imprisonment, accused of a variety of offences related to the "crime" of leading the Gezi movement, on the basis of an indictment that is filled with inconsequential and vacuous "evidence". This is without any doubt a consequence of the subservience of the judiciary to the executive under the present conditions of Erdoğan's despotic regime.[2] Whatever our differences of opinion with the victims of this hideous operation, we owe these people the duty of solidarity. Hence, a full settling of accounts with respect to the way the Gezi popular revolt was led will have to await a more democratic environment in Turkey where everyone is entitled to commentary.

---

2   For the official documents of the so-called main Gezi case, see T.C. İstanbul 13. Ağır Ceza Mahkemesi [Republic of Turkey İstanbul Assize Court No. 13], 2022: 613–616.

Secondly, we would like to draw the reader's attention to the fact that none of the contentious points to be discussed below hinges on the author's ideological, political and methodological stance alone. In each case, the decisive aspect of the argument we shall put forward is a matter of empirical verification. So, it is not simply a matter of taking a critical approach towards one ideological representation from within another, although that aspect is involved as well. Marxism requires a realistic and objective, though certainly not impartial, rendering of the material facts of the world and hence we do our best to base our opinions in a manner firmly saddled to the facts. "Truth alone is revolutionary" as Gramsci used to say.

The first point on which the record has to be set straight is that this was a country-wide people's rebellion that was not reducible to Gezi Park. Pick up any book on Gezi in Turkish or, for that matter, in English also, and you are immediately bound to see, if you yourself are not also blinded by the trees of Gezi Park, that Taksim and Gezi Park and the encampment there, as well as the different identity-based groups there gathered such as women, gay and trans people, anti-capitalist Muslims, to mention but those most commented upon, are overwhelmingly the topics of discussion (Göztepe, 2013; İnal 2013; Kara, 2014). Some studies, even book-length, do not stoop to mention some of the phenomena that occurred outside of the orbit of Gezi or Taksim square, questions that we will be raising in a moment, let alone venturing outside of İstanbul. The oft-cited figures of the Home Ministry, according to which over 3.6 million people engaged in action in 80 out of the 81 provinces of Turkey (T.C. İstanbul 13. Ağır Ceza Mahkemesi [Republic of Turkey İstanbul Assize Court No. 13], 2022: 316), are surely an understatement. The actual numbers on the streets, the squares and the parks were in all probability higher. Moreover, one should also not forget that many older women, the paltry and the sick joined in the movement by participating in *cacerolazos* (pots and pans concerts) from the safety and security of their neighbourhoods or their balconies and windows.

It is not only a matter of disregarding large numbers of people or geographic regions with their specificities, though. The distortion thereby accomplished relates even more importantly to the *essence* of the social, ideological, and political contradictions that came to the surface during the Gezi popular rebellion. This is the second major point, and we will try to explain this moving in concentric circles, taking the Gezi Park itself as our point of departure.

To start with, the meaning of Taksim Square cannot be reduced to an ecological sensibility. It is no doubt true that the protection of the trees of Gezi Park were the *triggering factor* for four days before the overpowering pressure of the masses drove the police from Taksim Square on the night of 31 May into

1 June 2013. It must also be emphasized that the resistance put up by ecologists grouped around Taksim Solidarity (Turkish: *Taksim Dayanışması*), a coalition of organizations that was formed in the spring to stop the onslaught planned by Erdoğan and his bureaucrats on this very important center of the city, was audacious and courageous. However, Taksim is not only those trees. It is also the square where fanatical bigots attacked and killed, in 1969, on a day that has gone down in history as "Bloody Sunday" (Turkish: *Kanlı Pazar*), two members of the large crowd of university students demonstrating against the visit of the Sixth Fleet of the US Navy to İstanbul, an event carved into the collective memory of the left in Turkey.

It is the square where the first free May Day demonstrations of the working class were held in the 1970s. Of these, the one in 1977, which brought together an estimated half a million workers and youth for the celebrations, was attacked by plainclothes agents firing from the hotels and other premises surrounding the square, resulting in 34 casualties from among the demonstrators. The memory of that day still reverberates in the spirit of all who celebrate May Day in Turkey (which reaches into the millions all over the country, if not terrorized by the police.).

It is also the square which was prohibited for May Day celebrations, as well as all other working class and left-wing demonstrations, by the ferociously repressive military dictatorship of the 1980s. Many young people died in the struggle to take back the square in the wake of the return to a parliamentary system and many of us were gassed and clubbed in the same struggle all the way to and including 2009 under the AKP. Only in 2010 was it finally opened to the masses, to be taken back again after a couple of years. In that self-same year of 2013, only one month before the taking of Taksim by the masses from the police on 1 June, tens of thousands of workers and youth tried to march to the square but were forcibly pushed back.

All of this means that Taksim is a very special location that has become engraved in the minds of all working-class and socialist fighters through successive events for over half a century. Generation after generation struggled to take it back from repressive bourgeois governments. It is our firm belief, though we certainly cannot adduce evidence for this, that on that fateful night of 31 May, the *overwhelming majority* of the people that thronged all the avenues and side streets around Taksim and fought until they conquered the square did not have in mind only the trees of Gezi Park, but this entire series of events that mark the servitude of the people of this country to a police state. This is not to belittle the ecological struggle and its protagonists. It is to set the record straight against a narrative that demeans the sensibility of hundreds of thousands if not millions of other people.

Intimately related to this first point is the further fact that the people's rebellion in İstanbul was not confined to the Gezi Park encampment, however outstanding that experience was. As important were the struggles that went on in working-class neighbourhoods and the poor shantytowns. Two among these stood out. Gazi, a predominantly Alevi and Kurdish neighbourhood with a long history of struggles against reactionary social forces and the repressive forces of the state, was one. The irony embedded in the similarity of the names of the two places, Gezi and Gazi, is emblematic in intimating the solidarity in unusual times between two socio-cultural environments at antipodes in normal times. An almost ticklish event occurred on the night of 15 June, in the wake of the driving of the Gezi dwellers from Taksim Square by the police. There was, of course, an explosion of rage all over the city. The crowd of which we were part naturally respirated tons of tear gas and was also treated, for the first time, to water cannon that bruised the skin. Late in the night, our thinning crowd received the support of a very large group arriving from Gazi, chanting, "Hold tight Taksim, Gazi is coming!" Gazi finally met Gezi in the same vortex of brute state violence!

The other neighbourhood that stood out in İstanbul was Sarıgazi. Police reports attribute special importance to two episodes in which the demonstrators attacked government buildings, evidently to take them over. We will come back to the more important of these later, but the one that the Sarıgazi crowd attempted to take was the district governor's office in Sancaktepe, İstanbul, which the crowd was not able to conquer, rather leaving it heavily destroyed before retreating in the face of fierce resistance put up by the police.

These two examples do not only show that there were very different socio-economic and political contradictions at play. The youth of Gazi or Sarıgazi do not even have enough pocket money to go visit Taksim, once the cultural center of İstanbul, and could not care less for either Gezi Park or its trees, when they themselves barely survive in a concrete jungle willfully infested with drugs by the authorities. Gazi and Sarıgazi were emblematic of the venting of the grievances of working-class youth, all the more so because they are Alevis or Kurds discriminated against. Ignoring the import of these dimensions of the people's rebellion leaves us in a delirious state of jubilation regarding the achievements of life in Gezi Park, which is not, or at least not the only, aspect we will face in future events.

Moving beyond the limits of İstanbul, there were many other cities that were constantly and fierily fighting law enforcement. Alongside Ankara, the capital city, and Izmir, the third largest, many cities such as Antalya, a gigantic tourism hub, Bursa and Adana, respectively the centers of the metallurgical and the textiles industries, and Hatay and Gaziantep in the southeast were the scene of feverish activity on the part of the masses. In some of these, Izmir, Ankara, and Antalya, as well as İstanbul, working-class districts, especially when these districts also coincided with the residential areas of the Alevi minority, were the venues of demonstrations day in and day out.

The province of Hatay, with its city of Antakya enjoying the legacy of a unique culture of inter-ethnic and inter-religious tolerance from time immemorial, was decisive for a very special reason: the province has a large population of Alevis of Arab ethnic origin (the *Nusayri*) and sits on the most sensitive segment of the 800-kilometer-long border (roughly 500 miles) between Turkey and Syria. One should remember that the Syrian civil war was started in late 2011 by fanatical Sunni forces that falsely claimed Assad's regime to be one in which the Alevi minority held a monopoly of power, oppressing not only Sunnis but all other ethnic groups and religious denominations. This was the basis of the support they received from the Erdoğan government as well as from Saudi Arabia and other Gulf countries. On the question of the Sunni-Alevi rift, Erdoğan's whole posture posed a dire threat to the Alevi minority of Turkey (numbering many millions and even tens of millions, although the exact figure is anybody's guess). Even the naming of the third bridge over the Bosphorus after Sultan Selim, nicknamed Yavuz (which translates as "cruel", "grim", "redoubted"), who, when fighting a war against Shia Iran in the 16th century, systematically massacred tens of thousands of Alevi civilian men (even Danişmend (1948: 7), a historian of extremely conservative views, admits so much), was a gauntlet thrown in the face of the Alevi minority. In Hatay, a province that was historically a bone of contention between Syria (when it was still under French mandate) and Turkey, a great part of the population is Arab as well as Alevi. So, Antakya and other cities in the province became the major battleground between the state forces and the people during the Gezi popular revolt. There is a striking fact about the casualties suffered by the masses during the battles waged against the police: 6 out of the 7 who died during the conflict were Alevi youth, three of them precisely from Antakya!

All this really shows that the people's rebellion was the ground on which the Alevi minority in Turkey was fighting for survival in the context of a rising Sunni fundamentalism under Erdoğan both regionally and domestically. The blindfolded gaze of liberal *cum* postmodernist ideology pushes this into the background when it does not ignore it completely.

Strangely enough, the cecity that is at play regarding space or geography is then transformed into a misconception concerning the temporal rhythm of the rebellion. In an overwhelming majority of accounts, the rebellion is limited to the month of June, some even going so far as to call it the "June movement."

And yet the spreading out of the movement to all the parks of İstanbul and later of Ankara, Izmir, etc. when Gezi Park itself was evacuated forcibly by the police on 15 June is highly appreciated by all involved as a creative alternative developed spontaneously by the mass movement against state repression. These forums or popular assemblies lasted until the small hours of the morning and represented a veritable occasion for grassroots democracy. In a certain sense, they were a premonition of the *"nuits debouts"* (nights awake) that the French mass movement was to create during the colossal struggle against the so-called Khomry labor law in 2016. These nocturnal assemblies in the second phase of the popular revolt in Turkey gave the rebellion a new lease of life, which was confirmed on the night of 24 June, when tens of thousands of people spilled outside one park in a central district of İstanbul in protest against the release of a police officer identified in a widely circulated video as having been responsible for the cold-blooded killing of a demonstrator in Ankara. Given the popularity of these forums, it is incomprehensible how, immediately after the movement subsided, almost universally the entire left limited the Gezi event to the month of June. This only becomes comprehensible when one realizes that for the majority ideologically imprisoned to imagining the entire event as the Gezi Park encampment experience, the show was over as soon as the park was evacuated by the police.

After a calmer month of August, the rebellion flared up once again in September. There were several foci that represented this revival: the struggle at the Middle East Technical University (Turkish: *Orta Doğu Teknik Üniversitesi*, ODTÜ) in Ankara, a traditional hotbed of subversive action; the town of Tuzluçayır near Ankara, which revolted against a construction project that combined a mosque with a *cem* house (the Alevi abode for religious activity), a project that smacked of the absorption of the Alevi faith into mainstream Islam; and a full-scale battle between demonstrators and the police in Antakya in the province of Hatay (when, in fact, the seventh casualty occurred). İstanbul also responded with a tactical retreat to the Asian side of the city because Taksim had been brought almost under siege by the forces of repression, lest the movement reconquered it. This new wave of revolt is also ignored probably because it is so heterogeneous and totally unrelated to the Gezi Park experience.

All in all, the experience of a people's rebellion that lasted for three months is reduced to a fortnight of the Gezi Park event, which undeniably was the apex of the entire process. For those who think that this debate on the temporal span of the rebellion is unimportant, we would like to point out the following: historical experience shows that in certain revolutions or uprisings, it is at the very end of the upheaval that the mass movement becomes the strongest.³ Recognizing the intricacies of the tempo and the rhythm of the mass movement will be helpful in future uprisings. Of course, for those who do not care about the victory or defeat of such movements, it is altogether a different matter.

Finally, an issue of considerable importance is the fiction of non-violence on the part of the mass movement during the people's rebellion. In reminiscences and commentaries on Gezi, participants who view the events through the liberal *cum* postmodernist lens glorify the experience for its peaceful, non-violent methods.⁴ This is truly amazing. The savage violence of the police during the first skirmishes at Gezi Park in the last days of May may have been met with patient non-violence on the part of the ecologists that had been camping there. However, the full-scale street battles of 31 May–1 June were only won through a posture of retaliation on the part of the demonstrators, in particular the socialist organizations and the football fan groups, who, adept at street-fighting, played a decisive role in winning the square on 1 June and keeping Gezi Park, if not the square itself, for an entire fortnight.

Who burned and overturned the police cars that dotted the whole area throughout the period of encampment? Who burned and destroyed the vans of the media, not without reason since mainstream media showed documentaries on the life of penguins while the whole country was up in flames? Who captured and eviscerated municipal buses that lay like fallen dragons around the square and acted as barricades against possible police assault for days on end? Who attacked the İstanbul prime ministerial office that stood at a distance of several kilometres to Gezi Park, fought the police into the small hours of the morning, used the heavy-duty machines that had been parked nearby as Trojan horses and forced the police headquarters to arrange for reinforcements

---

3 To cite but two examples, first, the 1905 Russian revolution, which started in January of that year, really came into its own from October on, when a general strike shook the entire country, which also had repercussions in early 1906 in the form of failed insurrections. The Egyptian revolution of 2011–2013, on the other hand, was the most resilient mass uprising of the present century and peaked three times. The first two were impressive insurrections that brought down Hosni Mobarak and ousted the Supreme Military Council of Marshall Tantaoui, but it was really the third episode that proved to be a world record-breaker when it brought out tens of millions of people all over Egypt on the same day, with the explicit intention of toppling the Muslim Brotherhood president Mohammed Morsi at the end of June 2013. Unfortunately, due to the extreme confusion of the revolutionary vanguard, this proved to be the swan song of the Egyptian revolution, since Abdel Fatah al-Sisi, then Chief of the General Staff, used the opportunity to take power upon himself through a Bonapartist coup.

4 In at least one case (Özel, 2014), this takes the form of the outlandish idea that Gezi signified "Turkey's search for a new definition of citizenship", as well as "an attempt to enlarge the liberal-democratic space in Turkish politics".

by sea in order to cope with the unstoppable pressure of the masses, who only narrowly missed in the end capturing that building that was of very high symbolic value? Who fought the police until the early hours of the morning of 16 June when Gezi Park was forcibly evacuated, throwing the gas canisters back to the police, sending Molotovs and projectiles of all sorts to push them back?

Closely related to this is the idea that Gezi has laid the ground for a tradition of tolerance in Turkey's politics. David and Toktamış (2015: 20) put this in crystal-clear form: "a wide array of social groups: Alevis, religious people, Kurds, women, Christians, Lesbian, Gay, Bisexual, Transgender and Intersex (LGBTI), Kemalists and football fans. The peaceful co-existence between these very diverse and, until then, antagonistic groups demonstrates that something greater happened at Gezi: the creation of a spirit of tolerance that may well sow the seeds for a new Turkey." Nothing of the sort has in fact happened. In this area as well the legacy of Gezi is nil. Alevis are under as life-threatening a threat as ever from the fanatical movements within the Sunni camp; gay and trans people have come under increasing ideological attack, given the atmosphere of the defence of the family in most Eastern European countries and the environment of rising fundamentalism in Turkey itself; and football fans, strangely included in this series of "social groups", are as fanatic as they have perennially been.

The reader may already have noticed that all of this has to do with Gezi Park itself, before the conquest of Taksim by the mass movement and after its loss to the police. We need not go into all the street-fighting that occurred *on a daily basis* in the other cities of Turkey, which the liberal identity-politics crowd has conveniently ignored up until today. It is nice for an intellectual to be able to enter Gezi Park in the evening on 1 June, set up one's tent without having to fight anyone, enjoy the festive atmosphere for a fortnight, fraternizing with all the different types of people that have gathered there, eat from the communal kitchen, and then by coincidence having absented oneself when the police attacked on 15 June, months later to say, looking back nostalgically at the entire experience, "oh, how peaceful was my Gezi, how pacific were the crowds"!

We cannot dwell longer on this question of violence versus pacifism, so vital for all great mass movements and *a fortiori* for revolutions. Let it be said though, in passing, that glorification of non-violence has been at the center of the entire experience of the Third Wave of World Revolution. Here again the discourse of the intellectuals and the practice of the plebeian masses diverge wildly. In all Arab revolutions there were willful acts of violence (attacks on police precincts, destruction of premises symbolic of hated power structures, forcible removal of unwanted government propaganda material and even exchange of fire between different forces of the army in Sudan), but all this is ignored rather than realistically reported. (We have taken up this question of the debate over violence in the Arab revolutions in Savran (2019: 53–56)). The author himself witnessed with his own eyes, when visiting Tunisia in 2013, the remains of various buildings that had served as the premises of the official party of the dictator Zine al Abidin ben Ali, burned and eviscerated by the people during the revolution, which lay there as instructive souvenirs of a hated despotism ousted by the power of the people.

It is not out of any veneration for violence that we remind the reader these facts. The luckiest revolution is the one that needs to make the least recourse to violence. It is only that principled refusal of violence is discussed nowadays in almost a puerile manner, in complete abstraction from the historical record and without coming to grips with the most elementary questions. Received opinion on Gezi reproduces this attitude in its entirety.

Let us end this questioning of conventional wisdom on the Gezi popular rebellion by returning to a point already made. Nowhere in the literature on Gezi have we come across even a short mention of the cycle of struggles that occurred in the wake of Gezi that we have already mentioned and will be taking up below. This again seems to be the result of that attitude of holding the experience of the Gezi Park fortnight between 1–15 June as if it were made of a different substance in comparison to all other social struggles and revolts. Behind that, we suspect, lies the liberal-postmodernist outlook that denigrates other forms of social struggle as outdated or primitive, which, as we shall try to show, is the unmistakable aspect of a certain type of class prejudice.

3 Under the Sign of the Third Wave of World Revolution

When we agreed to contribute to this initiative of a book on the tenth anniversary of Gezi, it was originally our intention to try to situate the Gezi rebellion within the international context since we believe that it is in fact a link in the chain of revolutions, rebellions, uprisings and protests that erupted one after another in the period 2011–2014. We will not be able to delve into this international aspect of things in a systematic manner for lack of space. Let us then explain, in summary form, what we mean by saying that the events in Turkey we are discussing are a link in the international chain of struggles.

We are of the conviction that revolutionary movements are, as a rule, of an international reach, even though there are many instances of "isolated revolutions", the most prominent ones being the English revolution of the 17th century and the Paris Commune of 1871. Apart from these and some other exceptional cases, even bourgeois revolutions developed in successive international waves in history. The age of democratic revolution in the Atlantic region, comprising the American and French revolutions, the spread of the revolution through Napoleonic wars throughout Europe and the Bolivarian revolutions of Latin America was the first such wave of bourgeois revolution. The so-called "spring of the peoples" of 1848–49 was the epitome of synchronised international revolution. Then came the revolutions of the East, with Russia (1905), Iran (1906), Turkey (1908) and China (1911) taking over the mantle of revolution from the West.

This is even truer of proletarian revolutions. These came in three successive waves in the space of the last one hundred years. The first wave of world revolution was kicked off by the Russian revolution of 1917, to be almost replicated by the German revolution of 1918–1923, followed by revolutionary crises in Hungary, Finland, Austria, Italy and Scotland, and accompanied by anti-colonial revolutions in many Middle Eastern and North African countries such as Turkey, Egypt, Iran, and Morocco. The Chinese revolution of 1925–27 and the Spanish revolution of 1931–39 may also plausibly be regarded as continuations of this first wave.

The second wave came in the midst of the Second World War and extended from the coasts of the Atlantic in western Europe to the Sea of Japan, comprising revolutionary struggles, some victorious, some defeated and some frustrated, in France, Italy, Yugoslavia, Albania, Greece, China, Vietnam and Korea, not to bring in other, more controversial cases in Asia. 1968 is a case that has to be discussed at length and so we will, for the sake of brevity, skip it and speak of what we consider to be the Third Wave of World Revolution. The most prominent geographic regions where this third wave has erupted are the Arab countries and Latin America, although lesser cases of turbulence can and should be evoked as well. The period between 2011–2014 saw the revolutionary rise of masses in Tunisia, Egypt, Yemen, Bahrain (though not Libya, which was an interregional and intertribal war from the very beginning, and not Syria, which turned into a sectarian civil war, seconded by international war, after the first six months). This revolutionary wave swept around the Mediterranean, giving rise to people's rebellions in many countries such as Spain (2011), Greece (2011) Israel (2011), Rojava-Syria (2012), Turkey (2013), Bosnia-Herzegovina (2014).

Let us, in passing, explain briefly how we distinguish between a revolution and a people's rebellion. A revolution always poses the question of power for the masses that have risen against the established order. If either objectively (i.e., in terms of material conditions) or subjectively (i.e., in terms of agency), the question of taking power does not come on the agenda, then the uprising in question cannot go beyond the limits of a popular revolt. However, within the turbulent vortex of feverish mass activity, a people's rebellion can imperceptibly slide into a revolutionary character. The distinction is important, in our opinion, in terms of the possibilities offered by revolution, on the one hand, and of popular revolt, on the other. A correct assessment of these possibilities is vital for the tactics of the parties and other actors inside the people's forces.

After having lost its elan as a result of the Bonapartist coup of General al-Sisi in Egypt in July 2013, the third wave of world revolution took another giant step forward in 2019. This time it was the turn of Sudan, Algeria, Lebanon and Iraq in the Arab world (with Iran, a non-Arab country, possibly included as a popular revolt during the events of November 2019). Latin America joined in this second phase, with Ecuador, Bolivia and Chile leading, joined later by Colombia and many others.

The pandemic resulted in a second interruption of the third wave, until very recently Sri Lanka displayed a classic case of an abortive revolution and Ecuador took up the relay in Latin America again. It is to be seen what new events will surprise the whole world between the writing of these lines and the publication of the book in which this chapter will take its place.

It is our firm conviction that the people's rebellion triggered by the Gezi events in Turkey was heavily influenced by the revolutionary ascent of the masses particularly in Tunisia and Egypt. Let us add to this a second element: Turkey being a West-looking country since the nineteenth century, the Occupy movement in the US, the very heart of the Western capitalist system, and the "squares movements" of Spain and Greece, in particular Plaza del Sol in Madrid and Syndagma in Athens, were also of non-negligible influence on the imaginary of particularly the educated population of the metropolitan cities. When these influences came together with the festering rage and frustration among the secularized, educated, and Westernized layers of the population, this cocktail erupted into a rebellion of the masses.

Of course, there are great differences between these countries with infinitely diverse features. Even between countries with a Muslim majority population, say Egypt and Turkey, the conditions are very varied. In some of these countries (e.g., Sudan and Turkey) the governments challenged were of an Islamist bent. In others, the Islamists were in opposition until the revolution succeeded in bringing down the old regime and then came into the fray opportunistically although they had contributed nothing to the ascendance of the revolutionary wave (e.g., Tunisia and Egypt). Most importantly, there are great divergences in terms of the class structures of the countries involved. It is really impossible to find great similarities between any of these countries. However, the fact that they are of the same wave of world revolution gives them a commonality that reaches beyond any of the differences that separate them. When one moves, the others follow in its steps and when one falters, others fall into despair alongside it. But most importantly the peoples of the different countries learn from each other that they can and must dare to take the administration of things into their own hands. This is invaluable.

4 The Class Character of Gezi and of the People's Rebellion

Already in the context of the Arab revolutions, issues of class structure and class agency became a bone of contention between the diverse commentators and political actors. The presence among the great masses of people of certain highly-educated, sophisticated layers of the population led to the birth of a myth of the "computer-savvy new class" leading these revolutions. This was especially true for the observers of the scene at Tahrir Square within the Egyptian revolution. One must not forget that Tahrir was paradigmatic for all subsequent mass movements, so the image of this new class of people, young men and women with aspirations for a modern life, leading, even "owning", so to speak, these revolutions was decisive. Fortunately, some researchers following the scene very carefully reported, analysed and thus definitively determined the part played by the working class in these revolutions, at least those of Tunisia and Egypt, a part that was quite inconsistent with the image that many commentators full of zeal for novelties tried to depict (Gjergji, 2013; Beinin, 2016).

As a result of careful study of the Arab revolutions we have found out that there is in fact a methodological problem that is often ignored here. This methodological problem is common to all countries from Egypt to Sudan to Turkey and needs therefore to be taken up with great seriousness if one wishes not to go astray in the analysis of these revolutions, whatever other differences remain in the class dynamics of the countries in question. The question is quite a straightforward one. The class composition of the major squares and encampment sites that act as the headquarters of these revolutions and rebellions is different from that of the rest of the troops of the revolution for a very simple reason: workers, breadwinners of families, and the residents of poor neighbourhoods and shantytowns, as well as the population of the smaller townships and satellite cities around the metropolises, cannot set up camp on a constant basis in the center of the metropolis for socio-economic reasons. An immense majority of these people lead a hand-to-mouth existence and so have to work every day. It is only members of those classes of people who already inhabit the central neighbourhoods of those cities with some reserve economic means that can enjoy the benefit of remaining in camps on squares such as Tahrir or Taksim or Syndagma or Plaza del Sol overnight and become permanent actors of these "headquarters".

Additionally, students who can spare a lot of time for these activities can also afford to take their place in these encampments. One should never forget that, whatever the different percentage of working-class and labouring peasant kids who can go to college in the different countries in question, the university has primarily become, in all countries with a certain degree of economic development, a site for the reproduction of the privileged educated classes of society (of this more in a moment) Thus, in most cases students are only a younger population section of the same classes we were talking about.

So, there is necessarily a considerable division between Tahrir and Mahalla, between Gezi and Gazi, between the center of Khartoum and Omdurman, on the one hand, where the Sudanese Professionals Association and the Forces for Freedom of Change have the upper hand, and the shantytowns and small townships, on the other, in which Resistance Committees have the say on everything. Everything, literally everything, looks different if you look at it through the eyes of a member of the Sudanese Professionals Association or through those of a member of the Resistance Committees. By the same token, for the outside commentator or analyst, things will look totally different whether you look at Tahrir or Mahalla, whether you look at Gezi or Gazi.

That seems to us one of the major reasons behind the entire confusion of the class character of both the Arab revolutions and the Gezi popular rebellion. Let us briefly go over the major claims about the class nature of the Gezi rebellion to see how this plays itself out. On the one hand, there is a quite influential characterization depicting Gezi as a "middle-class" phenomenon. Having praised the achievements of the AKP and Erdoğan in the spheres of economic growth and education in particular, Keyder (2013) concludes that this has led to the rise of "a new middle class in formation, whose members work in relatively modern workplaces, with leisure time and consumption habits much like their global counterparts. ... The Gezi protests were the first social movement to stem from this new reality." Here, the problem is that the very nature of the concept "middle class", this category of American sociology that means all kinds of things to all kinds of people, complicates the debate. We tend to believe that the analysts who insist on this definition of the class nature of Gezi imply thereby, most importantly, that this nature is *not* working-class.

On the other hand, those who react to this come forward with a clear statement: in their opinion, Gezi *was* working-class in nature although not in the sense of the industrial proletariat but in the sense of people who work in other kinds of jobs, who, nonetheless work for a wage for their living: teachers, bank clerks, workers in advertising or design companies, office workers, the professions etc. (Boratav, 2013: 15–20; Bürkev, 2013: 29–44; Tonak, 2013: 21–28, Tonak, 2014: 289–294). There is then a third position that claims that this is a new proletariat, which holds a college degree but can no longer enjoy the privilege of finding a secure job that the previous generations benefited from, a kind of precariat, in other words (Yıldızoğlu, 2013: 55–66).

The trouble with these positions is not so much that each of them is both right and wrong in a tautological sense (of that in a moment), but that they do not qualify their statement by defining which constitutive component of the Gezi popular rebellion they are thus characterizing. In case they are talking about the Gezi Park crowd setting tents there or constantly visiting, they are all of them right to a certain extent (to a certain extent only since their characterization of the layers in question, we believe, is wrong, as we will try to show in a moment). But if they are talking about the very real and no less significant component parts of the movement such as the youth of Gazi and Sarıgazi, the working populations of the predominantly Alevi neighbourhoods, the Tuzluçayır youth in Ankara or the people of Antakya, then they have gone completely astray!⁵

It is in fact a thankless, even futile job to try to define the class composition of a mass revolutionary movement or an equally massive people's rebellion solely on empirical observation. The reason is not hard to detect: as we know from historical revolutions and as we have been able to observe anew recently, such movements enlist people from very different backgrounds, walks of life and class positions to their cause.⁶ A revolution, in particular, is a very special situation in the life of a society, when everything is up for discussion, revision and transformation. So, people from even privileged classes may, if they are oppressed by certain conditions that exist in the *ancien régime* despite their class status, at least hesitate between the two camps of revolution or counter-revolution or even join the revolutionary side. But that case is simply an exaggerated complication seeking to bring home the fact that the presence within

---

5 The only serious treatment of the Alevi struggle within the Gezi uprising that we have come across is Gümüş (2013: 207, 230–33).
6 Here is a description of the diversity of the class make-up of demonstrators (this one is from Ankara, but the pattern is bound to be true elsewhere as well): "The bourgeois 'kids' of Çankaya, Oran, GOP [well-to-do, even posh neighborhoods of Ankara], the wives and children of the supers of the buildings, members of the middle class, public employees, students, homemakers, bohemians, would-be hippies ... Luxury cars support the action by constant honking. ... On the wall of a hotel on a side street, packages of milk, fruit juice, bottles of water have been placed. Whoever wants to takes one. As soon as the teargas cloud settles in, the doorman of the hotel comes out with a liquefied and diluted spray of 'Talcid' ... Everyone is filled with love for the hotel" (Çetin, 2013: 289–90).

revolutionary ranks of people from different classes really does not tell us too much about the class nature of the uprising. Rather, after having carefully and entirely cool-headedly marshalled the facts regarding who is on which side, what should be done is to determine which classes are active and efficacious in the unfolding of the revolution *qua classes* and what the mutual relations among those classes are. In particular, what one should look for is which class has or promises to have a *hegemonic* position in the revolution vis-à-vis the others.

So, the entire discussion on the class nature of Gezi is marred by two different methodological traps: first, what does one mean by "Gezi", the park or the entire people's rebellion? Without answering that question, any inquiry is hopelessly misplaced. And second, what actions in class terms are taken by the different classes to advance, retard or defeat the revolution and how these classes, *acting as classes*, interact with each other, in particular in hegemonic forms?

Viewed from this vantage point, our answer to the question of the class nature of Gezi is threefold. First, the Gezi Park camp was, despite the heterogeneity of the crowds gathered there, very clearly under the hegemony of the modern petty-bourgeoisie (Savran, 2014b). To provide a brief definition, this is the component of the petty-bourgeoisie that is reproduced by the modern conditions of production as opposed to the traditional petty-bourgeoisie (the small-holding peasantry, artisans and petty traders) that sees its conditions of reproduction lose ground by the year. The modern petty-bourgeoisie consists mostly of the professions with a high level of technical knowledge (medical doctors, engineers and architects, lawyers, pharmacists) who put this knowledge to use by opening up their own small business (cabinets, pharmacies, design studios, etc.) (Savran, 2007: 22–24). This class fraction is prone to ally itself in all countries with the educated top layers of the waged sections of the same socio-cultural group and the workers of the culture industry (such as digital experts, financial industry workers, culture industry workers, of which academics, etc.) (Savran, 2007: 37–38).[7] The hegemony we are talking about was

---

7   It should be noted that Boratav, mentioned above as one of the proponents of the idea that the working class formed the backbone of the Gezi movement, is, in fact, talking about the same layers ("highly-skilled, educated workers, together with their class comrades of tomorrow (students), with the participation of professionals."), (2013: 19). The difference lies in two decisive points: "the professionals" are petty-bourgeois in nature and the "highly-skilled, educated workers" are several extremely privileged top layers bordering the working class and only *semi-proletarians* in that they are not forced to sell their labor-power since they usually have the means to migrate into the ranks of the petty-bourgeoisie, which many of them do at some stage in their lifetime. Tonak (2013: 28) is in full agreement with Boratav. Bürkev

provided by the leadership of the Gezi Park resistance: The entire process was directed by the coalition of organizations that was called Taksim Solidarity, which was almost controlled completely by the professional organizations of engineers and architects and similar organizations. In this narrow sense, despite the profound differences between the two societies, there appears a very interesting parallel between the part played by the Sudanese Professionals Association up until recently and Taksim Solidarity as the leadership of the Gezi Park encampment and resistance.

Secondly, the components of the movement outside of Gezi Park were decidedly more plebeian in nature. Absent a rigorous type of survey or analysis on the class position of the different elements participating, the best characterization one could approximate to would be to say that from Gazi to Antakya the preponderant element was a combination of the working class, the urban poor, and the poorer sections of the traditional petty-bourgeoisie. Naturally, the youngsters from these classes held the front stage in the battles against the repressive forces of the state, as is common in all movements of resistance and contention. What is decisive, despite the presence of many industrial workers, etc. within the ranks of the demonstrators, is that the working class almost never intervened *qua* the working class. The workers present in the action were objectively workers, but did not act as members of a class determined to get the upper hand in a struggle against the ruling classes. Neither the demands nor the methods resorted to were those peculiar to the working class.

It is true that the Confederation of Public Employees' Trade Unions (Turkish: *Kamu Emekçileri Sendikaları Konfederasyonu*, KESK), the most left-leaning public employees' union, enacted its earlier declared sectoral strike on 5 June at Taksim square. It is also true that the Confederation of Progressive Trade Unions (Turkish: *Devrimci İşçi Sendikaları Konfederasyonu*, DİSK), the most progressive union confederation of industrial workers, declared that it would participate in KESK's appeal to turn that strike to a broader movement. But this was mostly formal. And it is significant that these two organizations, long-standing allies of the professional organizations of the modern petty-bourgeoisie, firmly in command of the Gezi Park resistance, declared a general strike only after the police forcibly evicted the campers outside of Taksim Square. This failure to act at the right time meant that that declaration of intention would remain only that, an act of good intentions.

(2013: 30–32) identifies the same layers, but characterizes them as an intermediary class with the structural characteristic of "losing out" and thus being absorbed into the working class. Startlingly, Bürkev concludes that "the question has a class character that is of a proletarian axis through and through".

The third aspect to be emphasized can thus be put very succinctly in light of what has been said so far. The working class was a *missing actor* in the Gezi uprising.

5   The Kurdish Movement and Gezi

The Kurdish question is, without doubt, one of the most important political issues in contemporary Turkey. The author of these lines is whole-heartedly in favour of the struggle of the Kurdish people for freedom and equality, including their right to self-determination, but deeply critical of the policies pursued domestically and internationally by the leadership of the movement since 2013 at the latest. This is not the place to discuss these issues of course, but the relationship of the Kurdish struggle to the people's rebellion was such a vital, even decisive issue that we need to look into the Kurdish question to the extent that it concerns the topic at hand.

The entire discussion on the relationship between the Kurdish movement and Gezi has unsurprisingly been fixated on a single issue: Did the Kurdish movement participate in the Gezi popular rebellion, or did it stand aside? The issue has been intentionally mystified by the spokespeople for the Kurdish movement and their many allies within the Turkish socialist movement. The muddling resides in a sleight of hand, whereby the question is answered *solely* with regard to Gezi Park. So, the geography of the Gezi popular rebellion, whose importance we have already discovered in discussing many diverse aspects of the phenomenon in its totality, once again comes to the fore.

Let us first provide the reader with a minimum amount of information that sheds light on the entire debate. 2013 was precisely the year when what was euphemistically called the "solution process", i.e., a process of negotiations between the AKP government and the Kurdish movement started. Full of uncertainties and ambiguities, it was nonetheless a renewed effort at solving the Kurdish problem that had beset the country for at least the previous three decades, after the guerrilla war started in 1984. It is our opinion that in taking this initiative the AKP was really going after the oil and natural gas supplies of the Kurdistan region of Iraq, but that discussion has to wait for another occasion. The process received the wholesale support of Abdullah Öcalan, the historic leader of the guerrilla movement, from his island prison (where he had been shut up since having been apprehended in Kenya by the United States and turned over to Turkey in 1999). It was also more or less willingly agreed to by the remaining PKK leadership from its headquarters in Qandil in Iraqi Kurdistan. The Peoples' Democratic Party (Turkish: *Halkların Demokratik Partisi*, HDP), the parliamentary party set up by the Kurdish movement together with a string of Turkish socialist parties and movements, was to act as the intermediary.

The "solution process" was, in our opinion, turned into a sort of alliance between the Kurdish movement and the AKP. The declaration made by Öcalan on the occasion of the Kurdish festivities of Newroz only months before Gezi harped on the commonality of objectives of the two movements, the AKP and the Kurdish movement, in the Middle East. Irrespective of whether this criticism of ours is correct or not, the "solution process" was the background for the adoption of the policy pursued by the Kurdish movement in relation to Gezi.

Secondly, let us very briefly deal with the aspect of the question as it regards Gezi Park itself before turning our gaze to the real issue. The HDP at first hesitated in providing support for the Gezi Park uprising, citing the presence among the crowds of a Turkish-nationalist tendency. This was rather a flimsy excuse since the tendency in question was rather weak. The real reason was the fear of alienating the AKP and losing the "solution process". However, in an astute tactical move, Öcalan stepped in and voiced his support and this led to the participation of the Kurdish movement in the Gezi Park encampment with its tent and its symbols. It is this participation in Gezi Park that is intentionally used to muddle the issue.

For what would really have been decisive for the fate of the people's rebellion would have been the participation of the Kurdish movement in Turkish Kurdistan. Had Diyarbakır, often called the capital of the region, moved forth as enthusiastically as İstanbul or Hatay, this would have created an earthquake. The Kurdish people are the most politicized and bold section of the citizenry and with Diyarbakır and many other cities of Kurdistan taking to and dominating the streets, with millions venting their anger and frustration with state policy on the burning Kurdish question as well as economic issues (for the Kurdish population is an underdog in this area as well), it is more than probable that the Erdoğan government would have been overthrown. This is how decisive the Kurdish movement's reaction was. And it failed at this fateful moment. Anyone confusing the two issues of what the Kurdish movement did in İstanbul and what it did in Diyarbakır is either too naïve or acting in bad faith.

It turned out that this was not only a chance missed for the people's rebellion, but for the Kurdish movement as well. But this will have to await our discussion of the Kobanê uprising of October 2014, an incident that is part of the cycle set off by the Gezi popular rebellion. Let us refrain from anticipating at this stage. Let us simply conclude this section by observing that during the people's rebellion the Kurdish movement was absent precisely where it was needed most, that is Diyarbakır and other Kurdish cities that surely would have left many Turkish-majority cities of the country in awe and envy had the leadership given the signal "Go!"

The Kurdish movement was thus the *second missing actor* of the rebellion.

6 Two Tactics of the Ruling Class in the Gezi Rebellion

A popular movement of the scale and power of the uprising that Turkey experienced in 2013 hardly ever fails to create hesitations and fissures in the ranks of the ruling class. Already, the ruling classes in Turkey were deeply divided face to the policies of the AKP government. The more powerful wing of the big bourgeoisie, under the roof of the Turkish Industry and Business Association (Turkish: *Türk Sanayicileri ve İş İnsanları Derneği,* TÜSİAD), which brings together the *crème de la crème* of the Westernizing-secular faction, deeply committed to NATO and the EU, had been severely critical of the government at times. Although it was extremely pleased by the ruthless policy of assault on the gains and rights of the working class pursued by Erdoğan (extensive privatization, growing commodification and commercialization of public services, attacks on the rights to unionize and to strike, flexibilization of the labor market, etc.), his orientation towards the Islamic world and his creeping Islamization of education, etc. caused increasing alarm in this section of the bourgeoisie. Unable to budge Erdoğan, it had grudgingly supported its pro-capitalist measures so far, but now that the people rose massively in defiance of the government and untiringly demanded its resignation, many from among the ranks of the *haute bourgeoisie* even stayed over at Gezi Park for a day or two. İnal (2013: 21) cites various other symptoms of the support Gezi received from the *crème de la crème* of the Turkish ruling classes.

This thoroughly comprehensible, though admittedly exaggerated, support to Gezi on the part of the Westernizing-secular wing was met halfway by a section of the leadership of the AKP itself. Let it be said clearly from the outset that Erdoğan himself took an entirely antagonistic attitude to the movement and even threatened a civil war of sorts by constantly referring to the "fifty per cent of the population that we hardly keep under control". However, Abdullah Gül, one of the founding leaders of the AKP, having been elected to the ceremonial though highly symbolic role of president of the republic, took a much more flexible position, agreeing in this with Bülent Arınç, the third member of the triumvirate that established the AKP and the acting prime minister for a brief period because Erdoğan was on a state visit to North Africa. The two, with the help of several other members of the cabinet, maneuvered in a blatant effort to sow division within the popular movement, pitting the "nice ecologists" with their "rightful concern for nature" against the "harmful elements", the "illegal organizations", i.e., the socialist and communist left in general. On this basis, they proceeded to start unofficial talks so that a solution, face-saving for both sides, could be reached.

Also active at this initial stage was Kemal Kılıçdaroğlu, the leader of the main opposition party, the CHP, a party that faithfully pursues the interests of the TÜSİAD bourgeoisie as its main goal. Let it be said in passing that an overwhelming majority of the millions who joined the people's rebellion were, without a shred of doubt, the regular electorate or even members of this party that poses as a left party of social democratic leanings. However, the leadership of the party kept decidedly aloof to the mass movement, even changing the venue of its planned demonstration in the early days from Taksim to another part of the city.

Thus, a powerful alliance of bourgeois forces, including a part of the top leadership of the AKP, was working for a negotiated solution. This section of the AKP leadership was, it seems, able to persuade Erdoğan to a watered-down version of negotiations with handpicked "representatives" of Gezi Park, which was held on the night of 13 to 14 June. (Some members of Taksim Solidarity were present at the meeting.) Erdoğan left the meeting in a nervous fit and no explicit plan was adopted for a peaceful solution.

On the night of 15 June, the park was forcibly evacuated and, on the 16th, Erdoğan held a rally of three hundred thousand fanatics bussed into another part of İstanbul. This was a war bugle.

7 How Did Gezi Park End?

We have briefly summarized these two different tactics of the ruling classes because the existence of the second, more conciliatory tone was instrumental in leading to the softening down of the leadership of the Gezi Park encampment, which finally facilitated the evacuation of the park. In other words, the Gül-Arınç overture convinced Taksim Solidarity to gradually empty Gezi Park in return for unsubstantial concessions on the part of the government. This then mollified certain elements of the mass movement, in particular the organized socialist movement, encouraged the option of attacking the park within the ranks of the government, and finally led to the crushing of the encampment. Let us now see how the process worked itself out in concrete terms.

After Gül and Arınç made their sounding out, there were explicitly positive responses from several leading figures of the mass movement in consultation with Taksim Solidarity. This led to the formulation of certain demands on the side of the mass movement and of an offer on the government's part. The demands formulated in the name of the movement by Taksim Solidarity were quite meek. For instance, despite days of savage repression, the blatant malpractice of using tear gas canisters as weapons in their own right by firing them directly taking mark towards the head of demonstrators, the use of troops without uniforms wielding nailed wooden bats, etc., the representatives only demanded the removal of some provincial governors, as if the real responsible instance were not the government and, in particular, the minister of the interior. We will see that even these meek demands were to prove valuable in the end. But much more central was the acceptance by the representatives of the offer of the government to hold a referendum on the question of whether the entire project of rezoning, i.e., the razing of the park to the ground in order to be replaced by a shopping mall in the form of a historic building. This was anathema to the majority of the people camped at Gezi Park for the simple reason that the judiciary, which at that point had not yet become a pliable instrument in the hands of Erdoğan, had again and again declared this rezoning project in contravention of all conservation legislation.

After the eventful meeting between Erdoğan and some handpicked representatives of Gezi Park, the secretary of Taksim Solidarity declared that an agreement had been obtained. The representatives then returned to İstanbul and in a very long meeting with representatives of all the organizations actively present in the park, tried to convince all present to accept what was presumed to be the offer by the government. This proved to be a tough job since none of the other demands out of the list of demands earlier formulated had been granted. The option of the referendum, as opposed to an outright abandonment of the project of rezoning by the government, the original demand of the mass movement, seemed a sort of capitulation on the part of the movement after all this struggle and self-sacrifice, after all the deaths and injuries and eyes lost. Moreover, with respect to police brutality, what was promised was simply an *internal investigation* of "excesses". Given the track record of the Turkish police and armed forces in investigating *their own crimes* (fully one and a half years after the Uludere/Roboski massacre, where 34 young Kurdish peasants were bombarded to death by the Turkish air force, not one single person had been prosecuted), the promise of an internal investigation was an insult on the intelligence of the masses!

Part of the argumentation in pushing for a compromise was that the people in the park were tired and that the support from the people of the city was dwindling. This argument proved to be entirely spurious for the "popular assemblies" that were meeting at the same time as the representatives' meeting was going on overwhelmingly opted for the continuation of the resistance until a more acceptable settlement was achieved.

All this was naturally played out in the open, the debate and the arguments put forth in defence of the diverging positions accessible not only to the masses, but thereby also to the government and the police thanks to the many agents of the government within the crowd. This mollification on the part of the presumed leadership of Gezi Park (a default leadership at best, as we shall have opportunity to discuss below), this hesitation and tergiversation persuaded the police that the time was ripe for an attack. The police had already made a first assault on Taksim on the 11th, but that had proved to be a semi-defeat for it. It did recover Taksim Square, but was not able to enter the park itself despite the inequality of arms. This clearly attests to the falseness of the argument that the people in the park were tired and slowly leaving, an idea that was defended with such zeal only three days later! The correct observation was rather to say that immediately after this attack by the police on the 11th, the number of people who visited the park after work increased and many came wearing hard hats, an explicit show of resolve to fight possible police assault.

The upshot of this is that it is superficial and wrong to say that it was simply the state's repressive apparatus that drove the park people out. At least as important was the success of the dual-track method of persuasion employed by the government circles and the willing submission of the unelected leadership of Gezi Park to this manoeuvre.

This was the subjective factor at play in the loss of Gezi Park. Behind this outcome were of course objective factors at play. We no longer need to speak at any length on the main and decisive objective factors, since we have already laid the ground for the explanation of this causality in the preceding sections, more particularly the section on the class nature of the people's rebellion and the section on the Kurdish movement. The decisive objective factors that led to the survival of Erdoğan in power were only two: the absence of what we have called the two "missing actors" within the entire historic event of the people's rebellion, i.e., the working class acting as a class and the Kurdish movement.

This is not a conclusion that we have only reached *ex post factum*. In an article written three days after Taksim Square and Gezi Park were conquered by the masses, on the 4th of June, this is what we wrote (Savran, 2013):

> The fate of the great popular rebellion in Turkey will be decided by the following questions: Will the Kurdish movement join the rebellion or will it implicitly side with the AKP government? And will the core battalions of the working class come forth with their class-based demands and forms of struggle?

8 The Socialist Movement and Gezi

The story of the socialist movement in Gezi Park is a tale of capitulation to political backwardness. It was the most striking shared characteristic of the participants in Gezi Park and later in the forums or public assemblies in all the parks of İstanbul and other cities that they were suspicious in the extreme of the existing political parties, not only mainstream ones but left-wing parties as well, of trade unions, and of all other such organizations. So much was perhaps understandable. Although it is not clear at all how much the younger generation of 2013 knew anything of the collapse of the twentieth century experience of socialist construction, even on the basis of conversations with their parents and grandparents, one may concede for the sake of argument that their suspicion may be granted some credibility because of the sheer weakness of the political and trade union organizations in question.

However, not only were the young Gezi crowd suspicious of existing organizations. They refused to be organized even when it was a question of themselves starting the process! There can be no doubt that this is an extreme instance of political backwardness. Politics in a mass society requires, by definition, the ordering of priorities, the making of decisions, and the setting up of cooperation and alliances between different groups so as to serve the purposes that one is pursuing. A solipsistic attitude is simply counter-productive since the necessity of politics in the above most general sense implies that no one lives in isolation from the rest of humanity and therefore needs to coalesce into one or more groups that are called organizations. One can surely be against *certain types* of organizations. But to be against organizing *per se* is self-defeating.

The socialist left in Turkey simply caved into this conception of the Gezi crowd. Many currents accepted this as the catechism of a new age. Alper Taş, a foremost leader of a well-established socialist current, provides a most illustrative instance of this attitude (Taş, 2013: 116). Even Oğuzhan Müftüoğlu, the historic leader of this same current, has said that all the political organizations of the left remained behind Gezi in every domain (cited in İnal, 2013: 33). It was as if such currents had finally been revealed the unassailable truth from this great eruption of the masses.

This went hand in hand with a naïve exaltation of this new generation. In a country where the left has been mesmerized by the role played by the generations of 1968 and then of 1978 in revolutionary politics, there was an incredibly rash talk of a new generation. It was rumoured that this generation, so disdained before Gezi for its depoliticization, was in fact very conscious politically. Strange then that ten years on nothing, *absolutely nothing* has remained of that generation in terms either of intellectual renewal or political acumen.

We do not know how those that so glorified the generation in question explain their baseless judgments of yesteryear.[8] For us, there is only one explanation: The left simply misread political naiveté and primitiveness, coupled with an unwarranted sense of righteousness, as originality.

This is shameful. Now, we are not talking about the youth of the park, but about the socialist currents of Turkey. This deception about the nature of the "Gezi generation" is a corollary of the failure of the left to study and analyse and understand the collapse of the twentieth century experience of socialist construction, coupled with the defeat suffered at the hands of the military in the early 1980s, a factor specific to Turkey. The price paid for this failure was the adoption of facile explanations that had nothing to do with the real world. The belief that a refusal to organize is the correct battle-cry of the future because young people who had not been interested in politics in the least up until then said so was the latest and most abhorrent of these quick-and-easy solutions to the most important intellectual problems that we have inherited from the twentieth century.

Other currents did not bow reverently to this primitiveness, but nonetheless did not challenge it for fear of isolation from the masses. The net result, a collective responsibility, was that the left failed to counter this self-defeating tendency rampant in the bosom of the movement. What should have been done was to tenaciously defend the *self-organization* of the Gezi masses. It is understandable that a spontaneous mass movement of the kind that Gezi was will not, in the initial stages of the struggle, wish to follow the leadership of parties or other kinds of organizations that it is not familiar with nor trusts. But to refuse to organize the mass movement even on entirely democratic basis is suicidal. This is not only because it leaves the movement vulnerable in its struggle against antagonistic forces, but also because it abandons the fate of the entire rebellion to the choices made by a leadership, Taksim Solidarity, which did not represent the inner forces of the mass movement. There is an immense paradox here: this is the fact that by refusing to elect its own representative bodies in the most democratic fashion, the movement *ipso facto* abandoned the leadership to a body that was composed of personalities and representatives that were *a relic of the pre-rebellion period* and so was not capable of representing

---

8 See, for instance, David and Toktamış (2015: 21), who write in the clearest contrast to our view, "Gezi acted as a trigger for the repoliticization of Turkish society and especially of younger generations, until then considered apathetic" or Karaduman (2014: 17), who still chides the left for their arrogance even as they admit that "Gezi has surpassed us" and "from now on, nothing will be the same".

the ebullition and effervescence created by the revolt itself. What had to be done was to elect a leadership that represented the spirit of the rebellion!

This is why we called Taksim Solidarity a "default leadership" above. When grassroots democracy is refused, a default leadership will take over, with what consequences we have already seen. As much is admitted by Can Atalay, a foremost member of Taksim Solidarity and today a victim of the travesty of justice of the Erdoğan regime, when he says (this in June 2013!) that with the advent of the Gezi Park eruption, the responsibility born simply surpassed the capacity of Taksim Solidarity, which was in his opinion the expression of different "life style" movements, and because no other organization was able to fill the vacuum, "a crisis of representation" was born (Atalay, 2014: 135–36, 148).

A second failure of the socialist left was to ignore the question of social classes. Class is a most decisive issue in situations where a mass eruption brings almost endless possibilities on the agenda. Neglecting or even ignoring the importance of the working class will always exact a heavy price on the movement, if only because through ruse and demagogy the reactionary party will try to win, and will succeed in their effort in many cases, this class to its side.

No attempt was made at Gezi to bring in the working class. It is true that partly, but only partly, as a result of its own fault, the socialist left has little influence among the masses of the working class at this beginning of the twenty-first century. However, two confederations of trade unions, one for workers (DİSK) and the other for public employees (KESK), are very much open to the influence of the socialist movement and although the former also looks to the CHP, we have already seen how the electorate and even the rank and file of this thoroughly bourgeois party had come under the spell of Gezi.

One method suggested itself in a very obvious manner. The mass demonstration that was planned for the second Sunday (9 June) could have been turned into a forum for workers' grievances as well. This could have also brought in progressive unions from the Confederation of Turkish Trade Unions (Turkish: *Türkiye İşçi Sendikaları Konfederasyonu*, Türk-İş), the largest union confederation in Turkey.

The socialist parties and movements in Gezi did not lift a finger in this direction. It was striking to see that when all the socialist currents participating in Gezi hung up their posters on the façade of a major cultural center overlooking Taksim square, there was only one party that mentioned the working class by calling trade unions to wage a general strike. The rest of the socialist movement simply ignored the importance or even the existence of that class.

A third shortcoming in the political stance of the socialist left was its failure to counter the propaganda that Erdoğan used against Gezi. This was in a way a simple continuation of what had been going on for the entire decade Erdoğan had been in power, less so in the first term (2002–2007), but much more marked from then on. Every time he ran into some deep trouble, political, economic or diplomatic, Erdoğan habitually laid the blame on "foreign forces", in other words the Western world. He did not neglect, concomitantly, to accuse his detractors within the domestic ruling class, i.e., the TÜSİAD bourgeoisie, as loyal collaborators of these "foreign forces". As a majority of the socialist left was intoxicated by the prospect of Turkey's accession to the European Union, which would transform Turkey overnight into a haven for democracy, peace, economic stability and workers' rights, not to mention national rights for the Kurds, an anti-imperialist rhetoric was shunned. This left Erdoğan's hand free to brainwash the plebeian masses, including the working class, into believing that the all-powerful imperialist countries of the West were after his head. As serious was the left's prevarication with respect to its political stance on TÜSİAD. Dimly aware of the contradictions between Erdoğan and TÜSİAD, a majority of the left, that same majority that regarded anti-imperialist propaganda as deleterious to the possibilities offered by EU imperialism, preferred not to talk about this social force that is supposed to be its primary historic foe.

Had the mass demonstration on 9 June been turned into a riposte to Erdoğan, challenging him to exit NATO and shut down the İncirlik base of the US in order to expose the shallowness of his supposed anti-Americanism and to nationalize the banks and shut down the casino that is the stock market if he wants to fight the so-called "interest-rate lobby", this might have made the other fifty per cent think twice about the sold-out character of the Gezi movement. Unfortunately, the illusions of the majority of the socialist left with respect to imperialism and the Westernizing-secular wing of the bourgeoisie precluded this policy and thereby abandoned the plebeian masses to Erdoğan's hegemony.

Fourth, the socialist movement capitulated easily to align with the attitude of Taksim Solidarity towards a compromise with the powers that be. We explained at length above how the compromise reached lacked sufficient guarantees with respect to the future of Taksim and Gezi and relied on Erdoğan's word of honour. We also underlined how little concession had been made by the government on the issue of police brutality. The rest of the demands were totally set aside. Under these conditions, given the continuing courage and combativity of the mass and given the overwhelming tendency of the "popular assemblies" to continue the resistance until an honourable deal was reached, the socialist left should certainly have rejected the agreement. On the contrary, all the major parties and organizations of the socialist left sided with the inadmissible agreement proposed by Taksim Solidarity.

A fifth point that should be raised is the fact that the socialist left did not intervene actively and in a correct manner in how the movement developed after the evacuation of Gezi Park and the setting up of forums or "popular assemblies" that gathered in parks around the city. The line to be adopted here, in our opinion, should have been similar to that defended above for the self-organization of the mass movement through democratically elected local representatives and an elected national leadership so that the forums did not get lost in a maze of outlandish demands ranging from the setting up of vegan kitchens to organizing socially responsible forms of trade in order to oppose the encroachment of big retail and also so that they did not degenerate into talking shops. Which is what happened to many of them as they died out towards mid-summer, when the wealthier layers, young and old, engaged in this activity, mostly belonging to the ranks of the modern petty-bourgeoisie, preferred to savour their recently won bravery and anecdotes of heroism on the beaches of the Mediterranean.

One final point has to do with the parliamentary cretinism of a majority of the socialist left, going from one extreme of almost total neglect of parliamentary work in the 1970s to total faith in electoral opportunities from the 1990s on. This infatuation with electoral politics continued despite the very strong signals indicated by Gezi that the conditions of Turkey made mass street politics a possibility and even a necessity. Very early on in the Gezi process, not only the uninitiated independent souls, but also socialists started to discuss what kind of electoral politics the Gezi experience could be turned into.

But the real blow came after the entire episode was over. As soon as the streets emptied in the wake of the flare-up of September that was discussed above, the entire left turned its face to the municipal elections of March 30, 2014. September to March, that is a six-month span. A country that has gone through such an earthquake and has not been able to solve any of the problems posed in a clear-cut manner might very well have seen a resumption of a similar kind of crisis in the space of those six months.

The author may perhaps be allowed a personal anecdote of a political debate between the leaders of close to a dozen political parties in September 2013, organized by the annual socialist conference of Karaburun, Izmir on the Aegean coast of Turkey. We found ourselves totally isolated when discussing the duties of socialists in the coming period. All socialist parties of some significance in Turkish political life that were present, including naturally the Kurdish movement, the strongest of them all, became fixated on the gains that could be made in the municipal elections of March, 30. We were the only ones to reject outright this kind of perspective, first, because the contradictions that had come to the surface in Gezi could lead to other eruptions of whatever specific character that simply could not be handled within the codes of electoral politics, and secondly, because elections were the terrain on which Erdoğan was still the strongest and no one should raise the hopes of the people as to the defeat of Erdoğan through electoral politics.

What happened in the aftermath of Gezi, we think, amply corroborated our outlook. Erdoğan won both the municipal elections in March 2014 and the presidential election, held for the first time through a direct popular ballot, in August of the same year. On the other hand, a corruption scandal of unprecedented gravity, involving Erdoğan's son and many of his ministers, broke out in December 2013 and once again threatened his seat only three months after the ending of the Gezi rebellion. There was a brief flare-up of the mass movement, but this died out soon. Then in October 2014, the largest Kurdish mass movement in the history of this country broke out. This will be discussed shortly. Just let it be said that these two episodes of December 2013 and October 2014 could have cost Erdoğan his seat, first as prime minister and later as president of the republic, had there been a serious sizable mass movement demanding his resignation. That was not to be, partly because this is not what the left had been preparing for.

9   The Cycle of Rebellions: from Gezi to the "Kobanê Serhildan" (October 2014)

The Gezi rebellion ended in September 2013. Only one year later the banner of rebellion was to be taken over by Turkish Kurdistan during the week-long "Kobanê Serhildan".[9] This was the deferred Kurdish Gezi. It was an event that was as important to the Kurds of Turkey as Gezi was important for the "West" of the country, that is, the geographical areas where Turks are the majority of the population.

This is not the place to give a detailed account of the entire series of events that led to the eruption of this uprising in an already long chapter. We will have to make do with a bare outline of the unfolding of the event and an emphasis on its overall relevance for socio-political struggles in Turkey, in particular in relation to Gezi.

The Kobanê serhildan was a result of the impact of the struggles of Syrian Kurds for autonomy in war-torn Syria on Turkish Kurdistan. The Syrian events started out in March 2011 as a popular revolt of the poor working population

---

9 "Serhildan" means "rebellion" or "insurrection" in Kurdish.

of the city and country under the impetus of the general Arab revolution and stayed that way for six months. Only in the fall of that year when the US and the reactionary Arab regimes, as well as the Erdoğan government in Turkey, changed course and started to arm the Islamists of the country did the conflict turn into a civil war with international ramifications. In the midst of that war, the Syrian Kurds, under the leadership of the PYD (Kurdish: *Partiya Yekîtiya Demokrat*, Democratic Union Party), ideologically affiliated to the PKK of Turkey, moved to establish autonomy in the Kurdish majority north and northeast of the country, under the name Rojava in summer 2012.

However, this was also the time when the Islamic State of Iraq and Sham (ISIS or Daesh) established its so-called Caliphate in the northern regions of Iraq and Syria. The relationship of the Erdoğan government to these two new formations contrasted sharply. Rojava was tolerated in the beginning but came to be considered a threat because it could pose an example of Kurdish autonomy within Turkey itself, and also because its consolidation meant more and more a strengthening of the PKK at least politically and ideologically if not militarily. The Erdoğan government's approach to ISIS, on the other hand, has been at best ambiguous and at worst supportive towards this *takfiri* reactionary organization (the concept *takfiri* implying that the movement assumed the power of postulating who is a real Muslim and who is not, thus attacking not only the presumed enemies of Islam but also those who explicitly defend and practice it, only according to its own understanding). ISIS had been attacking Kobanê, one of the cantons of Rojava, for several weeks when Erdoğan came forth, at the beginning of October 2014, and dropped the comment "Kobanê is about to fall", in a tone mocking the autonomy of Rojava. This let all hell loose in not only the Kurdish cities of Turkey, but also neighbouring cities such as Gaziantep, a heavily industrialized town with large Arab and Kurdish Syrian refugee populations, as well as all the metropolises of Turkey, since the policy of scorched earth pursued by the state from the 1990s on had led to the migration of millions of Kurds under compulsion.

For an entire week, millions of Kurds came out on the streets protesting Erdoğan and ISIS, marching day and night, whatever their political inclinations may be. All testimonies indicate that the sizeable minority of the Kurdish population living in Kurdistan proper in Turkey that systematically voted for the AKP rubbed shoulders with sympathizers of the Kurdish movement. One cannot exaggerate the importance of this event in terms of numbers, militancy, resolve, the outrage of the participants, and the resilience of the crowds in the face of attacks. The attacks came from three quarters: the repressive forces of the state, the counter-revolutionary armed forces among the Kurds themselves, and the fascists of the Nationalist Action Party (Turkish: *Milliyetçi Hareket Partisi*, MHP), i.e., the classical fascist party of Turkey, who are now allies of the AKP.

Some detail about these would give an idea to the uninformed reader about how the state and its repressive forces approached the serhildan. In many cities, the army was sent in to quash the rebellion, something that never came on the agenda during Gezi in the "West". In Diyarbakır, on the first night of the rebellion, hundreds of armed goons of the Free Cause Party (Turkish: *Hür Dava Partisi*, HÜDA-PAR), a notoriously reactionary Kurdish party already exposed for its criminal series of massacres of militants of the Kurdish movement in the 1990s but now protected and assisted by the government, attacked the crowds in several neighbourhoods, aided and abetted by the police special forces. In Gaziantep and Izmir, at least, there is incontrovertible testimony that militants of the MHP, making the signature hand sign of their movement, moved into neighbourhoods where Kurds lived and fired into crowds and even into homes, all the time accompanied and protected by the police special forces. Despite the brutality that the police displayed during Gezi, nothing of such proportions was even attempted there.

No wonder this left more than 40 or perhaps even 50 dead. And, more importantly, violence begot violence, there were casualties on all sides (including two senior police officers), police precincts and schools were burnt down, municipal buildings and other government premises attacked. So, Gezi in Kurdistan was immediately bloodied, on the very first day. This resulted in a total lack of comprehension in the "West" of Turkey. The Gezi Park crowd simply kept silent, and some liberal leftists even accused the Kurds of being "vandals" (a term originally used by the extremely reactionary Minister of Interior of the time). This was particularly abhorrent when one remembers that the Gezi participants had been called a similar name by Erdoğan himself, "çapulcu" ("*chapulist*" in its Anglicized version, meaning "marauder").

We have documented the significance, the humbling dimensions, the mass character of this event painstakingly and are referring to a number of articles, some authored and some collective (Gerçek, 2014a, 2014b, 2014c; Savran, 2014a). Unfortunately, they are all in Turkish.

Let us content ourselves with calling to the witness stand a most authoritative figure of the opposite side, Ahmet Davutoğlu, the prime minister of the time. Ten days after the events ended on 12 October, in other words after having had time to inspect the reports provided by his intelligence agencies, this gentleman pronounced, at a meeting of his fellow AKP bigwigs, the following sentence: "Should the solution process break up halfway, we will find ourselves unable to rule over that region" (Savran, 2014a). Lest there remain any doubts on the part of the reader, "that region" is obviously Turkish Kurdistan. We need insist no further on the importance of the serhildan.

However, that sentence also reminds us that this was still the time of the "solution process". That is why the government had another avenue open to it to try and stop the floodgates of rebellion. And because, despite the violence unleashed on peacefully demonstrating crowds, it could not put an end to the momentum of the rebellion it also used this alternative route. In an ironic twist of history, the government went to Abdullah Öcalan in his island prison and asked him to issue a declaration to the crowds admonishing them to return home. This was provided on the night of 7 October and the leaders of the HDP made Öcalan's message public in a press conference on the 8th. To put what followed into perspective, one needs to understand that Öcalan is considered no less as a *jefe máximo* by his flock than Fidel Castro used to be by the Cubans. Despite Öcalan's letter, the demonstrations went on until the 12th of October. Everything then shows, the geographic expanse of the revolt (35 cities), the heterogeneity of the crowds involving people of very different political persuasion, the resilience displayed despite the savage violence of the counter-revolution, the refusal of even the organization of the Kurdish youth to comply with Öcalan's admonishment (couched in very subtle diplomatic language in the document published by the organization), all go to show that this was a rebellion whose dynamics were *spontaneous* and if handled differently could have had a very different outcome, i.e. a Kurdish revolution proper.

Be that as it may, the main conclusion we need to draw in our present context is the following: Turkey went through two immensely explosive people's rebellions in the space of one year, but the actors of the two turned their back on each other. The Kurdish movement extended only diplomatic support to Gezi. And the Gezi Park crowd, as well as the rest of the Turkish population of the "West", with the exception of certain socialist currents, met the Kurdish rebellion with indifference if not hostility.

It is our conviction that, had the Kurdish movement thrown aside the so-called "solution process" during the Gezi people's rebellion, the two struggles could have been unified into one and Erdoğan could successfully have been ousted as prime minister. The tergiversation and prevarication of the Kurdish movement was penalized by the division sown between the "chapulists" of western Turkey and the "vandals" of Kurdish cities.

10 The Cycle of Rebellions: the Metalworkers' Gezi (May–June 2015)

The third episode within the cycle of revolts set off by Gezi was the metalworkers' Gezi, popularly acclaimed as the "metallic hurricane". Of the three, this was the least resounding in the short term and yet the most significant for the outcome of social and political struggles in the medium and longer terms.

In mid-May 2015, in one factory after another, in what appeared to be an unstoppable movement, metalworkers in their tens of thousands took recourse to a wildcat strike in order to quash the yellow gangster union that was painstakingly built by the military regime of the early 1980s in order to keep the commanding heights of the class struggle under the control of the bourgeoisie. Giant factories such as Renault, Fiat (under the brand name Tofaş, jointly owned by Stellantis and Koç Holding), and Ford were at the forefront of the movement. In some factories the work stoppage lasted for more than ten days with partial occupation. In some, such as the two manufacturing sites of Ford, the stoppage went on even longer.

This led to a wildfire of strikes in other factories, including Magneti Marelli Mako, Ototrim, Türk Traktör, Ford Otosan, and Valeo. It should be emphasized that this entire movement took place in a country where the right to strike has been constricted by the legislation promulgated under the military regime of the early 1980s and is strictly limited to disputes that arise in the collective bargaining process. This strike, on the contrary, found its sole source of legitimacy in the fighting spirit and the unity of the workers. Production came to a complete halt in these companies, many of which are industrial giants (up to six or seven thousand workers work in some of them). Moreover, the workers of the last shift to quit in each case remained inside the factory, spending the nights there, thus bringing these actions close to strikes with occupation.

The significance of this wildcat strike derived also from the strategic position of the metallurgical industry in the Turkish economy. The metal industry was (and still is) the top exporter in a country with a level of annual exports that totaled 160 billion USD in 2015. In recent years, the three top export products of the country have been cars, auto parts and accessories, and delivery trucks. Metalworkers thus find themselves in a centrally placed strategic position in the overall struggle of the working class in the country. Türk Metal, the yellow union against which the workers raised the banner of revolt, is the biggest union in the industry, with close to 140 thousand members, followed way behind by Birleşik Metal, with over 20 thousand members. The latter is affiliated to DİSK, a confederation that comes from a left-wing tradition, while Türk Metal is affiliated to the confederation Türk-İş, much more docile and pragmatic. Türk Metal has the most reactionary leadership structure in the entire panoply of unions affiliated to Türk-İş.

It should be pointed out that Türk Metal has been the flagship of the new order within the union movement set up in the early 1980s by the military regime. The confederation DİSK having been shut down by the junta and its leadership thrown in prison, Türk Metal was deliberately promoted into a position of dominance in the metal industry through the close collaboration of the military government and MESS, the bosses' association in the metallurgical industry. The reason for this well-thought-out strategy on the part of the bourgeoisie can be found in the fact that in the two-decade period before the coup, a period of great working-class militancy, the metalworkers' union affiliated to DİSK (Maden-İş as it was called) was at the vanguard of the struggles. The military regime was established precisely to stop this wave of great workers' struggles. Türk Metal was therefore designed to lull the metalworkers' fight into lethargy. This yellow union is of the US style gangster type and is more akin to a subcontractor company specialized in providing cheap and docile labor to metal companies than to a veritable union.

The movement of May-June 2015 was partially victorious, with the guaranteeing of full trade union freedom to the workers, renunciation of punitive layoffs on the part of the bosses, and some pay raise. But its real importance derived from the fact that it helped build a certain self-confidence in the metal workers, led to serious concerns of being overrun in the gangster union, contributed to a realignment in the respective positions in the industry of Türk Metal, the gangster union, and Birleşik Metal, the more class struggle oriented one, and, as a result, opened the door to successive waves of struggles in the metal industry.

An interesting detail that should be pointed out is that the metalworkers took up as their own some of the slogans that were a creation of the Gezi people's rebellion, in particular "This is only the beginning, the struggle will continue!", which itself bears not a very distant echo to a Parisian slogan of 1968: *"Ce n'est que le début, la lutte continue!"* In fact, this slogan was used in other workers' actions between Gezi and the metalworkers' action of May-June 2015. This shows that in the same way as Tahrir Square in Cairo became the paradigmatic reference point of all international movements in the period 2011–2013, so did the Gezi people's rebellion for all the different social forces that revolted against the established order during the cycle 2013–2015 within Turkey itself.

However, the real significance of the 2015 metalworkers' strikes with occupation lies in the fact that it brought forth on the stage of social struggles the sleeping giant, the working class, which, when it truly awakens, will shake

Turkey in the same way that Gezi and the serhildan have. There is no doubt that metalworkers will be among the vanguard of any proletarian movement that will, in future, gain momentum.

11 Conclusion

This chapter, we believe, does not need a lengthy concluding section. We will only add what seems to us a very significant aspect of the picture we have depicted here regarding the nature of the Gezi Park dimension of what was, as we have insisted throughout the chapter, a much more variegated and diversified people's rebellion.

Let us start out by saying that the critical outlook that permeates the chapter is really about the sorry state in which the left in general and its socialist component in particular have found themselves in throughout the last several decades. This state is not at all peculiar to Turkey but finds its expression, perhaps with certain nuances, in all countries. We have treated the root causes of this state of affairs at length in another recent article in English (Savran, 2022). The entire spectrum of criticism we have leveled at the Gezi movement and the various strata of its leadership, including the socialist parties and groups of the country with a Marxist background, owe their origin to the socio-economic and political conditions evoked in that article.

Among those conditions, the material *class basis* that has produced the contours of the so-called postmodern, identity-centered left is of paramount importance. We explained in the chapter we have just referred to that this entire current was the ideological-political expression of the needs and aspirations of certain class strata that rose to dominance in late twentieth-early twenty-first century capitalist society. The strata in question are the modern petty-bourgeoisie and its loyal ally, the educated semi-proletarian stratum that is at once a part of the proletariat, but simultaneously its negation.

These two strata have co-existed in many revolutions and people's rebellions of the twenty-first century with other laboring classes and strata of the population such as the working class proper, the urban poor and segments of the peasantry. What is interesting in the case of the Gezi people's rebellion is the following: although there was a general tendency in all revolutions and rebellions of the early twenty-first century whereby the central venue was rather a product of the higher classes participating in the movement, in the case of Turkey these strata were spatially separated from the rest of the classes and strata active in the movement in almost absolute isolation. In other words, the Gezi Park dimension of the movement was a laboratory of the political-ideological position and attitudes of the two strata in question, the modern petty-bourgeoisie and the educated semi-proletariat. It is true that the isolation was not complete since in many other cities such as Ankara, Izmir, Antalya etc. the separation in space was far from being as marked as that in İstanbul, but in the latter city the separation was so marked that Gezi Park in the first fortnight of the rebellion may legitimately be regarded as a laboratory case regarding the behaviour of the strata in question in as pure a manner as this can conceivably be achieved in the social sciences as opposed to natural sciences.

What we find is precisely the attitude that gives the chapter cited its title: this is precisely "the age of egoism" peculiar to the modern petty bourgeoisie and the educated semi-proletarian strata. This is why the world got to know so little of the part played by the Alevi communities of Turkey in the Gezi popular revolt, but everything about the "carnivalesque", highly intellectually-powered humoristic universe of the Gezi Park experience. Everything, or almost everything, the international audience has read or heard about the Gezi rebellion in Turkey is the narcissistic self-reflection of the modern petty-bourgeoisie and the educated semi-proletarian strata on their own experience.

We believe, on the contrary, that the Kurds of the Kobanê Serhildan of 2014 and the proletarians of the "metallic hurricane" of 2015 were as important as, if not more important than, these strata for the future of revolution and social change in Turkey in the coming period. These are what we characterized as the two "missing actors" of Gezi. Add to these the almost "invisible" actor of Gezi itself, that is to say the Alevis, and only then do you have the strategic actors (in addition to the Gezi crowd) of revolution and social change in Turkey.

Those whose viewpoint ignores these weaknesses of Gezi simply to concentrate on its indubitable achievements are bound to miss once again the chance of achieving victory in the next round of a mass explosion.

Bibliography

Atalay C (2014) Gezi direnişi. In: Kara A et al. (eds) *18 Brumaire'den Taksim Direnişi'ne Geziyi Soldan Kavramak.* İstanbul: Kalkedon, 135–153.

Beinin J (2016) *Workers and Thieves. Labor Movements and Popular Uprisings in Tunisia and Egypt.* Stanford: Stanford University Press.

Boratav K (2013) Olgunlaşmış bir sınıfsal başkaldırı: Gezi direnişi. In: Göztepe Ö (ed.) *Gezi Direnişi Üzerine Düşünceler.* Ankara: Nota Bene, 15–20.

Bürkev Y (2013) Sınıf, toplumsal muhalefet ve siyasal rejim açısından haziran isyanı. In: Göztepe Ö (ed.) *Gezi Direnişi Üzerine Düşünceler.* Ankara: Nota Bene, 29–44.

Çetin A (2013) Ankara gezi'sinden sahneler. In: İnal K (ed.) *Gezi, İsyan, Özgürlük*. İstanbul: Ayrıntı, 280-85.

Danişmend İH (1948) *İzahlı Osmanlı Tarihi Kronolojisi*, Volume 2. İstanbul: Türkiye Yayınevi.

David I and Toktamış FK (2015) Introduction: Gezi in Retrospect. In: David I and Toktamış FK (eds) *'Everywhere Taksim': Sowing the Seeds for a New Turkey at Gezi*. Amsterdam: Amsterdam University Press, 15-26.

Gerçek (2014a) *Tozun Dumanın Arasından Görülebilen (1): İç Savaş Kışkırtıcıları*. Available (consulted September 10 2022) at: https://gercekgazetesi1.net/ulusal-sorun/tozun-dumanin-arasindan-gorulebilen-1-ic-savas-kiskirticilari.

Gerçek (2014b) *Tozun Dumanın Arasından Görülebilen (2): Kürt Hareketinde Farklılaşma*. Available (consulted September 10 2022) at: https://gercekgazetesi1.net/ulusal-sorun/tozun-dumanin-arasindan-gorulebilen-2-kurt-hareketinde-farklilasma.

Gerçek (2014c) *Tozun Dumanın Arasından Görülebilen (3): Barzani Ne İşe Yarar?* Available (consulted September 10 2022) at: https://gercekgazetesi1.net/ulusal-sorun/tozun-dumanin-arasindan-gorulebilen-3-barzani-ne-ise-yarar.

Gjergji I (2013) The role of Egyptian workers in the 2011 uprising: A view from below. *Revista Sul-Americana de Ciência Política* 1(2): 19-37.

Göztepe Ö (ed.) (2013) *Gezi Direnişi Üzerine Düşünceler*. Ankara: Nota Bene.

Gümüş A (2013) Çukurova ve nusayri örneğinde şeriatçılığa ve metalaşmaya karşı duygu, akıl ve kültür kompartımanlarının varoluşsal direnci ve patlaması. In: İnal K (ed.) *Gezi, İsyan, Özgürlük*. İstanbul: Ayrıntı, 204-237.

İnal K (2013) Gezi: Tanım, failler ve roller. In: İnal K (ed.) *Gezi, İsyan, Özgürlük*. İstanbul: Ayrıntı, 15-40.

Karaduman Ö (2014) Önsöz – Gezi'yi soldan kavramak. In: Kara A et al. (eds) *18 Brumaire'den Taksim Direnişi'ne Geziyi Soldan Kavramak*. İstanbul: Kalkedon, 11-24.

Keyder Ç (2013) *Law of the Father*. Available (consulted September 10 2022) at: https://www.lrb.co.uk/blog/2013/june/law-of-the-father.

Marx K (1972) The Eighteenth Brumaire of Louis Bonaparte. In: Padover SK (ed.) *The Karl Marx Library*, Volume 1. New York: McGraw Hill, 245-46.

Özel S (2014) A moment of elation: The gezi protests/resistance and the fading of the AKP project. In: Özkırımlı U (ed.) *The Making of a Protest Movement in Turkey: #occupygezi*. London: Palgrave Macmillan, 7-24.

Savran S (2007) Sınıfları haritalamak: Sınıflar birbirinden nasıl ayrılır? *Devrimci Marksizm* (6-7): 9-49.

Savran S (2013) *"C'est Une Révolte, Pas (Encore) Une Révolution!"*. Available (consulted on September 10 2022) at: http://redmed.org/article/cest-une-revolte-pas-encore-une-revolution1.

Savran S (2014a) *"Çözüm Süreci Yarım Kalırsa O Bölgeyi Yönetemez Hale Geliriz"*. Available (consulted on September 10 2022) at: https://gercekgazetesi1.net/ulu sal-sorun/cozum-sureci-yarim-kalirsa-o-bolgeyi-yonetemez-hale-geliriz.

Savran S (2014b) Halk isyanının sınıf karakteri üzerine notlar. In: Savran S, Tanyılmaz K, and Tonak EA (eds) *Marksizm ve Sınıflar. Dünyada ve Türkiye'de Sınıflar ve Mücadeleleri.* İstanbul: Yordam Kitap, 295–302.

Savran S (2015) Class, state and religion in Turkey. In: Neşecan B et al. (eds) *The Neoliberal Landscape and the Rise of Islamist Capital in Turkey.* New York/Oxford: Berghahn, 41–88.

Savran S (2019) Arap devriminin dirilişi: Türkiye için dersler. *Devrimci Marksizm* (39–40): 13–62.

Savran S (2020a) 15-16 Haziran: Türkiye'de proleter devrimleri çağının açılışı. *Devrimci Marksizm* (43): 89–122.

Savran S (2022) The age of egoism. *Revolutionary Marxism 2022* [Annual English-language publication of *Devrimci Marksizm*].

Savran S (2023) *Bir İhtilal Olarak Millî Mücadele.* İstanbul: Yordam Kitap.

Savran S and Ülker E (2018) Historicizing the gezi protests. In: Özyürek E et al. (eds) *Authoritarianism and Resistance in Turkey.* Cham: Springer International Publishers, 33–41.

T.C. İstanbul 13. Ağır Ceza Mahkemesi [Republic of Turkey, 13th Assize Court of İstanbul] (2022) *Gezi davası dosyası* [*The Gezi case file*] [Retrieved from UYAP, the central filing system of the Ministry of Justice of the Republic of Turkey, on July 6 2022] https://hhgm.adalet.gov.tr/Home/SayfaDetay/uyap-vatandas-portal-bilgi-sistemi.

Taş A (2013) Gezi yeni bir yol açtı. In: İnal K (ed.) *Gezi, İsyan, Özgürlük.* İstanbul: Ayrıntı, 111–116.

Tonak EA (2013) İsyanın sınıfları. In: Göztepe Ö (ed.) *Gezi Direnişi Üzerine Düşünceler.* Ankara: Nota Bene, 21–28.

Tonak EA (2014) Haziran direnişi tahayyülleri. In: Savran S, Tanyılmaz K, and Tonak EA (eds) *Marksizm ve Sınıflar. Dünyada ve Türkiye'de Sınıflar ve Mücadeleleri.* İstanbul: Yordam Kitap, 295–302.

Yıldızoğlu E (2013) Gezi "olayı"nın sınıfı. In: Göztepe Ö (ed.) *Gezi Direnişi Üzerine Düşünceler.* Ankara: Nota Bene, 55–66.

CHAPTER 3

The Gezi Resistance at the Edge of Populist Rupture

Kürşad Ertuğrul and Aylin Topal

Recep Tayyip Erdoğan, whose political career first came to the fore when he became the Mayor of Istanbul in 1994, has had consecutive efforts to define Istanbul. In 2009, the Justice and Development Party (*Adalet ve Kalkınma Partisi*, AKP) government launched its efforts to turn Istanbul into a regional financial center for the Middle East and North Africa eventually becoming a global financial center competing with New York and London (Kalkınma Bakanlığı, 2015). In April 2011, then Prime Minister Erdoğan revealed his "biggest dream" of the "Istanbul Canal." Erdoğan's "crazy project" was a manmade waterway, a 40 kilometre-long, 150 meter-wide and 25-meter-deep canal between the Black Sea and the Sea of Marmara on the European side of Istanbul parallel to Bosphorus. Erdoğan noted that he imagines building a "new city" on both sides of this canal (Jones et al., 2011). In May 2013, Erdoğan announced the government's further redevelopment plans for Istanbul. The plans included the construction of a mosque –a project he had first uttered during his election campaign in 1994 before the local elections-in Taksim Square –the main square of İstanbul, and a historical military barrack in the Gezi Park– one of the few remaining green spots in Taksim Square. The plans also included "mega-projects" like a third airport and a third bridge over the Bosphorus.

These projects had created an accumulated discontent in civil society leading to a burst in June 2013. The Union of Chambers of Turkish Engineers and Architects (*Türk Mühendis ve Mimar Odaları Birliği*-TMMOB) and the Union of Chambers of City Planners (*Şehir Plancılar Odası*) immediately took a decisive position taking legal actions against the Gezi Park reconstruction project, while environment activists blocked entrance of the construction vehicles to the Park. These protests eventually spread over the country through the month of June after the police forces intervened by using excessive force on these protestors at Gezi Park at dawn of May 31. In the following weeks, millions rushed to parks in many provinces to protest, chanting, "[e]verywhere is Taksim, everywhere is resistance".[1]

---

1 According to the Gezi Report by the Human Rights Institution of Turkey under Turkish Ministry of Interior, 3.611.208 people actively took part in the 80 cities of Turkey throughout the insurgency and 5532 protest events were recorded (Türkiye İnsan Hakları Kurumu, 2014).

Erdoğan's reaction to the protests was uncompromising. Erdoğan's discourse reiterated the societal cleavage between Islamists and seculars to mobilize political support and consolidate its rule. Before Erdoğan flew to Africa on the 3rd of June, he claimed he was "barely holding back the 50 percent" of the country that voted for him from coming onto the street; in fact, he made the bold claim that "[t]here may be thousands of protesters on the streets" but he could "bring millions." (*The Economist*, June 15, 2013). Towards the end of June, the protests in and around Taksim Gezi Park were brutally dispersed by the police force, leaving 7 dead and 8163 wounded. Eventually, by mid-July, Taksim Square was dominated by infamous riot control vehicles armoured by water cannons and teargas bombs, along with a score of police officers patrolling the area at all times. However, the Gezi protests have left its bold mark, as "the Spectre of Gezi" continued to haunt Erdoğan regime, opening a new space for urban movements (Topal, 2014).

This study claims that while defining Istanbul as a global financial city with mega-projects has continued to be one of the projects of Erdoğan, there has been a growing opposition attempting to define the city with a focus on ecological justice, right to city, participation, and freedom. In the aftermath of the Gezi resistance, the centralized state power pressed for the continuation of the plans. The airport, the bridge, and the mosque are completed. The Istanbul Financial Centre (*İstanbul Finans Merkezi*) is still under construction, to be launched in early 2023, while the Istanbul Canal is still on the agenda, scheduled to be auctioned for its construction. At first sight, this picture could be a rather grey one, however, there have been increasing counter-efforts of defining urban space in İstanbul. In this sense, the Gezi Insurgency has been a significant moment for the "urban social movement" opposing the central government's projects. Gezi insurgency, originally, depended on the demand for urban self-management by and through autonomous communities and associations intervening in the imposed meanings on the city to raise their alternative understandings and concerns.

Our analysis depends on and is verified by open-ended, in-depth interviews we have conducted to make sense of and trace the lingering dynamics of the Gezi Insurgency in everyday life and assess its legacy. The key informants in this fieldwork were the representatives of the associations and civil initiatives that took an active part in the Gezi Insurgency, representatives of the consumer cooperatives formed in the aftermath of the Gezi Insurgency, representatives of the Istanbul City Council and the Republican Peoples Party (CHP). In our fieldwork, we tried to assess both the historical background of the Gezi Resistance and the living legacy of the Resistance ten years after its irruption.

1   Coming to Terms with the Urban Social Movement
     and the Populist Moment

When the Gezi Park insurgency erupted in Turkey during the summer of 2013, it appeared to be a part of the social protests sweeping the world from those in Iceland – the first wave of which had started in 2009 – to those in such diverse countries as Tunisia, Spain, Egypt, Greece, US, and Brazil in the early 2010s. In the social movement studies literature, this widespread protest wave of the 2010s has been distinguished from the previous ones; working class-based "old social movements", single issue-identity-based "new social movements" led by the new middle-class fragments (since the mid-1960s), and global justice movement organized around the World Social Forums through the 2000s in the form of broad, global class coalitions (Della Porta, 2015: 17). Della Porta (2015) defined this last, i.e. fourth, tide of social movements as "anti-austerity" led by those who are vulnerable to "precarization." In Della Porta's analysis, she remained cautious to include Gezi in this category. Della Porta was rightly cautious for there was no identifiable "anti-austerity" policy in Turkey at the time. Still, Della Porta's definition of the social basis of these movements as those under the impact of precarization was also too broad that almost everyone subjected to the conditions of neoliberal global capitalism may fall into this category. Pointing to the social, cultural, and demographic heterogeneity of the people supporting these insurgency movements, Castells (2012) emphasized that a cross-section of society from various backgrounds, ages, and conditions were the subjects in these action processes. The analytical framework Castells provides is also conducive to this diversity at the social basis of the struggles of those who strive to raise and represent their values and interests by creating platforms of "counter-power" through linking virtual and occupied public spaces against the institutionally and politically entrenched power which denies and disrespects them. The Gezi case as an "urban social movement" can be considered a part of this last wave of social insurgencies in this framework.

Available surveys and field studies (Gambetti, 2014; Konda, 2014; Yörük and Yüksel, 2014; Sophos, 2017) confirm that a cross-section of the society in terms of class backgrounds, gender, and age have participated in the Gezi Insurgency as a struggle against their oppression under the AKP government and its leadership. According to KONDA Report (2014), about 79% of the protestors were inexperienced in terms of activism, unorganized and unaffiliated. Social and political diversity has also been reflected by the variety of demands and concerns. What unified the protestors was their common experience of oppression, though the reasons why they had this sense of oppression[2] were different. Different groups, individuals, and class segments commonly targeted the authoritarian power. The common ground was a highly politicized expression of frustration under a structure of power that was getting more and more intrusive and authoritarian.

The political moment signalled a new political possibility, one that is attested by Laclau's (2007: 74) conception of populism. As the Gezi movement initiated a process of forming counter-power through articulating virtual[3] and occupied public spaces, it was instituting an "internal antagonistic frontier" between the "people" coming together in struggle and politically and institutionally established power configuration, i.e., people versus power as in the first precondition of populism in Laclau's analysis. Yet, in order for a new political subject to be constituted at this moment, it was also necessary to absorb the "unfulfilled demands" of the socially, politically, and culturally heterogeneous subjects in an "equivalential chain" to bring them together for a new modality of representation (Laclau, 2007). It was only through such an "equivalential articulation" that a "broader social subjectivity" (Laclau, 2007: 74) could be constituted as the basis of the new political subject both an outcome of a hegemonic articulation and the new subject for politics of hegemony (Şengül, 2015). Arguably, the Gezi Insurgency remained at the threshold of the second precondition for unleashing such a new dynamic in Turkish politics, still with significant political after-effects.

The Gezi Insurgency, despite its explicit political character, could not bring about a new political subject with popular identity, yet it led to significant social, political, and cultural outcomes as a strong case of an "urban social movement". Castells' definition of urban social movement structured around three basic goals resonates well with the Gezi case. Castells emphasized that not only the presence of three goals, but their conscious expression is the bedrock of an urban social movement. The collective action, characterizing an urban social movement, is based on these goals. Moreover, each goal "opposes another project in the city" (Castells, 1983: 319). The first one is to hold the city "organized around its use value" against the projects of commodification based on the logic of exchange value. In the case of the Gezi movement, the beginning point of the action process was government's project to convert one remaining

---

2 As Sophos (2017) cites from his field study "wearing an earring, being Alevi, drinking [alcohol]."
3 An early survey on Gezi protesters defined the Gezi movement as "online action" because of extensive use of social media and smart phones and tablets through the action process See: Bilgiç and Kafkaslı (2013).

public park at the city centre into a shopping mall and a residential area which was disguised as a restoration of an historic site. Hence, there was a clear popular resistance against this project of commodification based on the logic of exchange value. The second goal is the "search for cultural identity" in terms of the creation of "autonomous" local cultures and communities as a struggle for autonomous communication and control of social meaning. In the wake of the Gezi Insurgency and its aftermath, numerous neighbourhood associations have been established not only for the preservation of their commons but also for creating autonomous communities of communication and meaning creation. Proliferating assembly forms of direct democracy, the forums, through and after the Gezi movement can also be considered as a reflection of this goal. The third goal is the search for urban self-management via neighbourhood-level decentralization "in contradiction to the centralized state". While most of the protesters who later participated in the collective action were unorganized and unaffiliated, most of the organizations, especially neighbourhood associations, forming the Taksim Solidarity in 2012 against the government's project were raising and voicing this goal.

This structure of an "urban social movement" also explains the underlying social, political, and cultural heterogeneity in the social basis. The participants of the collective action process cut across the class, gender, and age categories as "they do not relate directly to the relationships of production, but to the relationships of consumption, communication and power" (Castells, 1983: 319). Therefore, Gezi is a case of "urban social movement" which created platforms of counter-power escalating from a defence of the city (in terms of its use value) and its communities demanding urban self-management toward being the centre of widespread social unrest against an authoritarian government and its leadership. In this sense, it is a part of the recent wave of social movements.

2 Tracing the Urban Dynamics and the Basis of the Gezi Insurgency

The third term of AKP rule that started with the elections in June 2011 may be called as territorialization of the party imposing conservative – religious moral and social norms on the society. AKP came to power with 34 percent of the vote casted in the national elections held on November 3, 2002. It was the first time in fifteen years that any party had been in a position to govern alone. The party was manifestly religiously oriented having its roots in the Turkish Islamic Movement. However, the party's leader, Erdoğan and his associates carefully distanced themselves from previous Islamic movement. They, rather, portrayed their party in the same lane as Western Europe's Christian-Democratic parties (*Milliyet*, February 4, 2002). However, the conservatism of AKP has become more evident as the Party consolidated itself in the subsequent local and national elections. Although such intentions had been present previously, since the end of 2012, the party explicitly revealed its vision to create a space of comfort identifying its territory. In October 2012, then Prime Minister Erdoğan revealed the future vision and projects of his Party, called "Political Vision 2023". He described the "new Turkey" as a "conservative democracy" with a new constitution shaping the system towards presidentialism or semi-presidentialism (Topal, 2016).

While the construction sector has become the locomotive of the Turkish economy, a new Turkey with spatial meanings was to be produced. On the more concrete policy level, the AKP governments ventured into construction and reconstruction of Turkey through an expansive urban regeneration undertaken by the Mass Housing Administration (*Toplu Konut İdaresi Başkanlığı*, TOKİ) since 2004 (Yalman, Topal and Çelik, 2019). AKP has intended to literally build its Islamic regime on the construction sector yielding mosques, skyscrapers, malls, double-wide roads, highways, airports, tunnels, and the like.

Istanbul as an historical monumental urban space came to be a territorial condensation of the reconstruction of the New Turkey vision (Topal, 2016). Istanbul has a special importance for Erdoğan as his political career shone in 1994 when elected as the Mayor of Istanbul on a religiously oriented Welfare Party (*Refah Partisi*) ticket. While running for the elections, constructing a mosque in Taksim Square was one of Erdoğan's projects for İstanbul (Çınar, 2018). The construction of the mosque, which had to wait until 2017, and several other projects intended to remake the city without taking into consideration its citizens.

The tripled property values particularly in İstanbul between 2001 and 2008 made the historical central city neighbourhoods the loci of capital accumulation (Karaman, 2008: 521). Starting from İstanbul, the MHA launched its urban regeneration projects in the squatter neighbourhoods, cornered in the high-rent city centre areas. While the urban regeneration projects turned former working-class neighbourhoods into gentrified locations by increasing the rent, dialectically, they have also accumulated discontent among the urban poor.

In tandem with this process, the right-to-city collectives, the leading members of which were mostly young graduates from urban and regional development departments of different universities, were forming in the neighbourhoods subjected to these urban regeneration projects with gentrification purposes. Some right-to-city collectives can be traced back to the 1999 Solidarity Volunteers and Earthquake Survivors Associations, which defended the right to decent shelter of the families that became homeless with the destruction of the 1999 Yalova (a nearby province to İstanbul) Earthquake that also destroyed some adjacent neighbourhoods of İstanbul. As several of our informants conveyed, as social mobilization increased, the 2009 local elections became a turning point in the formation of the rights movement concentrated in Istanbul. From 2009 onwards, the right-to-city and right-to-shelter collectives started to coordinate with the Social Rights Association (*Sosyal Haklar Derneği*, SHD) established in 2006 in İstanbul. The 2009 local elections in March led to some small-scale improvements, as AKP lost seven district municipalities to the main opposition party, the Republican Peoples Party (*Cumhuriyet Halk Partisi,* CHP), and lost its upper hand in the municipality councils. Faced with the relative success of right-to-city movements, AKP had to take a step back in its aggressive urban regeneration projects. These collectives searched for some ways to channel the dynamism they created in their movement in former working-class neighbourhood committees. The first strategy was to call for a united platform for all the existing neighborhood collectives (Topal, 2016, 2018).

In that context, the October 2009 Annual Meeting of Boards of Governors of the World Bank Group and the IMF together with the July 2010 European Social Forum (ESF) meeting in İstanbul turned into two timely opportunities for various collectives to unite (Topal, 2016). A group of activists founded a collective called *Direnistanbul* (in English: *Resistanbul*) to organize workshops, exhibitions, movie screenings, conversations, and activities against the World Bank (WB) and the International Monetary Fund (IMF). The meetings of Resistanbul joined many networks of activists, particularly combining the collectives organized in urban regeneration neighbourhoods and the activist youth. One year later, calling for a "socially and environmentally just transition in the economy" the ESF declaration underlined that "against those who try to create divisions between social and ecological justice, we assert that they do not contradict each other. They are, and have to be, complementary. Our vision is of a good life for all, not a nightmare of authoritarian eco-austerity" (ESF, 2010). During the ESF, these different collectives founded a new umbrella organization called the Urban Movements (*Kent Hareketleri*) whose "aim is to struggle collectively against the neoliberal attacks on our living spaces and cities" (Kent Hareketleri, n.d.). This organization established the coordination network among various associations and collectives, which, according to one activist informant "had been going through a survival crisis of their own." In other words, any individual group fighting for its particular interest came to grips that they must link their struggle to have an impact on the hegemonic strategy. In that context, "Urban Movements" as an umbrella organization could have been the core of a popularized social subjectivity if it could develop an "equivalential chain" inclusive of various demands on the city being represented and articulated through a specific one. This could only have been an outcome of a hegemonic political counter-project or a new populism with a new discourse as has been pointed out by Laclau.

During and in the aftermath of the 2011 general elections the full-fletched plans of AKP for Istanbul became crystalized. "Istanbul Vision 2023" meant a promising future for İstanbul to take part among the top ten finance centres of the world and a "global brand city of Turkey" (Aksoy, 2014: 27). In May 2013, Erdoğan further elaborated his plans for Istanbul redefining Taksim Square with a mosque and a symbolic Artillery Barrack including a shopping mall, in the adjacent Gezi Park. With the slogan of "let stability continue, let İstanbul grow", the Prime Minister also informed the public about the government's mega-projects like a third airport and a third bridge over the Bosphorus. These regeneration and mega projects intended to monopolize the definition of İstanbul urban space by erasing all the existing meanings, enclosing the space against rival meanings through the use of coercive disciplining poles of the state power (Topal, 2016).

Among all these 'crazy' projects, the plans for Taksim Square and Gezi Park triggered a massive reaction targeting the overall project of defining Istanbul's urban space. Representatives of the Union of Chambers of Turkish Engineers and Architects (TMMOB) and Union of Chambers of City Planners, together with environmentalist activists declared that they would not leave the Gezi Park to prevent the "construction" (read destruction) vehicles from entering the Park. Various organizations gathered under an umbrella organization, named The Taksim Solidarity, defending a collective right, "the right to the city" (Harvey, 2008; Kuymulu, 2013). On the 28th of May, these collectives pitched the first tents turning the Park into a camp area. In one of his speeches on the newly unravelling Gezi resistance, Erdoğan said that "these groups," upon establishing "themselves in a place," "refuse to leave" and "continuously terrorize the place" (*The Guardian*, 2013). In the same speech, Erdoğan also aimed to criminalize the protestors by saying 'those protesters in the Park are extreme groups'. Erdoğan infamously called them *çapulcu* (looters or marauders) and he warned, "the protesters would not be tolerated; they would be ousted from the Park by any means necessary". This utterance shows the threatening strength of the territorialization as giving space an identity of the resistance. Soon enough, on the dawn of the 31st of May came the violent attack of the police on the protestors as the government must have ordered that protestors would be ousted from the Park by any means necessary. The police using excessive force with tear gas and water cannons on the protestors burned the tents and destroyed the camp area. The evening of the same day, millions of people rushed into the public parks in their respective cities protesting both increasing authoritarianism precipitated by the violent police crackdown at Taksim Square and the neoliberal-*cum*-Islamist urban regeneration plan (Topal, 2018).

3   In Search of the Incarnations of the Spectre of Gezi: Living Gezi

The Gezi Resistance opened the space to a multidimensional horizon of meanings. The texture of space redefined by the Uprising was conducive to producing different but more or less coherent meanings that could co-exist together. In a very short time, the Park was transformed into an emancipated common space to harbour resistance against all forms of domination. The Park became the loci of expressing alienation, anger, and frustration against the relations of power diffused in society. It was a non-subjective resistance against an overt and subjective power. This non-subjectiveness was reflected in a description that was commonly used to refer to the ideals that the Gezi Resistance represented: "the Spectre of Gezi" (Topal, 2016).

When this communitarian life in the Park was brutally dispersed by the police force, the resistance evolved to manifest in different ways. The Gezi Resistance underlined the value of the urban commons. While the regeneration project intended to monopolize the urban space, the Gezi Resistance pushed forward the meaning of public space as an ongoing forum where everyone could speak and listen. Literally, the major public parks in Istanbul continued to be a truly open space to public speeches, lectures, concerts, rallying cries, and all forms of theatrical utterances (Topal, 2016).

Since the Gezi Resistance, there has been a growing number of effective civil initiatives organized around food, climate, and ecology trinity. The interviews for this study revealed that the Gezi Spirit has continued to gaze at the neighbourhood level through public park forums and solidarity networks. Our interviews suggest that the spirit has found its embodiment partly in the form of consumers' cooperatives established in the following years. As of March 2022, there are about 40 consumer cooperatives established in Istanbul. The interviews conducted with eight of the major cooperatives reveal the relationship between the Gezi Resistance and the foundation of the concerned organizations. The websites of these cooperatives and published interviews with the representatives of other cooperatives confirm the authors' interviews (Demirer, 2010). As clearly noted by the founder of Yerdeniz Cooperative, public park forums after the Gezi Resistance brought cooperatives into the strategy agenda of the civil initiatives (Birgün, 2021a). Similarly, Koşuyolu Cooperative founder Öztürk notes that cooperative members have gotten to know each other during the Gezi Resistance and the following park forums (Birgün, 2021b). Göztepe Cooperative founder also notes "the strategy of establishing a cooperative came out from the workshop discussions in the aftermath of the Gezi. We were seeking a new form of organization, and we organized our neighbourhood around safe food shortening rural and urban nexus" (Birgün, 2021c). Kadıköy Cooperative founders have also acknowledged that the idea behind the consumers' cooperatives has germinated in the public park forums and workshops at the neighbourhood level in the aftermath of the Gezi Resistance (Birgün, 2021d). In a nutshell, these social cooperative initiatives could be seen as the first institutional formation of the resistance, which continued to affect urban politics in a more coordinated fashion towards the local election in 2019.

Towards the local elections of March 2019, ecology, nature, and food have become significant issues on the public agenda. The main opposition party CHP's candidate Ekrem İmamoğlu made dozens of press releases during his campaign concerning these issues. Just a few months after assuming the mayor's office, İmamoğlu initiated the establishment of the first City Council of İstanbul in October. Although the institution of City Councils was first framed during the UN Rio Conference in 1992 as a unique governance mechanism of the cities, it had not been institutionalized before in Turkey. Thus, this initiation could be pointed to as a turning point for the creation of the idea of a new municipality in İstanbul by opening a new avenue for the grassroots defining the urban space. In March 2020, İmamoğlu, in his press release on Gezi Park, pointed out that

> the struggle that was put forward in Gezi was one of the most important struggles of Turkish history. I am now managing and coordinating the materialized form of that spectre by protecting the green (nature) and planning more human centred squares. That beautiful spectre was about protecting the city, the justice of city and the right to city.
> FISTIK, 2020

In order to understand the living legacy of the Gezi Insurgency at its decennial, we have also conducted expert interviews with significant figures who observed and experienced both the Gezi dynamics and its possible after effects in Istanbul and Turkey at large. In our interviews with Sencer Ayata,[4] an eminent sociologist and politician in CHP, and Eyüp Muhçu, the Chair of the

---

4 Interview has been conducted on June 22, 2022.

Chamber of Architects of Turkey (*Türkiye Mimarlar Odası*),[5] both emphasized "the social" character of Gezi with the point that it did not lead to a political representation nor to a formulation of new political ideas. In the view of Ayata, it was a "large-scale social protest" against increasing authoritarianism and oppression of life with a common demand for freedom. Muhçu noted that it was a moment expressing "social development" in terms of increasing awareness of right-to-city and environment, and a protest against long-running neo-liberalization process commodifying and privatizing the public spaces and resources with a rent-seeking concern leading to the transfer of wealth, corruption, and poverty. The latter process was, according to Muhçu, an oppressive, direct intervention in the life spaces of people as was epitomized by the government's project on Gezi Park. In that, the authoritarian government was aiming to remake/reconstruct Taksim Square as an embodiment of its hegemony as the symbol of the "new regime". In a way, Muhçu suggested, Taksim Square was projected as the "Kremlin square" of the "new regime". Muhçu concluded that it is in the wake of these processes that Gezi has been a struggle against the authoritarian-neoliberal encroachment to the city, social life, and civic freedoms.

Both Ayata and Muhçu underlined the socially and politically heterogeneous character of the protesters expressing the co-existence of diverse actors and identities against oppression. Ayata stressed the impact of this character of Gezi upon CHP in terms of increasing concerns for pluralist values in the party organizations and grassroots. While Ayata also admitted that this "legacy" of Gezi did not generate a direct political outcome by creating new political platforms, programs, or ideologies, Muhçu pointed to one significant outcome, that is, increasing significance of chambers (professional ones with a specialization on urban policies, planning and management like architects and city planners) and civil democratic organizations waging a struggle against commodifying and rent-seeking plans promoted by central and local governments which are detrimental for public life, resources and commons. Here Muhçu underlined that those organizations rather than established political institutions are more conducive to the co-existence of politically and socially diverse actors sharing an awareness of the right to city and environment with a concern for the protection of public spaces, resources, and commons. Ayata has made a parallel point by noting that while Gezi did not lead to direct programmatic and institutional representation at the political level, it unleashed a dynamic of new forms of political participation. This dynamic,

---

5 Interview has been conducted on June 29, 2022.

Ayata explained, can be attested in the form of new "social network organizations". As argued by Ayata, new social groups tend toward horizontal and flexible social networks, mostly operating through social media and/or internet platforms, outside of established hierarchical institutions. By so doing these social groups retain their autonomy, plural connections, and multiple identities. Ayata especially noted their significant impact in the 2017 referendum on constitutional changes (instituting a pseudo-presidential regime) in terms of sustained campaigns via these platforms for a "No" vote and their mobilization in the renewed (2nd round) mayoral election in İstanbul in 2019 in which the opposition candidate İmamoğlu drastically increased his vote.

Ayata, albeit cautiously, and Muhçu strongly affirmed the current tendency of expansion and strengthening of urban solidarity networks, neighbourhood associations, social organizations, and movements at the local level expressing civic sensitivity to the urban-public spaces, quality urban life, and right to city and environment as a significant after-effect of Gezi. In Muhçu's eyes, the establishment of the İstanbul City Council (*İstanbul Kent Konseyi*) is an important step in this direction as a significant outcome of the Gezi dynamic. Muhçu further underlines that there are strong local demands for the establishment of councils at the district levels.

In our interview with the Chair of the İstanbul City Council, Tülin Hadi,[6] she underlined that there is no direct relationship between the Gezi experience and the establishment of the Council, as this mechanism was already pre-defined yet dependent on the call of the mayor for being operational. Still, Hadi affirmed that the lingering legacy of Gezi is about participatory democracy, living and working together with political differences, creating dynamics of solidarity in terms of complementing one another via pooling a variety of abilities in collective efforts to meet the needs (cooperative practices) and persisting presence of the public agenda on climate, food and environment. Hadi emphasized that these ideals, which were raised through the Gezi experience, especially by the prefigurative[7] practices in the encampment area at the Park and forums, are in parallel with the concerns of the İstanbul City Council as a platform of governance. In this context, Hadi noted the significance of keeping and transmitting the memory of these ideals as a set of values to promote the lingering impact of the Gezi dynamics in shaping the future.

---

6   Interview has been conducted on August 3, 2022.
7   Tülin Hadi did not use this word in our interview but what she was pointing out was coinciding with the meaning of the term. As she was praising the collective efforts in putting into practice the ideals of a new life in solidarity in the Gezi encampment.

Hadi specifically underlined the importance of proliferation of consumers' cooperatives in the aftermath of the Gezi for the İstanbul City Council. Moreover, Hadi explained that the members of the City Council are thinking about possibilities of supporting the formation of new cooperatives in an expansive number of fields from construction and housing to logistics and energy. Hadi also informed that Kadıköy Cooperative (*Kadıköy Koopereatifi*) and Theatre Cooperative (*Tiyatro Kooperatifi*) are presently included in the İstanbul City Council, making it clear that formation and expansion of cooperatives across various fields has been a top issue to be extensively debated in the Council.

It seems that the impact of the Gezi protests and the following grassroots initiatives through cooperatives have managed to attain local participatory politics in the political agenda of the municipalities. The Istanbul City Council has been actively working through 21 working group teams on several issues and problems pertaining to the city. There are three working groups addressing the food, climate, and ecology concerns. An interview conducted for this study with the team leader of "Agriculture, Food, and Water Products" group indicates that these three groups are among the most active working teams meeting with the İstanbul City Council President Tülin Hadi regularly, publishing reports to the public, pressuring the mayor's office on their agenda. Perhaps, with the pressures exerted through these channels, the "climate, ecology, and food" issues have been the central pole of the İstanbul Metropolitan Municipality's 2030 vision plans.

As part of the initiatives on 2030 vision planning, the Istanbul Metropolitan Municipality (*İstanbul Büyükşehir Belediyesi*) commissioned a report outlining the food strategy of the city. The report was prepared by the leading critical academics working on agriculture and food politics. The document laid out the challenges of protecting the agricultural land and the agricultural producers while fighting against relevant social injustices, hunger, and malnutrition. Food security and food and water sovereignty of both producers and consumers were pointed out as the major objective of the documents. The climate crisis is acknowledged for its unequal impact on different sections of society and on nature with non-human beings. Policy alternatives for preventing and managing waste were also elaborated within the plan. Finally, the plan indicated the urgency of increasing resilience against natural catastrophes and managing various forms of crises.

The increased awareness about food, ecology, and climate change seems to have grown through the Gezi Insurgency. There have been increasing numbers of effective local grassroots initiatives bringing ecology and climate change into the public agenda campaigning against the Istanbul Canal and shifting policy outcomes in line with shorter-food-provisioning models like consumers' cooperatives and producers' markets in the aftermath of the Gezi Insurgency. This process cannot be conceived as a single-step political practice. Instead, a sound understanding would require tracing the nature of those integrant subjects and the social, cultural, and political processes of mobilization of different social actors into the Gezi movement and the ensuing consequences.

This mobilization brought Gezi protests to the edge of a populist rupture. However, it remained at the edge, as a popular, equivalential chain, could not be politically constituted as the popular basis of a new political identity. Still, this unprecedented massive counter-mobilization against the government's project on the city and its increasing authoritarianism created virtual and real counter-power platforms including a heterogeneous cross-section of the society. This vibrant dynamic of social opposition to the central government provided a ground for new initiatives on climate, ecology, and food. Therefore, the social dynamic unleashed by the Gezi insurgency opened up a horizon of future organizational structures such as consumers' cooperatives, and perhaps even the İstanbul City Council.

Our interviews, interestingly, attested to the gap between the political processes and the Gezi Insurgency as a social protest movement. There is an agreement about the social characteristics of the Gezi; heterogeneous social agents concerned with increasing authoritarianism and authoritarian interventions in city spaces coalesced together in their active protest against the central government and demanded participatory democracy, active participation in urban policies, and freedom. New forms of political participation and new practices of solidarity emerged out of these social action processes like consumers' cooperatives which would possibly extend into different spheres of social and economic life. As commonly noted by our interviewees, these dynamics did not generate or culminate into a new political representation, identity, or program but, nevertheless, unleashed vibrant social dynamics of solidarity, cooperation, and participation impacting life itself.

4   Conclusion

The need for new and creative forms of collective action with the ability to initiate long-lasting social change is growing every day. A collective resistance needs to define the common sense infusing everyday life with its own set of norms, values, and customs. While at the same time, the resistance should target the political power to topple the coercive and disciplinary state power. The resistance could collect the dispersed, pulverized, shattered will of people and bond them to a social organization committed to social change. For all these, there is a need to transform social mobilizations into a politically defined identity.

In our chapter, we argued that the Gezi Insurgency escalated toward the threshold of a populist political rupture yet remained an urban social movement culminating in a country-wide political protest against authoritarian power as represented by the central government and its leadership. The Gezi Insurgency, while remaining in the interstices of the social and the political, unleashed significant dynamics, especially at the local level, directly and indirectly affecting social and political life. These include spreading initiatives of solidarity at the neighbourhood-level such as consumers' cooperatives, increasing awareness of the right to the city as has been recalcitrantly defended by professional organizations like chambers of architects and chambers of city planners, formation of new organizations and dynamics of political participation both at the local and national levels, growing significance of the concerns on ecology, food, and climate, and a rising civic consciousness on the values of pluralism and co-existence with ideological-political differences. While it can be argued that these vibrations of the impact of the Gezi Insurgency are not necessarily observable through the political spectrum and for all sections of the society, it can still be projected that the dynamics of social, political, and cultural change may infuse more expansively as outcomes of these new initiatives become more observable and accessible. For said values, which we traced to the lingering impact of the Gezi Insurgency, are affirmative in themselves and can only be experienced positively in various spheres of life.

Bibliography

Aksoy A (2014) İstanbul'un Neoliberalizmle İmtihanı. In Bartu Candan A and Özbay C (eds) *Yeni İstanbul Çalışmaları: Sınırlar, Mücadeleler, Açılımlar*. İstanbul: Metis, pp. 26–47.

Bilgiç EE and Kafkaslı Z (2013) *Gencim, Özgürlükçüyüm, Ne İstiyorum? #direngezi Anketi Sonuç Raporu*. İstanbul: İstanbul Bilgi Üniversitesi Yayınları.

Birgün (2021a) "Yerdeniz Kooperatifi: İşleyişte Herkes Eşit" Birgün 16.03.2021. https://www.birgun.net/haber/yerdeniz-kooperatifi-isleyiste-herkes-esit-337727.

Birgün (2021b) "Koşuyolu Kooperatifi: Amacımız Mahalleye Sağlıklı Gıda Temin Etmek".

Birgün (2021c) "Göztepe Kooperatifi: Gezi Sonrasında Kurulduk" Birgün 16.03.2021. https://www.birgun.net/haber/goztepe-kooperatifi-gezi-sonrasi-kurulduk-337711.

Birgün (2021d) "Kadıköy Kooperatifi: Üreticilerle Aracısız Buluşuyoruz" Birgün 16.03.2021. https://www.birgun.net/haber/kadikoy-kooperatifi-ureticilerle-aracisiz-bulusuyoruz-337716.

Castells M (1983) *The City and the Grassroots*. London: Edward Arnold.

Castells M (2012) *Networks of Outrage and Hope*. Cambridge: Polity.

Çınar, E (2018) Yıl 1994 Belediye Başkanı Erdoğan Taksim Camii Projesini Anlatıyor, *Yeni Şafak* (November 14). Available (Consulted July 8, 2022) at: https://www.yenisafak.com/gundem/erdogan-taksim-camiini-boyle-anlatmis-3408743.

Della Porta, D (2015) *Social Movements in Times of Austerity*. Cambridge: Polity.

Demirer, G (2010) "Bütünün Hayrını Gözeten" bir Gıda Tüketim Modeli, *İklim Haber*, 17 March 2010. Accessed February 25, 2022 at: https://www.iklimhaber.org/butunun-hayrini-gozeten-bir-gida-tuketim-modeli/.

ESF (2010) *Final Declaration*, (July 4), Available (Consulted July 7 2022). http://www.europe-solidaire.org/spip.php?article17966.

Fıstık F (2020) Ekrem İmamoğlu Gezi Parkı'nda: "Gezi'de ortaya konan mücadele Türkiye tarihinin en önemli mücadelelerinden birisi", Medyascope (August 26 2020) Available (Consulted February 10 2023). https://medyascope.tv/2020/08/26/ekrem-imamoglu-gezi-parkinda-gezide-ortaya-konan-mucadele-turkiye-tarihinin-en-onemli-mucadelelerinden-birisi/.

Gambetti Z (2014) Occupy Gezi as Politics of the Body. In Özkırımlı Ö (ed) *The Making of A Protest Movement in Turkey #occupygezi*. London: Palgrave Macmillan, pp. 89–102.

Harvey, D (2008) "The right to the city" *New Left Review*. 53: 23–40.

Jones, S et al. (2011) Istanbul's New Bosphorus Canal 'to surpass Suez or Panama' *The Guardian*, 27 April. Available (Consulted February 5, 2023) at: https://www.theguardian.com/world/2011/apr/27/istanbul-new-bosphorus-canal.

Kalkınma Bakanlığı (2015) *Onuncu Kalkınma Planı (2014–2018): İstanbul Uluslararası Finans Merkezi*. Available (Consulted February 6, 2023) at: https://sbb.gov.tr/wp-content/uploads/2018/10/4Istanbul_Uluslararasi_Finans_Merkezi_Programi.pdf.

Karaman, O (2008) Urban pulse—(re)making space for globalization in Istanbul. *Urban Geography*, 29(6), 518–525.

Kent Hareketleri (n.d.) "Hakkımızda" Available (Consulted February 15, 2023) at: https://kenthareketleri.wordpress.com/hakkimizda/.

KONDA (2014), *Gezi Raporu*, http://www.konda.com.tr/tr/raporlar/KONDA_GeziRaporu2014.pdf, accessed June 7, 2015.

Kuymulu M B (2013) Reclaiming the right to the city: Reflections on the urban uprisings in Turkey. *City*, 17(3), 274–278.

Laclau E (2007) *On Populist Reason*, London: Verso.

Milliyet (2002) "Maşallah Maşallah!" April 11: p.1, Accessed July 5, 2023 at: http://gazetearsivi.milliyet.com.tr/Arsiv/2002/11/04.

Şengül, T (2015) "Urban Space and Politics in the Wake of Gezi Uprising" *METU Journal of the Faculty of Architecture* 32(1):1–20.

Sophos S (2017) Alone in the City: Gezi as a Moment of Transgression. In Hemer O and Persson HA (eds) *In the Aftermath of Gezi: From Social Movements to Social Change?* Cham: Palgrave Macmillan, pp. 65–85.

The Economist (2013) Descent into Confrontation. (June 15) Available (Consulted February 3, 2023) at http://www.economist.com/news/europe/21579487-prime-minister-chooses-toughness-over-talk-consequences-turkey-could-be-seriously.

The Guardian (2013) "Turkish protesters embrace Erdoğan insult and start 'capuling' craze", (June 10) Available (Consulted March 9, 2015) at: http://www.theguardian.com/world/2013/jun/10/turkish-protesters-capuling-erdogan.

Topal, A (2014) "A Specter is Haunting Turkey, the Specter of Gezi Park" *Global Dialogue: Newsletter for the International Sociological Association* 4(4). Available (Consulted February 10, 2023) at: https://globaldialogue.isa-sociology.org/articles/the-specter-haunting-turkey.

Topal, A (2016) "Taksim Square from the Ottoman Reformation Era to Gezi Resistance" in C. Berntharth (ed.) *Planning, Appropriation, Rebellions 1945–2015*, Leipzig: Spector Books.

Topal, A (2018) "From Tekel to Gezi Resistance in Turkey: Possibilities for a United Collective Social Rights Movement" in R. Sosa Elizaga (ed.) *Facing an Unequal World: Challenges for Global Sociology*, London: Sage.

Türkiye İnsan Hakları Kurumu (2014) Gezi Parkı Olayları Raporu. Available (Consulted February 3 2023). https://docplayer.biz.tr/1212206-Turkiye-insan-haklari-kurumu-gezi-parki-olaylari-raporu.html.

Yalman, G., Topal, A. and Çelik, Ö. (2019) "Changing Modalities of Urban Redevelopment and Housing Finance in Turkey: Three Mass Housing Projects in Ankara", *Journal of Urban Affairs* 41(5): 230–253.

Yörük E and Yüksel M (2014) Class and Politics in Turkey's Gezi Protests. *New Left Review* 89: 103.

CHAPTER 4

A Mirror to the Past, a Step to the Future

Kernels of Organized Movement in the Gezi Uprising

Gökhan Atılgan and Ezgi Kaya Hayatsever

> Even if I go back home now,
> I may come out again in a while
> Since these clothes and shoes are mine
> And since the streets belong to no one.[1]

∴

The Gezi Uprising was stylized as "çapulculuk" (meaning "looting" in Turkish) and seen as nonsensical and unhistoricised by the political agents who tried to violently oppress the movement. It was also romanticized by those who saw it as an unprecedented revolt. Both stylizations are based on non-dialectical reasoning, thus characterizing Gezi as "a bolt out of the blue."

In effect, the Gezi Uprising was neither nonsensical nor unhistoricised, for it had its specific causes and a history that resides within a broad context. Some analysts who realized this confined themselves to narrow or partial interpretations. A distinctive characteristic of such interpretations was explaining the uprising through atomistic approaches that were exclusively political, economic, ecological, or ideological. Another characteristic of these narrow or partial interpretations was their attempt at situating the interactions of Gezi solely within the context of its era, ignoring the legacy it had inherited from the history of Turkey (Atılgan, 2013).

The Gezi Uprising was a movement that embodied this historical legacy along with its possible manifestations in the future. The uprising carried the traces of social struggles in the modern history of Turkey; it shaped itself through the characteristics it had drawn from these struggles, without falling

---

1 This poem by Orhan Veli Kanık, translated into English by the authors of this chapter, was famously turned into a banner and hung from a cinema building in Taksim Square during the Gezi Uprising (Kanık, 1998: 49).

short of criticizing these qualities, before ultimately retreating from this stage of history and leaving behind characteristics of its own to be inherited or criticized. The Gezi Uprising was intertwined with the most daring instances of struggle in the modern history of Turkey as well as the other insurgent movements of its own era. It was both a part of a world-historical wave of social opposition and a moment of history for the social struggles in Turkey. In certain aspects, the Gezi Uprising drew inspiration from the world-historical wave it belonged while, from some other aspects, it inspired them. The Gezi Uprising indeed directed criticism to certain aspects of the legacy of social struggles in Turkey while amassing kernels of struggle from within these movements.

This chapter has two purposes. First, we discuss the legacy Gezi inherited from the struggles of laboring classes and socialist movements in Turkey, mapping out Gezi's critical engagement with this legacy and revealing the new forms this legacy emerged in through Gezi. Thus, we try to situate Gezi within the history of revolutionary and communal experiences in Turkey. Second, we aim to situate Gezi with respect to the other movements of its era. Hence, we evaluate the Gezi Uprising as a process in interaction with both the social struggles in the history of Turkey and the contemporaneous movements across the globe. As such, our perspective proposes an analytical engagement with Gezi both in temporal terms of the modern history in Turkey and the spatial terms of its contemporaneous world context, thus grasping Gezi both as a "relation" and a "process."

1   A Mirror to the Past

The Gezi Uprising was a new link in the chain of "history's accumulated achievements"[2] manifested in the previous resistances, revolts, instances of self-governance, practices of political organization, and communal experiences in modern Turkey. Yet, it was not a mere repetition of these experiences: it managed to creatively incorporate the brand-new ideas and potentialities of its own time, which were alien to past revolutionary experiences. This accumulated achievement was built upon the specific moments of the class struggles in Turkey. This achievement flourished in the cracks between the potential for a more advanced society and the violent attempts at hindering this potential, put forth by the uneven and combined development of economic, ideological,

---

2   The term is coined by Zygmunt Bauman (1978: 225).

cultural, sociological, and military structures in the tardy capitalism of Turkey, and carried the impact of the laboring classes and the socialists.

While sailing through some of the sparking moments of this accumulated achievement, we must remind the reader that there are many more moments that make up this accumulated achievement other than the ones mentioned here. In this accumulated achievement, one can immediately spot remnants of the workers' protests spanning from the resistance of 15–16 June 1970 to the TEKEL resistance in December 2009. Likewise, one could not ignore but notice trails of the struggles to protect nature, ranging from the 1990 resistance against gold mining in Bergama to the resistances against hydroelectric power plants in the Eastern Black Sea region in the 2000s. Further, there are also vestiges of popular movements such as the Alevi resistances in the 1970s and the several Kurdish *serhildans* (meaning "uprisings" in Kurdish) in the 1990s.

Last but not least, there exist echoes of youth movements that accelerated in the 1960s and the women's movement that became a public influence in the 1980s. Each and every one of these movements has contributed momentum to the accumulated achievement of the struggle of laboring classes in Turkey, and each and every one of them indicates a critical point in this struggle, linking it to the present and to the future. It is evident that the relation between these critical points will not be linearly progressive; for the rhythm of history is non-linear, after all. As we put forth a perspective that links yesterday to today and today to tomorrow, we do not think merely through references to history, nor do we romanticize the defeated moments of this accumulated achievement of history. Again, in our review of the wave of protests that occurred concurrently with Gezi, we do not aim to simply compare and contrast said protests with Gezi to see whether Gezi lacked certain characteristics those social struggles shared; to the contrary, our intention is to rather uncover the common legacy that can be derived from these contemporaneous movements.

We propose now to take a look at a number of significant experiences that contributed to the shaping of a new way of life, reaching out to Gezi through some of these struggles of laboring classes. But first, we propose to take a sweeping look through the historical context that formed the ground for these struggles and made them possible.

Turkey has a rich and robust history of social struggles by the oppressed classes; among these struggles come to the fore those of the toiling working class as well as youth movements. The 1960s, during which the dawn of industrial capitalism rose in Turkey, constitutes a turning point in this history. It was during this decade that the working class and university students, along with peasants, teachers, engineers and architects, doctors, policemen, public servants, artists, doormen, and shepherds as well as Kurds and Alevis, demanded more than they were getting, and thus emerged as actors in the scene of social struggles in Turkey under the conditions of developing capitalism. Accordingly, it was again during this time that each of these oppressed and exploited segments of society established their own organizations. The working class of Turkey established a political party, namely, the Workers' Party of Turkey (Turkish: *Türkiye İşçi Partisi,* TİP), and a union confederation, otherwise known as the Confederation of Revolutionary Trade Unions of Turkey (Turkish: *Devrimci İşçi Sendikaları Konfederasyonu,* DİSK). University students formed a number of organizations, including the Federation of Thoughts Club (Turkish: *Fikir Kulüpleri Federasyonu,* FKF) and the Revolutionary Youth Federation of Turkey (Turkish: *Türkiye Devrimci Gençlik Federasyonu,* DEV-GENÇ). Other social segments also created associations, unions, or professional organizations in accordance with the needs of their movements (Atılgan, 2016; Çelik, 2021). The socialists were also influential in organizing and building connections between various social struggles. In the 1970s, social struggles and socialist movements spread all around the country and attracted even more popular support than they did in the previous decade. Indeed, almost all of the oppressed groups in Turkey had risen in rebellion during the 1970s. On the one hand, these groups expressed their objections to, and criticisms of, the devastating consequences of the delayed development of capitalism in Turkey; on the other hand, they made an effort to transcend the capitalist conditions. In fact, there were several different attempts at envisaging how the production of goods and distribution of wealth, as well as democracy and cultural life, could be rebuilt anew. Having laid down the markers for the basic tenets upon which a new Turkey could be built, these attempts, which were later violently crushed at the hands of late capitalism, would prove to be anchor points for social struggles of the succeeding decades.

2   Innovative Settlements Project: the Experience of Participatory Democracy

One of the few important experiences that reached into the present from the depths of the history of struggles of the laboring classes in Turkey took place in the first half of the 1970s in the district of İzmit, the urban center of the province of Kocaeli in Turkey. İzmit's rapid development as an industrial city led to a serious housing problem and this was one of the most important issues on the agenda of local governance. A group of socialist architects and engineers, supported by the social democratic mayor in office at the time, offered an unprecedented approach to resolving the housing problem by launching the Innovative Settlements Project (Turkish: *Yenilikçi Yerleşmeler Projesi*) based on a participatory perspective (Çavdar, 1978; Ozan, 2016).

Before the adoption of this project, the workers' housing in İzmit was in the form of standard apartment buildings, which were designed and built with no regard whatsoever to the cultural dispositions, demands, and needs of the workers. The Innovative Settlements Project aimed at merging the technical skills of architects and engineers with workers' cultural dispositions and spatial habits. The project envisioned the active participation of all relevant parties in the decision-making processes about the settlements. Both individual and group meetings were held in workplaces, coffeehouses, and union offices with families of workers who were to become residents of the project. The objective of these meetings was to reveal the needs and preferences of the families and thus determine the various types of housing to be designed accordingly. In so doing, the workers who participated in the meetings took part in the modelling of the house they were going to live in. The project also included the workers as active subjects in the designing process of the common spaces of socialization that would be used collectively. The Innovative Settlements Project was abandoned before the houses could be built due to the obstructions by the central government and its hierarchical structures. Still, the project was a significant attempt that exhibited the potential of laboring classes to build a better life for themselves when included in a participatory democratic process.

The mentality instilled into the Innovative Settlements Project was entirely different from that of the current housing projects and activities carried out by the Housing Development Administration in President Recep Tayyip Erdoğan's Turkey (Turkish: *Toplu Konut İdaresi Başkanlığı*, TOKİ). There is a central decision-making process concerning the architectural design of TOKİ projects, and the residents are expected to choose one of the few options they are presented with and reshape their needs and habits in conformity with this space. Hence, the people directly affected by the consequences of such design decisions are completely excluded from the project and objectified. On the other hand, the Innovative Settlements Project of İzmit was imbued with the awareness of how the industrialized versions of architectural design could fragment and alienate the working class; indeed, the project had incorporated a participatory outlook that was in stark contrast with that of the TOKİ model of construction. The workers were at the center of the decision-making processes concerning design, and this very involvement allowed them to emerge as *subjects*.

Now is the time to remember the incident that sparked the Gezi Uprising. Taksim Square, where Gezi Park is located, is one of the most important center of secular lifestyle in Turkey. Erdoğan's Justice and Development Party (Turkish: *Adalet ve Kalkınma Partisi,* AKP) and its predecessor Islamist parties (such as The Welfare Party (Turkish: *Refah Partisi,* RP)), have always aimed at transforming Taksim Square through the construction of Islamist symbols. Erdoğan, emboldened by his electoral victories, was biding his time for realizing such a transformation of the square; not surprisingly, it was when his administration was strongest in terms of electoral support that Erdoğan took action. Erdoğan first ordered a mosque to be built in the square so that the most important symbol of Islam in Turkey, a minaret, would rise above the spatial heart of secular life. Erdoğan announced the rebuilding of the Artillery Barracks (Turkish: *Topçu Kışlası*), the historical military barracks of the Ottoman era, which was pulled down in 1940 to build Gezi Park in its place (Batuman, 2018). The Artillery Barracks was the center of the historical incident known as March 31. On this date in 1909, a group of religious reactionaries took to the streets, demanding the abolishment of the newly re-established Ottoman parliament.

The revolt was suppressed by The Army of Action (Turkish: *Hareket Ordusu*), formed by supporters of the Committee of Union and Progress (Turkish: *İttihat ve Terakki Cemiyeti*) in the military, who were the main actors in establishing parliamentary rule in the Ottoman Empire at the time. As a consequence, the Ottoman Sultan Abdulhamid II, who in time became a polarizing figure in Turkish politics, was dethroned.

Erdoğan has always proclaimed himself to be a great follower of Abdulhamid II. By building a mosque and rebuilding the Artillery Barracks in Taksim Square, Erdoğan wanted to shatter the position of the square as the center of secular life in Turkey. Erdoğan's aim was to reconquer Taksim Square through symbols belonging to Islam and the Ottoman era. However, this transformation was based on the will of a single person. Those people whose lives would be affected by this transformation were completely excluded from decision-making processes. The Gezi Uprising began with the protests against the uprooting of the trees in the area, where the military barracks would be built.

The objection raised by the Gezi Uprising against an authoritarian government emphasized the claim that decisions that affect citizens' lives could not be taken and implemented without them participating in the decision-making. One of the origins of this claim in Turkish history lies within the participatory democracy envisaged by the Innovative Settlements Project 50 years ago in İzmit. The laboring classes of Turkey, who took initial steps in participatory democracy half a century ago engaged in another leap forward during the Gezi Uprising.

3 Yeni Çeltek: a Step towards Self-Governance

Another experience of the laboring classes of Turkey that engaged in creating a new way of life took place in the mining town of Yeni Çeltek in the 1970s. The case of Yeni Çeltek is important for the patterns of solidarity and the kernels of communism it gave rise to, as well as revealing workers' skills for democratic representation, participation, and governance.

At the center of the Yeni Çeltek case was the Underground Mining Workers Union (Turkish: *Yeraltı Maden İşçileri Sendikası,* Yeraltı Maden-İş). The particular characteristic of this trade union was that it did not imitate its predecessors in its organizational structure and opted for building its own perspective and mechanisms through meetings with the workers that constituted its base. The previous union that was active in the area was a state-led one, in complicity with the employer firm. The president of this state-led union was engaged in trading the coals from the mines, using his position for personal gain, and had long instilled fear in workers who labored in conditions of slavery. In this suffocating atmosphere, Yeraltı Maden-İş was established by socialist engineers who claimed that those who produce should also be those who govern. The workers were initially reluctant to come to terms with such ideas, but this reluctance soon dissolved as groups of workers gradually came to organize themselves in the form of workplace committees and councils that held discussions concerning work conditions, rights, wages, and values. Through these discussions, the workers began to shape their own opinions about the organization of production and governance; in the course of building their own organization, they also gained self-esteem. According to the wife of one of these workers, for instance, her husband never put two words together prior to joining the committee meetings; after her husband became a spokesperson for one of these committees, there was "no shutting him up." (Akçam, 2004). Indeed, as workers engaged in discussions, they acquired consciousness not only about their own problems but also the problems of the country and the world (Akçam, 2004).

In the first collective bargaining process led by Yeraltı Maden-İş in 1976, the actual workers themselves, the diggers, the ground supporters, and the movers were at the bargaining table. The employers were shocked to see the mining workers themselves there, and they refused to hold face-to-face meetings with the workers. In response, the workers went on a strike to assert their demands and right to (self-)representation in the bargaining process. The strike received the locals' support, with peasant families supplying workers with meals and joining in the festivities during the strike. There were also public officials, small business owners, and the youth who showed their solidarity with the workers on strike. The 23-day-long strike ended when the demands of the workers were fully acceded to. Nothing would ever be the same in the workplace, as the workers had undergone a transformation, which, according to one of the workers, had bestowed upon them their own character (Akçam, 2004). The workers who used to be objects of the labor process were now the most active subjects in their working lives. It was so that one of the workers reported that the workers were now "happy to be workers" (Akçam, 2004). The miners, previously bereft and stricken, were now proud to be workers. They had learned how to stand up for themselves and to become subjects of a new life rather than victims of a life imposed upon them.

In the next collective bargaining process in 1980, the employers did not agree to the demands of the union of Yeraltı Maden-İş, claiming that their business was not yielding profits. Hence, the workers went on another strike, once again supported by peasants, shopkeepers, teachers, women, children, and the youth. The miners were able to build a circle of support that transcended the divisions of belief, ethnicity, and gender. In response, the employers announced that the mines would be closed, showing fake reports indicating that the mines ran dry. The miners reacted by occupying the mines and taking the production and management of the mines upon themselves. The workers, as the actual producers, had learned how to run the operation and management of the mines. The amount of coal they produced in 26 days exceeded the production of the previous management of their employers. The workers had also developed a new technical route to access the mine from the surface, which bore testimony to the superiority of workers' management skills.

As the workers became subjects of their own lives and set out to both manage themselves and produce for themselves, they also began to transcend the former workplace habits and relations. The miners dispensed with such mechanisms as bribery and wire-pulling for new recruitments; instead, they asked the local villages about those who needed employment the most and made lists of these individuals and hung them out at the entrance of the mine. In so doing, they were able to establish a transparent mechanism that provided need-based employment.

The new life that emerged in Yeni Çeltek extended to other social structures in the same area as well (Bütün, 2015). Just like the workplace committees of miners, the nearby townspeople also organized in the form of people's committees. The participatory and solidarity-oriented self-governance practices of miners became more and more prevalent in their locale.

The workers of Yeni Çeltek were also able to create kernels of communism in their struggle. The workers got rid of the black marketeers who sold overpriced coal to locals. The workers also abolished any intermediaries between the product of their labor and other laborers that would consume this product.

Having cleansed their prices from the profits of black marketeers and intermediaries, the workers set fair prices that enabled an equitable share of coal for everyone. The workers were also quick to realize that their practice of giving "one ton of coal for every household" was not fair and equitable: the number of people and the needs of each household were different. There was no real equality in giving the same amount of coal to households with elderly, children, or student households (Akçam, 2004). Additionally, the workers changed their methods of distribution, embracing the principle of "to each according to their need" rather than an equal distribution. Those who worked in Yeni Çeltek also provided coal for the poor, cultivating a feeling of solidarity and cooperation, one that is reminiscent of the concept of equality in Marx's *Critique of the Gotha Program,* where Marx pointed out that the "equal rights" based on the same criteria for everyone were in fact a right of inequality because "one worker is married, another is not" or "one has more children than another, and so on and so forth" (Marx, 2009: 11). Marx defined the understanding of equality Yeni Çeltek workers gave up on in their practices of distribution as "the narrow horizon of bourgeois right" and stated that true equality would only be possible through the principle of "each according to his needs," a principle which Yeni Çeltek workers lived up to in their deeds (Marx, 2009: 11).

This blossoming of a new life in the Black Sea region at the hands of the working class was obfuscated by the military coup on 12 September 1980. Many among the miners and union workers were imprisoned and tortured, some were even maimed in the process.

While the Gezi Uprising started at Taksim Square, it came to build its own circle of resistance, binding together both close and distant districts of İstanbul and even other cities. One of the origins of building such a circle of resistance can be traced back to Yeni Çeltek. The communal practices of need-based sharing and participatory decision-making beyond divisions of ethnicity and belief in the park resonated with the practices in Yeni Çeltek. There was a historical kinship between Gezi protesters who were active subjects, who acted collectively instead of submitting to a mere authority, and the workers of Yeni Çeltek, who became subjects of their own lives and regained their pride and dignity.

4 Fatsa: Almost a Commune

Another legacy of the history of working class struggles in Turkey which involved the formation of a new life was the local governance practices in Fatsa, a town in the midst of the Black Sea region. In the autumn of 1979, a socialist tailor named Fikri Sönmez, who was popularly known as Fikri the

Tailor (Turkish: *Terzi Fikri*), was sworn in office as the mayor of Fatsa with a landslide victory. This victory was the culmination of the ongoing practices of self-organization, direct democracy and self-governance in Fatsa (Bakır, 2021; Morgül, 2007). Fatsa thus presented a unique case of communal life reminiscent of the Paris Commune of 1871, illustrating the possibility of rupture required for radical social change (Acaroğlu, 2018).

The turning point in the local governance experience in Fatsa was the municipal elections in October 1979. However, the electoral success was the result of a whole process of revolutionary action. Some of the leaders of the Turkish revolutionary movement who were ambushed and killed by state forces in 1972 were from Fatsa, namely Ertan Saruhan and Nihat Yılmaz. After their deaths, these revolutionaries were reborn in the regional imagination of Fatsa as legendary heroes and their memory had facilitated the proliferation of revolutionary ideas among the population. Fikri the Tailor, a member of the Workers' Party of Turkey (Turkish: *Türkiye İşçi Partisi,* TİP) released from prison in 1974 and the mayor of Fatsa, was a comrade of these revolutionaries (Demirbilek, 2011).

The revolutionary youth and the revolutionary teachers in Fatsa were organized in the People's House (Turkish: *Halkevi*). The unconventional methods of education followed by these teachers had turned people in their favor. The communication between the people of Fatsa and these revolutionaries, who were also born and raised in Fatsa, was trusting, honest, and based on equal terms. Such factors contributed to the proliferation of revolutionary ideas among the people, who began to see the revolutionaries in a sympathetic light (Bakır, 2021).

On the other hand, there was the fact that the established order was not able to provide a happy and thriving life for the people of Fatsa. The basic means of livelihood for the people of Fatsa was growing hazelnuts, yet the production and cultivation of hazelnuts were carried out in extremely strenuous conditions. The producers needed to borrow money with a high-interest rate from the traders to meet their expenses during the production process. When they were unable to make their payments, they were forced to sell their harvest back to the traders at the minimum price (Bakır, 2021). Hence, the money they earned went back into the pockets of the traders. If they were late in their payments, they were insulted and humiliated by the traders. This combination of exploitation and humiliation went so much beyond endurance that the people felt a further affinity with the revolutionaries, who opposed the authority of the traders.

The revolutionaries began to contest the black-marketing practices of the traders, gaining the trust of the people. A strategy of the revolutionaries was to confiscate the stocks kept in the depots of the traders to be sold in the black market and then sell these goods for lower prices while making a fair payment back to the traders (Bakır, 2021). The people's committees, which were the basic form of self-organization in Fatsa, were born through this struggle against black-marketing (Bakır, 2021).

The peoples' committees were organized in every neighbourhood as units of self-governance through which people discussed their problems, suggested solutions to these problems and took action to alleviate the conditions. The demonstrations of "ending exploitation in hazelnut production" were organized by these committees (Bakır, 2021). The hazelnut producers, who previously did not believe that the traders would give them the price they demanded, saw that the demonstrations were effective, and the traders were forced to give them a fair price. This success increased self-esteem of the producers. Women, in particular, became more and more active in the struggle for rights (Bakır, 2021).

As the people of Fatsa moved from being the producing subject to being the governing subject, the peasants were also involved in the movement. The peasants elected their own "village representatives" and became part of the revolutionary transformation in Fatsa. The collectively developed consciousness and the collectively taking action rather than following a certain person or a certain group improved peoples' drive to take initiative. When the state did not build roads to distant villages, the people undertook the responsibility themselves and learned how to build roads (Bakır, 2021). The fruits of this self-organization and revolutionary consciousness derived from collective action were reaped in the 1979 municipal elections.

Fikri the Tailor, who was also born and raised in Fatsa, won said elections with a landslide victory in the midst of attempts to assassinate him. Through his initiative, eleven peoples' committees were constituted in the town, and these committees became the organs of governance in the municipality, addressing a number of issues ranging from domestic violence and birth control to building roads and accessing water. The meetings of the municipality were broadcast to people through loudspeakers, acquiring publicity in which all the citizens could participate. One-fourth of the population of the town became directly involved in municipal politics following the establishment of the committees (Bakır, 2021). The popular classes mastered self-governance through these practices, engaging in politics of participation.

One of the major problems of the town was the unpaved dirt roads. The inadequacy of the sewer system and the lack of maintenance caused the dirt roads to be flooded and turned into a sea of mud. The central government refused to supply funds to the leftist municipality for road building, thus trying to weaken the popular support for the mayor. The municipality and the peoples' committees reciprocated by initiating a campaign named "End the Mud." Women, children, workers, peasants, shopkeepers, and teachers of Fatsa suspended the course of their everyday lives and worked together to clear the roads of Fatsa. They managed to clear the mud in seven days. The mayor led the works himself, with a shovel in his hand. After the campaign, Fatsa had the look of an entirely new town. Festivities were held at the end of the campaign, celebrating the collective will and action of the people (Bakır, 2021). They were now able to identify their own problems, decide upon a course to resolve them, take action and succeed together, and celebrate together, feasting at the same table.

The consciousness of a new life inspired by the participatory governance of the municipality in Fatsa led to a transformation of the sharing practices of the people. In Fatsa, traditionally, the shells of hazelnuts were used in place of firewood in winter. Before the electoral victory of Fikri the Tailor, there were incidents of favouritism and unfairness in the distribution of shells. The committees implemented a truly populist policy of positive discrimination for the disadvantaged and prioritized the needs of the widows, the elderly and the destitute in the distribution of shells, which was the result of a communistic perspective ahead of its time (Bakır, 2021).

There were also cultural dimensions to the local governance practices in Fatsa. Fatsa People's Culture Festival in April 1980 became a site of attraction for progressive intellectuals and artists in Turkey (Aydemir, 2011). The festival offered choir concerts, bicycle races, theatre performances, movie screenings and art exhibitions. The people refused to listen to lengthy opening speeches and actively initiated the start of the festival themselves (Bakır, 2021). The women, men and children of Fatsa participated in a festive world of culture well beyond their time.

The experience of local governance in Fatsa, which resonated with the principles of governance and distribution in the Paris Commune, was perceived by the state as a serious threat that could spread through other regions of Turkey. Thus, a prefigurative coup was staged in Fatsa one month before the military coup of 12 September 1980. After the military operations that eradicated the progressive municipality in Fatsa, dozens of revolutionaries including Mayor Fikri Sönmez, as well as peasants, teachers, and workers, were tortured and imprisoned for many years.

The Gezi Uprising carried traces of the Fatsa experience as well, with its collaborative and non-hierarchical forms of decision-making. Gezi brought the legacy of Fatsa to Taksim Square through its intermingling of struggle and festivity, revolutionary action and art, resistance, and reconstitution.

5 The 1st of May Neighbourhood: Building a Slum Quarter

Another prominent experience of the laboring classes of Turkey echoed by The Gezi Uprising was the reconstruction of a slum quarter in İstanbul by impoverished working-class people and socialists in 1977 (Aslan, 2019).

İstanbul, as the industrial capital of Turkey, was a particular destination of internal migration flows from rural areas. The increase in migration led to housing problems in the city, and slum neighbourhoods were formed. These neighbourhoods became target areas for both revolutionary action and criminal networks in the 1970s. In a district called Kapanağılı, some of these criminal networks with links to both corrupt local government officials and armed gangs, i.e., the slum mafia, enclosed plots of land and sold them to recently migrated families at outrageous prices (Pamuk, 2015). In 1977, the socialist groups began to organize struggles against the slum mafia in Kapanağılı. These groups' aims were to divide the land into plots in accordance with the needs of the poor, to prevent the renting of slum houses for profit, to stop bribery and to set a common and controlled neighbourhood budget with equal contributions from the residents. These groups received great support from the residents and formed a people's committee for the realization of these aims, after which they began the construction of a slum neighbourhood with the assistance of revolutionary students along with socialist architects and engineers. The slum houses were planned in compatibility with the economic, educational and cultural activities of the residents, in a form that would enable socialization in the neighbourhood. The plan of the neighbourhood also enabled further integration with the city and public services. In the end, the neighbourhood that came to life was affordable, comfortable and integrated with the rest of the city. The neighbourhood, built by the common efforts of the socialists and people, was named the "1st of May Neighbourhood" (Turkish: *1 Mayıs Mahallesi*) in memory of the fallen members of the working class in the attack of May 1, 1977.

This slum neighbourhood, constructed by the shared labor and common reason of the working-class people and socialists, evidently challenged the capitalist conditions imposing mafia relations, exploitation, and lack of human dignity on the slums. Thus, the new identity given to slums by this revolutionary experiment was targeted by right-wing groups supported by the state. The slum houses were demolished; hundreds of residents who tried to protect their houses were detained, many of them were injured and nine of them were killed. However, the attack on the neighbourhood gave rise to an even bigger wave of solidarity: workers and socialists from other parts of İstanbul, as well as those from other cities in Turkey, rallied to Kapanağılı to reconstruct and revitalize the 1st of May Neighbourhood. The neighbourhood was rebuilt in less than two months.

The participatory initiative of the Gezi Uprising for the resolution of urban problems can be traced back to the urban experience of the 1st of May Neighbourhood. The hope of flourishing a new life through the common efforts of all parties involved in the Gezi Uprising, based on the voluntary presentation of skills and means, reflected the experience of the 1st of May Neighbourhood.

6   TİP: a New Experience of Socialist Organization

What Gezi lacked was a political organization that could enhance and carry into the future the values, relations, and forms of communication created during the uprising. Nevertheless, the first seeds of such a socialist party were sown in the 1960s in Turkey.

While the initial stages of the socialist movement in Turkey date back to the beginning of the 20th century, it was embraced by significant segments of society, particularly in the 1960s. The rise of social struggles coincided with this embracing of socialist movements, which flourished in the context of struggles of the oppressed segments of society for their rights. The ruling classes of Turkey, on the other hand, became politically vested in breaking the bonds between socialist movements and social struggles. Socialist movements were able to gain popular support to the extent that they could build internal relations with oppressed classes, thus popularizing socialism and assisting the manifestation of the people's potential for creating a new life. The Innovative Settlements Project, Yeni Çeltek experience, Fatsa experience, and the 1st of May Neighbourhood were such instances. However, socialist movements failed when they became external to the movement of oppressed classes, with their principles of "vanguardism" and "democratic centralism" shaping vertically hierarchical structures. In such cases, socialist movements failed to reveal the authentic experience of popular classes and carry them towards the future.

Socialists were able to lead the creation of new forms of struggle and future-oriented organizations throughout this exciting period when they interacted with the laboring classes, working and thinking collectively. However, as long as socialists stuck to vanguardism, individual leadership, centralism, and vertical organization, rather than to collective action, collective will, participation, and horizontal organization, their connection to the working class deteriorated and they were unable to herald new experiences to be carried into the future. The first socialist political party that followed the latter of these principles rather than the former was TİP. We now propose to take a look into the story of TİP, which displays characteristics of a socialist party that was absent during Gezi.

Established in 1961, TİP left a distinctive mark on socialist politics in the 1960s. TİP differed from both its predecessors and its successors in the sense that it was established by the authentic initiative of the working class. The workers established the party themselves, and socialist intellectuals were gradually integrated into the party in the later stages (Boran, 1968; Aren, 1993). This presented an original model of organization in the history of social struggles in Turkey. But there were other characteristics that made TİP a unique organization. One such characteristic was that the local organizations of TİP were formed by workers from different occupations such as farmers, shopkeepers, tailors, cobblers, and other craftspeople. Another original characteristic of TİP was the equal representation of intellectuals and the actual members of the working class in the decision-making branches of the party (Sargın, 2020). TİP was particularly careful about including the working class in preparing the speeches or written materials (Sargın, 2020). The editorial staff of the bulletin *Proleter* published by the party was entirely made up of workers. TİP also had the opportunity to address people from the radio, which was the main medium of the era for political propaganda, and a shepherd was included among those who would give a speech on national radio, addressing his fellow people (Aşut and Atılgan, 2021). This unprecedented incident in Turkish history demonstrated that the true leaders of TİP were indeed the working class. More than half of the parliamentary candidates of TİP in the elections the party participated in were members of the working class (Aybar, 2021).

TİP was able to go beyond the conventional organization of a socialist party in which socialist intellectuals and youth took it upon themselves to teach and lead people. The organization of this workers' party was entirely different from the 20th-century model of a "vanguard party" because factory workers, peasants, tailors, shepherds, farmers, and housewives were able to actively discuss, debate, and struggle together with scientists, lawyers, journalists, doctors and intellectuals from other occupations. TİP embodied the difference between an extrinsic form of politics, which dictates to the working class how to think, how to talk, and what to do, and an intrinsic form of politics that popularizes a party constituted by working classes themselves. This form of politics was captured by the slogan "Vote for Yourself" employed by TİP in the elections in the 1960s. Instead of being a party that defends the interests of the working class, TİP opted for being a party through which the working classes found their way into socialism in their efforts to represent their own interests. The ruling classes realized that the popularization of TİP among people added a new dimension to politics in Turkey. After the military coup on 12 March 1971, TİP was banned, and its executives were imprisoned.

The vast difference between a socialist party that takes action to lead the organic movement of certain segments of the working class and a popularized socialist party that was internally intertwined with the movement of the working class would make up a basic dilemma for the socialist movement in Turkey in later years. This dilemma eventually manifested itself in Gezi as well. Socialist parties or revolutionary organizations, which tried to dictate the action of the rebellious crowds through megaphones in Gezi, failed to recognize that the substance of Gezi had already surpassed all past phrases.[3] In the political climate that gave rise to Gezi, it was revealed that the political forms in which decisions were made by the central party organs and the party base built connections with the people to implement these central decisions were outdated. The forms of demonstration and protest in which a few people addressed the masses from the platform did not belong to the present or the future anymore. The rebellious masses enjoyed the privilege of collective debate, collective decision-making, and collective action, distancing themselves from old forms of politics and searching for new channels. The course of the Gezi Uprising revealed that it could have internalized the form of politics put forth by TİP in the 1960s. The socialist and revolutionary groups, while acting upon their feeling of social responsibility and their determination to resist political power, were only externally connected to Gezi in terms of both their structures and their mentality. This does not mean that the only key to success during Gezi was through the form of politics put forth by TİP in the 1960s; it is to say, rather, that people can only become the true subjects of political struggles through the contemporary versions of political organization with a high potential for popularization. The Gezi Uprising could have furthered its goals and its creative energies could have become more permanent through such a political party. However, when the Gezi Uprising took place, socialist and revolutionary parties in Turkey did not have functioning mechanisms that embodied effective, flexible, and rapid processes of decision-making, accountability in executive organs, and a participatory understanding of democracy. They lacked the capacity to develop a persuasive dialogue with the masses that spontaneously came together in Gezi and thus missed the opportunity to open up new channels to further the goals of the movement.

---

3   Herein the word "phrase" is used in reference to Marx's comparison in 18 Brumaire between the social revolutions of the 19th century and the revolutions of the previous centuries: "With the former, the phrase surpasses the substance; with this one, the substance surpasses the phrase" (2009: 4).

Gezi became a scene for prefigurative politics as it involved the mutual support of all the participants by all those who joined the uprising in accordance with their needs and skills. In fact, the Gezi Uprising involved collective mechanisms of debate, decision-making, action, and resistance, and transcended the strict, central, and hierarchical forms of organization by creating and testing reciprocal and creative forms of communication. As such, the uprising found ways of overcoming violence through intelligence and implemented non-exclusionary and non-discriminative patterns and providing the opportunity for free self-expression for all. Prefigurative politics includes the burgeoning of future forms of social relations, decision-making practices, cultural forms and human experience within the ongoing political practice (Boggs, 1977). Forming connections between the elements of prefigurative politics and past movements and giving these connections a permanent character and passing this character on to the future, could only be undertaken by socialist parties that drew lessons from the experiences of the 20th century. The working class of Turkey is yet to organize such a socialist party.

The deliberation provided by Gezi about the kind of life and the kind of country demanded by the popular classes shared common characteristics with the answers given to the same deliberation in İzmit, in Yeni Çeltek, in Fatsa, the 1st of May Neighbourhood, repeating some of these answers, criticizing some others and expanding the scope of yet others. As Marx says: "The social revolution of the nineteenth century cannot draw its poetry from the past, it can draw that only from the future" (2009: 3–4). The poetry of Gezi included verses from the past, voices from the present and melodies from the songs of tomorrow. The principles of the new life embodied by the Gezi Uprising were solidarity instead of egoism, courage instead of fear, creativity instead of mediocrity, assertiveness instead of passivity, collectivity instead of isolation, inclusion instead of exclusion, equality instead of discrimination, consent instead of coercion, altruism instead of contempt, horizontal communication instead of vertical, heterarchy instead of hierarchy, voluntarism instead of imposition, freedom instead of necessity, collective mind instead of individual reason. The resistance that defended these principles brought together singers, dancers, painters, poets, actors, comedians, city planners, architects, lawyers, publishers, restaurant owners, patisserie makers, hotel managers, taxi drivers, teachers, and photographers; united the old and the young in their support to the movement and spread to other parts of the city and other cities. The Islamist bourgeoisie and the state under its control, on the other hand, wanted to violently repress the life blossoming beyond the established order, just like their predecessors did in the modern history of Turkey. Eleven young people were killed during the Gezi Uprising. Forty-three people suffered serious injuries. In its attempt to recreate a future based on the despotic symbols of the Ottoman era, the Islamist bourgeoisie could not contain its violent animosity towards Gezi, whose song was directed towards another future.

Our argument that the Gezi Uprising is part of the accumulated achievement of the people of Turkey does not include a claim that the men and women in the uprising individually had the knowledge of this accumulation and organized their movement accordingly, that the uprising was shaped by the critical deployment of this knowledge. Rather, we mean to emphasize that Gezi was another moment of the class struggle in Turkey, which also gave rise to the Innovative Settlements Project, the 1st of May Neighbourhood, and Yeni Çeltek and Fatsa experiences in the past; as a matter of fact, Gezi is going to transfer some of this accumulation to the future endeavours of class struggle.

The Gezi Uprising was linked with the history of class struggle in Turkey as well as the contemporary movements in other countries. The uprising added certain elements to the accumulated achievement of local history and carried them towards a global level and reciprocally learned from accumulated achievements at the global level. We now propose to locate Gezi in the world-historical context of its own time and reveal its links with contemporary social struggles.

7   A Step to Future

As mentioned in the previous section, the Gezi Uprising has been analysed through many perspectives that focus on exclusively political, economic, or ideological aspects of the movement. In contrast with such analyses, our aim in this chapter is to bring to light the interconnections between the economic, political, social, and ideological facets of Gezi. Our perspective positions these different aspects of Gezi as various manifestations of peoples' reactions against the same totality of neoliberal capitalist relations. We argue that the outward analytical complexity of the Gezi Uprising is due to its unique blending of these reactions, which mirror the intricate infiltration of capitalism into all parts of public life. In order to build such a perspective, we put a particular emphasis on the social reproduction of labor and propose to assess these multiple facets of Gezi as differing yet linked reactions against the deteriorating conditions of the social reproduction of labor under neoliberal assault. Thus, the previous section of the chapter has focused on the instances from the history of Turkey in which laboring classes organized popular movements that went beyond lean political or economic demands and instead articulated a new way of living that benefits all, rather than some, embodying its potential to represent the common interest of the society as a whole.[4]

Analysing Gezi as a process and a relation involves focusing on not only the temporal continuities and breaks but also the relationalities that can be built between Gezi and its contemporary social movements and protests in different geographies. Hence, this section of the chapter focuses on the common dynamics of Gezi and other almost simultaneous protest movements in the world that took place in the span of less than a decade. Instead of explaining the aftermath of Gezi merely through the internal shortcomings of political actors in Turkey, we would like to delineate the converging and diverging characteristics of said movements with a focus on their meaning in the context of the social reproduction of labor. Such an outlook will in fact both allow us to discuss the so-called organizational failure of Gezi in a broader context and help us locate where Gezi falls among other seditious movements that rose against the restoration of the neoliberal regimes after the 2008 crisis and the accompanying assault on public life in various countries.

8 Social Reproduction Theory and Strategies of Class Struggle

The analysis of the social reproduction of labor, originally a Marxist concept that denotes the reproduction of labor power within social life, has received the most important and impactful contributions from feminist scholarship, which has mainly employed the term for the study of the institution of family and the role of unpaid domestic labor within the overall reproduction of capitalist relations (Mezzadri, 2019). Nevertheless, the concept supplies us with an analytical toolbox that presents valuable opportunities for the study of other aspects of this regeneration process. In fact, there has recently emerged a debate that tries to expand the scope of the concept to incorporate and analyse other aspects of the regenerative functions of social life.[5]

In her insightful contribution to this debate, Tithi Bhattacharya asks (Bhattacharya, 2017: 1–2):

---

4 Cf. Marx and Engels in *Communist Manifesto* (2016: 27–28): "The proletarian movement is the self-conscious, independent movement of the immense majority, in the interest of the immense majority. The proletariat, the lowest stratum of our present society, cannot stir, cannot raise itself up, without the whole super incumbent strata of official society being sprung into the air."
5 For collections regarding this debate, see: Bhattacharya (2017); Jaffe (2020); Arruzza and Gawel (2020).

> If workers' labour produces all the wealth in society, who then produces the worker? (...) What about the public transportation system that helped bring her to work or the public parks and libraries that provide recreation so that she can be regenerated, again, to be able to come to work?

This rhetorical question illuminates the fact that the daily life of a working person who sells her labor to access means of subsistence is a whole; the compartmentalization of time in the everyday life of such a person into so-called work-time and leisure-time, or into the fields of production by labor and reproduction of labor, is a social construct that has been established through the modern organization of work. Bhattacharya reminds us that though these two fields *appear* as separated, in fact, they form a "twain" in unity even under the capitalist mode of production (Bhattacharya, 2017: 74).

Building on Michael Lebowitz's (2003) concept of "second circuit" of production of labor power beside the capital's circuit of production of commodities, Bhattacharya argues that the second circuit of reproduction of labor involves the self-directed activity of the worker to satisfy her "social needs" (Bhattacharya, 2017: 81). These social needs are different from fixed biological needs as they are subject to historical change due to the variation of "the standard of necessity" through class struggle (Bhattacharya, 2017: 79). In other words, the standard set of goods and services required by the laborers in order to regenerate their power and will to work another day changes with respect to the historically negotiated concessions and achievements of the working class. The historical struggle to expand this standard set of goods and services ranges from the trade union demands to shorten the working day during the 19th century to the current demands for publicly subsidized healthcare (the 2010 Affordable Care Act known as Obamacare is a consequence of these demands) in the US.

Hence, while the working class fights to expand this standard, capital launches counterattacks to constrict this set even further. Bhattacharya characterizes the current neoliberal forms of this constrictive movement as a twin attack on the production in workplaces and the reproduction process in social life (2017: 90). On the one hand, at the point of production, the workers were intentionally and sometimes even coercively estranged from the trade unions which constituted the main representative entity of their collective will and the most influential instrument they had against the imperatives imposed on them by capital. On the other hand, financialised phase of capitalist accumulation swept over almost every working-class gain of the Keynesian era by privatizing health, education, social security and many other public provisions, including those in cultural and recreational areas cultural and recreational activities. Bhattacharya points out that the social reproduction of labor has been rendered more precarious and more vulnerable in the face of this "open class war" and neoliberalism eventually "succeeded in erasing a key sense of continuity and class memory" (2017: 90–91).

When societal antagonisms are defined as a clash between the social forces of capital and social forces of labor both in the field of production and in the field of reproduction, then the demands to expand the standard set of necessity become a part of class struggle as well. The demand for accessible and quality education, the demand for decent housing, the demand for unhindered access to a mentally and spiritually enriching public life becomes a demand of the whole working class to get their "share of civilization", to extend "their sphere of pleasure", to take their deserved share from the affluence produced by their own labor under capitalist relations (Bhattacharya, 2017: 92). Bhattacharya argues that the strategies of the working class organizations must take heed of the potential impact of the field of the social reproduction of labor on workplace struggles, emphasizing that these organizations have a better chance of making an impact when they are responsive to social needs as well as workplace demands.[6] In the case that the control over workplace relations is too tightly controlled for labor organizations to infiltrate the point of production, as it currently stands under neoliberalism, the better strategy may be to get involved in the lives of working people at the point of reproduction and organize the demands for social needs. Hence, the focus on the unity of production and the social reproduction of labor requires a shift in the strategical outlook of organized movements: rather than choosing one sphere over another and solely engaging with it, it might be more fruitful to broaden the focus and engage with working people in both spheres of life.

9 The Trajectories of 21st Century Social Struggles

As Bhattacharya points out, it is not a coincidence that rising social movements were mostly focused on issues concerning the field of social reproduction, such as access to public goods and the social impact of anti-austerity measures (2017: 86). The twin attack of neoliberal capitalism negatively impacted both the work experience and the everyday experience of vast segments of society. With the advent of the 2010s surfaced a series of protests and uprisings across

---

6 See Bhattacharya's discussion of the strategies of Chicago teachers strike in Bhattacharya et al. (2018).

the world, which began with the upheavals against the regimes of the Arab world and continued with an array of anti-austerity protests in South Europe, the Occupy movement in the US and mass uprisings in various Latin American countries. While the outcome of these protests went into diverging trajectories and were integrated into existing political projects of Islamist, or social democratic, or alternative neoliberal origin, initially they all involved a unique amalgamation of economic, political, and ideological demands. This unique amalgamation involved the demand of popular classes to hold and execute power in all spheres of life. The similarity of the grand framework of this demand and the simultaneity of said movements gave rise to a feeling of solidarity among the protesters around the world. Hence, these series of uprisings in all corners of the world were said to signal the initial stages of a third wave of the world revolution, following the first wave that famously culminated in the October Revolution of 1917 and the second upsurge that eventuated in the Chinese revolution of 1949 and the rise of post-war anti-colonialist movements in Asia and Africa (Savran, 2019: 14; Textum Dergi, 2021).

The differences between the uprisings were revealed as the anticipated next stage of the movements unfolded. While some of the movements gave way to more conventional forms of organization that pursued electoral success, others defied the expected democratic means of societal change, leading to violent and in some cases eventually devastating regime changes; and still some others seemingly led to no change at all, baffling the expectant observers and crushing the hopes of protesters. The seemingly rapid retreat of these movements created a vast disappointment and why these social movements did not create a "lasting impact" and did not lead societies, at least currently, towards social change became a topic of major discussion (cf. Hemer and Persson, 2017). However, the perspective that Savran puts forth in describing this wave of protests, as a specific moment of advancement in the course of a world revolution, allows us to analyse these protests as precursors in an ongoing process of social struggle, and it becomes even more important to see the links between the different courses this wave of protests followed.

While these struggles at the beginning of the new century took place within the span of a couple of years and shared certain characteristics from the outset, these very movements also contained particular qualities that eventually diverged their trajectories. The main shared characteristic of these simultaneous yet diverse seditionary movements was that they all included revolts against the onslaught of neoliberal capitalism on social life. The challenge these uprisings presented against neoliberalism was both the point of origin that united these uprisings and the very factor that differentiated them: all these movements raised an outcry against neoliberalism's conditioning of people's lives. As this conditioning took on different forms in each society according to the historical formation and character of capitalist relations, both the form and the trajectory of these movements variated in each geography. Again, said movements from this era involved the direct action of people who were increasingly subjected to the same process of proletarianization. Nonetheless, the dynamics of this process altered from country to country, bringing different sections of the working-class to the fore of the struggle and changing how the social base of the movement was perceived. Finally, despite this common proletarianization process, all of these movements were seemingly distant from the conventional working class struggles in their own histories. However, as the first section of this chapter has shown for Gezi, all of these movements also derived characteristics from their own histories of social struggle, yet reshaped these characteristics in the form of a struggle within the field of the social reproduction of labor rather than that of production, setting the ground for a re-merging of struggles in both of these fields, which were long perceived to be completely separated.

10   Converging Origins: the Challenge to Neoliberalism

One crucial aspect of the wave of protests in the 2010s was that they posed challenges to the specific forms of neoliberal policies implemented in their countries. This wave of protests was first sparked by the Arab Spring. The Arab Spring is often considered to be a "trumpet of sedition," to borrow a phrase from Neal Wood and Ellen Meiksins Wood, for the worldwide social and political struggles that followed the fall or destabilization of political regimes in the Arab countries, starting with Tunisia and Egypt (Wood and Wood, 1997). The rapid fall of the decades-long authoritarian regimes of Ben Ali and Mubarak following the popular street protests revealed the current fragility of these regimes in the face of the retreat of the support they received from powers of collective imperialism.[7] This display of fragility encouraged the various social forces that had a vested interest in the fall of these regimes, as well as the oppressed people of the region to take to the streets and squares with their own economic, political, and ideological demands. (Hanieh, 2013: 150). Thus, the dissent put forth by the Tunisian and Egyptian people spread throughout

---

7   For a detailed discussion of collective imperialism, see the collection edited by Ali Murat Özdemir (2014).

the region, igniting sparks of political change throughout the Arab region (Bayat, 2017: 10).

The overall political discourse both in the global political arena and media emphasized the political demands of the protesters, which, in a nutshell, aimed to secure their democratic freedom against authoritarian states. Notwithstanding, Hanieh argues that restricting the causes of the protests to the lack of "political freedom" would be a distortion, as these protests were strongly tied to the consequences of neoliberal adjustment policies and the impact of the 2008 global economic crisis (Hanieh, 2011). Hanieh also emphasizes that these neoliberal policies were implemented by a particular form of authoritarian power in Egypt. In Hanieh's eyes, this particular form of neoliberal rule characterized the struggle against neoliberalism as movements of dissent against authoritarianism, for it was the authoritarian regime in Egypt that was attempting to keep tight control over growing social dissent (Hanieh, 2011).

This growing social dissent had already been expressed in the form of labor strikes both in Tunisia and Egypt. In Egypt, there had been an ongoing series of strikes since 2006, led mainly by textile workers but also incorporating white-collar professionals and peasants which constituted the segments further drawn into the proletarianization process through the loss of land, privatization, and deregulation of labor relations. Moreover, these strikes were organized not by trade unions, which were already complicit in the patterns of neoliberalization adopted by the state, but by independent and local organizations by workers themselves. The links established between the workers' movement and the youth movement rematerialized later on in the form of the April 6 Movement in Egypt (Hanieh, 2011; Tuğal, 2016: 238–239). Hence, Amin points out the following movement of Egyptian people incorporated the youth "repoliticised" through these connections with the working classes, the forces of left discontent with the existing organizations and the middle classes that were caught in the wave of proletarianization but failed to find an outlet to express their dissatisfaction under authoritarian political conditions (Amin, 2016: 26). In Tunisia, the Tunisian General Labor Union (French: *Union Générale Tunisienne du Travail*, UGTT) was able to partly break from the authoritarian regime, recognizing the legitimacy of independent actions of discontent and attempting a dialogue between such social demands and the state (Beinin, 2016: 127). Such attempts by UGTT and the connections between the midlevel cadres of the union and the protesters led to a more unified composition during the 2011 protests in Tunisia (Tuğal, 2016: 241).

The challenge posed by the Arab Spring became a reference point for the following social movements of the decade, many protesters declaring their solidarity and sense of kinship with the movements in the Arab world, thus being classified as "Occupy Rebellions" (Bayat, 2017: 12). The slogan "Occupy!" was popularized by the Occupy Wall Street movement in 2011, during which the protesters who denounced the control of big business over American politics refused to leave Zuccotti Park in Lower Manhattan, New York City. The protesters denounced the collection of wealth in the hands of 1% of the society, represented by corporate institutions of neoliberalism in Wall Street, while the remaining 99% were increasingly pulled into poverty due to the very same neoliberal policies that added to the prosperity of 1% (Yangfang, 2012: 252–253).

This outcry against neoliberal forces in Occupy Wall Street both resonated with the Arab Spring protests (Hatem, 2012) and fuelled the social forces in the peripheral countries of Southern Europe, dissenting against the austerity measures implemented by their governments (Kellner, 2013: 264). In 2010 and 2011, a series of protests arose in Southern Europe against the fiscal policies imposed by the European Union (EU) in response to the Eurozone crisis. Starting with the Syntagma Square protests in Athens, Greece, the anti-austerity movement spread out to Spain, Portugal, and Italy. The protests were directed against severe cuts in welfare provisions, privatization of public services and the accompanying lack of open channels of communication between the political bodies and the people. However, as opposed to its counterparts in the Arab world, the anger against neoliberal policies in Southern Europe was directed towards the social democratic parties in government who gave full support to neoliberal policies, generating disappointment in their electoral base (della Porta, 2017a: 455). Hence, the protests indicated a withdrawal of popular consent from the political forces in power and a quest for new options that would be able to present policy alternatives.

A similar dynamic of disappointment was at work in Latin America as well: In 2013, Brazilian protesters took to the streets in an outcry against the increases in transportation fares, sparking the flames of what would turn into the June Uprising in Brazil. The mass protests that initially demanded the right to transportation evolved into a series of public action that reprimanded the submission of the center-left government of the Workers' Party (Brazilian Portuguese: *Partido de Trabalhadores*, PT) to neoliberal policies (Saad-Filho, 2013: 657). The Lula de Silva government of PT was the most significant symbol of the "pink tide" of the 2000s, during which leftist and center-leftist governments came to power in many Latin American countries, mobilizing the hopes and demands of popular classes against the neoliberal agenda followed by previous governments (Chodor, 2015). The PT government was supported by an "alliance of losers" of neoliberalism: the impoverished working class, the domestic capital losing its privileges to foreign capital and sections of the middle class, whose common denominator was merely their experience of loss under neoliberalism (Saad-Filho and Morais, 2014: 228). However, in the course of their political administration, the PT governments were severely criticized for surrendering more and more to neoliberal policies and letting down the laboring classes that carried PT to political power in the first place (Savran, 2006: 123). The PT government particularly under Dilma Rousseff alienated its primary base of the working-class by gradually shifting into a developmental variety of left neoliberalism after 2006, abandoning the inclusionary agenda the PT government had previously adopted (Saad-Filho, 2020: 20). In retaliation, the dissatisfied electoral base flooded the streets in a series of protests, beginning with the 2013 June Uprising.

Tonak argues that in each of these instances of popular uprisings, the economic demands of the laboring segments of society were more or less prioritized, while in the Gezi Uprising, no class demands or economic demands of any kind were articulated (Tonak, 2014: 301). While this is one of the crucial differences between Gezi and its contemporary social struggles, we argue that despite the difference in the articulation of demands, Gezi can still be conceptualized as a part of this third wave of world revolution as it also shares the basic connection built between the sphere of production and the sphere of the social reproduction of labor by these movements. Even when the working classes of the country were participating in the struggle through their mass organizations, the challenge to neoliberalism brought to life by these movements was focused not directly on reclaiming control of workplace relations or increasing wage levels. Rather, neoliberalism was challenged by reclaiming life in the sphere of the social reproduction of labor; more specifically, it came in the shape of reclaiming certain rights and liberties within this sphere, such as access to public transport, social security and public services, as was the case with Brazil and several European countries, and exercising political voice as citizens and the public use of urban space, as in the cases of the Arab Spring and of Gezi. However, each instance in this wave of social struggles painted this shared claim in their own colors depending on the historical actors and conditions of neoliberal capitalism in each country. As such, these demands acquired an anti-authoritarian character in the Arab region, an anti-EU character in Greece, an anti-corporate character in the US and an anti-commodification character in Gezi. It was the distinct character of this wave of struggles that rendered it possible to transform the discontent, which originated from the single phenomenon of the neoliberal attack on social life into a variety of movements that produced a diversity of political and organizational trajectories.

11 Diverging Trajectories: Mainstream Politics and Hijacked Energies

While the aforementioned movements share the common character of challenging varieties of neoliberalism, it is also evident that the differences manifested by neoliberal capitalism in each region led them towards a different trajectory in the aftermath of the movement. It is in this context that Asef Bayat asks whether the Arab revolts and the Occupy rebellions are of the same breed, despite their common roots in problematizing relations of inequality and precarity produced by neoliberal economies. Bayat further argues that the different political systems of these two regions gave rise to different political consequences: in electoral democracies, dissent took the form of popular movements with the aim of changing the political actors, such as in Spain, Brazil, Turkey and the US, whereas in the Arab countries under autocratic rule, dissent took the form of "refolutions," i.e., movements that aimed at forcing the state, or power blocs within the state, to alter the regime and carry out reforms (Bayat, 2017: 17–18). Thus, Bayat seems to suggest that the majority of the social struggles in this wave eventually delegated political action to systemic actors once again: in fact, Bayat emphasizes neoliberalism's capacity to instill compliance as well as dissent. With its ability "to structure people's thinking" and "to erase memory," neoliberalism presents market society as the only viable option despite the dissent and criticism it breeds (Bayat, 2017: 23). While Bayat also accepts that an egalitarian life blossomed in the squares all around the world, he argues that these squares existed in a liminal reality between the real and the unreal: these squares formed cradles within which a new way of life could blossom, but these patterns of new life could not be transferred to larger social structures as crowds dispersed and squares crumbled. Hence, the revolutionary aspects of square life could not withstand the forces of neoliberal restoration (Bayat, 2017: 14).

Bayat does make a very important point: all movements of this era seem to have shared the same fate in the face of restoration despite the differences in the trajectories they followed. The Arab Spring, while victorious in the sense that the social forces in struggle managed to overturn the ongoing regimes or alter the blocs in power, gave way to new governments or regimes that did not have the same vested interest in transforming the neoliberal patterns of distribution in society. The uprisings in Egypt and Tunisia that elevated the protesting masses to the status of equal citizens who have claimed their say in the political order were not accompanied by the structural transformations that would reflect this change in the level of the international order (Sune and Özdemir, 2012: 12). This refusal of the new regimes to stand against the global distribution of power relations limited the horizons of the movement to institutional restructuring rather than changing the underlying patterns of distribution to direct resources towards transforming unequal social relations. The uprisings in the Arab world are thus considered to be "stolen" from their true owners: the masses who protested against the institutional structure that allowed for the unequal, repressive, and exploitative neoliberal social relations (Uğurlu, 2014: 296–297). According to Achcar, the two major counter-revolutionary forces in the Arab world, the forces of the old regimes and the Islamic fundamentalist forces have used every means possible to weaken and marginalize the true progressive forces of revolution, who succumbed to the attacks from these forces due to material, organizational and strategic weaknesses (Achcar, 2020: 7). Thus, the transformative energy of Arab Spring was first hijacked by the Islamist organization of Muslim Brotherhood, who had at hand the political means of both incorporating and thwarting the demands put forth by the protesters, and then by the military coup under the leadership of Abdelfettah el-Sisi, which represented a synthesis of controlling the Islamist forces and achieving a common ground with the international allies of neoliberal restoration.

The uprisings in Brazil which aimed to turn around the PT government's shift from an inclusionary alliance with the working classes were confronted with counterforces as well. The movement in Brazil already involved the contradictory discontents of the competing groups it conflated together: the middle classes in the movement were dissatisfied with the expansion of citizenship to include the poor and the marginalized groups, opposing the transfer of resources to social assistance programs and public funds to further incorporate them into society. Concomitantly, the different segments of the working class and the poor demanded even further widening of citizenship and the reversal of the neoliberal policies that imposed cuts on these funds (Saad-Filho, 2013: 663). Hence, the uprising in Brazil was also stolen in a sense, albeit this time from within: the mainstream media under the control of the right-wing elites looking to circumvent PT entirely stopped criticizing the protests almost overnight and began criticizing the dysfunctional and undemocratic system upheld by PT governments (Saad-Filho, 2013: 658). This line of criticism during the protests would conclude with the impeachment of Dilma Rousseff and thereby carry the country back into the arms of authoritarian neoliberalism under the blundering right-wing leadership of Jair Bolsonaro.

Bolsonaro was often considered as an emulation of Donald Trump, who was elected president of the US in 2017. The Occupy movement had already been preceded by right-wing movements such as the Tea Party section within the Republican constituency founded by those who resented the effects of the 2008 crisis but blamed these effects on the policies of Obama administration

(Kumkar, 2018: 20). Trump administration tapped into the leftover resentment of these groups through his infamous slogan "Make America Great Again," which reflected the frustration of petty bourgeoisie of the Lower Midwestern and Southern regions of the US with the economic crisis and their fantasy of returning to a Golden Age of economic boom (Kumkar, 2018: 246). By hijacking the anti-corporate majoritarian outlook of the Occupy movement and rerouting the egalitarian demands expressed during the protests as adversaries of American people, the right-wing movement under Trump was able to mobilize industrial workers and rural populations, whose livelihoods were indeed threatened by deindustrialization and financialization (Fraser, 2017: 105). Thus, the fledgling egalitarian movement of the Occupy movement was robbed of any chance of connecting with a wider base and was instead confronted with a "Hobson's choice" between the reactionary populism of Trump supporters and progressive neoliberalism which combines "truncated ideals of emancipation and lethal forms of financialization" (Fraser, 2017: 104). Lacking both the discursive and the organizational capability to cope with the threat of destabilizing liberal democracy, the Occupy movement completely dissolved into the anti-Trump front, taking a stand with an alternate wing of the corporate establishment this very movement had initially wanted to drive out.

The only movements that gave rise to the formation of new political actors on the left spectrum rather than succumbing to those who were already on set were the ones in Southern Europe. The anti-austerity movement opted for creating its own political actors, who were expected to stand behind the collectively formulated demands against austerity policies, debt payments, and the fiscal and monetary impositions from the EU. Hence, Syntagma Square brought the Coalition of the Radical Left–Progressive Alliance, otherwise known as Syriza, into power in Greece, while the Indignados movement of Puerta del Sol produced Podemos in Spain; similar developments took place in Portugal and Italy, where left-oriented political parties strengthened their presence in representative democracy (della Porta, 2017b). The anti-austerity movement followed a political strategy that wanted to change the course of austerity policies by appealing to the representation of the democratic will of people in political institutions. While political parties such as Podemos and Syriza attempted to turn the tide towards a form of inclusionary populism, these parties were also forced to make significant concessions from their earlier positions in the course of political action. In the aftermath of its accession to power, Syriza infamously accepted a new deal with the EU that continued austerity measures and undertook Greece's debt to central European states, eventually abandoning its democratic-socialist ideals and transforming into a center-left populist party (Markou, 2021: 192). Podemos, in turn, failed to create an organizational structure that could be used to integrate the variety of demands from their supporters, instead taking a "verticalist turn" that concentrated power at the top of the party mechanism and put faith in a charismatic leadership of Pablo Iglesias Turrión (Nadal, 2021: 50–51). Hence, these parties were caught in conflictual positions: their abilities, even when they were in government, at best extended to partially remedying the neoliberal condition rather than implementing policies that would reverse the tide of austerity and the effects of economic crisis.

The unfolding trajectories and outcomes of the aforementioned movements may very well limit discussions over the protests in the 2010s into the confines of a success and failure dichotomy. From a perspective that prioritizes mainstream politics of existing institutions, elections, and liberal democracy, those movements that led to a change in the current configuration of power and politics in their respective countries can be deemed successful. Hence, the Arab Spring was successful in that the protests managed to haul up the authoritarian regimes, as was the anti-austerity movement in that it managed to create political actors that were able to infiltrate political mechanisms without completely altering the existing political structures. On the other hand, the Occupy movement seems to have lost to the rise of reactionary populism in the US, a fate shared by Brazil and most other "pink tide" countries. Similarly, the forces of Gezi seem to have dispersed without leaving any trace of a permanent organization behind. However, regardless of these movements' success or failure in terms of producing a lasting form of organization or achieving a regime change, it seems that all of these movements retreated against the forces of neoliberal capitalism in one way or another: while the Occupy movement in the US, the June Uprising in Brazil and the Gezi Uprising in Turkey gave way to a new phase of authoritarian neoliberalism, anti-austerity movement and the Arab Spring also failed to initiate fundamental change in distributive mechanisms; furthermore, the popular classes that spurred on these movements were eventually incorporated into processes of restoration of the neoliberal order. Not least, by resorting to the language of mainstream politics to obtain more concrete results, these movements negated their capacity to put forth an entirely new language.

Are we then to decide that this wave of protests was all in vain? At this point, we find it necessary to re-emphasize the perspective of "history's accumulated achievements" once again: the movements in Turkey's history of social struggles that lie within the heart of the Gezi Uprising were also forced to retreat if not downright crushed and overturned. However, the dynamics, values, and practices these predecessors to Gezi set forth persisted through history to reach Gezi, where they were incorporated into new meanings, new practices, and new forms of struggle. Similarly, the wave of worldwide protests in the 2010s set the ground for the emergence of a shared stance against the destruction wreaked by capitalism that proved to be the basis of worldwide solidarity and cooperation. Hence, if this episode of popular protests is seen as a stage in the world-historical revolutionary process, it is important to recognize that the process has not yet achieved closure. In the course of the protests, the people built up an experience of formulating dissent and constituting a formative collective will. This process of formation was cut short by the impact of rival social forces; however, it is this lived experience that obstructs the closure of this episode, along with the ongoing contradictions of the re-established neoliberal order. This experience illuminates the way forward for revolutionary action, rather than merely formulating commonsensical demands that could be met, incorporated or denied by the economic or political forces of neoliberalism. This shared stance was evident in the priority given to the practices of reclaiming public life and social needs in each instance of the wave of protests in the 2010s. Thus, the illumination and direction displayed by this shared stance can be better understood and followed as an effort to re-appropriate the sphere of the social reproduction of labor. While this demand for re-appropriation of the social reproduction of labor has only remained liminal in the unfolding of said movements, it is now the responsibility of revolutionary struggle to cultivate it.[8]

12   Conclusion

This chapter has focused on the relationality of Gezi with the process of social struggles in two dimensions, these being the historical dimension of the legacy Gezi inherited from the history of social struggles in Turkey and the geographical dimension of the simultaneous wave of social struggles in the world. By tracing the characteristics Gezi shares with other social struggles in these two dimensions as well as the divergent aspects, we attempted to shed light

---

8   In the case of Brazil, the revolutionary dynamic indeed made a comeback in the October 2022 elections, in which PT leader Lula da Silva, receiving 50.90% of the votes, reclaimed the presidency from Jair Bolsonaro. Following the election, Bolsonaro supporters raided the Congress, demanding military intervention against PT's victory, in an act reminiscent of the Capitol riots of Trump supporters in Washington D.C. on January 2021, after Trump lost the presidential election to Joe Biden. Refusing to be cowed, Lula condemned the riots as "vandal and fascist", signing a decree that provided the government with the authority to use force against the rioters.

on important potentialities Gezi carries for future political action, which we would like to further underline in concluding this book chapter.

It was a particular strength of Gezi to bring together different sections of the working class together in an unprecedented way. In his reminiscence of the Gezi days, Bulut (2022) points out that working-class youth from the poorer districts of Ankara used to flow into the central Kızılay square in the evenings, bringing fresh energy into the resisting crowds and carrying that energy back to distant neighbourhoods wherein other demonstrations took place (Bulut, 2022). In an era in which working-class lives are immensely fragmented, segmented, and separated from each other, in other words, in an era the working-class experience of everyday life is greatly isolated and alienated, Gezi created a chance for laboring people from various segments of the working class to meet, to get to know each other, to act together and to form a new way of life. This re-introduction of the segments of the working-class had its origins in the past resistance movements in Turkey, such as Fatsa, İzmit, and Yeni Çeltek, where the industrial and rural workers interacted with the student movement and the leftist intellectuals to constitute a collective will and formulate a popular strategy to alter their own life conditions. This past experience of working-class movements in Turkey also left a legacy of non-hierarchical, horizontal forms of organization, which was prefiguratively reflected in the Gezi Uprising.

This re-introduction of segments of the working-class to each other was also a characteristic of the square protests of the 2010s; however, the social struggles went into different trajectories, which led to further separation between different segments of the working class. Hence, this strength so evidently manifested in Gezi also became the downfall of the future trajectories of these movements: as the political consequents of these social struggles distanced their positions from those of the laboring classes and articulated mainstream political demands, they also ended up weakening the specific connection between segments of the working class and eviscerated their newly emerging potential of putting forth the basic principles of an anti-capitalist, participatory and democratic way of life.

Still, one should remember that the collective will to create such a social life and to determine the fundamentals of the democratic and participatory operation of such a society was there when the working class was struggling in unity. The laboring classes were struggling to take in hand not solely their economic well-being, nor merely their working conditions, but their ability to live a complete and fulfilling life, meeting not only basic needs but also social needs that have evolved and extended over time beyond what capitalism can supply. But this struggle for reclaiming the sphere of the social reproduction of labor was at its strongest when it was united with the struggle within the point of production. This should be the point of departure for any future consideration for social action and struggle. It therefore remains a quest for future social struggles to reconnect the discontent, the will and the hope emerging in the sphere of production with the discontent, the will and the hope emerging in the sphere of the social reproduction of labor.

Bibliography

Acaroğlu O (2018) Paris 1871 and Fatsa 1979: Revisiting the transition problem. *Globalizations* 16 (4): 404–423.

Achcar G (2020) From one Arab Spring to another. *Radical Philosophy* 2.07: 5–8.

Akçam C (director) (2004) *Devrimci Yeraltı Maden İş Sendikası Yeni Çeltek Belgeseli* [Motion picture]. Açılım Araştırma Belgeleme Filmcilik: İstanbul.

Amin S (2016) *The Reawakening of the Arab World: Challenge and Change in the Aftermath of the Arab Spring*. New York: Monthly Review Press.

Aren S (1993) TİP *Olayı*. İstanbul: Cem Yayınevi.

Arruzza C and Gawel K (eds) (2020) Special Issue: The Politics of Social Reproduction. *Comparative Literature and Culture* 22(2).

Aslan Ş (2019) *1 Mayıs Mahallesi: 1980 Öncesi Toplumsal Mücadeleler ve Kent*. İstanbul: İletişim.

Aşut A and Atılgan G (2021) *Proletaryanın Büyülü Kutusu: Türkiye İşçi Partisi Radyoda*. İstanbul: Yordam Kitap.

Atılgan G (2013) Diyalektik ile gezinmek: Dansa davet. *Duvar* 2(9): 20–26.

Atılgan G (2016). Sanayi kapitalizminin şafağında. In: Atılgan G, Saraçoğlu C and Uslu A (eds) *Osmanlı'dan Günümüze Türkiye'de Siyasal Hayat*. İstanbul: Yordam Kitap, 521–662.

Aybar MA (2021). TİP *Tarihi*. İstanbul: İletişim.

Aydemir O (2011) Gündelik yaşamda politik deneyim. Unpublished master's thesis, Ankara University, Ankara.

Bakır N (director) (2021) *Şu Fatsa'nın Yolları* [Motion picture]. Sol Kültür: Ankara.

Batuman B (2018) *New Islamist Architecture and Urbanism Negotiating Nation and Islam through Built Environment in Turkey*. New York: Routledge.

Bauman Z (1978) *Hermeneutics and Social Science: Approaches to Understanding*. London: Hutchinson of London.

Bayat A (2017) *Revolution without Revolutionaries: Making Sense of the Arab Spring*. Stanford, California: Stanford University Press.

Beinin J (2016) *Workers and Thieves: Labor Movements and Popular Uprisings in Tunisia and Egypt*. Stanford, California: Stanford Briefs.

Bhattacharya T (2017) How not to skip class: Social reproduction of labor and the global working class. In: Bhattacharya T (ed.) *Social Reproduction Theory: Remapping Class, Recentering Oppression.* London: Pluto Press, 68–93.

Bhattacharya T, Blanc E, Griffiths KD and Weiner L (2018) Return of the strike: A forum on the teachers' rebellion in the United States. *Historical Materialism* 26(4): 119–163.

Boggs C (1977) Marxism, prefigurative communism, and the problem of workers' control. *Radical America* 11(6): 99–122.

Boran B (1968) *Türkiye ve Sosyalizm Sorunları.* İstanbul: Gün Yayınları.

Bulut G (2022) *Ne Yapmalı İçin Hatırlamalı – Kim Yapmıştı? Mavi Defter.* Available (consulted August 1 2022) at: https://mavidefter.net/ne-yapmali-icin-hatirlamali-2-kim-yapmisti/.

Bütün O 2015) *Yedi Kat Yerin Altından Uğultular Geliyor: Yeni Çeltek'ten Soma'ya Maden İşçileri.* Ankara: Dipnot.

Çavdar T (1978) Toplumun bilinçlenmesinde araç olarak tasarım: İzmit yenilikçi yerleşmeler projesi. *Mimarlık* 154: 55–60.

Çelik A (2021) Labour in Turkey during the 1960s: The long hot decade of the working class. *Turkish Historical Review* 12: 265–293.

Chodor T (2015) *Neoliberal Hegemony and The Pink Tide in Latin America: Breaking Up with TINA?* New York: Palgrave Macmillan.

De Nadal L (2021) On populism and social movements: From the indignados to podemos. *Social Movement Studies* 20(1): 36–56.

della Porta D (2017a) Political economy and social movement studies: The class basis of anti-austerity protests. *Anthropological Theory* 17(4): 453–473.

della Porta D (2017b) Progressive and regressive politics in late neoliberalism. In: Geiselberger H (ed.) *The Great Regression.* Cambridge and Malden: Polity Press, 26–39.

Demirbilek S (2011) *Terzi Fikri: İki Darbe Bir Yaşam.* İstanbul: Ozan Yayıncılık.

Fraser N (2017) Progressive neoliberalism versus reactionary populism: A Hobson's choice. In: Geiselberger H (ed.) *The Great Regression.* Cambridge and Malden: Polity Press, 40–48.

Hanieh A (2011) *Egypt's Uprising: Not Just a Question of Transition, Monthly Review MRZine.* Available (consulted August 1 2022) at: https://mronline.org/2011/02/14/egypts-uprising-not-just-a-question-of-transition/.

Hanieh A (2013) *Lineages of Revolt: Issues of Contemporary Capitalism in the Middle East.* Chicago and Illinois: Haymarket Books.

Hatem MF (2012) The Arab Spring meets the Occupy Wall Street Movement: Examples of changing definitions of citizenship in a global world. *Journal of Civil Society* 8(4): 401–415.

Hemer O and Persson HÅ (eds) (2017) *In the Aftermath of Gezi: From Social Movement to Social Change?* Cham: Palgrave Macmillan.

Jaffe A (2020) *Social Reproduction Theory and the Socialist Horizon: Work, Power and Political Strategy*. London: Pluto Press.

Kanık OV (1998). *Bütün Şiirleri*. İstanbul: Adam Yayınları.

Kellner D (2013) Media spectacle, insurrection and the crisis of neoliberalism from the Arab Uprisings to Occupy Everywhere! *International Studies in Sociology of Education* 23(3): 251–272.

Kumkar NC (2018) *The Tea Party, Occupy Wall Street and the Great Recession*. New York: Palgrave Macmillan.

Lebowitz MA (2003) *Beyond Capital*. New York: Palgrave Macmillan.

Markou G (2021). Anti-populist discourse in Greece and Argentina in the 21st century. *Journal of Political Ideologies*, 26(2), 201–219.

Marx K (2009) *Critique of the Gotha Programme*. Moscow: Dodo Press.

Marx K (2009) *The Eighteenth Brumaire of Louis Napoleon*. Moscow: Dodo Press.

Marx K and Engels F (2016). *Manifesto of the Communist Party: A Modern Edition*. London and New York: Verso Books.

Mezzadri A (2019) On the value of social reproduction: Informal labour, the majority world and the need for inclusive theories and politics. *Radical Philosophy* 2.04: 33–41.

Morgül K (2007) A history of the social struggles in Fatsa. Unpublished Master's thesis, Ataturk Institute for Modern Turkish History, İstanbul.

Ozan ED (2016) İki darbe arasında kriz sarmalı. In: Atılgan G, Saraçoğlu C and Uslu A (eds) *Osmanlı'dan Günümüze Türkiye'de Siyasal Hayat*. İstanbul: Yordam Kitap, 663–752.

Özdemir AM (2014) *Kolektif Emperyalizm: Mağribden Maşrıka Dönüşümün Ekonomi Politiği*. Ankara: İmge Yayınları.

Pamuk O (2015) *A Strangeness in My Mind*. Translated by E Okalp London: Faber & Faber.

Saad-Filho A (2013) Mass protests under 'left neoliberalism': Brazil, June-July 2013. *Critical Sociology* 39(5): 657–669.

Saad-Filho A (2020) Varieties of neoliberalism in Brazil (2003–2019). *Latin American Perspectives* 47(1): 9–27.

Saad-Filho A and Morais L (2014) Mass protests: Brazilian spring or Brazilian malaise? In: L Panitch, G Albo and V Chibber (eds) *Socialist Register 50 / Registering Class*. London: Merlin Press, 227–246.

Sargın N (2020) *TİP'li Yıllar 1961–1971*. İstanbul: Sosyal Tarih Yayınları.

Savran S (2006) Brezilya'da Lula faciası. *Praksis* 14 Winter-Spring: 123–148.

Savran S (2019) Arap devriminin dersleri. *Devrimci Marksizm* 39–40 Summer/Fall: 13–62.

Sune E and Özdemir AM (2012) Rantçı devlet yazını üzerine deneme. *Uluslararası İlişkiler* 9(35): 3–31.

Textum Dergi (2021) *Neoliberalizmle Mücadele: Sungur Savran ile Söyleşi*. Available (consulted at August 1 2022) at: https://textumdergi.net/neoliberalizm-ve-mucadele-sungur-savran-ile-soylesi/.

Tonak EA (2014) Haziran direnişi tahayyülleri. In: Savran S, Tanyılmaz K and Tonak EA (eds) *Marksizm ve Sınıflar: Dünyada ve Türkiye'de Sınıflar ve Mücadeleleri*. İstanbul: Yordam Kitap, 289–294.

Tuğal C (2016) *The Fall of the Turkish Model: How the Arab Uprisings Brought Down Islamic Liberalism*. London and Brooklyn: Verso Books.

Uğurlu G (2014) Piyasanın Dostları - Toplumun Düşmanları: Mısır'da "Kolektif Emperyalizm" İzleği. In: Özdemir, A.M. (ed) *Kolektif Emperyalizm: Mağribden Maşrıka Dönüşümün Ekonomi Politiği*. Ankara: İmge Yayınları, pp. 275–302.

Wood EM and Wood N (1997) *A Trumpet of Sedition: Political Theory and the Rise of Capitalism, 1509–1688*. London: Pluto Press.

Yangfang T (2012) A review of the 'Occupy Wall Street' movement and its global influence. *International Critical Thought* 2(2): 247–254.

PART 2

Two, Three, Many Gezis

∴

CHAPTER 5

Gezi and the Yellow Vests Protests
"End of the World, End of the Month, Same Struggle?"

Antoine Dolcerocca, Sebla Ayşe Kazancı and Arca Özçoban[1]

In the early morning of Saturday, 8 December 2018, a large portion of Paris' 8th District, surrounding the Elysée Palace, was under complete lockdown: hundreds of Republican Guards and policemen were called in reinforcement and patrolled the area while the occasional drone hovered above. A helicopter of the French army idling in the courtyard of the Palace was standing ready to depart within minutes, "just in case." The helicopter's potential mission was to exfiltrate the President and take him to a safer place should the impending demonstration turn into an insurrection, overwhelm the security forces, and breach the enclosure of the Palace. On the third consecutive Saturday of weekly Yellow Vests marches, the French government staggered.

Five years earlier, in Turkey too, governing circles were entirely unprepared for the advent of Gezi, but the sheer panic that the protests triggered among the ruling classes is not the only commonality between these two cases. Maybe as a reaction, both protests also set off a level of repressive violence that neither country had witnessed against protesters in the recent past. Additionally, they were both sparked by an environmental issue: on the one hand, Gezi started in the eponymous park in the center of İstanbul, whose century-old trees were to be cut to build a giant mall modelled after an Ottoman military barracks; on the other, the Yellow Vests movement began following a governmental decision to increase taxes on diesel to finance the "Green transition." In a sense, then, both waves of protests were "environmental movements." Both also had sudden, unpredictable and grassroots origins, which took governments by surprise, as already mentioned, but also left on the side of the road most of the organizations that usually plan, organize, and lead mass social protests. Social media was then a key instrument not only to get organized but also to get informed, in a context where traditional news media were the object of broad distrust from protesters. With the absence of traditional institutions

---

1 Antoine Dolcerocca proposed the original idea, structured and wrote the article. Sebla Ayşe Kazancı and Arca Özçoban cowrote section 1.1.

as leading forces, both protests adopted a horizontal organization (or rather, lack thereof), without leaders, which made it difficult to co-opt the movement but, at the same time, blurred its message and rendered negotiations difficult. Finally, both movements involved a large majority of people who had never taken to the streets before, did not claim to represent any political group and both had an unusually high share of women participants (47% for the Yellow Vests and 51% for Gezi, much above the typical levels observed in trade-union demonstrations) (KONDA, 2014: 6; Algan et al., 2019).

Although these seven points of comparison could make the case for a striking parallel between these two movements, in this chapter, we contend that Gezi and the Yellow Vests are fundamentally different protests due to two central factors, i.e., the respective positions of the two countries in the world economy, and as a function of this, the class composition of each movement. This chapter starts with a brief introductory history of each movement by exploring the contexts in which they emerged and the forms the protests took. Then, in a second section, we focus on the first key difference between Gezi and the Yellow Vests, that is, the fiscal aspect of the former. In the same section, we also provide a concise history of fiscal unrest in France and propose to situate the Yellow Vests within that history. The third section is a comparative exploration of the sociology of the Yellow Vests and Gezi, the occupation, age, gender, and income levels of the protesters. In the fourth and concluding section, we turn to the problem of the relation between the environmental issue that ignited each of these protests, and the broader social and economic conditions in each country. For that, we organize our discussion around one of the slogans of the Yellow Vests: "End of the World, end of the month, same struggle".[2]

1 Gezi and the Yellow Vests Protests: Forms and Origins

1.1 *Gezi Protests*

Gezi Park protests started on May 27, 2013, with the participation of a small number of people who reacted to the uprooting of trees and the planned destruction of Gezi Park (a small yet symbolically important urban green space in İstanbul) to build a mall. The protest is widely interpreted as a reaction to the Justice and Development Party's (Turkish: *Adalet ve Kalkınma Partisi*, AKP) brand of "authoritarian neoliberalism" (Keyder, 2013a, 2013b) fuelled by a generalized rentier economy whereby the State commodifies land and

---

2 In French: *Fin du monde, fin du mois, même combat.*

public space via large projects (*"çılgın projeler"*, literally "crazy projects") built under public/private partnerships with corporations close to governing circles (Yeşilbağ, 2021).

A survey conducted throughout the country at the time indicated that 64% of people did not want any construction in the park. In İstanbul alone 75.5% of people opposed it (Metropoll, 2013). Erdoğan, then prime minister, disregarded both public opinion and the unfavourable ruling of the Cultural and Natural Heritage Conservation Board and went ahead with the project. The opposition to authoritarian neoliberalism and its rentier economy had been on the rise in the months leading up to Gezi: In fact, while there were less than 60 political protests across the country in July 2012, this number surged to a total of 150 in January 2013, 200 in March 2013 and 250 in May 2013, eventually culminating in more than 400 protests in June, during Gezi (Yörük and Yüksel, 2014: 109–110). This political discontent combined with growing nationwide environmental concerns then found an outlet with the Gezi protests.

Especially in the first days of the Gezi Movement, a considerable majority of the participants were from the relatively better-off, urban, and educated segments of the country. However, the movement quickly expanded to the working-class neighbourhoods of all large cities and even to smaller Anatolian towns and villages (Tuğal, 2013: 156). With the start of the unlawful destruction of the park, activists entered Gezi Park to perform a sit-in protest. The violence of police raids in the protest area (with the indiscriminate use of tear gas, pepper spray, and water cannons, and the death of eight civilians) was accompanied by the violent rhetoric of members of the government to describe the protesters. The tension escalated with the intensification of the violent rhetoric of the mainstream media, the general lack of coverage of protests, and the demands of the protestors. Twitter became a space to organize the Gezi protests and broadcast information. At a time when the government was trying to implement a media blackout and prosecute social media users, it motivated more people to join the movement against the repression. According to a pollster's report on Gezi, half of society thinks that the two key elements that increased the tension were the brutal police intervention and the prime minister's rhetoric (KONDA, 2014: 32–34). There is indeed a consensus among both participants and observers that the violence of the repression was a turning point and the trigger for the transformation of a local protest into a countrywide insurrection, whose key purpose was not to save Gezi Park anymore but to protest police violence, the curtailing of freedoms, and the rise of authoritarian neoliberalism, in other words, a broad anti-government and anti-AKP protest.

1.2 The Yellow Vests Protests

At the origin of the weekly country-wide protests was a planned tax hike on diesel, the most widely used fuel in France, and an essential commodity in rural and peri-urban areas where little to no alternative to the private car exists. For decades, diesel had been heralded as a cleaner alternative to gasoline, because of lower consumption levels and lower levels of CO_2 emissions. However, diesel combustion engines also release a much higher level of fine particulate matter (PM_{10} and $PM_{2.5}$) than gasoline, which has now become one of the most acute public health issues in cities globally, with particulate matter pollution levels regularly much above recommended thresholds. Studies have determined that diesel (in combination with intensive agriculture) is the main culprit for this explosion of particulate matter levels, and therefore has recently started to be phased out in many European cities (Cames and Helmers, 2013). Low Emission Zones (LEZ), which are being implemented in an increasing number of city centers, limit access to polluting vehicles and typically aim at phasing out diesel (as well as older gasoline-powered vehicles) within a few years. In Paris, one of the trend-setting cities on that issue, following the creation of the LEZ in 2019, which extends beyond the *périphérique* urban highway and consists of a vast area of 815km2 including more than 7 million inhabitants, the metropolitan administration is now planning to implement an absolute diesel ban (even including the most recent vehicles) as early as 2024, before the Olympic Games (RFI, 2022).

At the national level too, under the Presidency of Emmanuel Macron, diesel vehicles have been the target of environmental policymakers, as attested by the now defunct fuel tax hike that triggered the Yellow Vests protests. For decades, as part of the incentives to buy diesel vehicles, diesel fuel was subsidized and cheaper than gasoline (Ajanovic, 2011). The recent U-turn of French governments on diesel is best illustrated by Macron's "carbon tax," whose purpose was to align diesel prices on that of gasoline and make use of the additional tax revenues to finance policies towards the "Green transition". This, at least, was the official narrative.

This narrative was greatly undermined by an article of the Supplementary Budget Act of 2018, in which the government proposed that the planned 577 million euros collected through the carbon tax to finance the energetic transition be reallocated to the general budget, "in order to compensate for lower tax revenues than expected." (Assemblée Nationale, 2018) Incidentally, 2018 was also the year that saw the abolition of the Solidarity Tax on Wealth (*Impôt de Solidarité sur la Fortune*, hereinafter referred to as "wealth tax"), a progressive tax on households whose total net assets amounted to more than 1 million euros, which was one of Macron's key electoral promises. In the last year of its implementation, this tax incurred 4.2 billion euros of net fiscal revenue (Commission des Finances du Sénat, 2019). Therefore, at the end of 2018, to lower the budget deficit, the government decided to partly compensate for the lack of revenues resulting from the tax cut in favour of the few richest households in the country with a hike on the carbon tax for diesel fuel (Philippe, 2018). The carbon tax rise sounded bad enough on its own to modest households of rural and *"rurbain"* France, but its legitimacy –which stemmed from financing the energetic transition to combat climate change– took a serious hit when its purpose explicitly became one of compensating the suppression of the last progressive tax on wealth in Europe. As it happens, the reinstating of the wealth tax has been one of the main demands by Yellow Vest protesters, and during the 2022 electoral campaign for the French presidency, calls for a "climatic wealth tax" and other progressive tax schemes to finance the "green transition" became prominent from the left to the center, which shows the lasting influence of the Yellow Vests on the political sphere (Institut Montaigne, 2022).

The Yellow Vest protests erupted on November 19, 2018, after weeks of organizing on social media, and took two main forms: first, people permanently occupied traffic circles, filtering and slowing down traffic in strategic places; second, on Saturdays, yellow vests would converge towards Paris (or another large city) to march, usually on the *Champs-Elysées*, a form of protest reminiscent of those traditionally organized by trade-unions. In the first three months of the protests, the level of support for the movement reached a staggering three-fourths of the French society, while more than half of the French population defined themselves as "yellow vests" (even though some of them did not take part in either type of protests). Just as in the case of Gezi, the initial reason for the protest (here, the hike of the diesel tax, which was officially abandoned less than a month after the start of the protest) quickly moved to the background, and the Yellow Vests movement turned into an anti-Macron revolt. The movement, however, in clear contrast with Gezi, started as a fiscal revolt, and maintained this as a central aspect of the protest, even after the tax hike on diesel was abandoned. The next section examines the specificity of the Yellow Vests protest and situates it in the long tradition of fiscal revolts in France.

2   Fiscal Uprisings in France before the Yellow Vests

Fiscal uprisings have been a staple of French political history, before waning in the middle of the 19th century. *Ancien Régime* France was plagued by regular peasant revolts (often called *Jacqueries*, a derogatory term also used by some commenters to refer to the Yellow Vests), and the fiscal origins of the French Revolution have since established the concepts of consent to taxation and the associated notion of fairness of taxation as central themes of French political life. The *cahiers de doléances,* sent to the General Estates from all corners of France, were filled with complaints about the high levels of taxes and the inequality that resulted from the privileges awarded to the nobility and the clergy. The Declaration of the Rights of Man and of the Citizen (*Déclaration des Droits de l'Homme et du Citoyen*) of 1789 proclaimed the equality of all before the law but also the *equity* of each citizen's contribution to the functioning of the State, as stated in its Article 13: "For the maintenance of the public force, and for the expenditures of administration, a common contribution is indispensable: it must be equally distributed among all the citizens, *according to their abilities*".[3] (National Constituent Assembly, 1789) This article of the Declaration has since been used by proponents of progressive taxation to argue its legitimacy, in response to more liberal interpretations that consider progressive taxation as a breach of the principle of equality before the law (since wealthier citizens then have to contribute a higher percentage of their wealth or income than the rest of the population).

This difference in interpretation of the 1789 Declaration between French liberals and progressives illustrates the widely different roots of fiscal revolts in history: from liberal and anti-statist sentiments expressed in rather individual forms of protests to egalitarian impulses favouring more redistribution, generally taking the form of collective action. With the rise of progressive income tax at the beginning of the 20th Century, fiscal protests in France resolutely got anchored to the (far) right of the political spectrum, with regular demonstrations throughout the 1920s and 1930s. After World War II, Poujadism constitutes the last manifestation of a large-scale mobilization against taxation before a long period of relative calm, with high growth and the rise of the welfare State (Delalande, 2014).

The resurgence of fiscal protests occurred in the midst of the Great Recession following the 2008 financial crisis, with two radically different protests: in 2012, a group of internet start-up owners initiated an online campaign calling themselves *"Pigeons"* (literally translating as "pigeons" but roughly meaning "chumps"), protesting a new tax on capital gains announced by the newly elected Hollande government, which caved in quickly, cancelling the planned tax. In October 2013, the Red Caps (French: *Bonnets Rouges*) demonstrations

---

3   Our translation. Emphasis added by the authors.

erupted in Brittany, in opposition to the *ecotax*, a new taxation on highways targeting freight transportation and aimed at financing the green transition and encouraging the switch of freight transportation from road to rail. Unlike the Pigeons, the Red Caps organized crowded rallies and were responsible for the destruction of some of the infrastructures installed to collect the tax (overhead cameras, etc.) as well as numerous automated speed radars. This protest was successful as well, with the government deciding once again to abandon the implementation of the new tax. The Red Caps may initially seem like a rehearsal for the Yellow Vests: in addition to their colourful (both literally and figuratively) symbols and means of demonstration, both protests were initiated following a plan for a new tax on road transportation aimed at financing the green transition. However, both protests were radically different in terms of their geographical scope, their social make-up, and the demands of the protesters.

3 Are the Yellow Vests Protests Just Another Fiscal Uprising?

The Yellow Vests are arguably the first fiscal uprising in more than half a century that falls on the progressive side of the disagreement on the interpretation of Article 13 of the 1789 Declaration.

The first striking element of the Yellow Vests protest consists in its breadth: all regions of France were concerned somewhat equally, with roadblocks established in and around a large number of medium and large cities, or on major roads. Although all regions were involved, the protests had its roots mostly but not exclusively in peri-urban and rural areas, where there is simply no alternative to private vehicles and monthly gas expenses can often mount to several hundreds of euros. This is particularly true for independent workers visiting customers and patients, for example. In addition to this geographic breadth, the movement was initially very popular: 75% of the population supported the movement according to polls conducted at the beginning of the protests between November 2018 and January 2019, with more than half of the population expressing "support" or "sympathy" and 20% defining themselves as Yellow Vests. This level of support remained even after the degradation of a statue at the *Arc de Triomphe*, whose picture was on the front pages of many national and foreign newspapers on the following day and was used to portray the movement as dangerous. It was only in February 2019 that support for the protests significantly eroded: however, a year later, overall support was still at 55% (45% of support and 10% of Yellow Vests) (IFOP, 2018a, 2018b, 2019).

Initially, the institutional left, comprised of trade unions such as the General Labor Confederation (French: *Conférération Générale du Travail,* CGT) and political parties such as *France Insoumise,* was either ambivalent or outright hostile to the movement because it seemed to have been sparked by a conservative impulse, somewhat reminiscent of the *Bonnets Rouges* protests a few years before (Delalande, 2014). However, the protesters, in the first few weeks, benefited from a very favourable nay benevolent media coverage. The benevolent (over)exposure of Yellow Vest protesters on the news created a unique situation: for weeks, every single day, nonstop on the mainstream news channels, people (among which were notably many single women) who had never been highly politicized and had never participated in a demonstration, were being interviewed at their roundabouts and were allowed to express themselves freely and relay their demands, their concerns and their everyday issues, with the approving and sympathetic gaze of the news presenter. This was truly a unique moment in recent mass media history, where the audience could see themselves on the television. This phenomenon quickly pushed leftist leaders and sympathizers to recognize the progressive potential of the Yellow Vests. Genevieve Legay, one of many iconic yellow vest protesters recounted that before the first protest, as a long-time Association for the Taxation of Financial Transactions and Aid to Citizens (*Association pour la Taxation des Transactions financière et l'Aide aux Citoyens,* ATTAC) and French Communist Party (*Parti Communiste Français,* PCF) militant, she was somewhat hostile to the planned demonstrations and their central demand on the diesel tax. However as soon as the day after the first demonstration Legay realized that "this may have been what the left had been waiting for all these years": poor workers, especially working women, protesting their state of permanent survival, whereby they have nothing left as early as the 5th of each month, as soon as the rent and bills are paid (the "end of month" issue) (Carpentier, 2019). Legay immediately decided to join the movement, and, by February 2019, the most enthusiastic supporters of the yellow vests were left-leaning voters (Algan et al., 2019).

Another striking element in the Yellow Vests movement consists in its social composition and in the demands of the protesters, both of which have been the topic of intense discussions: initially, both the right and the left quickly tried to appropriate the protest and benefit from its aura in the rest of the population, more or less along the dividing line of the interpretation of Article 13 of the 1789 Declaration. On the one hand, the right, partly embracing a populist approach, claimed that protesters expressed their annoyance with both excessive and unfair taxation by the French state, exemplified by punitive transportation policies designed by a Parisian ruling class living a few dozen meters away from a metro station. On the other, the left asserted that protesters had nothing against taxes *per se* but against this regressive tax in particular, which would primarily affect more modest peri-urban and rural dwellers, therefore contradicting Article 13 of the 1789 Declaration and the principle of progressivity of taxation.

Did the Yellow Vests bear within their ranks the values of the French Revolution, or did they get co-opted by perfectly choreographed manoeuvres of entryism by *France Insoumise* and other leftist parties? What really happened in the first few weeks of the protest is still a matter of debate, which will surely never be decisively settled. And maybe it does not need to be. What matters is that Yellow Vests demonstrations have been filled with signs and mottos such as:[4] "Bring back the Wealth Tax," "Let's equitably share the cake, not the crumbs," "Who sows misery harvests wrath," "Our labor, their profits," and of course "End of the world, end of the month, same struggle" to which we will come back in the next section. The predominance of these sorts of slogans (on equity in taxation, social inequalities, the minimum wage, and even the environment) only increased in time and came to best represent the protests. Regardless of whether these notions were present in the protesters' minds from the start, or if they were dormant but later activated by clever leftist activism, the outcome is the following: By January 2019, the Yellow Vests were overwhelmingly a movement that denounced social inequalities and fought for a fairer world.

4 The Meanings of Gezi and the Yellow Vests

Determining the exact nature of the social classes that constitute either movement is not easy and has been the topic of heated debates among media commentators, pollsters, and academics. The nebulous, decentralized, and new-fangled characters of both movements render their analyses particularly delicate. However, in either case, many polls and analyses have been conducted, and if there is no consensus over the nature of the protests or the social profile of the participants, the debates usually revolve around two distinct positions.

In the case of the Yellow Vests, as we have seen, the movement was the object of keen interest of both the far right and the left, which equally claimed

---

4 The movement displayed an innumerable number of mottos, almost all of which were different from the ones we usually see in institutional demonstrations organized by trade unions. This is an entirely partial selection. As suggested, many slogans were also clearly anchored to the right or far right of the political spectrum, some of course including not-so-subtle references to intimate body parts, etc.

to respond to the demands of the protesters and to represent them. In parallel to these dividing lines, the treatment of the Yellow Vests protests by academics fell mainly within two camps, one that interprets the movement as a progressive one and another as a reactionary one. The progressive interpretation has been notably defended by Frédéric Lordon, who in the first few weeks of the protests wrote (Lordon, 2018):

> This is where the 'elites' are at: unable to see that there is no more time, that a whole world – theirs – is falling apart, that the breakdown will not be staved off by deferring or reducing taxes, and that they'll be lucky if the political institutions themselves are not caught up in the general collapse. Because it is not a 'social movement', it is an uprising.
>
> When any form of domination approaches such a tipping point, all the institutions of the regime, and in particular those of symbolic guardianship, rigidify in a profound misunderstanding of the event – wasn't this the best order possible? – coupled with a resurgence of anger, as well as a beginning of panic when the hatred against them bursts into the open and is suddenly revealed to their eyes.

Meanwhile, Alain Badiou (2019) interpreted the protests as being largely reactionary and did not expect anything progressive to come out of them, underlining that *"tout ce qui bouge n'est pas rouge"* (literally "All that moves is not red"):[5]

> Considering the movement – once again as it presents itself in its initial 'purity' – on the basis of its rare collective aspects, slogans, repeated statements, I find nothing in it that speaks to me, interests me, mobilizes me. Their declarations, their perilous disorganization, their forms of actions, their deliberate lack of general thinking and strategic vision – all this precludes political creativity. I am certainly not won over by their hostility to any embodied leadership, their obsessive fear of centralization, of unified collectives – a fear that confuses, as do all contemporary reactionaries, democracy and individualism. None of this is likely to pit against the utterly odious, despicable Macron a force that is progressive, innovative and victorious in the long run.
>
> BADIOU, 2019

---

5 The phrase was translated into English as "not everything that moves ahead is red" in Badiou's article for Verso: https://www.versobooks.com/blogs/4327-alain-badiou-lessons-of-the-yellow-vests-movement.

Such a radical difference of interpretation from the two leading figures of the French left is certainly due to the composition of the movement itself. The 2022 French elections have since demonstrated that the country is divided into three broad electoral blocs: a center-right block led by Macron composed of the conservative bourgeoisie; a left block led by Mélenchon's *France Insoumise* and supported by dwellers of the city center and their immediate periphery, that is to say by liberal educated classes together with the poor urban immigrant population; a right-wing nationalist block supported largely by less educated and poorer segments of peri-urban and rural France. It quickly became clear that the Yellow Vests were a combination of the second and third blocks, as polls have consistently shown that the overwhelming support for yellow vest protesters was coming from Le Pen and Mélenchon voters (IFOP, 2018a; IFOP, 2018b; IFOP, 2019). While Lordon focuses on progressive elements of the movement, Badiou emphasizes the reactionary ones, not only in its content but also in its form.

We argue that this difference of interpretation is reflected in the movement itself, in a concrete way. Following Emmanuel Todd's analysis, we can estimate that there are two main forms of Yellow Vests protests corresponding broadly to two demographics and two political orientations (Todd, 2020). On the one hand, in the traffic circles, a form of protest that is permanent and requires a lot of time and commitment, we observed mostly inactive people, either retirees or youth. These protesters have a monthly salary hovering around 1000 euros. This can be interpreted as the more communal and progressive aspect of the movement. On the other hand, protesters on the Saturday demonstrations in the city centers are slightly different: they are people who can afford the weekly trip and cannot stay in the traffic circles because they work. They usually are either independent workers or employees and have an average monthly income of 1400 euros. This form of protest corresponds quite well with the more reactionary aspects of the Yellow Vests that Badiou emphasizes.

However, what unites both categories (inactive poor and working poor, in other words, the proletariat together with the former and future proletariat) is that they have a salary below the median monthly income of 1700 euros per month. The Yellow Vests therefore were the coming together of some far right and far left voters, united by their class position and their education levels. Many commented that the "*banlieues*" steered clear of the demonstrations because of their hostility to it, but we see signs, notably in popular culture, that this was not the case: many rap songs have praised the Yellow Vests.[6] Activists

---

6 See Yoan Gwilman's thesis "Dans la même galère: Comment les Gilets Jaunes ont désamorcé Charlie", (cited in Todd, 2020).

in the suburbs have been sharing their sympathy with the Yellow Vests and said that the movement was an eye-opener. People in the banlieues realized for the first time that they shared the exact same problems with the white working poor and inactive: poor people get their hands blown off by police grenades and their eyes ripped apart by "flash balls" regardless of the neighbourhood they live in and their skin colour. Could the Yellow Vests, despite their failure which was coded in the structure of the movement, have been the trigger for a return to class politics?

Here, in complete contrast with Gezi, the level of participation and support for the Yellow Vests decreases as both income and education increase and there were almost no university graduates among the protesters.

In Gezi, the debates over the nature of the protest and its class composition were equally controversial. Indeed, there is a broad consensus that Gezi was about much more than the initial struggle over the fate of Gezi Park, and that it had its roots in years of social and political unrest in Turkey. Gezi Park was very much symbolic, in the sense that it was a reflection of all the other concerns over environmental and urban policies resulting from AKP's economic policies as well as rising authoritarianism and oppression. But then, who were the people demonstrating in Gezi, and why did they join the movement?

The interpretation of Gezi may be summarized as falling into three main approaches. The first of these is a political approach that understands Gezi primarily as a political and cultural reaction to AKP's policies in the ten years that preceded the protests. This approach contends that class holds almost no explanatory power in the case of Gezi, as the movement was too variegated and consisted in a cross-class protest (Yörük and Yüksel, 2014). The other two approaches, on the other hand, conceive class to be central to understanding Gezi. The first of these considers Gezi primarily as a working-class uprising. Korkut Boratav (2013) notably argues that those who joined the protests should be identified as the working class. In alignment with the standpoint of Yörük and Yüksel (2014), Boratav emphasizes that although professionals and self-employed individuals were present in the Gezi protests, these class segments did not constitute the majority of the protestors. Boratav instead identifies the majority of the protestors as highly educated workers, students (the future of the working class), and independent professionals. In addition to this class debate, Boratav also indicates that what motivated these groups was a product of class antagonism and that protestors struggled against the commodification of public spaces by the state and the bourgeoisie (Boratav, 2013; Tonak, 2013).

The last interpretation focuses on class as well but, instead of comparing the raw numbers of class participation, emphasizes the disproportionate participation (compared to their share in the rest of the population) of university graduates, professionals, and executives. Gezi then, was primarily a revolt of the "new middle class", whose members are faced with the contradiction between their potentiality and their reality, between their aspirations and their objective conditions. In that case, the direction of the Gezi protests was largely determined by the economic, cultural, and ideological concerns of the "new middle class" (Keyder, 2013a, 2013b). This last interpretation is the most convincing to us, as the staggering over-representation of professionals, intellectual laborers, and university graduates in the protests says much more about the movement than the higher numbers of workers or other categories. This, we argue, should therefore be the focal point of analysis if one is to understand the meaning of Gezi.

Now, we are coming to the fundamental difference between Gezi and the Yellow Vests, which we will examine in the next and concluding section, namely that more than 60% of Gezi protesters were graduates or students of Bachelor's level programs, while almost no university graduate participated in the Yellow Vests protests. The overrepresentation (compared to the whole population) of categories of protesters increases with income and education for Gezi, while for the Yellow Vests, overrepresentation increases as income and education levels decrease. How can we explain this crucial difference?

5 From Gezi (End of the World) to the Yellow Vests (End of the Month)

Despite their many apparent similarities, these two movements are radically different. Both protests were epoch-altering in their respective country and have been the latest mass protests to date. However, their radical difference lies in the vastly different positions of participants in the global division of labor, and their divergent experiences in terms of social mobility in the last twenty years.

The mounting global environmental crisis is characterized by a trade-off between enacting policies that improve the well-being of the planet, and policies that improve the well-being of people. In the case of the Yellow Vests, the trade-off was between people's purchasing power and the reduction of carbon emissions from transports. It looks at first as if we are left with a tragic alternative: if we increase taxes to finance the decarbonized energetic transition, we may have to deal with social unrest, misery, and other destabilizing consequences; and if we keep subsidizing fossil fuels to allow people to keep commuting at affordable costs, we will face other (climate-change-induced) costs down the road.[7] This, however, is a false alternative, as illustrated by one of the Yellow Vests mottos: "End of the world, end of the month, same struggle." It suggests that the solution to the environmental crisis (the "end of the world") cannot be found in isolation from socio-economic issues (the "end of the month") and that we are increasingly entering an area in which both issues are intricately connected.

As argued earlier, both movements were sparked by an environmental issue before quickly spreading beyond it and turning into broad movements of opposition to their respective government. The Yellow Vests and Gezi however approached the same issue from opposite angles. On the one hand, the Yellow Vests were largely composed of people with lower educational and income levels, with an astounding underrepresentation of university graduates. On the other, the Gezi protests were characterized by an equally astounding overrepresentation of university graduates, professionals, and independents. What then, explains such a crucial difference?

Our hypothesis is that Gezi was a progressive social movement led by an emerging middle class, while the Yellow Vests were a defensive social movement led by a downwardly mobile working class consisting of current and former workers including retirees as well as prospective workers such as students. To better situate these two movements, it is necessary to analyse them in relation to global income distribution, and even better, in relation to changes in income. The "elephant curve" showed that the benefits of globalization have been unequally distributed throughout the globe (Lakner and Milanovic, 2013: 31): the people who benefited most from income rise in the last 20 years (apart from the top 1%) were largely people situated in countries of the global South, while the middle class of advanced industrialized countries had their income stagnate or even slightly decrease over the same period.

In the French case, this stagnation of income and associated decline of the standards of living for a large portion of the population, particularly since 2008 is without a doubt the elemental force behind the rise of the Yellow Vests protest. These protests were a reaction to a declining standard of living following the imposition of neoliberal policies which organized labor and trade unions were unable to stop. Consequently, people who were never politicized or unionized and certainly never participated in any labor-union-organised

---

7 In the case of the Yellow Vests, the French government took the worst possible decision: it aggravated the social and economic distress of a large section of the population with the hike of the carbon tax on diesel, and "at the same time" abandoned its effort to build a low carbon economy by using the funds collected via the carbon tax for a completely different purpose, that is, giving a tax break to the 350.000 people of the country.

demonstration, took to the streets for the first time in their lives because they considered that their very survival was at stake. The high proportion of women in the protests, many of whom were single, is a clear sign of the urgency of the situation. The Yellow Vests, then, are one of the expressions of neoliberal globalization. It is the knee-jerk reaction of the downwardly mobile working class of the industrialized (or rather deindustrializing) core, longing for the better days of the recent past. This is a defensive social movement that tries to stop the increasing worsening of living conditions without the participation of trade unions and other institutions that have failed to do so or have been complicit.

In contrast to this, while standards of living in Turkey have stopped rising since 2015 or 2016, (and have even been declining since the early 2020s), the first decade of AKP's rule was characterized by a high level of foreign direct investments, rapid privatizations, and break-neck economic growth, which resulted in rising standards of living for a significant part of the population. Therefore, Gezi emerged in a completely different context than the Yellow Vests. Gezi could hence be interpreted as a progressive social movement led by the rising middle class of an emerging country. By this, we mean that the social classes leading the movement had benefitted from rising educational and living standards, either as an improvement of material conditions, or the opening of new aspirations and perspectives. In the first case, for the professional middle-class (well-off employees and self-employed), Gezi was a way of expressing that material well-being cannot come at all costs: while these classes had witnessed a significant improvement in their standards of living, they also faced a degradation of political conditions, a curtailing of freedoms, a worsening of environmental degradations, etc. In the second case, for university graduates who had not necessarily yet seen the fruits of their efforts in higher education, Gezi was a protest to denounce the disconnect between their aspirations, what was promised to them, and their material conditions (unemployment, high levels of exploitation, etc.).

In conclusion, we contend that both Gezi and the Yellow Vests can best be explained by the distributional consequences of globalization, as illustrated by the elephant curve, and by the objective and subjective (or anticipated) gains (or losses) of the participating classes, these being, a downwardly mobile working-class in the French case and an upwardly mobile (either objectively or subjectively) new middle class in the Turkish case.[8]

---

8   At the time of submission, France is engulfed in its greatest social mobilization since 1995, against a pension reform most economists describe as unjust. Following a rare consensus among all trade-unions of the country, millions are on strike and on the streets. As of 19

Bibliography

Ajanovic A (2011) The effects of dieselization of the European passenger car fleet in energy consumption and CO_2 emissions. In: *Proceedings of the 34th IAEE International Conference, Institutions, Efficiency and Evolving Energy Technologies.* Stockholm: IAEE.

Algan Y, Beasley E, Cohen D, Foucault M and Péron M (2019) Qui Sont Les Gilets Jaunes et Leurs Soutiens? *CEPREMAP and CEVIPOF* 3: 1–13. Available (consulted April 23 2023) at: https://sciencespo.hal.science/view/index/identifiant/hal-03393105.

Assemblée Nationale (2018) *Projet de Loi de Finances Rectificative n°1371.* Available (consulted March 26 2023) at: https://www.assemblee-nationale.fr/dyn/15/tex tes/l15b1371_projet-loi#_Toc529453513.

Badiou A (2019) *Lessons of the 'Yellow Vests' Movement.* Available (consulted March 26 2023) at: https://www.versobooks.com/blogs/4327-alain-badiou-lessons-of-the-yel low-vests-movement.

Boratav K (2013) *Olgunlaşmış Bir Sınıfsal Başkaldırı* ... Available (consulted March 26 2023) at: https://sendika.org/2013/06/her-yer-taksim-her-yer-direnis-bu-isci -sinifinin-tarihsel-ozlemi-olan-sinirsiz-dolaysiz-demokrasi-cagrisidir-korkut-bora tav-120919/.

Cames M and Helmers E (2013) Critical evaluation of the European diesel car boom – global comparison, environmental effects and various national strategies. *Environ Sci Eur* 25: 15.

Carpentier F (2019) *Entretien avec Geneviève Legay: 'Dès Que J'irai Mieux Je Reprendrai le Combat, Jusqu'à ma Mort'.* Available (consulted March 9 2023) at: https://www .revolutionpermanente.fr/Entretien-avec-Genevieve-Legay-Des-que-j-irai-mieux -je-reprendrai-le-combat-jusqu-a-ma-mort.

March 2023, all refineries and all ports of the country are occupied and all activity at a standstill. Macron's decision to trigger article 49.3 of the constitution to avoid debating and voting on the reform at the National Assembly has only intensified a latent political crisis which may be developing into a regime crisis. As in 2018, the level of support among the population is overwhelming (even higher, with polls reporting close to 80% of approval). As in 2018, the strategy of the government is that of relentless violent confrontation and provocation. As in 2018, the symbol of the yellow vest is now everywhere in demonstrations, only this time side-by-side with flags of trade-unions and political parties, as well as the usual provocative signs and slogans. This movement, which could be qualified as a merger of the Yellow Vests with the trade-unions, is superior to that of 2018 both quantitatively and qualitatively, and therefore represents a greater threat to the government, at a time when it is much weaker, with a meager relative majority at the National Assembly. If it is impossible to predict the outcome, a return to the status quo now seems entirely out of question.

Commission des Finances du Sénat (2019) *Rapport d'Information No 42 du 09/10/2019, Transformation de L'impôt de Solidarité Sur la Fortune (ISF) En İmpôt Sur la Fortune Immobilière (IFI) et Création du Prélèvement Forfaitaire Unique (PFU): Un Premier Bilan.* Available (consulted March 9 2023) at: http://www.senat.fr/rap/r19-042-1/r19-042-12.html.

Delalande N (2014) Le retour des révoltes fiscales? *Pouvoirs* 151(4): 15–25.

IFOP (2018a) *"Balise d'opinion #50".* Available (consulted March 9 2023) at: https://www.ifop.com/wp-content/uploads/2018/12/115209-Rapport-CN-SR-50.pdf.

IFOP (2018b) *"Balise d'opinion #51".* Available (consulted March 9 2023) at: https://www.ifop.com/wp-content/uploads/2018/12/115209-Rapport-CN-SR-51.pdf.

IFOP (2019) *"Balise d'opinion #80".* Available (consulted March 9 2023) at: https://www.ifop.com/wp-content/uploads/2019/11/116084-Rapport-CN-SR-N80.pdf.

Institut Montaigne (2022) *Rétablir l'ISF et le Transformer en ISF Climatique.* Available (consulted March 9 2023) at: https://www.institutmontaigne.org/presidentielle-2022/legislatives-2022/nupes/retablir-lisf-et-le-transformer-en-isf-climatique-2/.

Keyder Ç (2013a) *Yeni Orta Sınıf.* Available (consulted March 26 2023) at: https://bilimakademisi.org/wp-content/uploads/2013/09/Yeni-Orta-Sinif.pdf.

Keyder Ç (2013b) *Gezi Parkı Protestoları bağlamında Yeni Orta Sınıflar, Neo-liberal Dönüşüm ve Yoksulluk.* Available (consulted March 26 2023) at: https://bilimakademisi.org/wp-content/uploads/2013/10/Gezi-Parki-Protestolari-baglaminda-Yeni-Orta-Siniflar-Neo-liberal-Donusum-ve-Yoksulluk-_-KonusaKonusa.pdf.

KONDA (2014) *Gezi Report: Public Perception of the 'Gezi Protests' Who Were the People at Gezi Park?* Available (consulted March 26 2023) at: https://konda.com.tr/report/121/gezi-report?l=en.

Lakner C and Milanovic B (2013) *Global Income Distribution: From the fall of the Berlin Wall to the Great Recession.* World Bank Policy Research Working Paper No. 6719, Available at SSRN (consulted March 26 2023): https://ssrn.com/abstract=2366598.

Lordon F (2018) *End of the World?* Available (consulted March 26 2023) at: https://www.versobooks.com/blogs/4153-end-of-the-world.

Metropoll (2013) *Türkiye'nin Nabzı 'Gezi Parkı Protestoları Ve Türkiye'nin Otoriterleşme – Özgürlük Sorunu'.* Available (consulted March 26 2023) at: https://www.metropoll.com.tr/arastirmalar/siyasi-arastirma-9/1731.

National Constituent Assembly (1789) *Declaration of the Rights of Man and of the Citizen Adopted by the National Assembly during its Sessions on August 20, 21, 25 and 26, and Approved by the King.* Paris: Mondharre & Jean. Available (consulted April 21 2023) at: https://www.loc.gov/item/2021668069/.

Philippe B (2018) *Le Gouvernement Finance-t-il la fin de l'ISF Avec La Taxe Sur Les Carburants?* Available (consulted March 9 2026) at: https://www.capital.fr/economie-politique/taxe-sur-les-carburants-la-drole-de-mecanique-comptable-du-gouvernement-qui-pourrait-faire-polemique-1316576.

RFI (2022) *Paris Rolls Out Ban On Big-polluting Diesel Vehicles.* Available (consulted March 9 2023) at: https://www.rfi.fr/en/france/20220601-paris-rolls-out-ban-on-big-polluting-diesel-vehicles.

Todd E (2020) *Les Luttes de Classes en France au XXIe siècle*, Paris: Le Seuil.

Tonak A (2013) İsyanın sınıfları. In: Göztepe Ö (ed.) *Gezi Direnişi Üzerine Düşünceler.* Ankara: NotaBene Yayınları, 21–28.

Tuğal C (2013) 'Resistance everywhere': The Gezi revolt in global perspective. *New Perspectives on Turkey* 49: 147–162.

Yeşilbağ M (2021) Statecraft on cement: The politics of land-based accumulation in Erdoğan's Turkey. *Urban Studies* 59(13), 2679–2694.

Yörük E and Yüksel M (2014) Class and politics in Turkey's Gezi protests. *New Left Review* 89: 103–123.

CHAPTER 6

Re-visiting the "Populist Moment"

Geographies of Grassroots Movements and Left Populism in Greece, Spain and Turkey

Athina Arampatzi

The eruptive political landscapes of the past decade have brought to the fore the re-emergence of populist politics. Following the shockwaves felt by the 2008 global financial crisis in contexts where politics and contestation were being reduced to either technocratic management or repressed by authoritarian regimes, mass mobilizations and protest movements that took place in cities such as Athens, Madrid, and Istanbul underscored a severe crisis of representation underway. As Doreen Massey (2015: 5–6) pointed out, "this, in turn, opened up a space for populism: for the emergence of a different kind of voice—anti-establishment, grassroots, imbued with passion, producing meaningful talk and action". In this context, the "populist moment" that rose in Southern Europe as an alternative to the crisis of neoliberal hegemony (see Mouffe, 2018), along with its Eastern Mediterranean counterpart, has often acquired a pejorative or negative meaning in public discourse that tends to treat both its progressive and regressive political manifestations as de facto bound to reactionary forms of nationalism or "anti-political" (Beveridge and Featherstone, 2021). Nevertheless, as Beveridge and Featherstone (2021) argued, in contrast to what is often perceived as anti-political, once outside the logics and spaces of liberal state politics, such developments might bear positive connotations regarding the re-emergence of contentious and subaltern forms of democratic politics.

At the same time, the mass mobilizations and protest movements that came to denote a deep crisis of representation acquired different interpretations by recent scholarship, broadly focusing on their organizational characteristics and novelties, their common repertoires or continuities with past forms of collective action and new elements introduced (e.g. Sitrin and Azzellini, 2014; Castells, 2015; della Porta and Mattoni, 2015; Flesher Fominaya, 2015; Gerbaudo, 2016; Pettas and Daskalaki, 2021). Out of this scholarship, we may draw out two key analytical pathways into the workings of the recent protest movements, which either place the emphasis on their autonomous, horizontal, and rhizomatic forms of organization, or on a state-centered understanding of citizenship, institutional demands, and political representation. Without disregarding the analytical validity of these accounts, it is suggested that the key issue of political subjectification that these mobilizations underscored has been to an extent unattended to or treated under already established analytical categories or political identities, which fall short in accounting for the diversity, plurality, and heterogeneity of the emergent popular agency of protest movements. In this vein, this contribution[1] expands these debates, by developing a complementary reading of the protest movements in Athens, Madrid, and Istanbul through the lens of populism. In so doing, it calls attention to a plural reading of "a politics of different spaces" (Beveridge and Featherstone, 2021: 4), namely the conjunctural spaces from which particular ways of constructing "the people" and forms of left/progressive grassroots populism emerged in the three contexts; the institutional or non-state politics these pursued, impacting on the formal spaces of politics; and their diverse modal and temporal logics, and spatialities. Eventually, by adopting a geographical view of "the populist moment", the aim is to evoke a critical take on how left or progressive forms of democratic politics are articulated within *and* beyond the premise of national-state politics.

The chapter is structured in four sections. The first section outlines the political-economic context of neoliberal governance in Greece, Spain, and Turkey, by highlighting the particularities of each context and the ways neoliberal austerity and authoritarian rule instigated a crisis of political representation that gave rise to contestation and mass mobilizations. The second section synthesizes views and accounts of the mass mobilizations and protest movements in Athens, Madrid, and Istanbul and offers a re-reading of these through the lens of grassroots populism. Its three subsections pay attention to the respective specificities of the squares' movement in Athens, the 15M movement in Madrid and the Gezi Park uprising in Istanbul, as well as successive struggles that followed these in each city, by offering a view of articulations of new vocabularies of collective action under the common denominator of "the people". The third section locates the cross-articulations and synergies developed between the respective movements and the political actors of Syriza in Greece, Podemos in Spain, and the People's Democratic Party (HDP) in Turkey, by looking into the common elements of the discourses and left populist strategies adopted, as well as the discontinuities and ruptures induced in each case due to diverse structural, contextual or political representation factors. Finally,

---

1 Research in Spain and Greece has received funding from the European Union's Horizon 2020 research and innovation programme under the Marie Skłodowska-Curie grant agreement No 747313.

the concluding section critically engages with the possibilities and limitations identified through this comparative exercise regarding grassroots populist movements and left/progressive agendas, which still resonate in contemporary attempts to redraw the spaces of politics and challenge post-democratizing or authoritative political contexts.

1   Contextualizing Neoliberal Governance and Contestation in Greece, Spain and Turkey

The past decade has been crucial in re-defining analyses on economic crisis, neoliberal governance and contentious politics, drawing on contexts such as Greece, Spain, and Turkey, which experienced profound economic and socio-political re-articulations. Following the 2008 global economic crisis, critical scholars have drawn attention to the structural underpinnings and institutional reverberations, informed by analyses of neoliberal austerity governance as the primary crisis management mechanism. At the same time, an emphasis on the potential of radical ruptures to the neoliberal hegemony, through processes of politicization of societies and the generation of new political subjectivities against de-politicizing tendencies of neoliberal globalization, largely inspired scholarship to explore articulations of contentious politics, as expressed in instances of mass social mobilizations and urban uprisings occurring in cities such as Athens, Madrid, and Istanbul. Drawing on these debates, a contextualization of neoliberal governance and contentious politics follows, setting out the debate on the emergence of grassroots populisms in the three cities and an analysis of their distinct yet complementary geographies.

In Greece and Spain, the wide and deep repercussions of the economic crisis served as a catalyst for profound reconfigurations through the implementation of strict austerity governance (Karyotis and Gerodimos, 2015; Pavolini et al., 2015). Different from Spain, Greece had experienced a systemic disequilibrium, originating in unsustainable deficits of public budgets, mainly allocated to the international banking sector (Zettelmayer et al., 2013). In Spain, the economic shocks since 2008 primarily originated in an implosive real estate market, having a severe impact on the domestic banking sector which became overexposed to non-performing mortgage loans (di Feliciantonio and Aalbers, 2018). Further to the contextual particularities of the two Southern European countries regarding the origins of the economic recession, the mechanisms employed to manage the crisis by national governments and EU officials had common logic. Looking over the edge of bankruptcy, Greece was forced into negotiations to restructure its national debt, conditioned upon radical cuts in public expenditure. While initially presented as a prime solution, austerity governance not only failed to balance recession but rather aggravated economic conditions for large parts of the population, resulting in an unprecedented loss of welfare and living standards for post-war Europe. Concurrently, Spain witnessed a restructuring process that involved successive "rescue packages" directed to the banking sector serving publicly owned debt (Beswick et al., 2016). Along with the mass evictions and foreclosures, and the despair of hundreds of families bearing witness to the loss of their homes, this restructuring led to an overall steep devaluation of housing and land values. Therefore, different trajectories of economic crisis coincided under austerity rule in the two countries, having a significant impact on social welfare and urban governance.

The case of Turkey tells a different story as to the trajectories of neoliberal governance. Following a period of recovery after the 2001 economic crisis that seriously affected the country, fiscal austerity and strict structural reforms were adopted to manage the crisis and promote economic growth. While the seismic effects of the 2008 global crisis also had an impact on the Turkish economy, growth rates based on accelerated competitiveness in global markets witnessed rapid increases, without these being translated into well-paid employment and job opportunities for large parts of the population (Civelekoğlu, 2015). Within the particular sphere of Turkish neoliberal governance, scholars pointed out the prevalence of urbanization and the ideological connotation attributed to how space is envisioned in development projects (e.g., Gürcan and Peker, 2014; Özen, 2015; Rivas Alonso, 2015; Walton, 2015). In this regard, targeted land and infrastructure redevelopment, through mass privatization projects and foreign investments on previously publicly owned land, significantly boosted the construction sector in Istanbul among other places, as part of an ongoing governmental effort to create new investment opportunities through a series of urban regeneration and renovation schemes, including housing, airport, highway and power plant infrastructure (Özen, 2015). As Rivas Alonso (2015) argued, the Justice and Development (AKP) Turkish ruling party constituted its hegemony through the use of space, and policies actively promoting the commodification of urban spaces and the rebranding of entire neighbourhoods to accommodate affluent groups at the expense of previous low-income residents. This hegemonic form of neoliberal governance in Turkey was further fostered through a conservative religion-oriented dominant discourse and ideology, the complete absence of citizen deliberation around urban redevelopment projects and the silencing of dissenting voices under the guise of an economic success story (Civelekoğlu, 2015; Özen, 2015).

Critical scholarship interpreted the above developments at the global scale regarding the neoliberalization of governance by exemplifying what was arguably a deliberative redistribution of wealth, achieved through the creation, management, and manipulation of crises (Harvey, 2006). Bringing forward the structural origins of economic crises and the mechanisms operating to secure capital accumulation through capital devaluation, the crisis was interpreted in this view through the contradiction of creative destruction (see Holgersen, 2015). Specifically, regarding urban space, scholars pointed out how the fast-accelerating power of global financial capital and newly devised speculative mechanisms managed to transform immobile real estate property into highly mobile assets; thus, transforming urban space into an arena where crisis played out at the service of financialized capitalism (Fields, 2018; Marazzi, 2011).

Accordingly, at its ideological/ political premise, governance and institutions were confined in a depoliticizing discourse of austerity, which became the normalized narrative – and the "only alternative"-of restructuring policies and crisis management means (Peck et al., 2013; Tonkiss, 2013). Although austerity has already been part of previous neoliberalising mechanisms to roll back state expenditure, the economic crisis of 2008 and increasing speculative financialization since, prompted a crisis of local states across Europe, with far-reaching social and political implications (Davies and Blanco, 2017). By redefining the previously established relations between national states and sub-national entities, a new regulatory order was established over the past decade marked by a top-down, hierarchical exercise of governance through austerity and authoritative financial restrictions (Bayırbağ et al., 2017; Lippi and Tsekos, 2018; Peck, 2017). In this context, neoliberalising governance further encompassed a "post-democratic" (Crouch, 2004) dimension, meaning that political and managerial elites employed normalizing mechanisms for enforcing an increasingly depoliticized consensus, while citizen participation in decision-making processes became more and more diminished (Swyngedouw, 2007; 2009). As citizens were denied a voice over what was at stake and, simultaneously, gradually dispossessed of their homes, jobs, living standards, and reproductive means, these developments encountered strong critique and confrontation from social actors, expressed in mass social mobilizations in cities such as Athens, Madrid, and Istanbul.

2   Geographies of Grassroots Populism: Social Movements in Athens, Madrid and Istanbul

The past decade signified a multiplicity of novel meanings and renewed mechanisms of protest and collective action developing *in* and *out of* urban spaces. The vibrant crowds of the "Arab Spring", the "15M" movement in Spain, the

"Squares'" movement in Greece, the Occupy Wall Street movement in the USA, the Gezi Park and Taksim Square movement in Turkey flooded the streets, squares and public spaces of major cities around the world and challenged political representation and systemic injustices, while at the same time, articulating novel vocabularies of collective action, new ways of being and acting in common, and practices of democratic politics (Gerbaudo, 2014; Arampatzi, 2017b; García-Lamarca, 2017; Karaliotas, 2017; Purcell, 2021). Focusing on the common repertoires of these protests developing in cities such as Athens, Madrid, and Istanbul, we can identify continuities with past forms of mobilizations, such as the alter-globalization movement, as well as novel elements within repertoires of collective action. These included horizontal, leaderless, and networked organization within the encampments and occupations of *Syntagma* Square in Athens, *Puerta del Sol* in Madrid, and Gezi Park and Taksim Square in Istanbul; the vast use of digital media that managed to diffuse the protests' voice across the respective cities and connect with several other protest sites on a national and global scale; and new deliberative conceptions of democratic participation and inclusiveness, vis-à-vis established channels of political representation through formal political actors (della Porta and Mattoni 2015; Sitrin and Azzellini 2014).

The vibrant communication and exchanges established between the occupied public spaces and the common framings of the adversary, i.e. "political elites", "austerity", "repressive state" versus a framing of protestors as "we", "the people", "the 99%" etc. can be understood, as an emergent democratic agency opposing political elites and, at the same time, foregrounding a type of democratic pluralism (Kioupkiolis, 2016), through the fostering of translocal solidarities among occupied spaces and between protestors. The key common framing of "real" and "direct" democracy also involved a subsequent practice of inclusive pluralism in the assemblies and occupations, which eventually contested the function of political representation itself, rendering the crowds of the squares as active agents of a renewed political subjectification process (Prentoulis and Thomassen 2013). The resulting political subjectivities, in conceptual terms, departed from a normative perception of "true" or "right" democracy (Lorey, 2014). Rather they turned to the actually present and practiced participation through assembling in the squares. Hence, they created powerful ruptures, by opening up the possibility for new political subjects to emerge and assert a new understanding of a "presentist" democratic practice, which persisted in their aftermath (Lorey, 2014).

Re-visiting these mass social mobilizations, which occurred across different contexts and adopted pluralist repertoires to accommodate divergent political and cultural identities, ideological standpoints, and social backgrounds, we are presented with a process of political subjectification that involved a plural and hybrid popular agency that attempted to re-claim the political space of "the people" vis-à-vis the neoliberal hegemonic rule. This agency arguably re-politicized the failure of political representation in safeguarding equality, by challenging dominant perceptions of what "is" or "counts as" political (Prentoulis and Thomassen, 2013; Karaliotas, 2017). Thus, we may think of these movements as a popular agency that attempted to redefine politics and the ways it is being enacted in hegemonic discourse, by acting at a distance from the state and beyond rational interest-based collective action; nevertheless, articulating a critique that aimed to challenge and transform existing institutions (see Mouffe, 2018). As Castells (2015: 263) noted, "movements do not object to the principle of representative democracy, but denounce the practice of such democracy as it is today and do not recognize its legitimacy". In this sense, we can nuance a rather homogenizing view of "the 99%" or "the multitude" (Hardt and Negri, 2004) that is often ascribed to these movements and move beyond an understanding that pertains to a singular social subject and obstructs the negotiation of internal differences of protest movements.

Rather, opting for a reading of these movements through a plural agency that may act as a driver of radical democratic projects (Mouffe, 2005, 2013), we are then to reconsider political subjectification not based on pre-given singular identities, but as a processual construction of internally plural and, often, contradictive, political agency. Focusing, thus, on "doings, rather than beings" (Dikeç, 2013), as well as on their discursive logics, allows us to unearth the novel political subjects by looking into the very acts of protesting and the voicing of critique to existing forms of representative politics, which are necessarily defined through messiness and incompleteness in their becoming (Prentoulis and Thomassen, 2013). Therefore, we are not faced with the question of either opting for autonomy or hegemony, as a better-suited analytical lens into accounts of these movements or collective action in general. Rather than focusing on the mutual contaminations or crossovers between seemingly dichotomous or conflictual political identities (see Prentoulis and Thomassen, 2013; Eklundh, 2018), we may be better placed to understand the workings of recent mobilizations and grasp the possibility of radical emancipatory projects. Moreover, thinking of the constitutive elements of this plural agency and popular movements that emerged over the past decade, we are presented with a diversity of disparate social claims, demands or forms of political identities articulated in a "relation of equivalence" (see Laclau and Mouffe, 1985) and around a common denominator and adversary, namely "the people" versus "the elites" (see Mouffe, 2018). This relation is not based on an established shared identity, but rather on the commonly felt negation and repression of such demands by the existing political system. Here the notion of "populism" (see Laclau, 2005) helps us unpack this internally diverse and plural agency, as it does not necessarily refer to the actual content, particular interests, or ideological positions of movements; but rather to a "mode of articulation of whatever social, political or ideological contents" (Laclau, 2005: 34) or one of the logics, or one "way of doing politics" (Prentoulis, 2021:23). By employing the "grassroots populism" lens, the following discussion draws attention to the diverse geographies of social mobilizations and forms of popular agency that unsettled the hegemonic neoliberal configurations in Athens, Madrid and Istanbul.

2.1 Athens: "We Are Syntagma and We Are Everywhere! Direct Democracy Now!"[2]

On May 25 2011, thousands of people gathered in the central *Syntagma* Square of Athens, following a Facebook event organized by three citizens, with no affiliations to any political or activist organization. In response to what was already taking place in *Puerta del Sol* central square in Madrid, the goal of this gathering was to express the people's indignation against austerity measures voted by the government, as conditional of the country's "bailout" by the European Commission (EC), the European Central Bank (ECB) and the International Monetary Fund (IMF). This spontaneous act of indignation and call for collective action managed to bring in a large and diverse crowd that cut across ideological and social backgrounds, as well as political parties and previous social movement identities (Karaliotas, 2017; Arampatzi, 2017c). While initially, protestors self-identified with their Indignant Spanish counterparts, the occupation of *Syntagma* Square soon spread across the country, whereby similar events, protests, talks, and popular assemblies were organized in major cities, being transformed into what was coined as the "squares movement". Daily presence in *Syntagma* and slogans addressed at the adjacent Parliament building, the spatial organization of encampments and thematic work groups, cultural events, and open discussions, culminating in the formation of an open "popular assembly" at the lower part of *Syntagma*, lasted for more than two months and were occasionally faced with brutal police intervention aiming to disperse protestors.

Interestingly, the vocabulary of the square was indicative of the diversity and the heterogeneity of protestors, ranging from slogans against "corrupt, traitor politicians", demanding "popular sovereignty" and calling for "direct

---

2 Mottos from the *Syntagma* square protests in 2011, Athens Greece.

democracy" to address a malfunctioning political system that did not serve the people's demands. Political subjectification was thus taking place through these articulations of collective imaginaries that borrowed meaning from collective passions of anger, frustration, hope, solidarity, and interdependence. The square itself became in this way a staging ground of a collective will, a new kind of "radical we" that linked with prior movements, such as the alter-globalisation and the students' movements of the mid-2000s (Hadjimichalis, 2013; Pettas and Daskalaki, 2021). Contrary to a view of these protests as a unified whole, this identification with a "we" further portrayed internal divisions, which were spatially transposed between the popular assembly set up at the lower part of the square and the crowds gathering at the upper part (Arampatzi, 2017c). Karaliotas (2017) made an interesting conceptual distinction between "demos" and "ethnos" to demarcate such an internal differentiation, both signifying names for the "people", yet with different ideological connotations, namely the people as the foundation of democracy and the people as the cornerstone of the national state. It is through this view that we may grasp the hybridity of the *Syntagma* square protests through a plural populist ideal, which encompassed several understandings of a heterogeneous, hybrid "we" that did not abide by any prior subjectification to political representation, parties, or social movements.

Expanding a view of the squares' movement as a "populist moment" that re-defined the course of political developments in the context of the economic crisis in Greece, we may further identify the organic links it developed with other movements that started to emerge during and after the evacuation of the *Syntagma* square occupation in July 2011. Emblematic of these were the solidarity initiatives and networks that developed as a response to immediate necessity arising from the acute outcomes of austerity policies, i.e., radical cutbacks in welfare, public services, wages and pensions, and rising poverty and unemployment. The solidarity movement organised health provision, through social clinics and pharmacies, responding to a gasping health system; free education run by volunteers; community kitchens and food markets bypassing market intermediaries; time banks and alternative currencies. Through these initiatives, networks, and locally based groups, it managed to open up the political space for resisting austerity across neighbourhoods and foster new types of socio-economic conduct. By politicising the social reproduction crisis aggravated by the economic crisis (Pettas and Daskalaki, 2021), it also managed to foreground a socially transformative project, producing an empowering discourse on solidarity that took forward the popular political agency of the squares, vis-à-vis depoliticised discourses of charity, 'philanthrocapitalism' and the normalisation of the socio-political reality of austerity (Arampatzi, 2017a;

Edwards, 2008). Therefore, far from seeing the squares' movement as a mere "moment" in the political trajectory of the country, the spirit of *Syntagma*, its collective imaginaries and practices of organization were interweaved in the following period into novel social mobilizations, across Athens and Greece.

2.2 Madrid: "We Are Not Products in the Hands of Politicians and Bankers! Real Democracy Now!"[3]

Only ten days earlier than its *Syntagma* counterpart, on May 15th, 2011, the central Madrid square of *Puerta del Sol* was being occupied by protestors, following a nationwide demonstration called by the "Real Democracy Now" digital platform. While the demonstration across Spain instigated confrontations with police forces, protestors in Madrid remained in the square to articulate a critique against austerity measures and bank bailouts employed by national authorities to deal with the impact of the global financial crisis (Flesher Fominaya, 2015). Subsequently, an assembly was formed, organized around an encampment, which in the following days attracted thousands of people joining in support of the protestors' demands. Similar to Athens, the square occupation and encampment soon developed its own organization, with specific groups responsible for different tasks and logistics, while communication was established with other occupied squares across Spanish cities and beyond, Athens included. Although often faced with police crackdowns, the Sol occupation received vast social media attention, which soon worked to the advantage of voicing and diffusing its claims and discourse (Romanos, 2013). As social discontent grew over the stark apathy of political parties to tackle the impact of austerity, the Spanish "15M" movement straightforwardly targeted their critique at the political and financial elites who were rendered responsible for failing political representation and growing inequalities, as explicitly stated in their key motto that read: "we are not merchandise in the hands of bankers and politicians" (Gerbaudo, 2016; García Lamarca, 2017).

At the same time, and as protests and occupations of squares and public spaces spread across Spanish cities, the movement achieved to bring together a broad array of socio-demographics and backgrounds, overriding established ideological divisions through individual, leaderless deliberation and the side-lining of political parties, organizations and unions (Flesher Fominaya, 2015). The inclusive, open and process-based character of the 15M movement have arguably contributed to its success, managing to engage wide and large

---

3 Mottos from the *Puerta del Sol* square protests in 2011, Madrid Spain.

crowds. Another key achievement of this movement, according to García Lamarca (2017), was the challenging of hegemonic discourses and practices-dominant to the legitimation of the economic crisis—and the creation of alternative ones. These achievements were made possible due to the framing adopted by the 15M as a movement of "ordinary citizens" (Flesher Fominaya, 2015), a discourse employed to construct a vastly appealing common ground, a "popular identity" (Laclau, 2005) that, according to Gerbaudo (2016), cut across the divergent social demographics directly affected by neoliberal austerity. This popular identity, however, cannot be understood as a unified entity, rather, as Taibo (2013) showed, as a heterogeneous agency with "two souls" (and probably more), revealing tensions between demands around "real" or better democratic representation and autonomous politics that sought to disrupt the hegemonic order by acting outside state institutions (also see García Lamarca, 2017).

During and in the aftermath of the Sol occupation horizontal networked organization spread across Madrid. This de-centralization of the 15M movement further contributed to the formation of neighbourhood assemblies and local initiatives that resisted austerity and introduced the "insurgent practices" of the occupied square into concrete spaces and projects across the city (García Lamarca, 2017). Notably, the 15M movement developed support and close collaboration with the Platform for Mortgage-affected People (PAH), a key actor of the housing movement acting against evictions and foreclosures of mortgaged homes since 2009 (see Colau and Alemany, 2014). This support not only provided the housing movement with new impetus but further grounded the 15M movement in local contexts and popular projects to support those affected by the housing crisis and expand on the politicization of urban populations (di Feliciantonio 2017). The resulting dense networks across the city of Madrid permitted the expansion of collective action repertoires to meet the housing struggle demands, including legislative and direct actions to block evictions, and occupations of empty buildings to host people who had lost their homes (Romanos, 2014). In this sense, these alliances and convergences developed into further collective action, which diffused the popular agency of the occupied square across local contexts and disrupted the state of things of austerity politics (Blanco and Leon 2017). Subsequently, in the case of Madrid, political subjectification did not only occur on the basis of a popular identity and demands targeting political representation at the national scale alone. Rather the local scale of grassroots politics became prominent in struggles over other critical issues at the time, relating to the social reproduction of urban populations through housing.

2.3 *Istanbul: "The First Day, We Were [Labelled as] Terrorists; the Second Day, We Were Provocateurs; the Third Day, We Were Demonstrators; but on the Fourth Day We Have Become the People. Everywhere Is Taksim, Resistance Everywhere!"*[4]

In response to a municipal plan to redevelop the central Gezi Park of Istanbul, May 27 2013 marked the initiation of what would be an escalation of protests and mass social mobilizations of unprecedented intensity in Turkey's history (Gürcan and Peker, 2014). Faced with the demolition of a vital green space serving a densely inhabited urban area, a small group of environmental activists confronted developers and set up an encampment to prevent further work in the area (Gül et al., 2014). The encampment was soon to be anticipated by a forced eviction by the police, which instigated an approximately two-month protest cycle involving hundreds of thousands of people in Istanbul and other major cities throughout the country. Within these, Gezi Park and Taksim Square became the epicenter of this massive wave of mobilizations against the municipal and governmental urban renewal plan and what was perceived as a rising authoritarianism of the ruling AKP (Gürcan and Peker, 2014; Özen, 2015).

The redevelopment itself, including, among other projects, the reconstruction of an Ottoman-era monument, a shopping mall, and an opera house, was representative of a long period of governmental interventions to promote neoliberal marketization of urban space and policies that had targeted the cultural heritage of Istanbul and destabilized its social and environmental fabric (Gül et al., 2014; Civelekoğlu, 2015; Rivas Alonso, 2015). Further to foreclosing the possibility for egalitarian and heterogeneous urban spaces to exist in a neoliberalising city, as Gül et al. (2014) pointed out, the Turkish government had previously-and in this case-employed urban development as a means to promote an ideological and cultural agenda that would override the previous Kemalist heritage and establish its own hegemony. In this sense, for most protestors, according to Walton (2015), Gezi marked the unleashing of public dissent against an ongoing Turkish political culture of interventionism and pervasive illiberality, sealed by President Erdoğan's politics. Thus, what started out as a modest protest to protect a green space, swiftly turned into an outright popular uprising opposing the government, which managed to gather diverse political interest groups and individuals and became a symbol of resistance that shook the established dynamics of politics in Turkey (Gül et al., 2014; Gürcan and Peker, 2014; Yorük, 2014).

---

4   Mottos from the Gezi Park and Taksim square protests in 2013, Istanbul Turkey.

Following previous years' protest waves-such as the 15M in Spain, the squares' movement in Greece, and the Occupy in the USA and Europe—the Gezi uprising portrays common features with its predecessors. These include the occupation and symbolic use of public urban spaces, the vast use of digital media to diffuse communication and discourses, the open and heterogeneous participation of people with diverse backgrounds and the generalized expression of discontent against political and economic elites that sustained disparate groups and social demands (Özen, 2015; Walton, 2015). These social mobilizations revealed the importance of urban space in representing various and diverse values, symbols, ideologies, and meanings, and the passions symbolic places ignite among people (Gül et al., 2014). As Rivas Alonso (2015) pointed out, the Gezi protests in particular may be perceived as an agent of a new political culture that managed to challenge and subvert the rules of engagement in politics, while opening up space for new positions to re-negotiate citizenship and power. In this regard, we may think of the Gezi Park popular uprising as evocative of a novel meaning of collectivity and community that proclaimed heterogeneity and democratic participation over an established nationhood of retrospective homogeneity (Toktamış, 2015).

Therefore, the novel political subjectivities and practices that Gezi fostered around discourses of "justice versus injustice" did not crystallize around a specific identity, but rather on a plural multiplicity that brought together people of all ages and ideas or lifestyles, often contradicting and historically constructed in tension with each other (Walton, 2015). As a result, difference, as opposed to commonality, became the unifying glue of political engagement, overriding often opposing sides on the basis of a contiguous plurality (Rivas Alonso, 2015). This plurality was fostered through the struggle over the park that provided a platform to express a series of grievances, frustrations, and demands, which were ignored, repressed or could not be accommodated within the existing hegemony; thus, turning a particular struggle into a broader one (Özen, 2015). In the aftermath of the evacuation of Gezi Park and Taksim Square, and similarly to the Greek and Spanish cases, the new forms of popular agency of this movement were diffused across the city into public assemblies and local collective organizing, while protests were re-ignited a few months later, only to be met with enhanced police repression.

Based on the above, we are presented with a different reading of urban protests in Athens, Madrid, and Istanbul that evolved into multifaceted nationwide and locally based, networked movements. While borrowing elements from past waves of protests and collective organizing, originating in the political traditions of autonomous and Left politics, the protest movements in Greece, Spain, and Turkey weaved together such continuities into novel collective political imaginaries and identities, around democracy, participation, self-organization and self-management of spaces. As Prentoulis and Thomassen (2013) stressed, these elements suggest a particular articulation of autonomy and hegemony, articulated into a contiguous plurality and multiplicity through creative tensions encountered in non-institutional forms of organization, as well as state politics pursued. As shown through the three cases, such articulations of grassroots populism managed to overcome the confines of the "event", and the "moment" of eruptive protests and entered the temporal realm of locally grounded struggles in urban contexts. In this sense, and as rightly noted by Pettas and Daskalaki (2021), they overcame the often-short-lived character of protests and were able to build on resistance practices and community over time, methods that still resonate in more recent mobilizations.

Moreover, the articulations of grassroots populism encountered in these movements succeeded in fostering forms of political agency and community beyond the spatial imaginary of the nation-state, a sense of belonging that overrode nationhood established upon commonality, but rather on difference. The communication, action repertoires, exchanges, and diffusion of discourses and practices, translocally and across borders, thus, rendered these movements agents of a new plural understanding of how space may be negotiated in political activity. Finally, as Özen (2015) highlighted, by providing a voice to those not represented by the existing neoliberal hegemonic rule, these movements made visible and brought together a series of disparate social demands otherwise excluded, silenced, or ignored. This modality of grassroots populism of equivalential demands and social groups was crucial in foregrounding popular counter-hegemonic confrontation, also by developing synergies with existing and novel political actors that emerged in the three contexts. The next section discusses key insights into how these synergies were articulated, the possibilities opened up for democratic politics, and the discontinuities and ruptures of radical democratic projects.

3   Cross-Articulations and Disarticulations of Left Populist Politics: Grassroots Movements and Left-Wing Political Actors

Over the course of the protest movements in the three cities and in their aftermath, grassroots populism developed cross-articulations with established and novel left-wing political actors.[5] The electoral successes and rise of Syriza in

---

5   While a detailed discussion of the emergence of right-wing populism in the three countries falls outside the scope of this contribution, it may be noted that, regarding Greece, right-wing

Greece, the newly formed Podemos in Spain, and the People's Democratic Party (HDP) in Turkey, are representative in this regard of Left-wing populist actors that attempted to vindicate the negated and repressed demands of the popular agency of the protest movements, and articulate forms of pluralist democratic politics vis-à-vis the enclosed formal institutional spaces of politics. These political actors assumed a key role in materializing a hybrid mix of radical pluralism, by cross-articulating grassroots demands and horizontal networked mobilizations with vertical structures of party formations (Kioupkiolis, 2016). In their electoral agendas, common discourses and framings of "the people" and a fierce critique of institutions resonated with the protest movements and squares' occupations, focusing on reclaiming political representation and social rights for the common good (see Rubio-Pueyo, 2017; Ordoñez et al., 2018). What follows focuses first, on cross-examination of the discursive logics and strategies of left-populist agendas, and the ways they managed to establish antagonistic frontiers and relations of equivalence in the three different contexts; and second, on points of disarticulation, discontinuities, and ruptures in the synergies developed between the movements and political actors.

In Greece, against the backdrop of intensifying austerity and amidst growing discontent over the bailout agreements, the radical Left coalition party of Syriza saw its previous electoral rates rise fast. The active participation of party members in the occupied *Syntagma* Square in Athens and the weaving of links with the popular assembly, as well as the solidarity movement that developed in the aftermath of the protests, suggested a strategy on behalf of the party that sought to adopt the repertoires and claims of the movements (Karaliotas, 2021). In their discourse leading up to the 2012 national election, Syriza further developed a left-populist project that directly engaged the demands of the protestors (Katsambekis, 2015, 2016). For instance, raising issues of dignity, sovereignty, and social justice, while at the same time employing a discourse that drew a clear division between "us" versus "them", i.e., the people versus the political and economic elites. This was decisive in successfully developing a common language that would bring together disparate social demands, actors, and initiatives into a constellation able to challenge the hegemony of the ruling pro-austerity political parties.

As Kioupkiolis and Katsambekis (2018) showed, Syriza strategically chose to interact with the square's protestors horizontally, forging identification ties

---

nationalist populist discourses were represented in the agenda of the Independent Greeks party, which joined the coalition government of Syriza formed in 2015. In Spain, it was years later that the far-right VOX reflected such a tendency within the political spectrum, while in Turkey nationalist populist discourses were already part of the ruling AKP agenda.

through participation and aiming for popular unity, a social front that the party would effectively represent in the parliament. By transposing the grievances and discontent of the popular agency of the squares into the sphere of political representation, it managed to create a political space for relations of equivalence, or "chains of equivalence", to develop between diverse subjects, demands, identities, and actors (Stavrakakis and Katsambekis, 2014). As evident in the party's discourse, these equivalential actors and demands were pitted against the "establishment", namely the pro-austerity actors represented by the two larger parties of New Democracy and PASOK. The formation, thus, of a popular front was achieved through discursive means as well as active participation in the movements, resulting in the electoral rise of a previously minoritarian party. "They decided without us, we're moving without them" and "it is either us or them" were two key slogans employed by Syriza in their electoral campaign, which are indicative of the antagonistic frontier drawn between the majority of the people enduring the impact of austerity and a privileged minority enforcing it (Kioupkiolis and Katsambekis, 2018: 208).

In contrast to the pre-existing party of Syriza, which adapted its strategy to a left-populist agenda, Podemos in Spain were formed in 2014 and straight out of a turbulent period that placed political representation at the epicenter of contestation. Similar to Syriza, and even more so directly engaging with Laclau's (2005) theoretical premise (see Errejón and Mouffe, 2015), Podemos' formation came as a response to a crisis of representation of a political system that became more and more enclosed and dismissive of popular grievances. By adopting an agenda of social justice against the corrupt political elites, Podemos' discourse represented the anti-establishment sentiment of the social majority, as expressed in the occupied squares and protests across Spanish cities. Their electoral rise since the 2014 European parliamentary elections was indicative of a large base of voters that did not identify with the privileged minority of the political and economic elites but resonated with the increasingly precarious youth, often unemployed, educated urban citizens and students (Kioupkiolis and Katsambekis, 2018). Moreover, the party of Podemos, including its prominent academic and activist figures, sought to directly link with common sense, by presenting themselves as "decent ordinary people" who would connect with the disenfranchised majority, not from a vanguardist standpoint, but through employing participatory means (Flesher Fominaya, 2014).

As this was also the case for their discursive means, the party employed a communication strategy of direct and simple speech, clothes, and style, re-signifying and constructing new meaning for political representation in popular media outlets and digital social media (Briziarelli, 2018). This construction was based on a shared identification of "the people" against the "elites", i.e., "el pueblo versus la casta", represented by the two dominating parties of Partido Popular and PSOE, and became articulated by a common antagonism that divided the socio-political space (Kioupkiolis and Katsambekis, 2018). As Briziarelli (2018) highlighted, Podemos' alternative hegemony was based on a combination of elements and meanings, brought together in novel ways into a political construction that was externally articulated by an "us"-"them" antagonism, rather by an underlying common essence or political identity. Thus, their particular take on populism represented a modality of overcoming the diversity and heterogeneity of the plural popular agency of the 15M movement, by constructing a transversal chain of equivalence articulated into a popular unified front.

The People's Democratic Party (HDP) in Turkey is another case of a left-populist political actor that responded to a deepening crisis of representation. Formed in 2012 out of the broad participatory political platform of the People's Democratic Congress (HDK), HDP was inaugurated only a few months after the Gezi protests took place, in November 2013. At its inception, it adopted a straightforward left-leaning populist strategy to unify diverse and disparate struggles of the Kurdish movement, left-wing parties, NGOs, women's and LGBTQ+ rights organizations, environmental activists, trade unions, and ethnic groups' associations (Özen, 2015; Kaya, 2019). This strategy was constructed as antagonistic to the hegemonic Turkish nationalism embraced by the ruling AKP, which was based on the logic of one nation, one language unity and citizenship (Tekdemir, 2018). By bringing together unattended and excluded social demands, identities, interests, and groups that fell outside this top-down hegemonic consensus and representative channels, the party's strategy advocated an inclusive democratic left-wing populism that directly engaged the horizontal base of a diversity of social movements-including those individuals and groups that participated in the Gezi protests. Reflected in the party's agenda, this strategy weaved together a plurality of popular demands by placing emphasis on equal rights, social security, welfare, and solidarity (Tekdemir, 2018).

Its electoral rise in the 2015 national elections allowed HDP to enter the parliament, while in the previous year, the party had witnessed gains in the local and presidential elections. Leading up to the elections, HDP's discursive grammar assumed a role in the construction of an internally plural popular identity, which came as a response to the exclusionary politics imposed by the AKP's dominant discourse of Turkish nationhood (Tekdemir, 2018). For instance, as (Kaya, 2019: 12) noted, the "Call for a new life" by the party's leadership explicitly addressed those excluded and silenced to join up and participate against ethnic, religious, sexual, and class discrimination, by setting a political frontier against those who enforced such exclusion, i.e., the government. Regarding the identification of the common adversary, the party employed a discourse that explicitly personified the enemy as the political figure of President Erdoğan, representing a crucial symbol of the authoritarian neoliberal state (Kaya, 2019). By employing the slogans of "We into the parliament" and "Great humanity", HDP's discourse eventually aimed to bring together a plural and internally heterogeneous "we", along with the universal ideals of social justice and equality.

Following the electoral rise of these political actors, their discourses, agendas, and strategies, largely addressing "the people's" unmet demands towards social justice, were transformed and the synergies with the social movements of the previous period were redefined, discontinued, or ruptured. In this regard, we may identify two key factors that contributed to such disarticulations, broadly involving both endogenous and exogenous limitations. First, in all three cases the party's discourses and strategies had been identified with their charismatic leadership, key political figures that served as key symbols of reference for the parties and representing them in the public sphere. In the case of Syriza, and towards its rise to power in 2015, this became more evident as the party's campaign concentrated on the leadership role of Tsipras, which contrasted the prior strategy to promote plurality and horizontalism (Kioupkiolis and Katsambekis, 2018). Similarly, for Podemos, Iglesias assumed a key leadership role in the communicative strategy of the party, alongside other charismatic activists and academics that formed the party's core. In the case of the HDP, the run up in the presidential election of co-chair Demirtaş in 2014 was successful in raising the party's vote, while gaining great sympathy and establishing leadership among supporters and social movements (Kaya, 2019). The emergence of charismatic leaders within these political actors and the broad platforms, alliances, and coalitions they had forged with social actors may be further understood as a hybrid mix of verticality and horizontality.

Nevertheless, in the cases of Syriza and Podemos, the centralization of leadership on specific political figures took place alongside a centralization of decision-making, especially considering the transformations that Syriza underwent since forming a national government. In this regard, following its rise to power, Syriza did not actively take up its promise to actively promote civic participation and grassroots forms of democratic decision-making, thus tilting the hybrid mix of party-social movement politics towards a more vertical, statist, top-down representation and leader-led strategy (Karaliotas, 2021). Following the failed negotiations to block the continuation of austerity policies in the summer of 2015, and under the great pressure of a looming "Grexit" from the Eurozone, the voting of a new austerity package by the Syriza-led coalition government triggered internal tensions, leading to the rupture of alliances and synergies with social movements, party members and activists (Kioupkiolis and Katsambekis, 2018).

In the case of Podemos, while the party was witnessing electoral successes in local coalition governments in 2015 (see Janoschka and Mota, 2021), a similar transformation towards verticalism and bureaucratization of the previously formed participatory assemblies and fora led to the demobilization and disaffect of several of its supporters and active participants (Casero-Ripollés et al., 2016). As Kioupkiolis and Katsambekis (2018) pointed out, these discontinuities with prior base participants were also reflected in the 2015 national elections, when Podemos lost around a million of their votes, due to a weakening civic participation strategy and organized base; due to their shift to a more hierarchical and centralized party structure and decision-making; and, also, due to the transformation of its discourse, away from an anti-establishment radical left populism and towards a more moderate, center-left agenda, which was further reflected in the governmental coalition of Unidas Podemos with PSOE, following the 2020 national elections in Spain. In this sense, in their "institutionalized" phase, Podemos and Syriza had shifted their goals towards an opening up of politics in the narrow sense, by focusing mainly on state institutions and abandoning the left-populist project of constructing an alternative hegemony (Franzé, 2018; Karaliotas, 2021).

While in the case of Syriza, its left populist strategy was interrupted due to structural limitations imposed by the EU and the country's creditors as well as endogenous transformations of the party's strategy, in the case of the HDP's the exogenous factors proved crucial in the development of their alternative populist project. As Tekdemir (2018) showed, HDP's political influence was severely ruptured during a turbulent period of escalating violence, leading up to the state of emergency enforced by the Turkish government after the failed coup attempt in 2016. As the AKP government ceased negotiations on the Kurdish front, HDP was targeted by ultra-nationalist forces, due to its close association with the Kurdish movement, resulting in bombings and attacks with hundreds of casualties across Turkey. At the same time, the party was criminalized and stigmatized by the government and several of its members and key figures, including Demirtaş, were arrested and imprisoned (Özen, 2015, 2020). In the following elections of 2015 and 2019, HDP managed to remain in Parliament, but the political context in which it had risen to popularity had already radically changed (Kaya, 2019). The governmental authoritative tactics, thus, placed HDP under an ongoing threat of state repression which created critical limitations and discontinuities to the unfolding of its left-popular project; especially considering the already weak participatory channels within the party and the demobilization of a more radicalized youth associated with the Kurdish movement that blamed HDP for its pacifism and the distance it assumed towards armed conflict (Kaya, 2019).

4 Conclusions

This chapter proposed a view of the mass mobilizations and social movements that developed in Athens, Madrid, and Istanbul since 2011, through the lens of grassroots populism. Contextualizing these forms of contentious politics in their respective geographical and political-economic frameworks showed how different configurations of neoliberal austerity and authoritarian governance brought to the fore a commonly experienced crisis of representation, albeit with divergent socio-political origins and outcomes. Re-thinking these movements through the over-arching frame of populism, however, did not neglect their particularities and contextual trajectories; rather the choice of this conceptual frame was deliberate in order to place the emphasis on difference, diversity, plurality, and heterogeneity, as key traits of the various identities, interests, demands and actors that made part of these movements. The forms of popular agency that emerged out of the protests and occupations of urban spaces in the three cities further attested to a process of political subjectification that did not follow pre-given or established political identities. Rather, it was suggested that dichotomous readings of these movements of either pursuing autonomy or a new hegemony obscured the mutual contaminations and crossovers that actually took place during and in the aftermath of the mass mobilizations. By theoretically and methodologically employing the logic of difference that characterized the protest movements, the present discussion sought to underscore the temporal, modal and spatial logics of the contiguous pluralities forged in occupied squares, street protests, and localized struggles.

Moreover, focusing on the cross-articulations that grassroots populisms developed with left-wing political actors, the discussion placed an emphasis on the discourses and strategies pursued to accommodate the disparate demands, and attempts to transform the logic of difference into a logic of equivalence (see Laclau, 2005), by opening up the formal institutional spaces of politics. The articulations between the movements and left-populist agendas of political actors in each of the three contexts revealed common discourses regarding framing of "the people" versus "the elites" and the respective political systems, and strategies to form popular unity fronts to counter-austerity and authoritarian rule. By articulating hybrid forms of politics, between horizontal movements and vertical party structures, the political parties of Syriza in Greece, Podemos in Spain and the People's Democratic Party (HDP) in Turkey formed left-leaning populist agendas that employed a novel political vocabulary to address ignored, silenced or repressed social demands. Their electoral successes, however, marked a turning point, whereby the institutionalization of left populist agendas created discontinuities and ruptures to the equivalential relations built with and between movement actors. Especially regarding Syriza and Podemos, this turning point was marked by shifts towards more centralized forms of representation within the parties and weakening participatory means, as well as a turn to more moderate programmatic goals. These coupled with the structural limitations and pressures imposed by pro-austerity political forces resulted in the demobilization of parts of the movements. The case of HDP differed as to the defining impediments, considering that ruptures in the party's left-populist agenda occurred as a result of governmental repression and deepening socio-political conflict. Notably, Podemos managed to establish its strategy within local municipal coalitions and later become part of a national coalition government, yet with seemingly irreversible effects as to the party's previous relations with social movements.

Therefore, comparing through difference proved useful in bringing forward the particularities of each of the three cases, as well as broader contextual and structural dimensions that contributed to the socio-political developments under study. By adopting a geographical view into the workings of social movements and political actors, a novel reading of the forms of the popular agency was evoked, which enriches our understanding of left-populist politics more broadly. In this regard, it was suggested that the analysis of social movements that developed since 2011 in Athens, Madrid, and Istanbul evoked key dimensions of populist politics, which provide nuance to existing scholarship. Accordingly, we were presented with articulations of grassroots populism that managed to overcome the temporal limitations of short-lived protest events-or the "populist moment" as often perceived-and become grounded in locally based struggles and movements. This weaving of relations and synergies became further articulated with horizontal connections to political actors, which were nevertheless later foreclosed due to a turn of the latter towards centralized, party politics; thus, diminishing participation to the temporal confines of electoral campaigns and away from the every day, locally grounded workings of social movements.

Moreover, we may highlight the spatialities of grassroots populism, which fostered forms of political agency in and through local contexts, urban spaces, and everyday settings, thus adhering to spatial imaginaries that moved beyond the confines of the national-state spaces of formal politics. Contrarily, the aforementioned left populist actors, especially in their institutionalization phases, failed to overcome the limitations posed in this regard by pre-given state spaces of politics, with notable exceptions that actively engaged in a strategy of forging synergies and coalitions at the local scale of politics. Despite attempts to internationalize their left populist projects, the discourses and strategies adopted by the three political actors suggested a view of the people (or the peoples in the case of Turkey) that was internally plural and diverse; yet, however different to the hegemonic one, adhering to a view of nationhood as an all-encompassing spatial reference of politics. Additionally, regarding the modal logics of social movements, this contribution showed how a logic of equivalence was articulated during and in the aftermath of protests, starting from a particular topic, i.e., critique of failing political representation or an environmental issue as in the Gezi Park case, to articulate wider relations between disparate social demands, identities, actors and broader issues of social justice and equality. While initially adopted in their discourses and strategies, these modalities of equivalential relations constructed under a common denominator were later abandoned by left political actors, as their agendas were transformed and synergies with social movements loosened or ruptured. Indicatively, the radical left coalition of Syriza was later renamed to "Syriza-Progressive Alliance", adapting their name and discourse to address the middle classes, and dropping their previously populist vocabulary.

Subsequently, the forms of grassroots populism articulated through the social movements portrayed a series of possibilities to overcome the above limitations as manifested through formal politics. In an often fragile, experimental, contradictive, and incomplete way, they articulated a different kind of voice that proclaimed unity through difference. Despite severe limitations encountered, they foregrounded the "possibility of creating something beyond the existing political system" (Prentoulis et al., 2022: 126), by interrupting and attempting to transform the existing order (Özen, 2020). This possibility had long-lasting resonance, not necessarily limited to the three contexts under study, but also in subsequent left populist projects undertaken in different contexts and spaces, such as the Corbyn-led "Momentum" campaign in the UK or, more recently, the movement of "La France Insoumise" and the Mélenchon-led "New Ecological and Social People's Union (NUPES)" electoral coalition in France. Therefore, without disregarding the growing influence of exclusionary and right-wing forms of populism over the past period, future research may further develop insights into how left or progressive forms of populist agency take up the task of re-introducing conflict into post-democratizing forms of formal politics and challenging authoritative regimes in divergent contexts.

Bibliography

Arampatzi, A. (2017a) The spatiality of counter-austerity politics in Athens, Greece: emergent urban solidarity spaces. *Urban Studies* 54(9): 2155–2171.

Arampatzi, A. (2017b) Contentious spatialities in an era of austerity: everyday politics and struggle communities in Athens, Greece. *Political Geography* 60: 47–56.

Arampatzi, A. (2017c) Territorializing social movements: centralization and dispersal as spatial practices of counter-austerity struggle in Athens, Greece. *CITY: Analysis of Urban Trends, Culture, Theory, Policy, Action* 21(6): 724–736.

Bayırbağ, M.K., Davies, J. and S. Muench (2017) Interrogating urban crisis: Cities in the governance and contestation of austerity. *Urban Studies* 54(9): 2023–2038.

Beswick, J., Alexandri, G., Byrne, M., Vives-Miró, S., Fields, D., Hodkinson, S. and M. Janoschka (2016) Speculating on London's housing future. *CITY: Analysis of Urban Trends, Culture, Theory, Policy, Action* 20(2): 321–341.

Beveridge, R. and Featherstone, D. (2021) Introduction: Anti-politics, austerity and spaces of politicization. *Environment and Planning C: Politics and Space* 39(3): 437–450.

Blanco, I. and M. Leon (2017) Social innovation, reciprocity and contentious politics: facing the socio-urban crisis in Ciutat Meridiana, Barcelona. *Urban Studies* 54(9): 2172–2188.

Briziarelli, M. (2018) Podemos' Twofold Assault on Hegemony: The Possibilities of the Post-Modern Prince and the Perils of the Passive Revolution. In: Augustín, O.G. and Briziarelli, M. (Eds.) *Podemos and the New Political Cycle: Left-Wing Populism and Anti-Establishment Politics*. Switzerland: Palgrave Macmillan, 97–122.

Casero-Ripollés, A., Feenstra, R. A., and Tormey, S. (2016) Old and new media logics in an electoral campaign: The case of Podemos and the two-way street mediatization of politics. *The International Journal of Press/Politics* 21(3): 378–397.

Castells, M. (2015) *Networks of Outrage and Hope*. Cambridge: Polity Press.

Civelekoğlu, I. (2015) Enough is Enough: What do the Gezi Protesters Want to Tell Us? A Political Economy Perspective. In: David, I. and Toktamış, K.F. (Eds.) *Everywhere Taksim: Sowing the Seeds for a New Turkey at Gezi*. Amsterdam: Amsterdam University Press, 105–120.

Colau, A. and A. Alemany (2014) *Mortgaged Lives: From the Housing Bubble to the Right to Housing*. London: Journal of Aesthetics and Protest.

Crouch, C. (2004) *Post-democracy*. Cambridge: Polity press.

Davies, J. and I. Blanco (2017) Austerity urbanism: Patterns of neo-liberalisation and resistance in six cities of Spain and the UK. *Environment and Planning A* 49(7): 1517–1536.

della Porta, D. and A. Mattoni (eds., 2015) *Spreading Protest: Social Movements in Times of Crisis*. Colchester: ECPR Press.

di Feliciantonio, C. (2017) Social movements and alternative housing models: practicing the 'politics of possibilities' in Spain. *Housing, Theory and Society* 34(1): 38–56.

di Feliciantonio, C. and M. Aalbers (2018) The prehistories of neoliberal housing policies in Italy and Spain and their reification in times of crisis. *Housing Policy Debate* 28(1): 135–151.

Dikeç, M. (2013) Beginners and equals: political subjectivity in Arendt and Rancière. *Transactions of the Institute of British Geographers* 38(1): 78–90.

Edwards, M. (2008) *Just Another Emperor: the Myths and Realities of Philanthrocapitalism*. New York, NY: Demos.

Eklundh, E. (2018) Populism, Hegemony and the Phantasmatic Sovereign: The Ties Between Nationalism and Left-Wing Populism. In: Augustín, O.G. and Briziarelli, M. (Eds.) *Podemos and the New Political Cycle: Left-Wing Populism and Anti-Establishment Politics*. Switzerland: Palgrave Macmillan, 123–146.

Errejón, Í., and Mouffe, C. (2015). *Construir pueblo: Hegemonía y radicalización de la democracia*. Barcelona: Icaria.

Fields, D. (2018) Constructing a new asset class: Property-led financial accumulation after the crisis. *Economic Geography* 94(2): 118–140.

Flesher Fominaya, C. (2014) Spain is different: Podemos and 15 M. *Open Democracy*. Available (consulted 15 July 2022) at: https://www.opendemocracy.net/en/can-europe-make-it/spain-is-different-podemos-and-15m/.

Flesher Fominaya, C. (2015) Debunking spontaneity: Spain's 15-M/Indignados as autonomous movement. *Social Movement Studies* 14: 142–163.

Franzé, J. (2018) The Podemos Discourse: A Journey from Antagonism to Agonism. In: Augustín, O.G. and Briziarelli, M. (Eds.) *Podemos and the New Political Cycle: Left-Wing Populism and Anti-Establishment Politics*. Switzerland: Palgrave Macmillan, 49–74.

García-Lamarca, M. (2017) From occupying plazas to recuperating housing: insurgent practices in Spain. *International Journal of Urban and Regional Research* 41(1): 37–53.

Gerbaudo, P. (2014). The 'Movements of the Squares' and the Contested Resurgence of the 'Sovereign People' in Contemporary Protest Culture. Available (consulted 7 July 2022) at https://papers.ssrn.com/sol3/papers.cfm?abstract_id=2439359.

Gerbaudo, P. (2016) The indignant citizen: anti-austerity movements in southern Europe and the anti-oligarchic reclaiming of citizenship. *Social Movement Studies* 16(1): 36–50.

Gül, M., Dee, J., & Cünük, N. (2014) Istanbul's Taksim Square and Gezi Park: The place of protest and the ideology of place. *Journal of Architecture and Urbanism, 38*(1): 63–72.

Gürcan, E. and Peker, E. (2014) Turkey's Gezi Park Demonstrations of 2013: A Marxian Analysis of the Political Moment. *Socialism and Democracy* 28(1): 70–89.

Hadjimichalis, C. (2013) From streets and squares to radical political emancipation? Resistance lessons from Athens during the crisis. *Human Geography*, 6(2): 116–136.

Hardt, M and Negri, A. (2004) *Multitude: War and Democracy in the Age of Empire.* New York, NY: Penguin Press.

Harvey, D. (2006) Neo-Liberalism as creative destruction. *Geografiska Annaler: Series B, Human Geography* 88(2): 145–158.

Holgersen, S. (2015) Economic crisis, (creative) destruction, and the current urban condition. *Antipode* 47(3): 689–707.

Janoschka, M. and Mota, F. (2021) New municipalism *in action* or urban neoliberalisation *reloaded*? An analysis of governance change, stability and path dependence in Madrid (2015–2019). *Urban Studies* 58(13): 2814–2830.

Karaliotas, L. (2017) Staging equality in Greek squares: hybrid spaces of political subjectification, *International Journal of Urban and Regional Research* 41(1): 54–69.

Karaliotas, L. (2021) Geographies of politics and the police: Post-democratization, SYRIZA, and the politics of the "Greek debt crisis". *Environment and Planning C: Politics and Space* 39(3):491–511.

Karyotis, G. and R. Gerodimos (2015) *The Politics of Extreme Austerity: Greece in the Eurozone Crisis.* London: Palgrave MacMillan.

Katsambekis, G. (2015) The rise of the Greek radical Left to power: notes on SYRIZA's discourse and strategy. *Línea Sur* 9: 152–161.

Katsambekis, G. (2016) Radical left populism in contemporary Greece: Syriza's trajectory from minoritarian opposition to power. *Constellations* 23(3): 391–403.

Kaya, M. (2019) The potentials and challenges of left populism in Turkey: the case of the peoples' Democratic Party (HDP). *British Journal of Middle Eastern Studies* 46(5): 797–812.

Kioupkiolis, A. (2016) Podemos: the ambiguous promises of left-wing populism in contemporary Spain. *Journal of Political Ideologies* 21(2): 99–120.

Kioupkiolis, A. and Katsambekis, G. (2018) Radical left populism from the margins to the mainstream: A comparison of Syriza and Podemos. In: Augustín, O.G. and Briziarelli, M. (Eds.) *Podemos and the New Political Cycle: Left-Wing Populism and Anti-Establishment Politics.* Switzerland: Palgrave Macmillan, 201–226.

Laclau, E. (2005) *On Populist Reason.* London: Verso.

Laclau, E. and Mouffe, C. (1985) *Hegemony and Socialist Strategy.* London: Verso.

Lippi, A. and T. Tsekos (2018) *Local Public Services in Times of Austerity across Mediterranean Europe.* Basel: Springer.

Lorey, I. (2014) The 2011 Occupy movements: Rancière and the crisis of democracy. *Theory, Culture and Society* 31(7/8): 43–65.

Marazzi, C. (2011) *The Violence of Financial Capitalism.* Cambridge: MIT Press.

Massey, D. (2015) Editorial: Exhilarating times. *Soundings* 61: 4–13.

Mouffe, C. (2005) *On the Political.* Oxford: Routledge.

Mouffe, C. (2013) *Agonistics: Thinking the World Politically.* London: Verso.

Mouffe, C. (2018) *For a Left Populism.* London: Verso.

Ordóñez, V., Feenstra, R.A. and B. Franks (2018) Spanish anarchist engagements in electoralism: from street to party politics. *Social Movement Studies* 17(1): 85–98.

Özen, H. (2015) An unfinished grassroots populism: the Gezi Park protests in Turkey and their aftermath. *South European Society and Politics* 20(4): 533–552.

Özen, H. (2020) Reproducing 'hegemony' thereafter? The long-term political effects of the Gezi protests in Turkey. *Southeast European and Black Sea Studies* 20(2): 245–264.

Pavolini, E., León, M., Guillén, A.M. and U. Ascoli (2015) From austerity to permanent strain? The EU and welfare state reform in Italy and Spain. *Comparative European Politics* 13(1): 56–76.

Peck, J. (2017) Transatlantic city, part 1: Conjunctural urbanism. *Urban Studies* 54(1): 4–30.

Peck, J., Theodore, N. and N. Brenner (2013) Neoliberal urbanism redux? *International Journal of Urban and Regional Research* 37(3): 1091–1099.

Pettas, D. and Daskalaki, M. (2021) Solidarity and collective forms of social reproduction: the social and political legacy of Syntagma Square, Athens. *Social and Cultural Geography*. DOI: 10.1080/14649365.2021.1901973.

Prentoulis, M. and Thomassen, L. (2013) Political theory in the square: Protest, representation and subjectification. *Contemporary Political Theory* 12(3): 166–184.

Prentoulis, M. (2021) *Left Populism in Europe: Lessons from Jeremy Corbyn to Podemos*. London: Pluto Press.

Prentoulis, M., Agustín, O.G., Santamarina Guerrero, A., Featherstone, D. and Karaliotas, L. (2022) Reflections on the spaces of populist politics in Europe. *Soundings* 80: 123–151. DOI: 10.3898/SOUN.80.09.2022.

Purcell, M. (2021) Space and the desire for democracy in the 15M. *Transactions of the Institute of British Geographers* 46: 223–235.

Rivas Alonso, C. (2015) Gezi Park: A Revindication of Public Space. In: David, I. and Toktamış, K.F. (Eds.) *Everywhere Taksim: Sowing the Seeds for a New Turkey at Gezi*. Amsterdam: Amsterdam University Press, 231–250.

Romanos, E. (2013) Collective Learning Processes within Social Movements: Some Insights into the Spanish 15M/Indignados Movement. In: Flesher Fominaya, C and Cox, L. (Eds.) *Understanding European Movements: New Social Movements, Global Justice Struggles, Anti-Austerity Protests*. London: Routledge, 203–219.

Romanos, E. (2014) Evictions, petitions and *escraches*: contentious housing in austerity Spain. *Social Movement Studies* 13(2): 296–302.

Rubio-Pueyo, V. (2017) *Municipalism in Spain. From Barcelona to Madrid and Beyond*. New York, NY: Rosa-Luxemburg-Foundation.

Sitrin, M. and D. Azzellini (2014) *They Can't Represent Us*. London: Verso.

Stavrakakis Y and Katsambekis G (2014) Left-wing populism in the European periphery: The case of SYRIZA. *Journal of Political Ideologies* 19(2): 119–142.

Swyngedouw, E. (2007) Impossible/Undesirable Sustainability and the Post-political Condition. In: Krueger, J.R. and Gibbs, D. (Eds.) *The Sustainable Development Paradox*. New York, NY: Guilford Press, 13–40.

Swyngedouw, E. (2009) The antinomies of the post-political city: in search of a democratic politics of environmental production. *International Journal of Urban and Regional Research* 33(3): 601–620.

Taibo, C. (2013) The Spanish indignados: A movement with two souls. *European Urban and Regional Studies* 20(1): 155–158.

Tekdemir, O. (2018) Left-wing populism within horizontal and vertical politics: the case of Kurdish-led radical democracy in agonistic pluralism. *Journal of Balkan and Near Eastern Studies* 21(3): 335–349.

Toktamış K.F. (2015) Evoking and Invoking Nationhood as Contentious Democratization. In: David, I. and Toktamış, K.F. (Eds.) *Everywhere Taksim: Sowing the Seeds for a New Turkey at Gezi*. Amsterdam: Amsterdam University Press, 29–44.

Tonkiss, F (2013) Austerity urbanism and the makeshift city. *CITY: Analysis of Urban Trends, Culture, Theory, Policy, Action* 17(3): 312–324.

Walton, J. (2015) 'Everyday I'm Çapulling!': Global Flows and Local Frictions of Gezi. In: David, I. and Toktamış, K.F. (Eds.) *Everywhere Taksim: Sowing the Seeds for a New Turkey at Gezi*. Amsterdam: Amsterdam University Press, 45–58.

Yörük, E. (2014) The long summer of Turkey: the Gezi uprising and its historical roots. *The South Atlantic Quarterly* 113(2): 419–426.

Zettelmeyer, J., Trebesch, C and M. Gulati (2013) The Greek debt restructuring: an autopsy. *Economic Policy* 28(75): 513–563.

PART 3

Dissenting a Step Further beyond Gezi

CHAPTER 7

Watchmen as AKP's "Brownshirts"?
Regime Debate and Police Order in the Post-Gezi Period

Selin Dingiloğlu and Çağlar Dölek

The post-Gezi period in Turkey has been characterized by an intensification of a multifaceted political and economic crisis, as discussed in an extensive volume of critical literature elsewhere (Babacan et al., 2021; Bedirhanoğlu et al., 2020; Şahin and Erol, 2021). The transformation of state coercion and the intensification of social and political violence have played a crucial role in this crisis-ridden period, raising alarming concerns over Turkey's becoming a police or fascist state *par excellence* (Berksoy, 2022; Işık, 2022; Kars Kaynar, 2018; Kaygusuz, 2018; Yarkın, 2022; Yılmaz 2021). The recent debates on the reinstatement of the historically peculiar watchmen (Turkish: *bekçi*) system as an urban auxiliary policing strategy provide a crucial example in this regard.

The Law on the Neighbourhood Watchmen, numbered 7245, was enacted in June 2020 amid a widespread public reaction (Resmi Gazete, 2020). The law has frequently been associated with the need for creating a novel, politically loyal social control unit within the police organization after the Gülenist coup attempt in 2016. The Gülenists, as close allies to the Justice and Development Party (Turkish: *Adalet ve Kalkınma Partisi*, AKP) throughout the 2000s, had exerted an overwhelming dominance over the national police force and other sectors of the state, such as the judiciary. Following the attempted coup, the AKP government undertook mass purges in the police organization and dismissed about thirty-three thousand police officers over their alleged links to the Gülenists (Anadolu Ajansı, 2019). Some commentators relate the reinstatement of an expanded watchmen system and the recruitment of new (and politically loyal) cadres to an urge to overcome the staff deficit in the rank-and-file of the police organization (Ahwal News, 2020; Al Monitor, 2020; San, 2020; Sharma, 2017). Although the exigency of mass purges might have played an immediate role, explaining the revival of the watchmen system on this ground has two significant shortcomings: First, by narrowing the focus on the Gülenist-AKP conflict, it might overlook the multifaceted matrix of social and political contradictions that underlie the Islamist-nationalist bloc represented by the political alliance between the Nationalist Movement Party (Turkish: *Milliyetçi Hareket Partisi*, MHP) and AKP, thereby failing to conceive the contested socio-political context that has led to the reconfiguration of the security architecture in Turkey. Second, such questioning does not answer why the personnel deficit was not overcome by enhancing the regular police forces with new and loyal recruits instead of reinstating an auxiliary policing agency.

The opponents of the new law put it in the general context of AKP's securitization policies that aim at criminalizing any social and political dissent by establishing a police state. The new law indeed grants the watchmen discretionary powers similar to those of the police, including stop and search, the use of lethal force, and even intervention in demonstrations upon ministerial discretion. Connected to this point, the critics of the law link the enhanced revival of the watchmen system to the fortification of a police state with such tendencies as the normalization of arbitrary practices, discretionary violence, and legal impunity (Aktan, 2020; San, 2020). While highlighting the new law's continuity within the broader making of a police state is crucial, the above-posed question remains in the air: Why was it deemed necessary to introduce a separate and auxiliary policing force?

This chapter tackles this question by exploring the reinstatement of the neighbourhood watchmen system via a dialectical reading of policing and proletarian marginalization in the context of utterly contradictory social and political dynamics of *fascistization* in Turkey. Whereas a comprehensive engagement with the recently heated "regime transformation" debate in Turkey is beyond the frontier of this chapter (see Babacan et al., 2021; Bedirhanoğlu et al., 2020; Berksoy, 2022; Kaygusuz, 2018; Tuğal, 2016; Yılmaz, 2021), we intend to contribute to this debate by exploring how the process of *fascistization* signifies a peculiar form of paramilitary mobilization with a contradictory class character that also informs the authoritarian state form and the carceral regime in the making in Turkey. With this goal in mind, we first discuss the contested social and political dynamics and appearances of proletarian marginalization in Turkey in its world-historical context. Then, we explore how the watchmen system as an urban policing unit assumes a legally ambiguous space in the architecture of policing, creating politically convenient opportunities for the mobilization of *lumpenised* social groups in accordance with the Islamist, nationalist, and authoritarian agenda of the ruling bloc.

1   Fabricating a Violent Urban Order: the Dialectics of Crime and Policing in the AKP Era

> Since capital, the direct or indirect control of the means of subsistence and production, is the weapon with which this *social warfare* is carried

on, it is clear that all the disadvantages of such a state must fall upon the poor ... If the worker can get no work he may steal, if he is not afraid of the police, or starve, in which case the police will take care that he does so in a quiet and inoffensive manner.

ENGELS, 2008 [1892]: 25; emphasis added

Exposing a vivid description of the conditions of proletarian living in mid-nineteenth century England, Friedrich Engels uses the notion of "social warfare" to critique the structural processes of dispossession that create the conditions of radical dependence of the proletariat on what Ellen Meiksins Wood (2003: 9) calls "the impersonal imperatives of the market". Unfolding itself in the historical formation of the wage form under "the logical sequel of the principle involved in free competition" (Engels, 2008 [1892]: 132), this social war fabricates pauperism on a massive scale, resulting in the constant rebounding of a surplus population. Likewise, the "virtual pauper" represents a dialectical category in Marx's original exposition of the proletarian, conceived not as a synonym for wage labourer in its mere sociological sense; the notion of the proletarian instead implies dispossession, expropriation, and radical dependence on the market (Denning, 2010: 81). The question of subsistence thereby becomes a contested terrain for labour and capital, a terrain through which the fundamental contradiction characterizing capitalism unfolds itself in everyday life: the contradiction between private appropriation and social (re)production. Whereas the historical specificity of capitalism is to organize this contradiction based on a real and superficial distinction between the economic and the political, fabricating a fetishized separation of state power from class power (Bonefeld, 1992; Clarke, 1991), the proletarian masses are socially constituted and politically administered amid this contested process of social warfare.

Representing a world-historical project for the restoration of the class power of capital at the expense of labour (Harvey, 2005), neoliberal globalization has arisen on a contested process of marginalization of proletarian life in the countries of the global South and North alike (Wacquant, 2008). Reflecting an intensified social warfare *à la Engels,* the massive scale of slum formation on the urban margins of the global South has given way to the making of "the informal sector", which was politically coined in the 1970s to reckon the generalized system of "wageless life" for the labouring masses (Denning, 2010: 81–86). The countries of the global South have experienced "urbanization without industrialization" which delinks economic growth from employment generation (Davis, 2006: 14). This structural tendency of "jobless growth" deepens class inequalities while forcing masses into precarious conditions of working and living. The system of wageless life, therefore, animates proletarian struggles for survival, signifying a complex repertoire of subsistence that has been morally, politically, and legally denounced by the ruling classes and the state, and thereby subjected to various forms of regulation, surveillance, containment, and repression. As the vast literature on "survival strategy" maintains, the urban poor in the global South continue resorting to practices such as petty theft, begging, prostitution, and drug dealing to counter the adverse consequences of precarious living in the era of neoliberal globalization (Auyero, 2000; Bayat, 1997; Schneider and Susser, 2003).

To the extent that proletarian struggles for subsistence come in direct contradiction with the discipline of capital in a financialized neoliberal order, we need to develop a relational perspective on the complex dynamics of the concomitant constitution of work-poverty-unemployment-crime (Hall et al., 1978: 189). On methodological and theoretical grounds, the empiricist project of bourgeois social science, including its sociological and criminological variants, tends to conceive them as distinct, externally related empirical facts. Such a myopic perspective not only fails to explain the underlying dynamics of the co-constitution of such phenomena, but also, and perhaps more importantly, this perspective reproduces the marginalizing gaze of the state in fabricating the political categories of the poor, the indigent, and the criminal. The reifying logic of such a project thereby constantly produces "suitable enemies" (Christie, 1986) for the deployment of state violence while mystifying the socially produced criminogenic conditions. The proletarian life characterized by the essential precarity of wage labour is subjected to the criminogenic conditions of social (re)production reflecting the discipline of capital over society at large. To scrutinize the dialectical relationship among work, poverty, and crime, therefore, we need to view these phenomena not as isolated facts, but as moments in social warfare *à la Engels,* within which the class power of capital is being reproduced as a social relation while the regime of private property assumes its contested hegemony in everyday life. In a nutshell, the social reality of crime and the corresponding political strategies of criminalization signify a dialectical process that necessitates a dynamic understanding of crime "only as a relation between … crime and control" (Hall et al., 1978: 185). This relational and dynamic perspective on the nexus of work-poverty-unemployment-crime conceives the proletarian as a dialectical category that is co-constituted with police power amid the socially contradictory and politically open-ended process of the formation of wage-labour as the only available means of subsistence (Dölek, 2019: 178).

Viewing recent transformations in Turkey through these dialectical lenses of crime and control seems significant to understanding the contradictory social dynamics of the making of a violent urban order in Turkey in the 2010s. A new wave of dispossession on the part of the country's working classes has been rooted in generalized precarity, persistent unemployment, and indebtedness under the discipline of a financialized economy (Çelik, 2015; Karaçimen, 2014; Şahin and Erol, 2021). The rise of a stagnant surplus population has been an outcome of this process, reflecting often controversial everyday struggles for living on precarious, flexible, part-time, temporary, and intermittent forms of employment (Oğuz, 2020). Precarious living, therefore, signifies a generalized condition of the country's proletarian masses.

This process also animates the contested making of advanced marginality (*à la* Wacquant, 2008) in a peripheral context, i.e., the formation of spatial clusters of chronic poverty that has been interpenetrated with various sorts of common criminality, with everyday violence it constantly generates. In this context, we see the rise of illicit economies (drug enterprises, petty theft, illegal sex work, etc.) on the part of the dispossessed populations in Turkey (Engin, 2015; Mercan and Şen, 2020; Ünal-Reşitoğlu and Altan, 2022). Arguably, the social war that has increasingly characterized the urban margins has arisen based on the actual formation of illicit (Turkish: *gayrimeşru*) economies of survival. The social reality of common "criminality", coupled with the everyday violence it produces, therefore, represents an essential component of proletarian life, conditioning the character of the ongoing social war and associated strategies of policing in contemporary Turkey.

A 2021 report by the Turkish Statistical Institute (Turkish: *Türkiye İstatistik Kurumu,* TÜİK) on the number of "convicts received into prison by type of crime and province where the crime was committed" between 2011 and 2020 provides a striking picture in this regard (Eren, 2021). Accordingly, the most common crimes in 2020 are as in the following: assault (15.7%), theft (15.2%), traffic crimes (5.9%), opposition to the Bankruptcy and Enforcement Law (5.3%), and production, commerce, use and purchase of drugs (4.7%). In the last decade, as Eren demonstrates (2021), assault and theft have become the most common crimes, reflecting the increasing levels of poverty, inequality, deprivation, and associated issues of interpersonal violence in everyday life. As a matter of fact, the punitive control of common crimes such as theft, drugs, and interpersonal violence, represents a constitutive dimension of the authoritarian state formation in Turkey (Gönen, 2020: 262). Considered in conjunction with the recent rise of working-class suicides (Yücal and Kabalay, 2022), the systematic character of workplace "murders" (İSİG, 2023), violence against women (HRW, 2022) and against immigrant communities such as Syrian refugees (Farooq, 2021), as well as the politically fabricated massacres amid "natural catastrophes" (Aktaş and Karakaş, 2023), the ongoing social warfare has already assumed a violent character on a massive scale in the country.

The violent character of the social war gains a distinctly political form amid a "hostile conjuncture" (Karataşlı and Kumral, 2019) of urban warfare conditioned in the geopolitical context of the Syrian crisis. That is, the social war rooted in the violence of capital accumulation, dispossession, and marginalization of proletarian life has also been accompanied by the urban warfare embarked upon by the state against the Kurdish national movement in the country. Reflecting Turkey's adoption of 'new military urbanism' (Graham, 2009), the counter-insurgency warfare against the Kurdish movement, designed especially in the 1990s via extra-legal actors such as the Gendarmerie Intelligence and Counter-Terrorism Organization (Turkish: *Jandarma İstihbarat ve Terörle Mücadele Teşkilatı*, JITEM) and para-military groups such as village guards (Turkish: *korucular*), assumed a distinctly urban form since the early 2000s. Identifying a historical continuity in Turkish paramilitarism, Ayhan Işık lists a number of actors of various legal and extra-legal characters during the AKP period, including International Defence Consultancy Construction Industry and Trade Inc. (Turkish: *Uluslararası Savunma Danışmanlık İnşaat Sanayi ve Ticaret A.Ş.*, SADAT), the Gendarmerie Special Operations (Turkish: *Jandarma Özel Harekat*, JÖH), the Police Special Operation Department (Turkish: *Polis Özel Harekat Dairesi*, PÖH), watchmen, Osmanen Germania, and the so-called "Esedullah" team (Turkish: *Esedullah timi*) (2022: 4). Especially during the 2015–16 urban warfare waged against the youth groups of the Kurdish national movement, JÖH, PÖH, and Esedullah were utilized in the large-scale destruction of the Kurdish-populated cities where thousands of civilians were killed (Işık, 2022: 7; Üngör and Işık, 2021: 31). In the process, such paramilitary groups as JÖH and PÖH were reinforced and incorporated more systematically into the hierarchical networks of the armed groups (Işık, 2022: 8). Failing in its attempt to draw a clear dividing line between the Kurdish people and the Kurdistan Workers' Party (Kurdish: *Partiya Karkerên Kurdistanê*, PKK), the state, with the active participation of such paramilitary groups, targeted everyone, "making no distinction between civilians and militants" (Işık, 2022: 9). The cities where the most destruction and deaths occurred are Cizre (province of Şırnak); Sur, Silvan, and Lice (provinces of Diyarbakır); Nusaybin and Dargeçit (provinces of Mardin); Şırnak Center, Silopi, and Idil (provinces of Şırnak); and Yüksekova (province of Hakkari) (Üngör and Işık, 2021: 32).

We, therefore, observe an intensified interpenetration of political strategies rooted in this twin warfare. For instance, urban renewal, as a neoliberal project of displacement and commodification, has provided a politically productive opportunity for the AKP government to link these two fundamental processes (Dölek, 2020). The massive mobilization of police power through urban renewal processes has been materialized with the transposition of strategies for urban warfare against the Kurdish movement into a large-scale campaign against any kind of "suitable enemy" in the rest of the country. The institutional agents of "security" such as national and local police departments, as well as provincial security directorates have assumed a proactive role in the process. In November 2012, for instance, the Ministry of Environment and Urbanization (Turkish: *Çevre ve Şehircilik Bakanlığı*) received a request from provincial security directorates of sixteen large provinces, including İstanbul, Ankara, İzmir, Diyarbakır and Adana, on the identification of certain slum (Turkish: *gecekondu*) regions as the primary areas of demolition as part of the ongoing urban regeneration projects. The ideology of security informing such a request was based on a strategic, albeit ambiguous, conflation of "terror, drug-dealing and public disorder" as closely interlinked problems in *gecekondu* neighbourhoods depicted as "crime zones" (Hürriyet, 2012).

This crime-terror nexus has thus been decisive in the transposition of violent policing strategies that were primarily employed in Kurdish-populated cities to urban centers in the western part of the country. As Zeynep Gönen (2020: 272) demonstrates, especially in the 2010s, the war on drugs became "a fully-fledged wartime mobilization" that depoliticized urban social problems and contradictions, subjecting marginalized populations to increasingly paramilitarised police power, while incorporating dispossessed masses into the carceral regime in the making. Whereas this transposition has become normalized in the post-Gezi period, the establishment and proliferation of fortified military outposts (Turkish: *kalekols*) need particular attention. As heavily armed military stations established especially during the 2013–2015 Peace Process (Turkish: *Barış Süreci*) in the Kurdish-populated provinces (Üngör and Işık, 2021: 31), *kalekols* have been deployed in the western parts of the country as a new spectacle of militarized policing (Dölek, 2020: 284), as part of a broader strategy against the political mobilization of racialized and marginalized populations (Yonucu, 2022).

Whereas the laboring masses have increasingly witnessed the deterioration of their material conditions of living in a fragile, debt-driven financialized economy, this process of deepened social insecurity has been articulated into a politically contested process of what we call *the marginalization of proletarian life* in the country. The "security" architecture of the Turkish state, including policing, courts, and prisons, we argue, functions as a contested carceral regime based on the contradictory fabrication and constant reproduction of various facets of marginalization in the everyday lives of the dispossessed masses in Turkey. More specifically, the carceral regime in the making incorporates different sectors of laboring masses as fragile subjectivities in social control such as police officers, private security guards, watchmen, or other paramilitary forces loyal to the ruling bloc. The country's nascent carceral regime also criminalizes precarious sectors of the population via vividly racialized and gendered strategies of punitive control. What is important here is to observe the contradictory dynamics of these two tendencies as two sides of the same coin. That is, we need to view the production of crime (and thereby criminals) and the fabrication of crime control (and thereby social control agents of various sorts) as relational processes.

Table 7.1 provides a vivid illustration of the "control dimension" of this relational process. Compiled from the annual reports of the General Directorate of Security from 2006 through 2021, the table demonstrates the dramatic rise in the number of police personnel during the AKP years, making Turkey one of the most policed countries in Europe (Fleck, 2022). For the purposes of this chapter, what is also important to highlight is that the number of watchmen recruited began to increase even before the enactment of the Watchmen Law in 2020. As the investigative journalist Nurcan Baysal underlines, the reinstatement of the watchmen was conditioned in the Turkish state's counter-insurgency politics against the Kurdish movement during the 2015–16 urban warfare. This auxiliary policing unit was designed to provide vernacular support such as intelligence gathering to the armed forces during the clashes, rather than "neighbourhood security" as proclaimed by the AKP government. Accordingly, in April 2016, the provincial governments of Şırnak, Hakkari, Diyarbakır, Şanlıurfa, and Mardin began recruiting watchmen, well before their diffusion in the western parts of the country such as İstanbul in August 2017 (Baysal, 2021). Rooted in the urban warfare against the Kurdish national movement, the revival of the watchmen system is thus an important recent case in the transposition of violent policing strategies.

We need to read Table 7.1 in conjunction with another important auxiliary policing force: private security. The sector has already become one of the largest private security sectors in Europe with the employment of over 350 thousand private security guards in everyday life. Besides, the number of persons with private security certificates has surpassed 1.5 million (Hürriyet, 2022). These numbers point out a fundamental dynamic concerning the social composition of the labor force in Turkey: a considerable portion of the country's proletarian masses has been incorporated into the private security sector under conditions of deepened precarity and social insecurity within an effective strategy of policing the poor through the poor (Dölek and Rigakos, 2018: 7). Besides, quite parallel to the revival of the watchmen system in the context

TABLE 7.1 Number of police and watchmen

Years	Total number of police	Watchmen	Ratio
2021	316,509	29,626	9.36%
2020	313,225	29,242	9.33%
2019	307,813	21,319	6.92%
2018	276,094	11,398	4.12%
2017	264,879	4,653	1.75%
2016	251,954	4,295	1.70%
2015	260,679	3,149	1.20%
2014	256,904	3,521	1.37%
2013	250,557	3,793	1.51%
2012	242,228	3,981	1.64%
2011	232,647	4,227	1.81%
2010	218,255	4,468	2.04%
2009	209,246	4,870	2.32%
2008	198,491	5,249	2.64%
2006	181,196	10,726	5.92%

SOURCE: ANNUAL REPORTS OF THE GENERAL DIRECTORATE OF SECURITY (2006–2021)

of the urban warfare against the Kurdish movement, the private security has been politically redesigned via a recently initiated Project for Cooperation and Integration of Public Police and Private Security (Turkish: *Genel Kolluk-Özel Güvenlik İşbirliği ve Entegrasyon Projesi,* KAAN) with a specific aim of integrating systematically the private security sector into the political architecture of policing at large. Not surprisingly, this redesign reflects how the social warfare of capital, and the urban warfare of the Turkish state, are intimately connected. The former Minister of Interior Süleyman Soylu explains this connection in a nutshell:

> The PKK terror is not only related to the mountains, rural [areas/regions]. [Its] intellectual base [and] personnel recruitment are produced in cities. The city is not only composed of spatial settlement. To the contrary, [city] is the arena when human[s] establish *security relations* at the backdrop of this spatial appearance. Therefore, urban security, and especially

the security of such large, global cities as İstanbul, is a matter of special expertise and capacity and private security is part of this *work*.
İÇİŞLERİ BAKANLIĞI, 2022; emphasis added

The "security relation" in the making reflects a contradictory process of the incorporation of precarious masses as fragile subjectivities in social control such as police officers, private security guards, nightwatchmen, or other paramilitary forces loyal to the ruling bloc. At this point, we need to explore how the watchmen system as an auxiliary policing strategy assumes a legally ambiguous space in the architecture of policing, creating politically convenient opportunities for the mobilization of *lumpenised* social groups in accordance with the Islamist, nationalist, and authoritarian agenda of the ruling bloc. In light of the above-presented reading of social warfare in relation to urban warfare, it is imperative to develop a closer analysis of the watchmen system in the broader political architecture of policing in Turkey.

2   Watchmen in the Political Architecture of Policing

As repeatedly noted by the parliamentary opposition, the new system is fundamentally characterized by ambiguity and arbitrariness in the watchmen's legal status, and thus in their duties, entitlements, and potential ways of deployment. A closer look at this newly fabricated system seems significant to understand how arbitrary power informs the entire political architecture of policing in contemporary Turkey and thereby presents a politically productive opportunity for the forces of order to connect this new policing unit to *fascistization* process in the making.

First, a fundamental legal ambiguity characterizes the powers assigned to the watchmen system. While extending the powers such as stop and search and the use of lethal force to the watchmen, the Watchmen Law goes well beyond the already ambiguous and arbitrary "reasonable doubt" principle that the Law on Police Duties and Entitlements (Turkish: *Polis Vazife ve Salahiyet Kanunu*, PVSK) has been based on. During the bill's committee hearings, for instance, the Peoples' Democratic Party (Turkish: *Halkların Demokratik Partisi*, HDP) parliamentarian Filiz Kerestecioğlu highlighted that the absence of any specification in stop and search would allow watchmen to engage in discriminatory practices based on politically biased considerations or social and moral prejudices (Türkiye Büyük Millet Meclisi, 2020a). As a matter of fact, the watchmen system has already assumed a specific role of policing the "morals" of society, in tandem with the Islamist, conservative, and nationalist political agenda of the ruling bloc. At this point, we need to connect the "morality police" in question to a broader debate on police power. As critical policing scholars have well maintained, the fabrication of wage labor through police power has been compounded by a simultaneous project of moral regulation. With a strategic agenda of fabricating a new moral order, the police have been instrumental in the violent imposition of an urban order that reproduces gendered and racialized dynamics of social inequality (Neocleous, 2000: 99–100). Since the definition of morality is a contested/controversial issue, the policing of morals offers a politically productive opportunity for police power to exercise discretion as a form of everyday law-making on the part of the forces of order. From the perspective of those positioned at the receiving end of this everyday politics of law and order, policing signifies a permanent deployment of emergency powers and violence. The watchmen violence against sex workers in Turkey is a paradigmatic example in this regard (Tar, 2018).

In a similar case of ambiguity, the Republican People's Party (Turkish: *Cumhuriyet Halk Partisi*, CHP) parliamentarian Ibrahim Kaboğlu refers to the bill's sixth article that mandates watchmen to "take preventive measures until general law enforcement officers arrive in order to prevent demonstrations, marches, and disturbances that may disrupt public order." Kaboğlu emphasizes that "disturbance" is a legally void term because it is not defined in the relevant articles of the constitution (Türkiye Büyük Millet Meclisi, 2020b). In a similar vein, the İyi Party (İYİP) parliamentarian Mehmet M. Çulhaoğlu points out that the article does not specify what kind of "preventive measures" are implied (Türkiye Büyük Millet Meclisi, 2020c). This ambiguity in defining "disturbance" and "preventive measures" indeed tells us a familiar story behind the foundational contradiction in modern police power. The police assume "an impossible mandate" (Manning, 1977) due to the complex and contradictory nature of the everyday realization of capitalist accumulation. Given the contradictory repercussions of the twin warfare underway, as we noted above, crime control and order maintenance become essentially open-ended processes that position the police as agents in "justice without trial" (Skolnick, 1966) that operate in the pendulum of legality and illegality. As Brogden notes, this signifies a fundamental "irony" in police work because it is "the lowest of the low, the street constable, unlike in other 'professional' occupations, [that] is the one who can exercise the maximum discretion at work" (cited in Neocleous, 2000: 99). The law-making and law-preserving functions of state power, as Walter Benjamin reminds us, are thereby dissolved in police power (1999: 287). The legal ambiguity inscribed into the watchmen system, therefore, represents not a mere political move on the part of the ruling bloc, but an expression of this foundational ambiguity underlying police power in the form of discretion. For this discretionary authority is not a mere matter of disproportionate and arbitrary use of force; it instead represents a core feature of police power. As Neocleous contends, "without discretion police power cannot function" (2015: 358). That is why such ambiguous notions as "disturbance" and "preventive measures" that characterize the watchmen system in Turkey are foundational elements connecting policing to its essential function: "violence work" (Seigel, 2018). Policing in general, and the watchmen system in particular thereby signifies a political organization of a violent urban order that characterizes the social warfare underway (See, among many others, Bianet, 2021).

A similar ambiguity arises in relation to the physical space of watchmen's duties. The spatial domain of the watchmen is specified as *mahalle* (neighbourhood) and *çarşı* (marketplace). The criticisms in parliament and the media focus on both the vagueness of the *mahalle* as an administrative unit and its insubstantiality as a social realm within contemporary urban cultural and spatial clusters (Batuman and Erkip: 2019: 6; Sevinç, 2020; Topuz, 2020). The same holds true for the *çarşı*, which has no legal definition in administrative, criminal, or constitutional law and can thus range from old bazaars to shopping malls and districts. Furthermore, the law allows for the deployment of watchmen in "hot spots" where there is a crowd – and thus a risk of crime – for short shifts (Batuman and Erkip, 2019: 9), as opposed to the old watchmen who were only responsible for "securing" public order in their specific locality. The watchmen can thereby be deployed "nowhere and everywhere." Operating via arbitrary and open-ended definitions of "morality" and "disturbance" and thereby "public order", the watchmen system signifies a spatial project in containing the everyday contradictions of the social war underway. For instance, this urban policing unit assumes a frontier agency role in the violent pacification of complex and contradictory strategies of survival at the arsenal of the dispossessed populations, including petty theft, drug dealing, and sex work. Besides, the spatial dimension of this nascent policing unit signals the political strategy of "controlling the streets", a peculiar concern of the current power bloc, a controversial issue that is connected to our discussion on the process of *fascistization* below.

3   The Watchmen as AKP's "Brownshirts"

We should connect the above discussion on discretion to Benjamin's critique of violence and police power, and underline that the political organization of the watchmen system as such reproduces the "ghostly appearance" of police power in the lives of the dispossessed. As Benjamin (1999: 287) contends, the "formless" power of the police, this "nowhere-tangible, all-pervasive presence" operates through intervention "in countless cases where no clear legal situation exists, when they are not merely, without slightest relation to legal ends, accompanying the citizen as a brutal encumbrance through a life regulated by ordinances". This ghostly presence armoured by an almost limitless set of discretionary powers connects police power to *fascistization* processes underway. The system, we contend, fabricates a permanent state of emergency in the lives of the dispossessed along the lines of an Islamist, conservative, and nationalist agenda of the ruling bloc. We thus need to introduce another dimension of the debates over the new watchmen system in the context of the recently heated regime debate and historical fascism. Parallel to the purge-and-recruitment cycle of the police organization in recent years, the AKP-loyal cadres have allegedly filled the posts of the new system, raising concerns over their becoming a proto-fascist militia organization reminiscent of Mussolini's Blackshirts or Hitler's Brownshirts.

In addition to the arbitrariness provided by the legally vague frameworks, the discretionary powers in the hiring process raise concerns that the AKP government is designing a party militia disguised as an auxiliary police force to criminalize and suppress any forms of social and political dissent. The provincial governors, mandated by the Watchmen Law, assume an active role in the recruitment process, which not only results in a dual hierarchy in the lines of authority but also allows for political manipulation in the recruitment process. Despite the fact that the law classifies them as security-related civil servants, the watchmen are exempt from the civil service exam and instead hired based on their performance in a separate exam. The interview by a committee presided over by the governor accounts for fifty per cent of their score. Opposition parties claim that this specific recruitment mechanism is purposefully designed to strengthen AKP's discretionary power in manipulating the composition of watchmen in order to establish a party militia. They report that the lists of "eligible candidates" are submitted by AKP's local branches to the governors, and in some cases, governors who refuse to hire them are dismissed. Therefore, critics of the new watchmen law claim that the main goal of this legal venture is to create a loyalist armed force particularly in the service of AKP's autocratic and authoritarian regime (see Filiz Keresticioğlu's speech in Türkiye Büyük Millet Meclisi, 2020a; Hakkı Saruhan Oluç and Lütfü Türkkan's speeches in Türkiye Büyük Millet Meclisi, 2020b; Mahmut Tuğrul's, Aydın Adnan Sezgin's and Hüda Kaya's speeches in Türkiye Büyük Millet Meclisi, 2020c; Hasan Subaşı's speech in Türkiye Büyük Millet Meclisi, 2020d).

This characterization of the watchmen as an exclusive armed force tasked with ensuing the survival of an oligarchic group embodied in AKP or the

President Erdoğan and his close circle is the primary link that contextualizes it in the debate over AKP's new (security) regime. During the plenary sessions in the parliament, for example, the HDP parliamentarian Hakkı Saruhan Oluç portrays the watchmen as a special paramilitary force that is designed to "melt the security of the regime, state and society into one-man's security" (Türkiye Büyük Millet Meclisi, 2020b). In her account of the transformation in AKP's security politics throughout its governmental period, Özlem Kaygusuz (2018) conceptualizes the recent redesign of the security architecture as a shift from the neoliberal security state (NSS) to the politics of regime security (RS). Drawing on the literature on neoliberal security paradigm (Boukalas, 2014; Boukalas, 2015; Bruff, 2014), Kaygusuz emphasizes that the NSS is designed as "a permanent state of exception around a massive surge in coercive state activity" in order to effectively manage the growing social and political unrest in the face of 2007–08 global crisis in the neoliberal capitalist economy. The NSS strengthens already existing authoritarian elements in liberal democracies by legalizing the use of excessive state power, disempowering the check and balance mechanism, and shifting away from consent-building policies in favour of coercion. Coercive institutions and practices are restructured not only to manage the economic crisis but also to keep it from becoming a political one. The distinguishing feature of RS is that the ruling elites regard their own survival in power as a primary security concern and associate it with the survival of the state. Therefore, the *reinforced* coercive apparatus serves as the guardian of the ruling party, alongside an autonomous and all-powerful decision-making network under the president's command (Kaygusuz, 2018: 17). As a result of a deep fusion between the governing party and the state, the structure and operation of the security apparatus is determined by a party or an oligarchic network.

The political background that allows for this paradigm shift can either be an intra-elite confrontation or an intensified class conflict. Kaygusuz (2018: 8–13) contends that in the Turkish case, it is mainly the political struggle between the AKP government and the Gülen movement, on the one hand, and between the Islamists and the secularist/modernist segments of the state, on the other. Between 2006 (when the accession negotiations with the European Union were halted) and 2013 (the time of the Gezi protests), the AKP government established the NSS by empowering police through enhanced discretionary powers to manage the social unrest that would eventually arise due to dissatisfaction with the neoliberal policies implemented, and it has proven effective in suppressing popular and class-based opposition to the neoliberal policies until the Gezi protests. Although the Gezi events, the rising Kurdish political movement, and Gülenists' corruption investigations (17–25 December 2013) all contributed to the AKP regime adopting a regime security paradigm, it is primarily the intra-elite conflict with the Gülen movement that demonstrated the NSS's inadequacy.

While the intra-elite fragmentations and new political and institutional constellations based on them have an undeniable impact, particularly on the reconfiguration of security architecture, the social fault lines along class-based, ethnic, sectarian, and regional fractures play an equally important role in both the emergence and design of the new security regime. Actually, the social dimension is not entirely absent in the debates over the new law. It is especially apparent in the argument that, by reintroducing the watchmen system, AKP is attempting to strengthen and multiply security apparatuses in order to deal with potential social unrest in the face of recent ever-intensifying pro-capital redistribution policies that have deteriorated economic conditions for large segments of wage-earners on an unprecedented scale. However, addressing the social class factor solely as the object of surveillance, control, and coercion in security politics would obscure not only the dialectics in the political formation of classes but also what we believe to be the true peculiarity of the new security architecture: the establishment of security clusters that mobilize the masses. The "qualitative upgrade" provided by the watchmen system to the AKP regime's security policies is based on potential instrumentalization of it in this regard as well as the expansion of the arbitrary and discretionary powers. This point is especially important in the context of discussions about regime transformation. Rather than assessing the changes in the AKP regime's security policies by tracking them along a spectrum from less to more authoritarian, and measuring authoritarianism solely by autocratic or oligarchic elements, we propose invoking the *fascistization* debate in accordance with the security regime.

In fact, critics of the watchmen law in parliament and the media cite several examples from historical and contemporary authoritarian regimes to establish organizational parallelism with the watchmen (see Lütfü Türkkan's speech in Türkiye Büyük Millet Meclisi, 2020b; Aydın Adnan Sezgin's speech in Türkiye Büyük Millet Meclisi, 2020c). The historical German fascism is considered particularly relevant with its deployment of the Sturmabteilung (SA) organization—colloquially referred to as the brownshirts-as a paramilitary force loyal to the Nazi party and Hitler. The historians of Nazi Germany extensively chronicle the fragmentation within the security apparatus and confusing task duplications between police and SA forces; the formation of SA as a special organization directly loyal to the Führer; or the reinforcement of the police with the SA as an auxiliary force (Broszat, 2013; Feuchtwanger, 1995; Sewell: 2014). The institutionalization of the Nazi security apparatus does indeed set an example that bears some striking resemblance to the watchmen system. But too much focus on the institutional design-as an independent variable-and especially on the autocratic manipulation of and control over them (the "Führer absolutism" as analogous to the "one-man regime") may have a blind spot on the multifaceted societal matrix of power relations in general and complexes of inter and intra-class relationships that are peculiar to fascism in particular. Any comparison to fascism can only provide insight if it also elaborates on these matrices and complexes. For, fascism denotes a specific form of mass politics as well as a specific form of authoritarian state.

Cihan Tuğal (2016) emphasizes in his analysis of the AKP authoritarianism in terms of fascism that while there is a global shift to the extreme right in many regimes, fascism is distinguished from the rest based on "a political party's extensive civic networks ... and mass mobilization, which runs deeper than loose right-wing networks." One cannot simply identify AKP's new path with historical fascisms due to the peculiarities of both Turkish case and historical time, as Tuğal contends. Despite historical and structural incompatibilities, however, one thread that connects interwar fascisms to AKP's (neo-fascist) regime is violent mass mobilization through paramilitary right-wing nationalist or Salafi-jihadist organizations as well as mafia leaders, with the lines between them and the official security forces blurring, as noted above.

While the watchmen system is not a typical paramilitary organization, it is closely related to the fascist model of paramilitary mass mobilization in many ways. Firstly, and most obviously, the legal ambiguities discussed above place it in the grey zone between official law enforcement and extra-state paramilitary practices. The aforementioned mechanisms of political interference in the hiring process also allow for potentially overlapping recruitments in paramilitary organizations and the watchman system. Moreover, fascism deploys forms of paramilitary violence not only to circumvent the legal and institutional constraints of the ordinary rule of law; the arbitrary powers wielded by coercive apparatuses and the "state of exception" are also integral parts of liberal democracies and thus far from a "fascist exception." Fascism is distinguished by the mobilization of masses through extra-state or (semi-)official channels, so that "the mass" becomes the agency of arbitrary power and political brutalization.

Debates about this aspect of fascist mass mobilization can be found in studies of historical fascism under the loose rubric of lumpenism. Arguments about the social composition of the watchmen connect to these debates, but only in a scattered and indirect way. We need to dig deeper into perceptions of the watchmen's social profile because they have important implications for both the marginalization and criminalization of the urban poor and the *fascistization* thesis.

4 The Watchmen as an "Army of the Lumpens"

Allegations of the formation of a party militia under the guise of watchmen reveal more than mere concerns about political loyalism. The social composition and contradictory class character of this new armed force is also a major source of concern. The watchmen are often portrayed as "a furious army of fools" with a criminal tendency, recruited not only from the ranks of AKP supporters, but also from the lower orders of society, creating a dichotomous perception of potential criminals as opposed to "security men" based on the following assumptions: Watchmen may become easily integrated to the local networks of petty theft, drug enterprises, sex work and such, since-unlike the policemen-they are usually recruited from the local community and not subject to mandatory rotation in duty station (see Lütfü Türkkan's speech in Türkiye Büyük Millet Meclisi, 2020b). Aside from possible links to illicit economies, the attribute of criminal tendency implies the watchmen's likelihood to engage in arbitrary acts of violence against the citizens. This assumed likelihood is, on the one hand, grounded in their political militancy, which can lead to selective hostility toward specific groups. Given the opportunities for political profiling during recruitment processes, it is more than a coincidence that the majority of their reported violent acts target political dissidents or social groups that have been systematically marginalized and criminalized by the Islamist-nationalist rhetoric. The watchmen, as "the morality police", exercise arbitrary, abusive, and brutal interventions to individuals and social gatherings in the parks or other public spaces (see Lütfü Türkkan's speech in Türkiye Büyük Millet Meclisi, 2020b; Hüda Kaya's speech in Türkiye Büyük Millet Meclisi, 2020c; Kocabaş, 2020; sendika.org, 2022; soL, 2019, 2022). As critical scholars working on racialized and gendered dynamics of policing in Turkey have demonstrated, selective violence against the Kurdish people, the Alevi population, immigrants, women, the LGBTQ+ community, and sex workers is not the exception but the rule for the politics of the police in contemporary Turkey (Gönen and Yonucu, 2011; Gönen, 2016; Hülagü, 2020). The watchmen system, therefore, operates to even deepen this racialized and gendered politics of moral order in everyday life, as we have noted above.

Beyond the general politics of the police, however, we need to critically evaluate the watchmen's social profile and associated contradictions in its class character as foundational dimensions in their political and ideological engagements in everyday life. The watchmen are typically depicted as a horde of delinquent, young, male paupers who can be easily provoked to "drag the public life into a field of political tensions (…), into a scene of violence manufactured by the government" (Hakkı Saruhan Oluç's speech in Türkiye Büyük

Millet Meclisi, 2020b). It is widely assumed that the despair of pauperized, marginalized, and uprooted young males will most likely lead to reckless violence if given the authority to use coercive force. Opponents of the law claim that it allows the AKP government to exploit this policing unit to form a loyal "paramilitary army recruited from an ignorant herd with only a degree of secondary education and no proper vocational training" (Zeynep Özen's speech in Türkiye Büyük Millet Meclisi, 2020a).

The watchmen's brutality is thus frequently attributed to their lack of education and vocational training in parliamentary debates. Watchmen receive significantly less vocational training (approximately 90 days) than other law enforcement forces, with only a few hours of courses on topics such as universal human rights and the domestic legal system. This insufficient training is seen as one of the primary reasons underlying watchmen's arbitrary acts of violence. It is, however, the question of general educational level that complicates the ways watchmen's social composition is profiled. According to the law and relevant regulations, the watchmen must be under the age of 30 and have at least a high school diploma or equivalent. Many opposition deputies warn about the dangers of distributing firearms to a group of poorly educated males in their twenties.

According to the National Police Department statistics, while the majority of watchmen are high school graduates, more than one-third have a college or university degree (including more than three hundred watchmen with a postgraduate degree). Based on these statistics, MHP deputy Ümit Yılmaz strongly opposes the label "ignorant herd" (Türkiye Büyük Millet Meclisi, 2020c). The opposition parties, however, emphasize that this rate is an indication of the government's disastrous economic policies, which have resulted in extremely high rates of unemployment among university graduates, rather than success in terms of recruitment policies. Figures by the Turkish Statistical Institute demonstrate that the youth unemployment rate is nearly 25%, while researchers estimate that the actual rate is as high as 40%, including those who are not actively looking for work out of desperation and are thus excluded from official statistics. Even more strikingly, the rate of youth unemployment among university graduates is the highest (28.3%). Several speeches by opposition party deputies point to these figures as the primary pull factor attracting young people to the public and private security sectors:

> In Turkey, there are three institutions you can go to find a job: you can be either a police officer, or a sergeant, or, with the last regulation, a watchman (...) 20 per cent [of the recently employed watchmen] are university graduates. We have established too many universities, overcrowded

them, and instead of offering [graduates] job opportunities, now we tell them to go and become a watchman.
ERKAN AYDIN'S speech in Türkiye Büyük Millet Meclisi, 2020c

As a result, the opposition's rhetoric on the social composition of the watchmen alternates between criminalizing and victimizing the urban poor. Watchmen are portrayed as either an ever-present and potentially violent band of uneducated, declassed young paupers easily organized into fascist stormtroopers by AKP, or as an average group of impoverished urban youth crushed, deprived, and misled by the AKP regime's failed policies. What manufactures these mutually exclusive attributes of agency and victim is the misleadingly isolated focus on who the watchmen are. Instead of looking for fixed sociological categories to profile them, we need to examine the social and political power relations within which they operate.

At this point, we can use the frequent mention of the historical German fascism as an opportunity to elaborate on the controversies over the watchmen's social composition-not necessarily to assume direct applicability to the Turkish case, but rather to provide a methodological template. While commenting on the watchmen's rampant acts of violence which began even before they were granted the new law's entitlements, Lütfü Türkkan (Türkiye Büyük Millet Meclisi, 2020b) draws a comparison between the SA forces and them:

> do you know what this bill on watchmen looks like? It looks like the 2020 version of the law enforcement [units] in Nazi Germany (...) In Hitler's Germany, the national socialists had a political militia that was notorious for acting brutally and inciting street brawls (...) They called them brownshirts (...) What we are witnessing now is the government's attempt to adapt Hitler's regime guardians wearing brownshirts to present days.

The social foundation of paramilitary violence and brutalization in politics is a familiar topic in debates on the class character of fascist mass movements, particularly in relation to the "lumpen" social origins and political tendencies of such paramilitary forces (Auerbach, 2019; Barrow, 2020; Hallas, 1985; Jones, 2019; Sewell, 2014). Historians of fascism affirm that many contemporaries—including Marxists—characterized the class composition of Nazi paramilitary forces as predominantly lumpen-proletarian. When we examine the references to the role of lumpenism in historical fascism both then and now, we see that the term "lumpen" can refer to a wide range of people, from gangsters and criminals, "the bands of mercenary thugs from the dregs of society," (Sewell,

2014) that is, the lumpen proper, to an indefinitely large segment of dispossessed, impoverished, and unemployed masses.

While this epithet can easily echo marginalization and criminalization of the paupers, the Marxist uses of the concept usually go beyond any fixed sociological category implying a certain layer of population, and signify a notion of lumpenization as a political *process* that shapes inter and intra-class *relations* (Dingiloğlu, 2022). Even when the term "lumpen" appears to refer to an indistinct group of "degenerated paupers" as the class base of fascist movements, Marxists are concerned with why and how certain proletarian (and petty-bourgeois) segments are marginalized and criminalized – "lumpenised", so to speak-rather than who the lumpen *is*. And lumpenization is seen as an outcome of the peculiar circumstances fabricated by the economic and political crisis of capitalism. The fascist movement organizes and mobilizes the frustration and despair among the petty bourgeoisie and impoverished proletariat as a result of widespread dispossession and unemployment, with the financial and political support of the ruling class. As Trotsky (1972: 6) contends: "Through the fascist agency, capitalism sets in motion the masses of the crazed petty bourgeoisie and the bands of declassed and demoralized lumpen proletariat—all the countless human beings whom finance capital itself has brought to desperation and frenzy".

Paramilitary organizations enlisting "crazed petty bourgeoises" and "declassed lumpen proletariat" are one instrument of this mobilization, which not only allows the fascist movement to broaden its social base but also serves the rule of capital in general. Just before the words quoted above, Trotksy (1972) makes the observation that fascism arrives at the moment when "the 'normal' police and military resources of the bourgeois dictatorship, together with their parliamentary screens, no longer suffice to hold society in a state of equilibrium". In his seminal work on fascism, Arthur Rosenberg (2012 [1934]: 152) similarly identifies "the peculiar tactic of using stormtroopers" as a specific characteristic of modern fascism, and refers to two overwhelming factors in diagnosing the conditions that make the instrumentalization of stormtroopers possible, if not necessary: firstly, the deepening social and political unrest which, albeit not forming "a state of open civil war" yet, do not allow normal conditions to prevail; consequently and secondly, "the complete disintegration of the normal state power" which prevents the state authorities and government from using "standard and regular state authorities against the opposition" (Rosenberg, 2012 [1934]: 153). When the state ceases to be the political "embodiment of the general, public interest" in the face of the legitimacy and authority crisis, ruling groups "begin to look around for other means" to "restore the legitimate authority (Rosenberg, 2012 [1934]: 153). This is the point where "the anger of the people", "the upright citizen who still believes in God, King, and Country" emerges as the social embodiment of public order. The "rage of the patriotic masses", of course, has to be manufactured and organized—otherwise, there would not have been a crisis (Rosenberg, 2012 [1934]: 153). It is carried out through, among other things, the extra-legal paramilitary forces which in many cases are converted into a sort of auxiliary police. Their arbitrary powers enhanced with legal vagueness is a symptom of this "disintegration of normal state power" as much as a deliberate design.

Rosenberg, too, confirms the lumpen character of these forces. The widespread acts of violence are perpetrated by the "hordes of professional criminals", that is, the lumpens proper, who are attracted to these forces due to the possibility of plundering with total impunity (Rosenberg, 2012 [1934]: 155). Nonetheless, Rosenberg emphasizes an additional source of recruits contributing to the brutality: "the powerful temptation for all impoverished individuals who had come down in the world to join the stormtroopers" stems from the fact that "as members of these fascist bands that were tolerated by the authorities, they were suddenly wrenched from being non-entities to becoming powerful elements in whose hands lay the fate of their fellow human beings" (Rosenberg, 2012 [1934]: 155).

The lumpen debate, as invoked by historical fascism's mass mobilization strategies, has illuminating implications for discussing the Turkish case of the watchmen system mainly in terms of the social composition of the watchmen and their possible deployments. While political profiling during the hiring process lends credence to the suspicion that Islamist and nationalist networks are embedded in the night watch system, it should not be overlooked that such coercive apparatuses are not merely an instrument to mobilize pre-existing loyalist reserves, but also to recruit or organize new ones. Given AKP's loss of support particularly among the well-educated urban working class and the liberal middle classes, it is reasonable to expect the AKP regime to rely more on "thugocracy" (à la Mohammadi; see Dabashi, 2010: 128) especially as regards the street mobilization against any popular dissent. Watchmen, as an armed force created for close surveillance and control of the streets, may thus exhibit lumpen character in many cases. However, it is more about the *lumpenising* effect of the night watch system on the impoverished groups through empowering them with access to discretionary power and arbitrary violence than it is about recruiting the already present "lumpen hordes." This process of mass lumpenization, when integrated into the "usual" modalities of police violence, actualizes the aforementioned dialectical process which generates both subjectivities and subjects of social control from laboring masses by, among other things, manipulating the rage of the impoverished into a fascist "politics of ressentiment". In relation to this particular point, it is animated by the economic and political crisis of the class rule as much as by deliberate designs of an authoritarian or fascist party, and thus operates within the larger context of the social and political regime of the rule of capital.

5 Conclusion

The reinstitution of the watchmen system represents the latest addition to a web of policing agencies mobilized for the fabrication of a violent police order characterized by the permanent deployment of discretionary violence against all forms of political dissent and marginalized populations. In this regard, the peculiar contribution of the night watch system to the police regime lies primarily in how the discretionary power is embodied and perpetrated as a form of a permanent state of emergency, which characterizes the tradition of the oppressed, as Benjamin reminds us.

The legally vague framework of the night watch system amplifies the formless power of the police to the extent that paves the way for the formation of a paramilitary force. Furthermore, their ambiguous position in the bureaucratic hierarchies of the security clusters and their recruitment based on political hiring with no proper vocational criterion or training places the watchmen among the "lowest of the low" –in terms of "professional" capacity and identity–while also equipping them with greater discretionary power in policing. The specific design of the night watch system strongly suggests that watchmen may become one of the mediums of brutalization of politics via lumpenised mass mobilization. This is the primary reason why this newly introduced policing agency should be viewed in the light of not only the fortification of the police state but also of the *fascistization* process in Turkey.

This approach would allow us to further elaborate on the implications of the watchmen for the regime debate in Turkey. Given the grounded assumptions about the erosion in AKP's bases of social and political power, as well as its urge to secure its own survival in power, it is reasonable to assume that the watchmen are intended to function as a party-militia in the service of the AKP regime. Their frequent deployment specifically against the political dissents of the Islamist-nationalist ruling bloc strongly confirms this assumption, too. However, the integration of "auxiliary" forces such as the watchmen and of the extreme-rightist networks organized as paramilitary groups into the security architecture may perform additional functions that are particularly relevant in organizing the racialized and gendered (anti-Kurdish, anti-immigrant, anti-feminist, and anti-proletarian) violence, which appears to be the global formula of the neofascist revivalism in the face of deepened proletarian marginalization. Therefore, the potential utilizations of the watchmen-and the renewed security regime in general-beyond the exclusive interests of an autocratic elite group, or the "one-man regime", need to be examined closer and further by the prospective studies, especially in terms of the violent mass mobilization that fabricates and organizes the "anger of the upright citizen" and the "rage of the dispossessed" against the citizenry and the dispossessed.

Bibliography

Ahwal News (2020) *Turkish Opposition Warns New Legislation Could Turn Watchmen Paramilitary Force.* Available (consulted July 4 2022) at: https://ahvalnews.com/security/turkish-opposition-warns-new-legislation-could-turn-watchmen-paramilitary-force.

Aktan I (2020) *Nóemi Lévy-Aksu: Bekçilere Silah Vermek İttihat ve Terakki'nin Fikriydi.* Available (consulted June 24 2022) at: https://www.gazeteduvar.com.tr/yazarlar/2020/02/02/noemi-levy-aksu-bekcilere-silah-vermek-ittihat-ve-terakkinin-fikriydi.

Aktaş AK and Karakaş KC (2023) *The Massive Death Toll from Turkey's Earthquake is No Natural Disaster.* Available (consulted February 28 2023) at: https://jacobin.com/2023/02/turkey-earthquake-disaster-relief-neoliberalism-erdogan.

Al Monitor (2020) *Turkey Rounds Up Scores of Citizens with Alleged Gulen Links.* Available (consulted July 4 2022) at: https://www.al-monitor.com/originals/2020/06/turkey-arrests-warrants-gulen-coup-erdogan-crackdown-feto.html.

Anadolu Ajansı (2019) *İçişleri Bakanı Soylu: 17–25 Aralık ve 15 Temmuz sonrası KHK ile 33 bin Kişi ihraç edildi.* Available (Consulted February 14 2023) at: https://www.aa.com.tr/tr/politika/icisleri-bakani-soylu-17-25-aralik-ve-15-temmuz-sonrasi-khk-ile-33-bin-kisi-ihrac-edildi/1591165.

Auerbach W (2019) *On the Lumpenproletariat: A Historical Reconstruction and a Conceptual Critique.* Available (consulted April 17 2021) at: https://mcmxix.org/2019/03/26/on-the-lumpenproletariat/#_ftnref105.

Auyero J (2000) *Poor People's Politics: Peronist Survival Networks and the Legacy of Evita.* Durham and London: Duke University Press.

Babacan E et al. (eds) (2021) *Regime Change in Turkey: Neoliberal Authoritarianism, Islamism, and Hegemony.* London and New York: Routledge.

Barrow CW (2020) *The Dangerous Class: The Concept of the Lumpenproletariat.* Michigan: University of Michigan Press.

Batuman B and Erkip F (2019) 'Night Hawks' watching over the city: Redeployment of nightwatchmen and the politics of public space in Turkey. *Space and Culture* 0(0): 1–14.

Bayat A (1997) *Street Politics: Poor People's Movement in Iran*. New York: Columbia University Press.

Baysal N (2021) *Bekçilik Sistemi Kamu Güvenliğine Tehdit Haline Gelmiştir*. Available (consulted August 02 2022) at: https://ahvalnews.com/tr/bekcilik-sistemi/bekcilik-sistemi-kamu-guvenligine-tehdit-haline-gelmistir.

Bedirhanoğlu P et al. (eds) (2020) *Turkey's New State in the Making: Transformations in Legality, Economy, and Coercion*. London: Zed Books.

Benjamin W (1999) *Selected Writings*, Volume 1, 2 and 3. Cambridge: Harvard University Press.

Berksoy B (2022) Apparatuses of denunciation, neoliberal governmental rationality, and the potential for a fascist turn: The Case of Turkey in the 2010s. *Comparative Studies of South Asia, Africa, and the Middle East* 42(1): 36–50.

Bianet (2021) *Bekçi Şiddeti Meclis Gündeminde*. Available at (consulted August 2 2022) at: https://m.bianet.org/bianet/siyaset/244121-bekci-siddeti-meclis-gundeminde.

Bonefeld W (1992) Social constitution and the form of the capitalist state. In: Bonefeld W et al. (eds) *Open Marxism: Dialectics and History*, Volume 1. Cambridge: Pluto Press, 93–132.

Boukalas C (2014) No exceptions: Authoritarian statism. Agamben, Poulantzas and Homeland Security. *Critical Studies on Terrorism* 7(1): 112–130.

Boukalas C (2015) Class war-on-terror: counterterrorism, accumulation, crisis. *Critical Studies on Terrorism* 8(1): 55–71.

Broszat M (2013) *The Hitler State: The Foundation and Development of the Internal Structure of the Third Reich*. New York: Routledge.

Bruff I (2014) The rise of authoritarian neoliberalism. *Rethinking Marxism* 26(1): 113–129.

Çelik A (2015) Turkey's new labor regime under the Justice and Development Party in the first decade of the twenty-first century: Authoritarian flexibilization. *Middle Eastern Studies* 51(4): 618–635.

Christie N (1986) Suitable enemies. In: Bianchi H and van Swaaningen R (eds) *Absolutism: Towards a Non-Repressive Approach to Crime*. Amsterdam: Free University Press, 42–54.

Clarke S (1991) *The State Debate*. London: Macmillan.

Dabashi H (2010) *Iran, the Green Movement and the USA*. London and New York: Zed Books.

Davis M (2006) *Planet of Slums*. London and New York: Verso.

Denning M (2010) Wageless life. *New Left Review* 66: 79–97.

Dingiloğlu S (2022) Sınıf, Ahlak ve Siyaset: Marx ve Engels'te Lümpen Kavramı. *Praksis* 58: 109–128.

Dölek Ç (2019) Thieves, kabadayis, and revolutionaries on the margin: A social history of the police in the Altındağ slums in Ankara, Turkey (1920s-1970s). Unpublished doctoral thesis, Carleton University, Ottawa, Canada.

Dölek Ç (2020) 'The law of the city?' Social war, urban warfare and dispossession on the margin. In: Bedirhanoğlu P et al. (eds) *Turkey's New State in the Making: Transformations in Legality, Economy and Coercion*. London: Zed Books, 276–294.

Dölek Ç and Rigakos G (2018) Private security work in Turkey: A case study of precarity, militarism, and alienation. *Critical Sociology* 0(0): 1–22.

Engels F (2008 [1892]) *The Condition of the Working Class in England in 1844*. New York: Cosimo.

Engin C (2015) LGBT in Turkey: Policies and experiences. *Social Sciences* 4(3): 838–858.

Eren M (2021) *'Uyuşturucu' Suçları 10 Yılda 7 Kat arttı*. Available (consulted June 22 2022) at: https://m.bianet.org/bianet/insan-haklari/253819-uyusturucu-suclari-10-yilda-7-kat-artti.

Farooq U (2022) *How Killing of Syrian Refugee Marks an Alarming Trend in Turkey*. Available (consulted on September 13, 2022) at: https://www.aljazeera.com/news/2022/1/12/turkey-news-log-jan-12.

Feuchtwanger EJ (1995) *From Weimar to Hitler: Germany, 1918–33*. London: Palgrave.

Fleck A (2022) *Europe's Most Heavily Policed Countries*. Available (consulted October 4 2022) at: https://www.statista.com/chart/16515/police-officers-per-100000-inhabitants-in-the-eu/.

Gönen Z (2016) *The Politics of the Crime in Turkey: Neoliberalism, Police, and the Urban Poor*. London: Bloomsbury Publishing.

Gönen Z (2020) The war on drugs: A view from Turkey. In: Bedirhanoğlu et al. (eds) *Turkey's New State in the Making: Transformations in Legality, Economy, and Coercion*. London: Zed Books, 260–275.

Gönen Z and Yonucu D (2011) Legitimizing violence and segregation: Neoliberal discourses on crime and criminalization of urban poor populations in Turkey. In: Bourke A et al. (eds) *Lumpen-City: Discourses of Marginality / Marginalizing Discourses*. Ottawa: Red Quill Press, 75–103.

Graham S (2009) Cities as battle space: The new military urbanism. *City* 13(4): 383–402.

Hall S et al. (eds) (1978) *Policing the Crisis: Mugging, the State, and Law and Order*. London and Basingstoke: Macmillan.

Hallas D (1985) *The Comintern*. London: Bookmarks.

Harvey D (2005) *A Brief History of Neoliberalism*. New York: Oxford University Press.

HRW (2022) *Combatting Domestic Violence in Turkey: The Deadly Impact of Failure to Protect*. Available (consulted September 16 2022) at: https://www.hrw.org/sites/default/files/media_2022/05/turkey0522_web.pdf.

Hülagü F (2020) Domesticating politics, de-gendering women: State violence against politically active women in Turkey. In: Bedirhanoğlu et al. (eds) *Turkey's New State in the Making: Transformations in Legality, Economy, and Coercion*. London: Zed Books, 245–259.

Hürriyet (2012) *Önce Bizi Yıkın!* Available (consulted June 23 2019) at: https://www.hurriyet.com.tr/ekonomi/once-bizi-yikin-21903189.

Hürriyet (2022) *Özel Güvenlik Görevlileri Gündemde*. Available (consulted September 23 2022) at: https://www.hurriyet.com.tr/yazarlar/dr-huseyin-h-serdar/ozel-guvenlik-gorevlileri-gundemde-42108020.

İçişleri Bakanlığı (2022) *Bakanımız Sn. Soylu: Kolluk kuvvetlerimize 350 bin kişilik bir güvenlik desteği sağlamayı hedefliyoruz*. Available (consulted October 1 2022) at: https://www.icisleri.gov.tr/bakanimiz-sn-soylu-kolluk-kuvvetlerimize-350-bin-kisilik-bir-guvenlik-destegi-saglamayi-hedefliyoruzIrdem I et al. (eds) (2020) *Güvenliğin Kurumsal Yönetiminde Destekleyici Polislik: Bekçilik Örneği (Rapor)*. Ankara: Polis Akademisi Yayınları.

İSİG (2023) *At least 1843 workers lost their lives in work-related murders in 2022*. Available (consulted February 22 2023) at: https://isigmeclisi.org/20828-at-least-1843-workers-lost-their-lives-in-work-related-murders-in-2022.

Işık A (2022) Turkish paramilitaries during the conflict with the Kurdistan Workers' Party PKK. *The Commentaries* 2(1): 1–11.

Jones M (2019) Foundation violence: Atrocities and the birth of German democracy. *Bulletin of German History* 65: 37–58.

Karaçimen E (2014) Financialization in Turkey: The case of consumer debt. *Journal of Balkan and Near Eastern Studies* 16(2): 161–180.

Karataşlı SS and Kumral S (2019) Capitalist development in hostile conjectures: War, dispossession, and class formation in Turkey. *Journal of Agrarian Change* 19(3): 528–543.

Kars Kaynar A (2018) Withering constitutional state? Recent 'Police State' discussions in Turkey. *Research and Policy on Turkey* 3(1): 90–102.

Kaygusuz O (2018) Authoritarian neoliberalism and regime security in Turkey: Moving to an 'Exceptional State' under AKP. *South European Society and Politics* 23(2): 281–302.

Kocabaş I (2020) *Bekçilere Verilen Yetkiler Kadınları Endişelendiriyor. Birgün*. Available (consulted on September 2, 2022) at: https://www.birgun.net/haber/bekcilere-verilen-yetkiler-kadinlari-endiselendiriyor-287129.

Manning P (1977) *Police work: the social organization of policing*. 2nd edition. Long Grove: Waveland Press.

Mercan BA and Şen M (2020) Advanced marginality and criminalization: The case of Altındağ. *Turkish Studies* 22(4): 603–635.

Neocleous M (2000) *The Fabrication of Social Order: A Critical Theory of Police Power*. London: Pluto Press.

Oğuz Ş (2020) Türkiye'de yedek işgücü ordusu ve farklı biçimleri: Hane halkı işgücü anketlerinden gözlemler, 2004–2013. *Praksis* 53: 141–170.

Resmi Gazete (2020) *Çarşı ve Mahalle Bekçileri Kanunu*. Available (Consulted February 14 2023) at: https://www.resmigazete.gov.tr/eskiler/2020/06/20200618-7.htm.

Rosenberg A (2012 [1934]) Fascism as a mass-movement. *Historical Materialism* 20(1): 144–189.

Şahin CE and Erol ME (eds) (2021) *The Condition of the Working Class in Turkey: Labor under Neoliberal Authoritarianism*. London: Pluto Press.

San S (2020) *Erdogan's Private Police Force: A New Blow to Turkish Democracy*. Available (consulted June 23 2022) at: https://www.opendemocracy.net/en/north-africa-west-asia/erdogans-private-police-force-a-new-blow-to-turkish-democracy/.

Schneider J and Susser I (2003) *Wounded Cities: Destruction and Reconstruction in a Globalized World*. Oxford and New York: BERG.

Seigel M (2018) Violence work: Policing and power. *Race & Class* 54(9): 15–33.

Sendika.org (2022) *İzmir'de Trans Kadınlara Polis ve Bekçi İşkencesine Karşı Açıklama*. Available (consulted June 17 2022) at: https://sendika.org/2022/07/izmirde-trans-kadinlara-polis-ve-bekci-iskencesine-karsi-aciklama-trans-kadinlara-baskinin-boyutu-acikca-iskenceye-vardi-661923/.

Sevinç M (2020) *Muhafazakar Semt Ahalisinin Bekçi Sorunu Var Mıdır?* Available (consulted June 4 2022) at: https://www.gazeteduvar.com.tr/yazarlar/2020/03/03/muhafazakar-semt-ahalisinin-bekci-sorunu-var-midir.

Sewell R (2014) *Germany from Revolution to Counter Revolution*. London: Wellred Books.

Sharma S (2017) *İstanbul Nightwatch: Guns Replace Kindly "Uncles" of Past*. Available (consulted 2 July 2022) at: https://www.middleeasteye.net/news/istanbul-night-watch-guns-replace-kindly-uncles-past.

Skolnick JH (1966) *Justice without Trial: Law Enforcement in Democratic Society*. New York: John Wiley and Sons, Inc.

soL (2019) *Seğmenler Parkına İçki Baskını: Artık Parklarda İçki Yasak*. Available (consulted June 17 2022) at: https://haber.sol.org.tr/turkiye/segmenler-parkina-bekci-baskini-artik-parklarda-icki-yasak-258322.

soL (2022) *Kadıköy'de 16 Yaşında Kız Çocuğu Önce Bekçiler Tarafından Taciz Edildi, Ardından Gözaltına Alındı*. Available (consulted June 17 2022) at: https://haber.sol.org.tr/haber/kadikoyde-16-yasindaki-kiz-cocugu-once-bekciler-tarafindan-taciz-edildi-ardindan-gozaltina.

Tar Y (2018) *Mahalle Bekçileriyle Birlikte Tehdit, Hakaret ve Şiddet Arttı*. Available (consulted June 22 2022) at: https://kaosgl.org/haber/mahalle-bekcileri-ile-tehdit-hakaret-ve-siddet-artti.

Topuz AD (2020) *Bekçi Baba 2: Önce Sopa Vardı*. Available (consulted June 17 2022) at: https://www.gazeteduvar.com.tr/yazarlar/2020/02/03/bekci-baba-2-once-sopa-vardi.

Trotsky L (1972) *Fascism: What It Is and How to Fight It*. New York: Pathfinder Press.

Tuğal C (2016) *In Turkey, the Regime Slides from Soft to Hard Totalitarianism*. Available (consulted July 10 2022) at: https://www.opendemocracy.net/en/turkey-hard-totalitarianism-erdogan-authoritarian/.

Türkiye Büyük Millet Meclisi (2020a) *İçişleri Komisyonu 2'nci Toplantı (28 Ocak 2020)*. Available (consulted June 2 2022) at: https://www5.tbmm.gov.tr/develop/owa/komisyon_tutanaklari.goruntule?pTutanakId=2493.

Türkiye Büyük Millet Meclisi (2020b) *Genel Kurul 93'ncü Birleşim (2 Haziran 2020)*. Available (consulted June 2 2022) at: https://www5.tbmm.gov.tr/tutanak/donem27/yil3/ham/b09301h.htm.

Türkiye Büyük Millet Meclisi (2020c) *Genel Kurul 94'ncü Birleşim (3 Haziran 2020)*. Available (consulted June 2 2022) at: https://www5.tbmm.gov.tr/tutanak/donem27/yil3/ham/b09401h.htm.

Türkiye Büyük Millet Meclisi (2020d) *Genel Kurul 97'nci Birleşim (10 Haziran 2020)*. Available (consulted June 2 2022) at: https://www5.tbmm.gov.tr/tutanak/donem27/yil3/ham/b09701h.htm.

Ünal-Reşitoğlu H and Altan B (2022) The role of criminal networks in involvement and progression in the drug market in Adana, Turkey. *Journal of Crime and Justice* 46(4): 1–15.

Üngör UU and Işık A (2021) Violence against the Kurds in the Turkish Republic. In: Jongerden J (ed.) *The Routledge Handbook on Contemporary Turkey*. London and New York: Routledge, 24–36.

Wacquant L (2008) *Urban Outcasts: A Comparative Sociology of Advanced Marginality*. Cambridge and Malden: Polity.

Wood EM (2003) *The Origin of Capitalism: A Longer View*. London: Verso.

Yarkın G (2022) Turkish racism against Kurds: Colonial violence, racist slurs, and mob attacks. *The Commentaries* 2(1): 77–90.

Yılmaz Z (2021) Turkey's regime transformation and its emerging police state: The judicialization of politics, everyday emergency, and marginalizing citizenship. In: Mackert J et al. (eds) *The Condition of Democracy: Contesting Citizenship*, Volume 2. London and New York: Routledge, 166–184.

Yonucu D (2022) *Police, Provocation, Politics: Counterinsurgency in İstanbul*. Ithaca: Cornell University Press.

Yücel Y and Kabalay B (2022) Suicidal economy of Turkey in time of crisis: 2018 crisis and beyond. *Critical Sociology* 0(0).

CHAPTER 8

In Search of the Labor Movement in Turkey
A Panoramic Review vis-à-vis the Gezi Uprising

Ezgi Pınar and Adem Yeşilyurt

In the heydays of the Gezi uprising in June 2013, Atatürk Cultural Center (Turkish: *Atatürk Kültür Merkezi,* AKM), which was then located at the entrance of Taksim Square in İstanbul, was fully decorated with various posters, banners, flags, and slogans. On the façade of AKM, the grotesque and eclectic panorama of the Gezi Park uprising could easily be recognized: On the one hand, the posters and slogans of the socialist movement seemed dominant, but there were also Turkish national flags and a poster of Mustafa Kemal Atatürk, the founder of the Republic. Some were calling for the resignation of then Prime Minister Recep Tayyip Erdoğan; others were calling for revolutionary struggle and socialism. In 2018, only a few years after this picture was engraved in the collective memory of the participants of the Gezi uprising, the historic AKM was demolished. In its place, the new Opera building decorated with Islamic motifs was opened in late 2021 with the initiative of the Justice and Development Party (Turkish: *Adalet ve Kalkınma Partisi,* AKP) as a symbolic sign of their resentment. On the other side of Taksim Square, opposite where AKM once stood, a magnificent mosque was built and opened to worship in 2021, symbolizing the victory of the ruling power. On one of the biggest posters at the façade of AKM during the Gezi days, there was a slogan written in bold, calling "Unions to duty for a general strike" (Turkish: *Sendikalar Göreve Genel Greve*). The only response to this demand was a one-day strike organized by the unions, to the disappointment of the protesters. The presence of the different fractions of labor and the organized labor movement during the Gezi movement was a hot and contentious topic even during the uprising. Based on an overview of this discussion, this chapter aims to provide a panoramic review of the labor movement in Turkey vis-à-vis the legacy of the Gezi uprising. Putting aside the discussions about the class character of the Gezi uprising, we argue that a labor-centered analysis of Gezi helps us to understand the labor politics in AKP's different periods and hence the situation of the labor movement today.

The Gezi uprising in 2013 has been a very significant moment in Turkish history for both the political regime and social movements. Its impact on the political scene in Turkey and whether it marks a shift towards an authoritarian regime have been discussed widely. "Authoritarian turn" (Babacan et al., 2021: 1–2) is the most prevalent discourse in analysing the recent political developments in Turkey and discussions on whether AKP's response to the Gezi uprising indicated such a turn is an important part of this discourse. According to the advocates of the "authoritarian turn" thesis, the rule of AKP can be divided into two periods. In this viewpoint, the first period is seen as a decade of political liberalization with the effects of the European Union anchor, and the second period, which is said to begin with the Gezi uprising, is argued to be an era of the gradual increase of authoritarianism ever since AKP turned to authoritarian policies. When we look from an institutional and security-centered perspective, authoritarian practices are more evident in the aftermath of the Gezi uprising. However, in this chapter, we, from a labor-centered perspective, will argue that it is more of a continuity rather than a rupture or turn in authoritarianism of AKP. We will be addressing the authoritarianization processes from the organized labor side by discussing the labor politics during the AKP governments and labor's reaction and position towards it. While doing so, the main focus of the chapter will be the link between the Gezi movement and organized labor, and AKP's labor containment strategies. In the face of the decline of working-class politics, and the lack of labor in the current dominant analyses of Turkish politics, it is valuable to engage with a labor-centered political economy perspective when looking at the historical and political crossroads. This perspective is very much inspired by the conceptualization and theorization of labor-centered development by Benjamin Selwyn, which is a critique and reversal of the political economy of capital. According to Selwyn (2016: 3), "the objective of the political economy of capital is to preclude the emergence of the political economy of labor, or at least to incorporate and neutralize it." The very emergence of capital, however, relies on labor as the Marxist labor theory of value suggests. Capital-centered and state-centered analyses would then always overlook the political economy of labor, which is not limited to the economic sphere but "is generated through laboring-class collective action and organization" (Selwyn, 2016: 3). Accordingly, political and social phenomena should also be analysed from the point of view of labor. Labor-centered approaches pay attention to labor as a social and political agent not only on the empirical ground but also at a theoretical and historical level. Analysing the Gezi uprising, a significant experience of historic value, from this point of view would contribute not only to the literature on the Gezi uprising but also to the aforementioned theoretical attempts.

For a labor-centered analysis of the Gezi uprising, we will first inquire into discussions of Gezi's class character and involvement of the organized labor movement in the uprising. By refusing the popular middle-class theses, we follow the Marxian class analytic approach of Gürcan and Peker (2015) who describe the catalyst of the Gezi Park protests as "an alliance of various wage-earning class fractions [...] led by service-sector employees and the educated youth, and comprised white- and blue-collar workers" (2015: 324). Despite the problems and challenges of proletarianization and authoritarian neoliberalism, we observed insufficient support for the Gezi Park events on the part of the organized labor movement. In this chapter, we examine this insufficient support of the organized labor movement to the Gezi uprising and the criticisms aimed at the role of traditional trade union organizations. We will also shed light on the newly emerging organizational capacities for labor based on the Gezi Park experience. It remains imperative to bridge discussions on the Gezi uprising to the labor movement and labor politics insofar as the Gezi uprising is seen as a turning point in the recent political history of Turkey.

Although the conclusion is the absence of a direct and explicit relationship, a labor-centered perspective can still enable us to discuss the labor movement with respect to the sociological and political legacy of the Gezi Park process. Adopting such a perspective renders the implications of the Gezi Park protests on the labor movement more visible and allows us to better observe, for instance, decision-making processes and organizational capacities during the occupations of spaces, spreading of pre-existing factory occupations, place-based organizations, and the case of neighbourhood forums,[1] etc. Although the organized labor movement could not function as leverage for the protests because of the insufficient support of their member base, it should be interpreted in line with the protracted authoritarian character of the labor regime during the successive AKP governments. Nevertheless, the legacy and the lived experience of the Gezi protests have lasting effects on the labor movement as we see in the strikes, actions, and new types of organizations.

Methodologically, our analysis of the labor movement vis-a-vis the Gezi uprising builds upon surveying the present literature, probing into the relevant statistical data regarding the worker unions as per the categories established by the Ministry of Labor and Social Security (Turkish: *Çalışma ve Sosyal Güvenlik Bakanlığı*, ÇSGB) and examining the controversial news articles on the subject matter. This chapter, therefore, constitutes an attempt to critically review and examine the existing material on the Gezi protests focusing

---

1 Gezi protesters established neighborhood forums in various cities. Street protests were eventually transformed into public meetings, gatherings, protests, solidarity events and other activities organized by neighborhood forums which represent "a new, but influential societal actor in Turkey's changing political climate" (Ergenç and Çelik, 2021: 1039).

on the labor movement. Our analysis concentrates on both the changing and unchanging characteristics of labor policies of the AKP governments, and the actions and reactions of the unionized labor, or lack thereof, against these policies since the onset of the Gezi uprising. While the history of authoritarian labor regimes in Turkey is not limited to the AKP rule, the successive series of AKP governments brought along a significant deepening of neoliberal authoritarianism. Even though the Gezi movement is mostly accepted as the moment of authoritarian turn, it is not plausible to conceive this moment as a radical turn from a labor-centered perspective (see Pınar, 2021). Revealing the historical background of the current condition and profile of labor in Turkey would allow us to expose both continuities and changes in the labor regime, which would, in turn, help us understand Gezi in a broader socio-economic context. As first argued by the Greek philosopher Parmenides of Elea, "nothing comes from nothing," and as the French chemist Antoine L. Lavoisier (1965) expanded on it, nothing becomes nothing but only changes; as such, we believe that the legacy and remainders of the Gezi movement can still be sought within the society. This heritage may not be currently noticeable at first sight, but it still is worth investigating.

1 An Inquiry into the Class Character of the Gezi Uprising

The questioning of the labor movement brings us to the discussion of the class character of the Gezi Park protesters. Up until now, the Gezi Park protests, and the class identity of the protesters, have been problematized from various theoretical perspectives (cf. Boratav, 2013a; Göztepe, 2013; Keyder, 2013; Tonak, 2013; Tuğal, 2013; Öngen, 2014; Gürcan and Peker, 2015; Özden and Bekmen, 2015; Yörük and Yüksel, 2015). Some have conceptualized Gezi as a collective working-class action against neoliberalism while others conversely described it as a middle-class revolt. Some have even argued that Gezi was an exclusively ideological uprising of the secularist social segments while others have simply attributed Gezi's emergence to the popular discontent of the so-called Generation Y in the face of the conservative interventions to their lifestyles. From a labor-centered political economy perspective, the class characteristics of the participants of the Gezi uprising have been a hot topic both during and after the Gezi Park protests. Even among Marxist scholars, there exist critical nuances. For some Marxists, the Gezi uprising was a movement of workers but not entirely a working-class movement. Yet, Gezi has been conceived to be a full-fledged wage-labor movement and predominantly a working-class movement at the same time for others. What is crucial in this regard is the shared experience of rising precariousness during AKP's neoliberal authoritarian era. The rising proletarianization of white-collar professionals such as doctors, engineers, and lawyers exemplifies the precarity in contrast to middle-class theses. Herein, we discuss different interpretations of the role of class in the Gezi Park protests in detail with reference to the studies in the relevant literature.

There exist three prevalent lines of thought in the currently available literature regarding the class characteristics of the Gezi movement (Yörük and Yüksel, 2015: 136). First and foremost, the Gezi movement is considered a (new) middle-class revolt against the conservative politics of AKP. One of the pioneers of this line of thought was Çağlar Keyder. For Keyder, Gezi protests were mainly composed of new middle classes, which represent the highly educated intellectual labor in urban centers who are relatively autonomous from the employers (Keyder, 2013: 1). While Tuğal (2013) also defines the Gezi Resistance as "an occasionally multi-class, but a predominantly middle-class movement" in which "generously paid professionals" constitutes the core of the participants, Yardımcı-Geyikçi (2014) links the protests of the urban middle class with their representation problem in the party politics. In line with Keyder and Tuğal, Wacquant (2014), in his oration at Boğaziçi University, defines the Gezi Park protesters as "the new cultural bourgeoisie of intellectuals, urban professionals, the urban middle class, rising to assert the rights of cultural capital". Gürcan and Peker (2015: 323) rightly challenge Wacquant's argumentation as Wacquant's culture-oriented analysis reduces the Gezi movement to Gezi Park in Taksim and overlooks the counter-hegemonic nature of the protests across the country. The second line of thought underlines the role of the working classes with different degrees. For instance, Boratav (2013a: 15) argues that the Gezi resistance represents "a matured class-based uprising" of the working class against the so-called middle-class tributes. In addition, Tonak (2013: 28) employs a larger definition of working classes by introducing the criterion of whether the people in question are in a position to sell their labor power for their livelihood or not, and includes potential workers, students, the unemployed, and even retirees in his analysis. For Yıldızoğlu (2013: 62), Gezi protesters were mainly based on a new fraction of the proletariat, notable for its effective labor and employment within the sectors of information and communication technologies. The third and last line of thought emphasizes the multitude of disorganized subjects. Following Michael Hardt's conceptualization of multitude to examine the Gezi uprising (Semercioğlu and Ayyıldız, 2014), Yörük and Yüksel (2014: 122) do not consider class as an explanatory variable for the Gezi protesters and instead characterize Gezi as a "popular movement driven by political demands, in which all social classes participated proportionally" against the authoritarian and conservative policies of the government. Yörük and Yüksel (2015: 159), therefore, argue that most of the Gezi protesters come from a proletarian background even though most of the middle-class members of the society participated in the protests. They conclude that the Gezi protests were not motivated by class-based demands, but rather by political demands that brought together all the classes for anti-government protests (Yörük and Yüksel, 2015: 165).

The above-mentioned three lines of thought differ significantly from each other. The discussions and attempts associated with these positions to define the class content of the protests are beyond the scope of this chapter. Nonetheless, there is a contention commonly shared by all these positions, that is, the visibility of the white-collar precarious workers and professionals. Also, for Özatalay (2014: 183), the only socio-economic category relatively less affected by cultural and generational differences with a significant prevalence in the Gezi resistance was the white-collar "service class" composed of managers, professionals, and workers. It was also possible to observe their organizational presence in Gezi Park. Informally established white-collar worker organizations such as the Platform for Plaza Action (Turkish: *Plaza Eylem Platformu*) and the Flight to Join Us (Turkish: *Kaç Bize Gel*) were actively involved in the protests during and after the Gezi uprising. As demonstrated by Begüm Özden Fırat (2021), perhaps the most significant aspect of the Gezi uprising was hidden in the various encounters it provided for different segments of society. Those of different classes, identities, ethnicities, etc. came together at Gezi Park and experienced a way of living together in the Gezi commune. In the action repertoire of the Gezi uprisings, we observe street art and protest graffiti, social media engagement, street demonstrations, occupation of spaces, and establishment of neighbourhood forums for democratic decision-making processes. In fact, even years after the Gezi Park protests in 2013, neighbourhood forums, such as those in Ankara, were still active as a commoning practice (see: Ergenç and Çelik, 2021). We believe the occupation of parks, factories, workplaces, and other public spaces, along with the formation of forums, are in line with the memory of the working-class movement and were therefore also used widely in the post-Gezi period by the labor movement.

Gezi has been discussed with its potential for its contribution to, and/or impact on, a radical political change that would mean democratization of Turkey. Democratization is the other side of the coin, the political opposite of authoritarianism. The question is who the possible actors, carriers of the democratization processes, would be. Hence, the representative capacity of the movement, as well as the social segments involved in the Gezi uprising, become relevant to the debates around both democratization and authoritarianism.

Following this, to what extent the laboring classes, specifically the low-wage and unskilled segments of labor who had joined or supported Gezi, becomes a concern of not only scholarly but also political nature. Drawing inspiration from the above discussions on the class character of the Gezi Park protests, the labor-centered political economy perspective puts forward the social power of labor, which may in return eliminate some of the drawbacks in the previous debates on the Gezi uprising.

2 The Question of "Strike Flop" and the Role of the Organized Labor Movement

The one-day strike of the trade unions during the Gezi protests on June 17, 2013, was met with disappointment because of the low level of participation and the organizational weakness of the trade unions. One news piece headlined "The 'Gezi strike' flop of the trade unions!" by a pro-government online media outlet in Turkey even mocked the general strike of the organized labor movement (İnternethaber, 2013). While five large labor organizations were calling for a general strike, the news poked fun at the low participation rate by arguing that only the "masters/chiefs" of the trade unions participated in the strike. Two days later, one of the prominent columnists of the so-called "pool media", a term used to indicate the pro-government media allegedly financed by AKP (Bulut and Karlıdağ, 2016: 17–18; Irak, 2016: 9–10), wrote about the same issue under the title of "Strike flop" and criticized the devaluation of the importance of the general strike to "a symbolic support action to the little-bourgeoisie uprising at Taksim" (Ardıç, 2013). We are aware of the fact that these are prejudiced and malignant news and opinions in line with defamation campaigns targeting the political opposition in Turkey. Pro-government media outlets took advantage of the situation that arises from the case of trade unions and the self-criticism of the Gezi protesters. Therefore, we need to question the basis of their arguments to examine the labor movement vis-à-vis the Gezi uprising.

Although there are various sociological analyses and survey studies on the participants of the Gezi Park protests which will be analysed below, there is little evidence of the participation of the different segments of the laboring classes in the uprising and the neighbourhood forums that were formed following the protests. Among the constituents of the Taksim Solidarity (Turkish: *Taksim Dayanışması*) are two trade union confederations and several professional chambers, including those of engineers, architects, and physicians. Said trade confederations are the Confederation of Public Employees' Trade Unions (Turkish: *Kamu Emekçileri Sendikaları Konfederasyonu*, KESK) and the Confederation of Progressive Trade Unions of Turkey (Turkish: *Türkiye Devrimci İşçi Sendikaları Konfederasyonu*, DİSK). The rest, significantly HAK-İŞ Trade Union Confederation (Turkish: *Hak İşçi Sendikaları Konfederasyonu*, HAK-iş) and also the Confederation of Turkish Trade Unions (Turkish: *Türkiye İşçi Sendikaları Konfederasyonu*, TÜRK-İŞ), shared the same discourse with the government regarding the Gezi movement (Erdinç, 2014:168). DİSK and KESK organized a work stoppage and a protest march to Gezi Park on the 4th and 5th of June 2013 (Tekgıda-İş Sendikası, 2013; Cumhuriyet, 2013a). From the beginning of the Gezi uprising, there was a demand for a general strike from trade unions to accelerate the social and political impact of the uprising. However, these confederations could not meet this demand, which was also one of the reasons why these unions were accused of not taking an active role during the Gezi movement (Gazetenisan, 2013; Alçın, 2013). They organized the one-day strike (Dünya, 2013; Cumhuriyet, 2013b), but the strike remained merely a protest march, to which the participation was limited, as a result of DİSK's failure to mobilize their members (Milliyet, 2013).

Besides its impact on the general political atmosphere, Gezi has generally been discussed from within sociological (cf. Yörük and Yüksel, 2015; Tonak, 2013) and, in particular, urban-sociological perspectives (cf. Alonso, 2015; Gümüş and Yılmaz, 2015; Karasulu, 2015). There are also various surveys on the class origin and social profile of the participants (see KONDA, 2013; 2014 and GENAR, 2013). These surveys show that the protesters were of various wage-earning classes and shared the common experience of working under precarious conditions. Gürcan and Peker (2015: 329) also draws attention to the class locations of the protesters in the KONDA (2013) and GENAR (2013) surveys, respectively as wage-earners (52% and 53.8%), students (37% and 24.1%) and unemployed (6% and 10.8%). This objective condition of precariousness and the accompanying sentiments are not only a matter of current socio-economic life but also involve protesters' concerns for their future due to the economic ambiguity under the AKP government. According to the KONDA survey (2014: 9), the majority of the participants in Gezi were senior university students, new graduates, and new employees in the job market. In fact, half of the Gezi participants had a university degree while this is only the case for a tenth of the Turkish population (KONDA, 2014: 10).

In addition to the class origins and social profile of the participants, the motivation of the Gezi protesters also varies. The leading reason for those who partook in the protests was the perceived lack of freedom. Others cited they joined the protests because they were against violations of rights and dictatorship (KONDA, 2014: 19). It is apparent that anti-authoritarianism constituted the essence of the Gezi uprising. Looking at the demands and the program of the Taksim Solidarity, the leading actor of the Gezi movement, one cannot easily depict it as a totally working-class movement (Arslan, 2013; Öztaşkın, 2013). Although DİSK and KESK were supporting the Gezi uprising at the discursive level, even the mobilization of their members to the movement was very limited and they were accused of failing to act as leverage for the movement in general. We argue that the weak link between the large majority of the traditional working-class population and the Gezi protesters is an outcome of a protracted authoritarian labor regime. This definition of the labor regime is inspired by Özden et al.'s (2017: 202) analysis of the political regime in Turkey. The political regime in Turkey, albeit with ongoing political and economic crises, maintains itself with further authoritarian measures. Similarly, an authoritarian labor regime is maintained in Turkey by responding to the crisis and capital accumulation strategies of the power bloc (cf. Bozkurt-Güngen, 2018). For instance, following the 2008 financial crisis, there arose the need for a new accumulation strategy (Akçay, 2015) which would bring about changes in labor politics that would be increasingly effective in the post-2012 period (Akçay, 2018). This trend would only continue to intensify with the declaration of a state of emergency against the attempted coup d'état on July 15, 2016. The attempt was seen as a "gift from God" by the AKP government, to which Erdoğan himself admitted (Şık, 2016); as such, the failed coup attempt facilitated a surge in the magnitude and prevalence of state violence and rising authoritarian measures under the pretense of fighting against the coup plotters.

This trend goes hand in hand with the decreasing unionization rate since 1980. Yet it changes with the pro-government unionization trend increasingly after the coup attempt in 2016. A recent report by DİSK (2020) puts forward that from 2013 to 2020, the increase in the number of members of HAK-İŞ was about 300%, while it is 44% for TÜRK-İŞ and 84% for DİSK. When we look at the statistics during the Gezi movement, we see a rate of 6.3% trade union density in 2013, and a differentiated distribution of unionization (OECD.Stat). For instance, when we look at the distribution of workers within the trade union confederations, we see that DİSK, which is one of the constituents of the Taksim Solidarity and openly supported the Gezi movement, comprised only 11% of unionized workers in 2013. In the same year, 71% of the unionized workers were members of TÜRK-İŞ, followed by 16% in HAK-İŞ and 3% in independent trade unions (T.C. Çalışma ve Sosyal Güvenlik Bakanlığı, n.d.a).

In their work in which they compare the labor movements in Brazil and Turkey, Özden and Bekmen (2015) argue that the initiative and impact of the labor movement were limited in the Gezi uprising and that trade unions were ineffective during the uprising in 2013. Kaygısız (2014:118–119) notes that there was an increase in labor protests in 2013; and further states that almost every single day workers in a workplace took action which often lasted for a long time (2014: 118–119).[2] Especially DİSK and its affiliated unions initiated widespread action in various regions of the country during this period (Kaygısız, 2014: 118–119). This tendency can be observed from the data presented by the Ministry of Labor and Social Security Working Life Statistics Strikes and Lockouts by Years. According to this dataset (T.C. Çalışma ve Sosyal Güvenlik Bakanlığı, n.d.b). There is a dramatic increase both in the number of workers involved in strikes and, also, in the lost working days due to strikes. The number of strikes in 2013, which amounted to 16632, is almost twenty times more than those in 2012 and the days lost due to strikes in 2013, which were registered as a total of 307,894 days, is nine times more than those in 2012. Although there was seemingly no direct and organic link between the Gezi uprising and the organized labor movement, the spirit of the protests appeared to have had a positive impact on the motivation for protests among the workers. Indeed, there were various prominent struggles in the post-Gezi periods such as the 2013 Turkish Airlines (Turkish: *Türk Hava Yolları*, THY) strike in multiple cities, especially in İstanbul at around the same times as Gezi, the 2014 Greif strike and occupation in İstanbul, the 2014 Yatağan resistance in Mugla, the 2015 "metal storm" mainly in Bursa and the surrounding region, and the 2018 Flormar resistance in Kocaeli (Gürler, 2021: 325). The occupation was a frequently used action in different labor protests along with the formation of councils and workplace democracy (Gürler, 2021: 325). Although the Gezi uprising and the associated organizational experience brought about critiques towards traditional trade union organizations in the face of their passiveness, the lived experience and the legacy of the Gezi protests became observable in the following periods.

3   Dissolution and Recomposition of the Organized Labor in Progress

Dissolution of labor corresponds to a globally valid paradigm shift in industrial relations and in the balance of power relations between labor and capital. The impoverishment of labor, the erosion of its organizational capacity and the diminishing of its collective power (Pınar, 2021: 33–36) have been an

---

2   The suspension of collective agreements in 2012, as per the Law No. 6356 on Trade Unions and Collective Bargaining Agreement came into force on November 7, 2012. Pursuant to this, hundreds of thousands of workers in hundreds of workplaces simultaneously carried out collective bargaining in 2013. Another reason for the increase in the protests in 2013 was the resumption of the government's work on the law, especially the severance pay, which would deeply affect the working life (Kaygısız, 2014: 115).

ever-increasing international trend due to the neoliberalization of labor markets. In Turkey too, changes in the labor politics and organizational power of the laboring masses have been in line with this trend. Especially from the 1980s onwards, the new legislations and regulations governing trade unions, collective agreements and strikes rebalanced capital-labor relations to the detriment of the laboring classes. During this time, the organizational capacity of the working class was further corroded by the adoption of new flexible modes of production, with flexible work hours and precarious forms of employment, all of which resulted in the segmentation of the working class in itself. In short, the question of new forms of labor organizations and resistance strategies vis-à-vis the increasingly authoritarian and populist labor containment strategies has since the 1980s been on the agenda. Resituating Gezi into this wider context of the neoliberal authoritarian transformation of industrial relations, Boratav (2013b), Öngen (2014: 9–10) and a number of others (cf. Tonak, 2013), underlined the working-class character of the uprising and understood Gezi as a reaction to rising precarity. However, the admitted motivations and objectives of those who partook in the Gezi uprising, as well as their socio-economic profiles, seem in discord with such analyses. In the words of Oğuz and Ercan (2015: 114):

> The uprising was unexpected, not in the sense of a lack of previous struggles leading up to May 2013, but in the sense that the various types and fields of social struggle (such as those by public employees, professionals, students, feminist and ecological movements) came together for the first time. However, certain sections of the working class, especially industrial labor, remained politically underrepresented among the Gezi protesters. This was a result of how the neoliberal policies advanced under the AKP rule disorganised the working classes through deunionisation, low wages, precarisation, intensification of workloads, erosion of social benefits and increasing workers' debts.

Coşkun (2019: 77) also argues that AKP was still a popular political option among the laboring classes even if the party's power and hegemony had weakened during the Gezi uprising. Gezi was a moment of both weakness and strength for the government. When the social and political crisis deepened, the government began to increase the usage of the repressive apparatuses of the state. The harsh attitude of the government against all kinds of social opposition after the Gezi process induced a sense of fear among the public and a general state of indifference to workers' calls for solidarity, which in turn resulted in the deterioration of labor as a political actor. For instance, Yatağan Thermal

Power Plant (Turkish: *Yatağan Termik Santrali*) workers were in a long-lasting struggle against the power plant's privatization since September 2013; however, the increased pressure by the government after the Gezi uprising, when coupled with the effective silence of the TÜRK-İŞ and the lack of support from the local people, impeded the Yatağan protests from growing larger (Eren, 2019: 2654).

The hegemonic power of AKP, over which was a broad social consensus, was shaken during the months-lasting Gezi days despite AKP's continued attempts to retain political power by adopting different political strategies and calling in the aid of various political partners. A result of this was not merely the sustenance but further advancement of the authoritarian labor regime in Turkey, which was inherited by the AKP government from the new right tradition in Turkey. Since its first term, AKP has been known for its success in establishing both intra-class and inter-class alliances. The formation of interclass alliances by the AKP governments was not achieved through addressing the laboring classes per se but through its focus on the masses, both the poor and the subaltern. Social welfare and its reorganization had a significant place in the discourse and the policy agenda of AKP without direct reference to the laboring classes, which had lost their acquired rights and political ability to defend these rights with the 1980 coup d'état. In fact, at the end of the 1970s, the working-class movement was strong enough to defend workers' interests against those of the capitalist classes in Turkey. Furthermore, the late 1970s marked a period of hegemonic crisis for the ruling classes when workers' social opposition was robust owing to the organizational power of the working class. The 1980 coup d'état, which widely targeted organized segments of society, including trade unions, was a milestone in Turkish labor history and the making of an authoritarian state (see: Margulies and Yıldızoğlu, 1984; Boratav, 2008). The institutional power and the heritage of such labor organizations were curbed down afterward, either directly or indirectly.

Neoliberal labor politics and legislation aimed for the dissolution of organized labor and derived its strength from de-unionization. By 2008, the rate of trade unionization in Turkey had decreased to 6.51%, resulting in trade unions having no effective power in processes such as collective bargaining and collective agreement (Şafak, 2009). According to International Labor Organization (ILO) statistics, Turkey ranked 85th out of 104 countries in terms of unionization in 2016 (ILOSTAT n.d.a). Concerning collective bargaining coverage, Turkey, with a rate of 5.9%, ranked 72nd out of 85 countries in 2016 (ILOSTAT, n.d.b). In addition to low unionization rates, as Gürcan and Peker (2015: 329) already point out, structural capacities of the labor decline because of rising unemployment, privatizations, sub-contracting, outsourcing, and contract manufacturing. Furthermore, de-unionization during the neoliberal restructuring of the labor market in Turkey was accompanied by a gradual decrease in real wages. One significant indicator of the weakening of labor rights and the labor movement, in general, is the share of labor in the national income. A joint report by ILO and the Organisation for Economic Co-operation and Development (OECD) in 2015 points to a tendency of decline in the labor share of national income all around the world, in a time period from 1990 to 2009 (OECD, 2015: 3). The same report also indicates that this decline is more pronounced in developing countries than in advanced capitalist countries; indeed, of all the countries in the report, Turkey is demonstrated to have had the largest rate of decline over the period of 1995 to 2012 (OECD, 2015: 6). Reports also show that there were always prolonged structural problems with the Turkish labor market (World Bank, 2006: ii-ix) such as unemployment, especially among the youth and the educated labor reserve, the size of the informal economy, inefficiency, low technology and inability to create jobs (see also Yeldan, 2007:14). In a low-tech industrial setting, labor-intensive employment strategies are common; accordingly, such strategies were employed by the AKP governments for years as the main capital accumulation strategy. In Turkey, the ratio of labor income to national income was in an accelerated decline since 1999 and it was calculated to be at 47.67% in 2017 (Duman, 2019: 353). According to the latest data provided by ILOSTAT Explorer (n.d.c), Turkey ranked 153rd among 178 countries with 39.2% labor income share in GDP. While Switzerland is at the top of the list with 68.8%, Turkey is followed by such countries as Sri Lanka and the Syrian Arab Republic with 38.9% (ILOSTAT Explorer, n.d.c). Along with the accumulation strategies that brought about the aforementioned rates, in line with Weyland's arguments (1999: 389), the capacity of trade unions was also reduced by governmental regulations that made "labor laws more flexible" and undermined "unions' financial sustenance, and fomenting divisions in their midst".

May (2006: 94) argues that the management of employment was a key issue of social policies in industrialized societies with welfare systems, where wage workers receive most benefits and legally protected social provisions. In Turkey, the opposite seems to be true at an ever-increasing level as employment becomes even more irregular, flexible and insecure. The employee, who is entitled to certain individual and collective labor rights, vanishes from the policy agenda. Moreover, the precarious structure of the labor market and the financialization of daily life have been forcing workers to depend more on credit to sustain their income. Debt has a disciplining effect and pressures workers into incorporating existing uneven labor relations. Debt is considered one indicator of an authoritarian labor regime together, among such other indicators as low wages and a high proportion of the unemployed or underemployed labor force (Anner, 2015: 3). As a matter of fact, Anner stresses that precarious and vulnerable conditions facilitate disciplining and exercising control over labor. An important step in the precarization of labor in Turkey was the inauguration of a new Labor Act in 2003, followed by various regulations such as the Employment Packet (Law No. 5763) in 2008 and the National Employment Strategy in 2014.[3] In a flexible and precarious labor market, the indebted worker consents to longer work hours, lower wages, compulsory unpaid leaves, and hard-working conditions (Karaçimen, 2015: 753). These factors solidified the de-unionization tendency among labor that had already faced "combined effect of trade liberalization, financialization, and privatization in the first decade of the 2000s" (Gürcan and Mete, 2018: 13).

In addition, while in debt, laborers become more and more subordinate to the government and existing power relations as the subjects of authoritarian populist politics. Clientelist and paternalist social policies in the form of political Islamist welfare politics of the AKP have substituted the labor politics based on individual labor rights and the collective bargaining power of trade unions. This transformation, to put it in Gramscian terms, does not "allow different segments of the working class to transcend their economic-corporate moments on the basis of the solidarity of interests, albeit in the purely economic field" (Yalman and Topal, 2019: 4) and instead prevents the working class from forging their interests into a (national) political moment.

Neoliberalization of the labor market together with the post-Fordist production regime and accumulation strategy is the fundamental impetus behind the reconfiguration of the relations of capital and labor. This new regime of labor relations labormarked by the increasing capital mobility, high-levels of mechanization and decreasing wages or shift of production to the low-wage countres, also came to mean the abolishment of traditional corporatist relations between trade unions and capital organizations on the one hand, and the limited democratic participation and control of labor on the other (Tauss, 2012: 57). Although the paths of neoliberal reconfiguration may differ between core and peripheral countries, "work in the global era is characterized by rising insecurity, increased intensification, more flexible organizational forms, and altered power relations between employers and employees" (Bandelj et al., 2011: 808). These global developments together

---

3   These new regulations concerning the labor market coincide with the outlined periodization of the AKP. They are attempts to maintain the party's hegemony, which also requires the stability of the processes of capital accumulation and needs to meet the interests of the Turkish internationalized bourgeoisie.

form the structural dimension of the diminishing of the labor class as a collective social actor in politics. While the collective power of the laboring classes and the trade unions waned, atomization and isolation of labor became the main tendency within labor relations. As Clua-Losada and Ribera-Almandoz (2017: 30) put forth in their work on the authoritarian neoliberalization of labor relations in Spain:

> Authoritarian neoliberalism deepens the isolation effect in labor relations by further individualizing labor laws and weakening collective bargaining processes and institutions. A key characteristic of this isolation effect on labor has been the clear erosion of collective bargaining systems and labor legislation.

De-unionization has long been a significant strategy of the labor management by the AKP governments. AKP carried out the legacy of authoritarian measures of the labor regime following the 1980 coup d'état which gradually led to changes in the composition of trade unions and confederations. In 2012, the *Law on Trade Unions and Collective Bargaining Agreements No. 6356* was enacted, easing the process of forming a trade union and increasing trade union membership. The law empowered administrative committees within the trade unions and thus provided the legal basis for strengthening pro-AKP trade unions (BSB, 2015: 70) or, in rather general terms, collaborationist unionism (Gürcan and Mete, 2018: 9). The law brought about both increased de-unionization and corporatist tendencies in trade unionism. New legislation governing threshold and sector-wise regulations, which went into effect on the eve of Gezi, served to overcome the dominance of TÜRK-İŞ among unionized labor in Turkey and paved the way for the empowerment of HAK-İŞ supported by both the government and employers' associations ran by the Islamist bourgeoisie (Çelik, 2012).

With all these authoritarian neoliberal measures effectuated, the power balance between labor and capital drastically favoured capital even before the onset of the Gezi uprising. In the period that led up to Gezi, labor in Turkey was besieged by conditions of precarious and low-waged employment, daily life in debt, a decrease in its organizational capacity, and containment strategies such as paternalism and corporatism. In the aftermath of the Gezi uprising, the labor movement continued to suffer from worsening conditions, especially with such blows as the 2016 coup d'état attempt, which served to rationalize the nationwide state of emergency imposed by AKP, and the recent COVID-19 pandemic, which similarly restricted labor in the workplace and elsewhere. In his report on labor's collective rights under the regime of the state of emergency and afterwards with the pandemic, Koçak (2021) shows us various rights violations in different lines of business and cases, particularly with respect to the right to work, protection against anti-union discrimination, right to strike, freedom of assembly and association. And Odman et al. (2021) keep an account of the labor rights violations during the pandemic lockdowns and afterwards. In their case-by-case analysis, they demonstrate different faces of authoritarian pressures by taking advantage of the state of emergency and the pandemic.

4 Concluding Remarks and Further Issues under Pandemic Conditions

In this chapter, we examined the relationship between the organized labor movement and the Gezi Park protesters. More particularly, we assumed a historical viewpoint to shed light on the sociological and political legacy of the Gezi Park protests, with particular respect to the labor movement. From a labor-centered political economy perspective, we defend that Gezi does not constitute a historical turning point for the political regime but rather points to a continuation of authoritarianism. Despite our criticism of the lack of sufficient involvement of the organized labor movement in the Gezi uprising, we also noted several lasting impacts of the latter on the former. Prefigurative politics (Ertuğrul, 2022: 224), as in the case of the establishment and continuation of neighbourhood forums, have had a lasting effect on the labor movement in the post-Gezi period. We observe the emergence and proliferation of new place-based worker organizations, which differ from the traditional working-class unions, and aim to organize white-collar workers, in particular.

Labor and the labor movement have confronted two different crises in the last few years. The nationwide state of emergency over the period of 2016 to 2018 in the aftermath of the coup attempt on July 15, 2016, and the recent pandemic crisis since the beginning of 2020 have resulted in severe rights violations and the banning of strikes and further worsened economic conditions of labor with rising levels of precarization and unemployment. During the state of emergency, for instance, the İstanbul Airport strike was conspicuous for the police brutalism and long detention periods the workers and unionists faced. The negative economic effects of the pandemic were cemented by the irrational economic policies of the government; consequently, the official annual inflation rate was above 84.39% in November 2022 according to the Turkish Statistical Institute (TÜİK, 2022a). As a Turkish government agency attached to the Ministry of Treasury and Finance, it has published suspicious statistical data in recent years. In the same month, the Inflation Research Group (Turkish: *Enflasyon Araştırma Grubu*, ENAGrup), composed of independent academics, announced the annual inflation rate as 170.70%, slightly more than twice the official data (Duvar English, 2022). The so-called "middle-classes" almost disappeared from the Turkish socio-economic context with ever-increasing precarization and a decrease in purchasing power. The discontent in the society became widespread cutting across different segments of the working society. The containment of labor became a much more crucial and difficult question for the AKP government under the conditions of such a socio-economic crisis. Additionally, Turkey has been under a currency crisis since August 2018 and the situation was only exacerbated during the COVID-19 pandemic. At the time we penned this chapter, the national minimum wage per month in Turkey decreased to around $250 per month towards the end of 2022 with the depreciation of the Turkish lira and it has been increased to $455 in January 2023 by means of a 55% in previous six months and a 100% hike in the last year (Reuters, 2022). The youth unemployment rate has risen to 26.1% in June 2020 during the first peak periods of the pandemic (TÜİK, 2020) and currently remains at 17.8% in November 2022 (TÜİK, 2022b). Consequently, the demand for employment in delivery jobs has significantly risen, particularly in the grocery and food delivery sectors during this time. Companies in these sectors adopted the model of uberization, by hiring individual couriers with precarious conditions, which contrasted with the conditions of traditional full-time and part-time employment. The dissatisfaction and resentment of couriers peaked in early 2022 and culminated in mass protests of motorcycle couriers in the streets and on social media. In response, trade unions organized several strikes in the delivery sector. Although there were some notable success stories in a few companies, most of the companies preferred to turn a blind eye to the ongoing actions and demands of their employees. As was the case with the Gezi uprising, these mass actions and protests were not originally mobilized by organized trade unions. Instead, it was the workers themselves who first occupied the workplaces, as well as the headquarters of delivery companies, even before the involvement of the trade unions and, as with the Gezi uprising, the carnivalesque scenes in the streets were widespread during these events.

 The current state of affairs demonstrates that there still is room for effective protests, collective action, and new forms of organization, which seem to be in the course of making, through both workers' actions that push beyond the limits of present forms of organization and creative attempts at self-organizing. While Gezi precipitated a whole new protest culture with new forms of organizations, it was also a call to the labor movement as we saw in the slogans, social media, and at the forefront of AKM building calling "Unions to duty, to general strike". The experience of Gezi is now an innate part of the collective memory of the Turkish working-class movement. The changing role of the organized labor movement in the Gezi uprising and in its aftermath is a substantial question worthy of more discussion, which is why we named this chapter "In Search of the Labor Movement in Turkey", after the famous novel of Marcel Proust, *In Search of Lost Time*.

Bibliography

Akçay Ü (2015) *AKP, TÜSİAD ve Küresel Kriz: Yeni Bir Kalkınmacı İttifaka Doğru (mu?)*, Available (consulted March 26 2023) at: https://sendika.org/2015/04/akp-tusiad-ve-kuresel-kriz-yeni-bir-kalkinmaci-ittifaka-dogru-mu-umit-akcay-baslangic-256456/.

Akçay Ü (2018) Neoliberal populism in Turkey and its crisis. *Berlin School of Economics and Law, Institute for International Political Economy* (Working Papers 100/2018). Available (consulted April 21 2023) at: https://www.ipe-berlin.org/fileadmin/institut-ipe/Dokumente/Working_Papers/IPE_WP_100.pdf.

Alçın S (2013) *Genel Grev Genel Direniş*. Available (consulted March 26 2023) at: https://www.evrensel.net/yazi/58549/genel-grev-genel-direnis.

Alonso C R (2015) Gezi Park: A Revindication of Public Space. In David I and Toktamış K F (eds) *'Everywhere Taksim': Sowing the Seeds for a New Turkey at Gezi*. Amsterdam: Amsterdam University Press, 231–248.

Anner M (2015) Labor control regimes and worker resistance in global supply chains. *Labor History* 56(3): 292–307.

Ardıç E (2013) *Grev Fiyaskosu*. Available (consulted March 26 2023) at: https://www.sabah.com.tr/yazarlar/ardic/2013/06/19/grev-fiyaskosu.

Arslan M (2013) *Gezi Direnişinde Sendikalar: Örgütsel Yenilenme İçin Fırsat*. Available (consulted March 26 2023) at: https://ayrintidergi.com.tr/gezi-direnisinde-sendikalar-orgutsel-yenilenme-icin-firsat/#_ftnref2.

Babacan E, Kutun M, Pınar E and Yılmaz Z (2021) Introduction: Debating regime transformation in Turkey: Myths, critiques and challenges. In: Babacan E et al. (eds) *Regime Change in Turkey: Neoliberal Authoritarianism, Islamism and Hegemony*. London: Routledge, 1–11.

Bandelj N, Shorette K and Sowers E (2011) Work and Neoliberal Globalization: A Polanyian Synthesis. *Sociology Compass* 5(9): 807–823.

Boratav K (2008) *Türkiye İktisat Tarihi 1908–2007*. Ankara: İmge Kitabevi.

Boratav K (2013a) Olgunlaşmış bir sınıfsal başkaldırı: Gezi direnişi. In: Göztepe Ö (ed.) *Gezi Direnişi Üzerine Düşünceler*. Ankara: Notabene, 15–20.

Boratav K (2013b) *Sözün Bittiği Yer*. Available (consulted March 26 2023) at: https://haber.sol.org.tr/yazarlar/korkut-boratav/sozun-bittigi-yer-77931.

Bozkurt-Güngen S (2018) Labour and authoritarian neoliberalism: Changes and continuities under the AKP governments in Turkey. *South European Society and Politics* 23(2): 219–238.

BSB (2015) *AKP'li Yıllarda Emeğin Durumu*. İstanbul: Yordam Kitap.

Bulut S and Karlıdağ S (2016) Relationship between media ownership and news process in Turkey from the political economy perspective. *Journal of Media Critiques* 2(7): 11–34.

Çelik A (2012) *Sendikal Ayrımcılık ve Yasaklar Manzumesi*. Available (consulted March 26 2023) at: https://www.birgun.net/haber/sendikal-ayrimcilik-ve-yasaklar-manzumesi-4366.

Clua-Losada M and Ribera-Almandoz O (2017) Authoritarian neoliberalism and the disciplining of labour. In: Tansel CB (ed.) *States of Discipline: Authoritarian Neoliberalism and the Contested Reproduction of Capitalist Order*. London: Rowman & Littlefield Publisher, 29–46.

Coşkun MK (2019) AKP ve işçi sınıfı. *Devrimci Marksizm* (39–40): 63–79.

Cumhuriyet (2013a) *Emekçiler Destek için Grevde*. Available (consulted March 26 2023) at:207https://www.cumhuriyet.com.tr/haber/emekciler-destek-icin-grevde-425790.

Cumhuriyet (2013b) *Sendikalar Greve Gidiyor*. Available (consulted March 26 2023) at: https://www.cumhuriyet.com.tr/haber/sendikalar-greve-gidiyor-428144.

DİSK (2020) *COVID-19 Günlerinde Sendikalaşma Araştırması*. Available (consulted March 26 2023) at: http://arastirma.disk.org.tr/?p=2042.

Duman A (2019) Türkiye'de emeğin değişen payı ve gelir dağılımı. *Çalışma ve Toplum* 1(60): 349–370.

Dünya (2013) *Gezi için Genel Grev*. Available (consulted March 26 2023) at: https://www.dunya.com/gundem/quotgeziquot-icin-genel-grev-haberi-214755.

Duvar English (2022) *Turkey's Independent Academics Announce Annual Inflation Rate as 170 Percent*. Available (consulted March 26 2023) at: https://www.duvarenglish.com/turkeys-independent-academics-announce-annual-inflation-rate-as-170-percent-news-61598.

Ercan F and Oğuz Ş (2015) From Gezi resistance to Soma massacre: Capital accumulation and class struggle in Turkey. *Socialist Register* 51(1): 114–135.

Erdinç I (2014) AKP döneminde sendikal alanın yeniden yapılanması ve kutuplaşma: Hak-İş ve ötekiler. *Çalışma ve Toplum* 41(2): 155–174.

Eren C (2019) Özelleştirme kıskacında işçi hareketi: Yatağan işçilerinin 2013–2014 direnişi. *Çalışma ve Toplum* 63(4): 2639–2682.

Ergenç C and Çelik Ö (2021) Urban neighbourhood forums in Ankara as a commoning practice. *Antipode* 53(4): 951–1269.

Ertuğrul K (2022) Gezi insurgency as 'counter-conduct'. *Middle East Critique* 31(3): 221–240.

Fırat BÖ (2021) *Doç. Dr. Begüm Özden Fırat – Gezi Direnişi ve Sonrasında Örgütlenme ve Eylem Pratikleri.* Available (consulted March 26 2023) at: https://www.youtube.com/watch?v=26aeS-ndwFg.

Gazetenisan (2013) *5 Haziran Grevi: Uyarı Grevi Yetmez, Genel Greve!* Available (consulted March 26 2023) at: https://www.gazetenisan.net/2013/06/5-haziran-grevi-uyari-grevi-yetmez-genel-greve/.

GENAR (2013) *Gezi Parkı Profili.* Available (consulted March 26 2023) at: https://www.geziarchive.net/reports.

Göztepe Ö (ed.) (2013) *Gezi Direnişi Üzerine Düşünceler.* Ankara: Notabene.

Gümüş P and Yılmaz V (2015) Where did Gezi come from? Exploring the Links between Youth Political Activism before and during the Gezi Protests. In David I and Toktamış K F (eds) *'Everywhere Taksim': Sowing the Seeds for a New Turkey at Gezi.* Amsterdam: Amsterdam University Press, 185–197.

Gürcan EC and Peker E (2015) A class analytic approach to the Gezi Park events: Challenging the "middle class' myth". *Capital & Class* 39(2): 321–343.

Gürcan EC and Berk M (2018) The combined and uneven development of working-class capacities in Turkey, 1960–2016. *Labour History* 60(3): 1–19.

Gürler D (2021) 20. yüzyıldan 21. yüzyıla işçi denetimi bağlaminda fabrika işgalleri ve işgal fabrikalari hareketi. Unpublished doctoral thesis, Kocaeli University, Kocaeli.

ILOSTAT (n.d.a) *Statistics on Union Membership.* Available (consulted March 26 2023) at: https://ilostat.ilo.org/topics/union-membership/.

ILOSTAT (n.d.b) *Statistics on Collective Bargaining.* Available (consulted March 26 2023) at: https://ilostat.ilo.org/topics/collective-bargaining/.

ILOSTAT (n.d.c) *Labour Income Share as a Percent of GDP.* Available (consulted March 26 2023) at: https://www.ilo.org/shinyapps/bulkexplorer54/?lang=en&segment=indicator&id=LAP_2GDP_NOC_RT_A.

İnternethaber (2013) *Sendikaların 'Gezi grevi' fiyaskosu!* Available (consulted March 26 2023) at: https://www.internethaber.com/sendikalarin-gezi-grevi-fiyaskosu-5486 22h.htm.

Irak D (2016) A close-knit bunch: Political concentration in Turkey's Anadolu Agency through Twitter interactions. *Turkish Studies* 17(2): 336–360.

Karaçimen E (2015) Interlinkages between credit, debt and the labour market: Evidence from Turkey. *Cambridge Journal of Economics* 39(3): 751–767.

Karasulu A (2015) 'We May Be Lessees, but the Neighbourhood is Ours': Gezi Resistances and Spatial Claims. In David I and Toktamış K F (eds) *'Everywhere Taksim': Sowing the Seeds for a New Turkey at Gezi.* Amsterdam: Amsterdam University Press, 201–214.

Kaygısız İ (2014) 2013 Yılı işçi eylemleri üzerine bir değerlendirme. *DİSK-AR* (2): 108–121.

Keyder Ç (2013) *Yeni Orta Sınıf*. Available (consulted March 26 2023) at: https://bilimak ademisi.org/wp-content/uploads/2013/09/Yeni-Orta-Sinif.pdf.

Koçak H (2021) OHAL *Rejiminde İşçilerin Kolektif Hakları: Avrupa Kökenli/İlişkili İşletmelerde Sendikal Örgütlenme Hakları. Association for Monitoring Equal Rights, Truth Justice Memory Centre and Netherlands Helsinki Committee*. Available (consulted April 21 2023) at: https://www.esithaklar.org/2021/06/ohal-rejiminde-iscile rin-kollektif-haklari-avrupa-kokenli-iliskili-isletmelerde-sendikal-orgutlenme-hakl ari-baslikli-raporumuz-yayinda/.

KONDA (2013) *Gezi Parkı Araştırması Kimler, Neden Oradalar ve Ne İstiyorlar*. Available (consulted March 26 2023) at: https://konda.com.tr/rapor/77/gezi-parki-arastirm asi-kimler-neden-oradalar-ve-ne-istiyorlar.

KONDA (2014) *Gezi Raporu Toplumun 'Gezi Parkı Olayları' algısı Gezi Parkındakiler kimlerdi?*. Available (consulted March 26 2023) at: https://konda.com.tr/rapor/67/gezi -raporu.

Lavoisier AL (1965) *Elements of Chemistry, in a New Systematic Order Containing all the Modern Discoveries*. Translated by R. Kerr Dover: New York.

Margulies R and Yıldızoğlu E (1984) *Trade Unions and Turkey's Working Class*. MERIP *Reports*, 121 (January/February). Available (consulted April 21 2023) at: https: //merip.org/1984/02/trade-unions-and-turkeys-working-class/.

May M (2006) Employment policy. In: Hill M (ed.) *Social Policy in the Modern World: A Comparative Text*. Oxford: Wiley-Blackwell, 93–116.

Milliyet (2013) DİSK *ve* KESK *Yürüyüşten Vazgeçti*. Available (consulted March 26 2023) at: https://www.milliyet.com.tr/siyaset/disk-ve-kesk-yuruyusten-vazgecti -1724055.

Odman A, Arıkan B, Işıklı E, Can E, Düğmeci D, Koçak H, Çobanlı K, Solum Ş, Tezer T and Çetinkaya Y (2021) "Kapanmadan açılmaya Covid-19 döneminde emekçi hakkı ihlalleri". In: Kendir H, Koçak H and Demiray R (eds) Pandemiye *Rağmen: 2020–2021* KODA *Etkinliklerinden Seçmeler*. İzmit: Kocaeli Dayanışma Akademisi, 156–186.

OECD (2015) *The Labour Share in G20 Economies*. Available (consulted April 21 2023) at: https://www.oecd.org/g20/topics/employment-and-social-policy/The -Labour-Share-in-G20-Economies.pdf.

OECD.Stat (n.d.) *Trade Union Dataset*. Available (consulted March 26 2023) at: https: //stats.oecd.org/Index.aspx?DataSetCode=TUD.

Öngen T (2014) *Prometheus'un Sönmeyen Ateşi: Günümüzde İşçi Sınıfı*. İstanbul: Yordam Kitap.

Özatalay C (2014) Gezi direnişi: Antikapitalist mi, alter-kapitalist mi? In: Öğütle VS and Göker E (eds) *Gezi ve Sosyoloji*. İstanbul: Ayrıntı Yayınları, 170–185.

Özden BA and Bekmen A (2015) Rebelling against neoliberal populist regimes. In: David I and Toktamış K (eds) *Everywhere Taksim Sowing the Seeds for a New Turkey at Gezi*. Amsterdam: Amsterdam University Press, 89–105.

Özden BA, Akça İ and Bekmen A (2017) Antinomies of authoritarian neoliberalism in Turkey: The Justice and Development Party era. In: Tansel CB (ed.) *States of Discipline: Authoritarian Neoliberalism and the Contested Reproduction of Capitalist Order*. London: Rowman & Littlefield Pub, 189–210.

Öztaşkın M (2013) *Sendikalar Gezi'de Neredeydi?* Available (consulted March 26 2003) at: https://www.youtube.com/watch?v=8LFjRboiJnY&ab_channel=Mercek Alt%C4%B1.

Pınar E (2021) A labour-oriented perspective on regime discussions in Turkey. In: Babacan E et al. (eds) *Regime Change in Turkey: Neoliberal Authoritarianism, Islamism and Hegemony*. London: Routledge, 32–48.

Reuters (2022) *Turkey Raises Monthly Minimum Wage by 55% for 2023*. Available (consulted March 26 2023) at: https://www.reuters.com/markets/turkey-raises-monthly-minimum-wage-by-50-2023-2022-12-22/.

Selwyn B (2016) Theory and practice of labour-centred development. *Third World Quarterly* 37(6):1–18.

Semercioğlu C and Ayyıldız D (2014) Interview with Michael Hardt. *Mesele Dergisi* (90): 16–19.

Şafak C (2009) *İşçilerin sendikalaşma oranı yüzde 6,51* Available at: https://sendika.org/2009/01/iscilerin-sendikalasma-orani-yuzde-651-can-safak-27893.

Şık A (2016) *Allah'ın Büyük Lütfu*. Available (consulted March 26 2023) at: https://www.cumhuriyet.com.tr/haber/allahin-buyuk-lutfu-644388.

T.C. Çalışma ve Sosyal Güvenlik Bakanlığı (n.d.a). *6356 Sayılı Sendikalar Ve Toplu İş Sözleşmesi Kanunu Gereğince; İşkollarındaki İşçi Sayıları ve Sendikaların Üye Sayılarına İlişkin 2013 Ocak Ayı İstatistikleri Hakkında Tebliğ*. Available (consulted March 26 2023) at: https://www.csgb.gov.tr/media/1688/2013_ocak_6856.pdf.

T.C. Çalışma ve Sosyal Güvenlik Bakanlığı (n.d.b). *Yıllara Göre Grev ve Lokavt Uygulamaları Strikes and Lockouts by Years 2008–2021*. Available (consulted March 26 2023) at: https://www.csgb.gov.tr/media/31747/grev_lokavt.pdf.

Tauss A (2012) Contextualizing the current crisis: Post-fordism, neoliberal restructuring, and financialization. *Colombia Internacional* (76): 51–79.

Tekgıda-İş Sendikası (2013) *Gezi ve Sendikalar*. Available (consulted March 26 2023) at: https://www.tekgida.org.tr/gezi-ve-sendikalar-19708/.

Tonak A (2013) İsyanın sınıfları. In: Göztepe Ö (ed.) *Gezi Direnişi Üzerine Düşünceler*. Ankara: Notabene, 21–28.

Tuğal C (2013) "Resistance everywhere": The Gezi revolt in global perspective. *New Perspectives on Turkey* 49: 157–172.

TÜİK (2020) *İşgücü İstatistikleri, Haziran 2020*. Available (consulted March 26 2023) at: https://data.tuik.gov.tr/Bulten/Index?p=Isgucu-Istatistikleri-Haziran-2020-33790.

TÜİK (2022a) *Tüketici Fiyat Endeksi, Kasım 2022*. Available (consulted March 26 2023) at:https://data.tuik.gov.tr/Bulten/Index?p=Tuketici-Fiyat-Endeksi-Kasim-2022-45800.

TÜİK (2022b) *İşgücü İstatistikleri, Kasım 2022*. Available (consulted March 26 2023) at: https://data.tuik.gov.tr/Bulten/Index?p=Isgucu-Istatistikleri-Kasim-2022-49384.

Wacquant L (2014) 'Urban Inequality, Marginality and Social Justice In the City'. Available (consulted April 20 2023) at: https://archive.org/details/LoicWacquantInequalityMarginalityAndSocialJusticeInTheCity.

Weyland K (1999) Neoliberal populism in Latin America and Eastern Europe. *Comparative Politics* 31(4): 379–401.

World Bank (2006) *Turkey Labour Market Study Report No. 33254-TR*. Turkey. Available (consulted April 20 2023) at: https://documents1.worldbank.org/curated/en/869781468310746230/text/332540TR0Labor1ver0P0791890iPUBLIC1.txt.

Yalman GL and Topal A (2019) Labour containment strategies and working class struggles in the neoliberal era: The case of TEKEL workers in Turkey. *Critical Sociology* 45(3): 447–461.

Yardımcı-Geyikçi Ş (2014) Gezi Park protests in Turkey: A party politics view. *The Political Quarterly* 85(4): 445–453.

Yeldan E (2007) Patterns of adjustment under the age of finance: the case of Turkey as a peripheral agent of neoliberal globalization. *PERI Working Papers* (126): 1–24.

Yıldızoğlu E (2013) Gezi "olayı"nın sınıfı. In: Göztepe Ö (ed.) *Gezi Direnişi Üzerine Düşünceler*. Ankara: Notabene, 55–66.

Yörük E and Yüksel M (2014) Class and politics in Turkey's Gezi protests. *New Left Review* 89: 103–123.

Yörük E and Yüksel M (2015) Gezi eylemlerinin toplumsal dinamikleri. *Toplum ve Bilim* 133: 132–165.

CHAPTER 9

The Legacy of the Gezi Resistance and Its Effects on Turkey's Socialist Movements of the Past Decade

Eren Karaca and Özgür Balkılıç

The brevity of the month-long Gezi Park protest event belies its importance in Turkey's recent history. The June 2013 uprising was the apogee of previous collective movements, and the event had widespread effects on subsequent political developments over the last decade. The heterogeneous elements that came together at the protests, the resistance's similarities and differences with other mass movements, the new political and social organization practices that emerged, and the political subjectivities that were added to the social movements' repertoire have thus far been the focus of many scholarly works aiming to understand the spirit of Gezi (see Ertuğrul, 2022; Farro and Demirhisar, 2014; Karataksanis, 2016; Karayakalı and Kaya, 2014; Özdemir, 2015; Yetkin and Şimşek, 2017). However, ten years later, it is clear that more effort is needed to explain this progressive mass movement beyond framing it as nostalgia, an anomalous case, or simply a different flavour of social activism. This chapter will contribute to the literature by looking at the movement with a broader lens in order to understand its transformative effects. To analyse its impact fully, the demands of the resistance for political and social change in the country deserve to be contextualized and evaluated against emerging possibilities for progressive change.

We believe that the most immediate path to progressive transformation is through socialist movement which seeks to replace the current political and social order with a radically new one. There emerges a need, for both practical and theoretical concerns, to realistically evaluate how Turkey's socialists described the resistance and what steps they took after Gezi. Bringing a historical and political context to the movement's demands and the progressive, emancipatory ideals that arose from the protest will fill a gap in the literature. We find it important to consider the resistance both as a political subject affecting the current struggle of the socialist organizations and as a historical subject shaping Turkey's recent past towards a socialist future. This chapter, therefore, will focus on the legacy of Gezi within socialist organizations by describing how those groups variously analysed and interpreted retrospective readings of the resistance over that decade. This chapter's central question will help us grow our understanding of the impacts of the resistance on the politics and organization of Turkey's active socialist organizations, how those organizations define this effect, and what kind of ties they established with the Gezi Resistance over the last decade.

Considering the apparent lack of mass support for socialists today, we can say that the socialist organizations in Turkey could not (re)organize the resistance into a revolutionary struggle after Gezi with clearly defined goals and a shared agenda. This is, in fact, a self-critical assessment shared by nearly all the extant socialist organizations. In general, the organized left would agree that the Gezi wave itself was a climactic moment, one that was beyond the abilities of the socialist left back then to recapture it and one that was so widespread that the organized socialists remained incapable of leading it with their organized power in that point in time.[1] Notwithstanding, it is clear that socialist organizations moved quickly to articulate their political discourse through the demands made by this popular movement and re-evaluated their strategies accordingly. The political atmosphere after Gezi, with AKP's crises-ridden but lingering power in politics and the failure of the parliamentary opposition to defeat AKP's one-party government, also led to a political context that affected the strategies of the socialists. In light of all the aforementioned, this chapter will first survey the scholarly literature on Gezi and then proceed to summarize Turkey's political atmosphere in the aftermath of the Gezi Resistance; the chapter will thereafter conclude with evaluating the post-Gezi strategies of four different socialist political parties, these being namely, the Communist Party of Turkey (Turkish: *Türkiye Komünist Partisi*, TKP), the Left Party (Turkish: *Sol Parti*), the Workers' Party of Turkey (Turkish: *Türkiye İşçi Partisi*, TİP) and the Labour Party (Turkish: *Emek Partisi*, EMEP).

1   Unfinished Questions on the Legacy of Gezi

Early post-Gezi literature primarily offers analysis of the participants in the Gezi Resistance, rather than evaluating the organizations involved. Although we cannot say that the debate was fully elaborated upon, evaluating the Gezi

---

1   The Freedom and Solidarity Party (Turkish: *Özgürlük ve Dayanışma Partisi*, ÖDP), which later became the Left Party, published an assessment on the resistance in July, right after the protest was at its peak in June, stating the following: "It is a fact that the revolutionary-socialist movement [...] tended to integrate with this wave as a whole, and in this sense, it made an important contribution to the resistance. Although it is an uprising beyond the current power of the left, it is possible to talk about a wave that integrates with the left" (ÖDP, 2013a).

Resistance as a so-called "middle-class movement" and identifying the Gezi Resistance participants as such have a significant presence in the literature. Keyder (2013: 4) asserts that "a line of struggle that came to the fore with the emergence of the new middle class" and the accompanying "sensitivity to issues such as individual freedom, environmental awareness [and] oppression of the state" overlap with the Gezi Resistance. Similarly, Wacquant (2014) opines that lower classes are excluded from the resistance of the urban middle class so that the latter could preserve its hegemony over space, and even in this sense, the middle class differentiates itself from the lower class. Tuğal (2013 166) also thinks it is more appropriate to call the resistance a middle-class movement since the participants are predominantly middle-class or "generously paid professionals."

Critics of these analyses argue that any study which merely relies on the profiles of the participants of the movement is limited in scope, and continuity becomes a problem unless we situate the movement within the general political context of Turkey. For example, Aytekin (2017: 204) claims that the so-called middle and lower classes were together on the streets, united by the elements he calls "aesthetic political acts," such as "music (both popular and 'high' music), dancing, graffiti, and other forms of street art, puppet show, video art, ironic slogans, football fans' chants adapted to politics, poetry, public book readings, standing, jumping, arbitrary noise, ornamenting barricades, and so on." Saraçoğlu (2015: 299) also argues that the resistance is a "class movement" in terms of the "demands it puts forward and the political/ideological impact it creates," the power bloc it confronts, and the political/economic/ideological line represented by this bloc.

Against arguments that presumed the resistance to be of a middle-class character, the renowned Marxist economist Boratav (2013) contends that the working class was not absent in the Gezi uprising even if workers' organizations and their programs did not actively partake in the resistance. Boratav concludes that the Gezi Resistance is by definition a reaction of the labouring classes to AKP policies, considering how the movement started and the nature of its demands. Gürcan and Peker (2015) bring a broader perspective to this discussion by rejecting the liberal left's assumption that there is an irreconcilable opposition between spontaneity and leadership. The well-known liberal leftist figures in Turkey defined the protesters as the main actors in instances of aggression and violence and further asserted that the Taksim Solidarity Platform and socialist organizations were responsible for the murdered protesters (Gürcan and Peker, 2015: 27–30). The scholars underline how these figures were influential in discrediting the collectively organized street protests during Gezi and how they accused the organized struggle of not being "innocent" and of seeking to profit from the movement (Gürcan and Peker, 2015: 30). Bringing a class perspective to define the Gezi Resistance, therefore, has been an important intervention of the critical and Marxist scholars against the liberals' arguments that demonized the organized power of the people. Indeed, the organized left was in the streets with well-organized actions throughout the entirety of the Gezi uprising. The socialists were always visible with their calls to strengthen the people's voice, and their presence was obvious in the organized forces they displayed in street protests, through their newspapers, slogans and visual materials they contributed to the movement (Gürcan and Peker, 2015; Aytekin, 2017).

Critical scholars also rightly make a substantial effort to situate the resistance within a historical-social totality, rather than looking at it as an event that started and ended in a strictly defined period (Gürcan and Peker, 2015; Yörük, 2014; Yücesan-Özdemir, 2016). This view allows us to see the impact of the earlier organized movements on the emergence of the Gezi Resistance, even if it seemed to be a spontaneous outburst of the people's anger against the ruling government in June 2013. In the view of Yücesan-Özdemir (2016: 9–10), the question of whether it was the middle-class who took to the streets impedes an analysis of what made the Gezi Resistance possible, scrutiny of which requires a broad analytical-political perspective. Yücesan-Özdemir further asserts that it is only through this analytical-political perspective that the Gezi Resistance could be thoroughly contextualized in relation to the changing course of politics and everyday-life practices in Turkey. Different forms of popular outcries of dissidence and dissent, which had previously come to materialize in the Tekel Resistance, the wave of protests against hydroelectric plant constructions, struggles of the urban poor, and women's demonstrations, were fundamental pathways that led up to the Gezi Resistance. Similarly, Savran (2010) asserts that the working-class movement in Turkey had made a great stride forward, especially with the Tekel Resistance that took place in 2010. In addition to this class activism, it is possible to systematically process the political and economic environment that triggered this activism in the recent history of Turkey; one such analysis is put forth notably by Gürcan and Peker (2015), whose contribution examines the political, economic and ideological opportunities, namely the objective factors that lead to collective action in the Gezi Park protests.[2]

---

2 According to the authors, there are three sets of opportunity structures: (1) the political-structural fix-AKP's hegemonic alteration of place and space (drastic urban renewal, destruction of green spaces, Islamizing Taksim's landscape, etc.); (2) the political regime/

A holistic examination of historical-social context is valuable when examining the leadup to Gezi. Inspired by the critical works mentioned, this chapter will examine such context by extending the analysis into the post-Gezi period and by focusing on the socialist organizations that claim to carry class-based movement to the future. We think there is much to add to the literature as we sift through a period where AKP still takes a leading role in shaping Turkish politics, yet the political scene is turned upside down almost daily. In this sense, the analyses in this chapter will necessarily exceed theoretical abstraction and evaluate the remaking of the political scene in Turkey in the aftermath of the Gezi Resistance, with a particular focus on the organised left.

2   The Post-Gezi Political Atmosphere and the Socialists

Two seemingly distinct positions have shaped the mainstream politics in the post-Gezi period of Turkey. AKP vigorously and incessantly denounced the Gezi uprising and alleged that a series of events, including the Gezi uprising, were plotted by a coalition of subversive domestic forces –such as the Gülenist network, the Kurdistan Workers' Party (Kurdish: *Partiya Karkerên Kurdistan*, PKK) and its followers, and the so-called radical and illegal leftist movements- with support from foreign governments in order to illegitimately overthrow the elected government. Considering the utmost importance of judicial processes in building up and consolidating AKP's power in the last twenty years, it was not unexpected of Erdoğan to accuse participants of the Gezi and its leading figures, without offering any substantial evidence, of being terrorists and bandits who had spoiled the mosques by taking shelter there with beer bottles in their hands during the heyday of said events, in an effort to undermine the legitimacy of the movement. Erdoğan has used this type of rhetoric again recently and targeted the Gezi Resistance and protestors, saying that they are "rotten" after the trial of seven Gezi participants in late April 2022; a trial which ended with heavy sentences for the accused (Cumhuriyet, 2022). The results of such court decisions are another judicial triumph for Erdoğan and AKP. One of the governing party's main tactics to consolidate its regime was to deal with its opponents by condemning them for engaging in "criminal acts," and planning to disrupt recent improvements in the country that AKP has undertaken.

---

state capacity-Islamic, security-oriented, authoritarian state; (3) international politics-AKP's unsettled strategy in international relations (Syrian conflict, bombings).

The increasingly authoritarian attitude of AKP aims for the total elimination of its rivals, a strategy that results in a hegemony crisis. The party constantly exploits and deepens the existing political cleavages and creates new ones by consolidating its electoral base through a vigorous nationalist, Islamist, and chauvinist political discourse that imagines perpetual enemies within and outside Turkey. Party policy also excludes almost half of the population voting for or supporting AKP's opponents. With this strategy, the current government makes no effort to convince one half of the population of its ideological discourse, instead preferring to explicitly and intentionally divide society into two opposing groups and situate itself as the leader of one of these partisan camps, resulting in never-ending political chaos. Karahanoğulları and Türk (2018) underline that the power struggles and resulting changes in the executive branch of the Turkish state have been utilized by the governing party to deepen the cleavages between AKP supporters and its opponents and that they use divisiveness as a ruling strategy. Yaşlı (2018) also argues that AKP's failure to convince nearly half the population of its vision for society was the apparent symptom of a hegemony crisis. Although Yalman (2015, 2019) is reluctant to define this political chaos as a hegemony crisis, he agrees that perpetual turmoil is a constructive method which the ruling party uses to bring in more oppressive policies.

This crisis-ridden ruling strategy exposed itself vividly during the Gezi events, wherein nearly 10 million people took to the streets. In the aftermath, AKP acted quickly to create a counter-myth to Gezi. The government put the Gülenist coup attempt on July 15, 2016, and the social mobilization that AKP organized after this attempt in the center of such a counter-myth, presenting AKP as the sole rescuer of democracy. With this, the party also indicated that it could tolerate and encourage the street politics of its supporters. Erdoğan himself actively encouraged the people to take to the streets on the night of the Gülenist coup attempt, declaring the people killed that night martyrs and the day July 15 a countrywide national holiday. However, AKP continued to take a stern attitude to preclude any anti-AKP movement in the streets.

Meanwhile, the mainstream political parties who were encouraged by the Gezi protests to dethrone AKP embraced the events in their own ways. For example, when seven people were sentenced to imprisonment for organizing the resistance, Meral Akşener, whose nationalist İyi Party had been founded as a split within the traditional fascist movement in Turkey, spoke about Gezi as an important resistance against the oppressive regime of AKP. She argued that the uprising infused the people who suffered from this regime with the hope of overcoming it.[3] Similarly, CHP chairman Kılıçdaroğlu occasionally talks about the resistance to call for support from anti-AKP masses, emphasizing the demand for democracy in the resistance. However, this seemingly welcoming attitude towards the Gezi Resistance, in addition to the use of a pro-Gezi stance during the ensuing political struggles regarding Gezi as a strategy to undermine the party in power, has been accompanied by deradicalization of the uprising in two main ways: Firstly, while the mainstream opposition parties have supported the primary demand of the Gezi Resistance, the overthrow of the AKP government, the opposition's strategy was to avoid street mobilization as much as possible or organize street movements that would unfold strictly under their control. CHP and its leader, Kılıçdaroğlu, have characterized street politics as a provocation insidiously supported by AKP because it leads to an open battle between government supporters and opposition parties and further drives the country into chaos.[4] CHP therefore avoided the protests and even prevented its supporters from engaging in social protests during critical political turning-points in the post-Gezi period by failing to organize any rally after the much-debated and controversial 2017 presidential referendum.[5] Nevertheless, mainstream opposition parties did not entirely refrain from engaging in street politics. For instance, CHP held a "Justice March" in late spring of 2017 to protest the arrest of its deputy, Enis Berberoğlu, who was charged after videos of the National Intelligence Organization's arms shipments were provided to a journalist, thus violating state security laws. Although several other figures, including journalists, artists, recently dismissed university professors, and politicians who were not necessarily affiliated with CHP, joined in this nearly month-long march, the main opposition was cautious about losing control and feared the march may turn into a more radical and lasting street movement.

The second way the opposition parties adopted to derail the "radicalism" of the Gezi resistance was to insist on ending AKP's rule through an electoral process, rather than intensified street protests. CHP was the most prominent actor in channelling the "spirit of Gezi" toward elections and calling for participants

---

3   In her speech in 2022, Akşener says: "From the beginning to its derailment with all kinds of provocations and interventions by Mr. Crisis [Erdoğan], Gezi was a stance and resistance of our youngsters against the colonial regime in its 10th year, including idealists and leftists, religious and secular people, women and men" (soL, 2022).
4   CHP leader Kılıçdaroğlu has repeatedly stated that going out on the streets is not within their policy, addressing both the government and the public (BBC News Türkçe, 2022).
5   Kılıçdaroğlu explained why he did not participate in the protests against Turkey's Supreme Electoral Council (YSK) together with the CHP supporters by saying, "There were very serious speculations that there would be people with bats and even guns on the streets" (Sözcü, 2017).

and supporters of Gezi to take action at the ballot box. CHP's campaign during the 2014 municipal elections, done under the umbrella of the spirit of Gezi (Cumhuriyet, 2013), demonstrated the first signs of such a strategy, in the immediate aftermath of the movement. In fact, the party continued to refer to the Gezi uprising during the following elections; the chair of the party's main branch in İstanbul claimed that they would undertake election campaigns based on the Gezi movement for the 2015 general elections, and the party declared that the 2018 general election campaign was inspired by the citizens who participated in Gezi (Cumhuriyet, 2014).

As for the People's Democratic Party (HDP), despite its predecessors being the most prominent institutional body of one of the most powerful social movements – namely, the Kurdish movement – after the 1980 coup d'état in Turkey, it followed a cautious and hesitant policy towards the Gezi uprising in its initial phase. This cautious attitude was mainly to protect the extant peace negotiations underway between the AKP government and the PKK. One of the co-chairs of the Peace and Democracy Party (BDP),[6] Selahattin Demirtaş, declared during the first days of the events that although the party stood behind the central demands of the protestors, there were some political actors embedded within the group who sought to turn the action into an excuse for military intervention to overthrow the government, and this led the BDP to stay off the streets.[7] This cautious policy was replaced with a more welcoming attitude in the latter days of the protest, and in its aftermath. In the party's June 2015 general election campaign, BDP adopted the motto, "We will prevent you from being the president," referring to Erdoğan. At this time, Demirtaş referred to the Gezi uprising as a movement that should inspire the HDP to struggle against AKP and its oppressive policies. However, to its dismay, the Kurdish movement seemingly embraced an open attitude towards Gezi as an alternative political force in the streets but lost its mobilizing capacity when the government exerted violent oppression and thereby paralyzed both the legal and illegal aspects of the Kurds' resistance. This ongoing political oppression was embodied in the arrest of Demirtaş under different charges in 2016

---

6   BDP was the Kurdish political party from 2008 to 2014 until its entire parliamentary caucus joined HDP after the 2014 elections.
7   In his statement, Demirtaş said: "The democratic demands put forward in Gezi Park are the democratic demands that the BDP can embrace and stand behind. In this respect, we were on the side of the Gezi Resistance. ... But some other things also started: 'Can we create a popular movement that will overthrow the government and lead it towards a coup? Or can we channel this popular movement into a coup?' ... That's why we kept a distance. We will not be with those who want to create a coup from here" (soL, 2013a).

and his approximately five-year imprisonment, starting in 2018. AKP's attack has eroded both the HDP's powerful influence in mainstream politics and the capacity of the Kurdish movement to engage in mass-mobilization, thus weakening an important actor on the national political scene.

Considering the general dynamics of a political stage, wherein either the legacy of the Gezi movement has been denounced and forcefully repressed or it has been used as a symbol to leverage votes, the traditional organized leftist movements seemed to stand as the leading prospect of keeping this street movement alive, albeit at a different scale. It was the socialist organizations that infused this large popular movement with more elaborated and precisely defined ideological and political directions and strategies. Their goal was not just to replace the existing government, but also to radically transform the current political and social structure. Some of these political organizations, in fact, have boldly acted and woven their discourse and strategies around "the Gezi spirit" to further their cause. However, the ensuing political chaos, which has forced every actor to adopt a rigid choice of being either pro-AKP or anti-AKP, has restricted the capacity of these groups to follow an independent and socialist policy line. Despite their bold claims of offering an alternative political agenda and strategy to every aspect of mainstream politics, and depending on street politics to enforce their demands and ultimate goals, they have been under significant pressure, particularly during the election periods, to ally with the various anti-AKP parties found in mainstream politics. When resisting such alliances, they have been accused of dividing the electorates whose primary demand was to get rid of the government, leading to further accusations that they are working for the benefit of the party in power.

Even so, some leftist groups have sought to be an ally of more mainstream anti-AKP forces without giving up their strategy of building up street politics and their ultimate socialist goals. They invoke "the Gezi spirit" over and over again to give a rational basis for such a strategy, saying that Gezi was a political moment in which various political and social movements and social groups acted together to bring down the current oppressive government. In other cases, however, some socialist organizations follow an independent political agenda and construct alliances on a third front to inspire socialist sentiment among the general population. Several of them have started alliance talks with other socialists aimed at finding a common strategy independent from mainstream politics, especially for the elections in 2023, and to create long-lasting partnerships. In addition, since the Kurdish movement's influence, and therefore the HDP's influence, on the left has not faded, talks of collaboration between various parties to come together under the HDP's banner continue.

We can summarize the place of socialist parties in this political picture by underlining two important observations: First, in the first five-year period after Gezi, the socialists had difficulty organizing the anti-AKP masses into an independent socialist line, even though AKP increased its aggression against protestors and AKP opponents. Socialist groups were under constant pressure from mainstream politics, especially during election periods which are critical times in Turkey, and especially when the HDP had a prominent role as the second-strongest opposition in parliament. Under these circumstances, some socialist organizations and influential figures adopted the strategy of acting together with the CHP and HDP at certain moments, thinking that a firmer commitment to an anti-AKP front would be timely. Those who did not identify with this front asserted that such a commitment would undermine the progressive ideals of Gezi. Secondly, in such a challenging environment, the current strength of the socialist front was insufficient to call the masses to organize in its name. Although the strategy of strengthening the socialist option has taken more concrete steps in the last two years, the elections in 2023 surely rekindled the debates about which strategy would be best to prevent AKP from forming another one-party government or to dethrone Erdoğan from the presidency. Yet the latest elections only confined the debate to the question if it was right for the leftists and socialists to support the strongest opposition of Erdoğan, Kemal Kılıçdaroğlu.

The following detailed examination of the socialist parties will derive its conclusions primarily by referring to this political picture. In the rest of this chapter, we will evaluate the strategies of four influential socialist parties and their ways of engaging in the Gezi spirit during the post-Gezi period in Turkey. These organized movements represent different strands and traditions of Turkey's Marxist groups, namely the Communist Party of Turkey (TKP; KP from 2014 to 2017), the Left Party (Sol Parti; ÖDP until 2019), the Worker's Party of Turkey (TİP, predominant cadres of which had led HTKP from 2014 to 2017), and the Labor Party (EMEP). Despite lacking their former strength, they still represent the most significant and organized political structure of the Turkish socialist left. We reviewed the public statements, online newspapers, and theoretical publications of these parties in order to understand their position and strategies related to the Gezi Resistance.[8] We also added one political alliance to our analysis, the United June Movement (Turkish: *Birleşik Haziran Hareketi*, BHH), which emerged in 2014 and included the participation of some of the

---

8   We would like to express our gratitude to Aydemir Güler, Önder İşleyen, and Nuray Sancar for making it easier for us to find the documents we were looking for, and to get more clarity and information about the steps taken by the parties after the resistance.

more leftist primary organizations. This group was included not only because it is the most well-known socialist alliance, but also because it claims to represent the Gezi spirit and it promotes the continuation of street politics. Of course, the entire canvas of the Turkish left has always been a more colourful picture than can be captured in a single study. Still, we believe that evaluating the relationship between the lingering Gezi spirit and the politics and strategies of these traditional parties including the BHH will offer us a general framework from which to adequately analyse the legacy of the Gezi event, the most popular progressive insurgency in Turkey's recent past.

3   The Socialist Left in the Early Post-Gezi Period

Organized socialists had long been encouraged by the proliferation of the workers' and social movements in Turkey, particularly in the early 2010s. Their next step in June 2013 was to take to the streets with hundreds of protestors and express their organized support for the demands of such a popular movement. Socialist organizations repeated their call almost every day to join the resistance, and many answered that call, becoming participants and organizers of meetings even while their fellow members were detained by police. Their printed and online newspapers and broadcasts played an essential role during the heyday of the resistance since the government-controlled mainstream media did not report news from the streets. For example, the "press sponsors," those who stood as the spokespersons of the protestors, had leading roles in the organization of the "Gazdan Adam" ("Man of Pepper Gas") festival, which was held at the beginning of July, just when the street protests began to fade. The event was organized "to strengthen the struggle that started with the Gezi Park resistance and spread all over the country and to shout once again the demand for the government to resign" (soL, 2013b). The socialist left's own press, TKP's soL, and ÖDP's Birgün, were among the prominent media outlets organizing the event. In June 2013, TKP's newspaper reached a circulation of around 20,000, and ÖDP's popular newspaper, Birgün, had a circulation of about 15,000 (Gürcan and Peker, 2015: 99).

The efforts to define the movement were more explicit right after the climax of the protests. The importance of the event and where it fell in the history of Turkey's social movements, and the potential it left behind for the development of an alternative future, became central themes in socialist writings. Among the various leftist groups, there was a common opinion expressed about the historical importance of the movement. For example, in its 2014 political report, TKP defines the resistance as follows: "The June Resistance brought together a large group of laborers on an enlightened and emancipatory axis, and in this sense, it helped to cross a critical threshold for the struggle for socialism" (Komünist Parti, 2014). Moreover, their party program was revised after Gezi mentioned the resistance as proof that the country's progressive achievements have not disappeared, despite the reactionism created by capitalism (Komünist Parti, 2015). A similar evaluation is found in the party's theoretical publication of August 2013 when their Secretary General wrote, "The June Resistance should be evaluated on two different planes. On the vertical plane, it is a very important social mobilization in itself, which contains the possibility of turning into a revolutionary upsurge, and on the horizontal plane, it disrupts the long-term asymmetrical balance of power that has been going on for over 30 years in favour of the ruling classes in Turkey" (Okuyan, 2013). In a statement made during the days of the resistance, ÖDP similarly describes the resistance as "the turning point of the country's re-establishment and the destruction of the oppressive and exploitative order. Now we all have to keep moving forward from here" (ÖDP, 2013b). ÖDP also published a note on Gezi after a meeting of the House of Representatives in July 2013. The importance of the uprising is defined by the party with the statement, "This resistance movement, which did not leave challenging the AKP regime to the elections and the ballot box ... and found a solution in its own words and actions, restored the collective self-confidence of the people who had been suppressed and weakened for many years" (ÖDP, 2013a). In one of its earliest evaluations of Gezi, EMEP also stated that the uprising "is a manifestation of the reaction built up by the policies of the government that victimizes its own population" and that it shows the reflex of the masses against the anti-democratic politics of the AKP government (EMEP, 2013).

The Gezi Resistance, therefore, is considered both as an explosive backlash to the reactionary and market-oriented AKP and as a turning point for the people to recognize their power against the AKP's hegemony. The event is further recognized as an important step taken towards constructing an alternative future. Socialists also repeated the importance of being organized in order to articulate the demands of the masses with greater strength, particularly when the liberals started to discredit organized actions in the resistance. Targeted by liberal left interpretations that categorized the organizations in attendance at the protests as "sectarian opportunists" (Gürcan and Peker, 2015: 30), the socialist left, from the very outset of the protests, held a strong line against calls to remain unorganized, insisting that the movement can only be carried into the future by organizing the various dynamics and actors it engaged with. ÖDP put that "It is obvious that such a movement can only be carried out with a strong organization that is ready for this with its position, relations, and ties on social/class grounds" (ÖDP, 2013a) and TKP similarly said "The diversity of the masses in the movement … is a situation that takes its existence from the movement's having a common direction and the social sensitivities on which it is based. The essential thing is to organize these sensitivities and to increase their resistance against disruptive and intimidating interventions" (Komünist Parti, 2014).

However, despite presenting a united front on some issues, the socialists also held certain contrasting opinions that stemmed from their organizations' traditional differences, particularly when deciding how best to organize for the socialist cause. For instance, according to TKP, these mass movements must gain a more elaborately defined political goal. While battling against opposition from within, the party aimed to organize those who sought more than voting AKP out. According to TKP, the main opposition party CHP and the other strong actor HDP undermined the sources of resistance and delayed AKP's failure by turning themselves into liberal projects. TKP also repeatedly argued that the end of the street protests would not mean an end to the ideals of the resistance. On the contrary, if the Gezi resistance was defined only by street politics, it would be tantamount to handing over the movement's ideals and hopes to the parliamentary opposition and thereby making them disappear. Thus, TKP defined the task of reproducing the progressive and emancipatory ideals and political direction of the resistance in various ways as a weapon of struggle against AKP and the exploitative order, with an emphasis on constructing a socialist alternative organized under the party (TKP, 2013).

ÖDP, on the other hand, has taken a different stance on how the Gezi dynamics should be organized in the near future. At first, the party argued that "organization models stemming from the grassroots initiative and based on horizontal organization and flexible relations" should come to the fore by taking lessons from the new trend that emerged in Gezi. In this sense, ÖDP placed a particular emphasis on the park forums, in which people were invited to open debates in urban parks, especially in İstanbul. The forums, which became one of the symbols of the Gezi resistance, were grassroots initiatives that should be encouraged by the socialists to continue the struggle, according to ÖDP.[9] While acknowledging that these forums were useful in promoting communication among the laborers, TKP suggested that forums would not be sufficient to respond to the need to organize an anti-establishment struggle. TKP's Kemal Okuyan (2013) asserted that the search for an alternative power

---

9 For an overview of park forums and their impacts on the future of Turkish politics, see: Ramazanoğulları (2022).

would not emerge from the forms of organization created by the resistance, referring to the park forums, because the resistance reflected the reaction of the people to the governing power, but not their search for power. He insisted on focusing on the political organization that would strengthen the will of the people.

ÖDP's emphasis on strengthening grassroots initiatives and organizing the anti-AKP opposition in widespread forums and committees would come to the fore in a later attempt to unite socialists after Gezi. In addition to endorsing these forums, which should be developed in a way that would aid the self-organization of the people, ÖDP argued that there should be no intervention from above in this organizational structure, and commented on the matter by saying, "the negativities created by the approaches thinking that getting organized means 'gathering in their own unique organization' in the narrow sense should be eliminated" (ÖDP, 2013a).

EMEP had a different theoretical approach to the interactions between groups involved in popular movements, such as the Gezi Resistance. Briefly summarizing the demands of the movement as democratic and necessary to fulfill the goals of a socialist struggle, EMEP was then inclined to blend them with the Kurdish movement's demands, along with political strategies embraced by HDP. EMEP's strategy of embracing the Gezi movement was closely connected to the "immediate task" of uniting democratic forces, which were at the time associated with the People's Democratic Congress (HDK), itself an alliance with the pro-Kurdish BDP and several socialist movements established for the 2011 general elections. The resolutions of the 7th Congress of EMEP, convened in December 2014, announced that the party would work together and organize this front, representing the "widest bases possible" against imperialism and reactionism (EMEP, 2015). Later, EMEP would carry such a policy forward outside the socialist bloc established after Gezi, but within a democratic front that prioritizes the solution of the Kurdish problem as an urgent need.

Significant steps were taken by the most prominent socialist parties to come together after the resistance when the need to organize a socialist alternative after Gezi and the related discussions were most intense. TKP, for example, led a movement called the Left Front (Sol Cephe). In its first meeting, the front was positioned as a class-based response to the disorganization of the uprising. Therefore, the organizational power of the front was to be utilized and strengthened with local assemblies (soL, 2013c). At the same time, ÖDP also launched a movement called the United Opposition Movement (Turkish: *Birleşik Muhalefet Hareketi*, BMH), aiming to spread the grassroots movement of forums across the country. The first of these had a short lifespan because theoretical, political, and strategic disagreements within TKP resulted in the establishment of two different parties in 2014, dissolving the Left Front. While one faction, namely, the Communist Party (Turkish: *Komünist Parti,* KP), argued for the party to recognize the importance of such wide-reaching movements and use them as convenient channels for organizing the masses to party politics, the other faction, bearing the name People's Communist Party of Turkey (Turkish: *Halkın Türkiye Komünist Partisi,* HTKP) after said split, decided that it was best for a socialist party to prioritize establishing alliances with emerging social movements and broader opposition dynamics.[10] In 2017, leading cadres of HTKP came to organize TİP, a new socialist party bearing the same name as the first socialist political party to win representation in Turkey in the 1965 general elections, while KP eventually continued its political life under the name TKP.

After TKP's split, the second initiative, ÖDP's United Opposition, held a meeting in Ankara that hosted several different organizations (with the participation of KP and HTKP separately) and socialist individuals. In this first meeting, the participants announced that they had established the BHH, the most visible socialist front to emerge after Gezi. Many academics, independent journalists, activists and writers, and different political parties and movements took part in this alliance. As mentioned, the common goal of socialist parties, that of being organized to better affect change, is the most crucial step toward strengthening social opposition and realizing the Gezi demands. This idea was therefore the basis for socialists to come together under the BHH flag. The first public declaration of the group stated that "we have decided to struggle and build the future by bringing together all the egalitarian, emancipatory, progressive, revolutionary and pro-peace dynamics of [Turkish] society, [including the] resistance movements, and opposition forces" (soL, 2014a). Afterward, the BHH sought to spread the movement's influence and organizational base through forums and assemblies held in different provinces. At the end of 2014, the first countrywide assembly of the BHH convened and published a statement to announce that the movement's struggle would continue (soL, 2014b).

However, the BHH encountered its first difficulties in June 2015, when differences of opinion among the participants appeared surrounding which political strategy they should adopt for the elections that year. The election strategies of the main opposition, CHP and HDP had gained popular support by targeting AKP and especially Erdoğan. But that success also brought division amongst the socialists. At the start of those discussions, some participants

---

10 For an interview, in Turkish, consisting of answers to the questions asked to the representatives of these two parties, see Gültekin (2014).

of BHH argued that the group should openly support HDP in the elections, but the majority opposed this view (Gazete Duvar, 2018). Although very different election strategies were proposed, the general consensus within the movement was to refrain from defining any clear strategy for the elections in order to maintain the group's independent attitude. In a March 3rd televised statement, a BHH spokesperson said, "The United June Movement does not negotiate with any side, especially CHP and HDP, over the concern of representation in the parliament ... However, as a requirement of this independent stance, we also want to share with the public that we will be in solidarity with the forces that convincingly embrace society's demands during the election process" (Cumhuriyet, 2015).

Nevertheless, one TKP leader, namely Aydemir Güler (2015), thought this strategy could politically paralyze the BHH and the socialists within it, and that socialists should show a clear and decisive stance regarding the elections. In the absence of such clarity, according to the KP, the trend toward aligning with CHP and HDP in the name of opposing AKP would be strengthened, finally leading to a liberal stance that would wipe out any progressive gains won by the Gezi Resistance. Accordingly, and without a formal announcement, KP severed its association with the BHH and entered the elections with their own candidates. The party took no active role in the movement thereafter. Immediately following the June 2015 general elections, other parties, and movements also left the BHH, citing different concerns over the electoral debates, or the broader movement's inability to fulfil its initial promises.

With these groups going their separate ways, the general election of 2015 constituted a turning point in the relationship between the socialist left and the Gezi resistance. As summarized in the previous section, while the extant dynamics of mainstream politics have always left little space for socialists to manoeuvre, this was particularly true during the election periods. The two main opposition parties, CHP and HDP, convinced the larger anti-AKP masses to undermine the AKP through the elections by articulating the primary demand of the Gezi, "Government, Resign!" as part of their election strategies. And, in fact, HDP passed the 10% threshold in the June 2015 elections, thereby preventing AKP from becoming a one-party government again. However, AKP's response was to unlawfully avoid a coalition government, creating a political stalemate. AKP also increased state violence, carrying out intense military operations in the Kurdish regions in an attempt to retake power in the November elections. Under the circumstances, the socialist movements, which tried to fortify a socialist alternative after Gezi, lost momentum in their quest to become an influential and independent political alternative, leading some socialist movements to ally with the main opposition parties. If we define the legacy of the Gezi movement based on the most apparent demands of the masses, namely the resignation of the AKP government, the mainstream opposition succeeded in convincing the masses that the only way to get rid of the AKP was to concentrate anti-AKP forces during the elections, but it is a strategy that has, so far, failed.

4   After the 2015 General Elections

The two election periods of 2015 represented a key point in Turkish politics in general, and for the organizational strategies that were employed to meet the demands of the socialist cause that rose to public consciousness through Gezi. The political organizations that remained within the BHH were ÖDP (later Sol Parti) and HTKP (later TİP). The politics of this new period were initially shaped by AKP's oppressive policies against the Kurdish movement, policies which were accelerated after the June 2015 elections and accompanied by increasing violence. Then, the horror atmosphere of state violence further intensified when the so-called Gülenist network failed to overthrow the government via a coup d'état on July 15, 2016. Immediately following the coup attempt, the governing party declared *etat de siege* and began ruling the country through extraordinary decrees announced by the AKP government alone.

Understandably, this period of violence and uncertainty initially paralyzed the opposition, the socialist movements and the activities of the BHH just after the elections. However, in an effort to revive the movement once more, the BHH took another considerable step to prevent AKP from consolidating its power. In line with its strategy of organizing the Gezi dynamics through assemblies in different parts of Turkey, the BHH campaigned with a powerful "NO" movement for the upcoming presidential elections in April 2016. This movement gained momentum with the "1 million letter" campaign, when BHH participants distributed letters to citizens, visiting their homes and calling them to stand against and say "NO" to "the one-man regime, the dictatorship, and the presidential system." The movement acknowledged that the meaning of "no" might differ for some political movements, but the campaign would focus on strengthening a general "NO" without trying to unite the various groups (Birgün, 2017). However, the constitutional amendment package, which includes the abolition of the parliamentary system, the adoption of the presidential system, and the granting of executive power to the party-member President, was approved in April 2017 with 51.41% yes votes to 48.59% no votes.

After the 2017 referendum, the BHH went through a period of dissolution, proving that the election periods after Gezi have further whittled the socialists down to an ineffective position in the general political arena. As another example, with the new general election atmosphere that emerged in 2018, the BHH has been further depressed with fiery debates over which strategy should be followed. While ÖDP, which has since changed its name to Sol Parti, insisted on maintaining the BHH's independent position, TİP, once organized under the name HTKP, has decided to allow its leading figures to be listed as HDP candidates. In fact, two candidates of TİP were elected to the parliament as a result of its cooperation with HDP and these deputies, alongside two others who broke with their parties and joined TİP, formed the party's own group. In short, the socialists' lack of policy agreement during election periods ultimately led to the downfall of the BHH movement.

The dissolution of the BHH can be considered another turning point for socialist organizations in Turkey since it marked the end of their use of specific strategies that referred to the Gezi uprising. It was the end of an era when Gezi dynamics were used specifically to fortify an independent socialist line which was not aimed at just replacing the existing government, but also at the total and radical transformation of the nation's political and social structure. After the 2018 elections, socialist parties used Gezi more generally as political leverage, especially on the anniversary of the movement each year. Furthermore, it has prominently been the socialist parties who have defended the uprising, categorizing it as the people's struggle against the AKP government, and Erdoğan, who has vehemently criminalized and condemned Gezi, labelling it a devilish plot. TKP's Güler (2016) and Okuyan (2018), for example, postulate that the political turmoil that led to despair among the general population prevented any further mass mobilization, but Gezi remains one of the most momentous political events for the socialists and the general population, and it continues to provide hope for better times to come. The Gezi Resistance will not be repeated, but it proved the possibility of similar uprisings from which the socialist movement could derive popular strength.

Like TKP, ÖDP, who had relied on the legacy of Gezi after the two elections in 2015, also lost its specific focus on Gezi during the transition to the presidential system and dissolution of the BHH. Although a considerable proportion of the country had shown an uncompromising attitude towards the ruling party and mobilized in the streets in unprecedented numbers, ÖDP felt that more moderate resistance and political opposition could not prevent the ultimate establishment of AKP's Islamist/fascist regime. The party therefore argued that socialists must shift their strategy from forestalling the establishment of AKP's regime to overthrowing it since the rise of the presidential system had fortified the power of the regime. The party's official political evaluation and strategy was also confirmed by replacing the name ÖDP with Sol Party in late 2019 (Birgün, 2019). EMEP, on the other hand, continues to embrace the Gezi legacy as it inspires successive social movements nationally and internationally. Today, EMEP uses the Gezi anniversaries to reiterate the need for an independent and democratic Turkey, and the experiences and achievements inherited from the Gezi uprising are part of their strategic communications (EMEP, 2020). However, despite recent talks with TKP and Sol Party to raise an independent socialist front, EMEP, like TİP, never completely severed ties with HDP (Gazete Duvar, 2022). Currently, an alliance of seven movements, including HDP, TİP, and EMEP, is advancing separately from the socialist bloc led by TKP and Sol Party.

Among these socialist parties, TİP stands out as one that still designs its politics and strategies with a considerable rhetorical reference to the Gezi uprising. Its official webpage opens today with a photo from the uprising and a headline saying: "while the Gezi will eternally perpetuate, tyrants will vanish." In fact, TİP's leader, Baş, (2014) explained the division within the TKP in 2014 by referring to the necessities of a new era brought about by the Gezi uprising that had forced the socialist/communist movements to redefine their theoretical assumptions and political strategies. As such, the Gezi uprising, for TİP, was a milestone for the Turkish socialist movement. In their current political program, TİP declares their political priority and primary goal as the overthrow of AKP – or the Palace Regime in their political parlance – which they contend would be an important blow to the capitalist class and the imperialist forces who have supported the government from its earliest days (TİP, 2022). For TİP, the dissolution of such a regime via mass mobilization and through an alliance with social movements or other opposition parties would give socialists more significant influence in the new political stage and make them more prepared for their final struggle (Baş, 2021).

In this regard, the relatively recently founded TİP follows a populist-leftist rhetoric that divides Turkish politics between the tyrant, referring to Erdoğan and his supporters, and the masses who are suffering under the AKP's oppressive policies. Given this divide, the urgent task of the socialists is to fight by organizing, interacting, and allying with every kind of popular movement and street protest that seeks to undermine the power of the AKP, including the Gezi resistance. The party argues that the socialists who have been assigned this task must be a part of these larger movements through internal engagement with them, rather than merely demonstrating the need for a socialist consciousness from outside the group (Çulhaoğlu, 2014). Relying on such principles, HTKP was one of the main actors within the BHH with their efforts to influence grassroots social movements from the inside.

However, after the two elections in 2015 in particular, TİP's cadres adopted the policy of allying with the mainstream opposition parties, namely CHP and HDP, without abandoning their strategy of mass movements to dethrone the AKP. The group cited three main reasons for this approach. Firstly, the strategy would unite the general opposition to the single cause of wiping out the current regime, from which the socialists could potentially gain too much. Secondly, by doing so, they would have interacted with the grassroots Kemalist and Kurdish movements and infused the larger masses who supported them with the cause of socialism. In fact, TİP's chairman, Erkan Baş, appeared as one of the central figures in the Justice March in 2017, which was arranged by the CHP's leader, Kılıçdaroğlu, to interact with the anti-AKP social groups and continue "their march which they have taken on since Gezi" (T24, 2017). Lastly, these alliances would have offered the socialists a chance to take part in parliament, meaning they could possibly derail parliamentary procedures in the name of socialism and use this advantage to call for larger mass actions without necessarily losing their ultimate aim of overthrowing the capitalist order. Then, Baş was chosen from the ranks of HDP as one of the general assembly candidates for the 2018 elections. Baş explained this move as the Kurdish movement handing over "revolutionary responsibility" to the socialists since both groups had been violently oppressed by the Palace regime after 2015 (Demokrathaber, 2018). TİP believes their representatives' election to parliament and their new independent party group have allowed them to expand the socialist cause (Baş, 2021). The politics and the rhetoric adopted by TİP still claim to interact with street politics and to reiterate and consolidate the demands of the Gezi uprising. The party has so far found no significant mass support, yet the May 2023 election results provided another milestone for TİP, which kept its visibility in the political arena with its parliamentarian opposition.

5   Conclusion

This chapter evaluated the post-Gezi decade actions of Turkey's socialist organizations which embraced the demands of the Gezi uprising and (re)organized it for a transformative change by discussing its meaning and legacy and creating alliances that would stir the masses to action. Besides being a practical need for the socialist struggle, the necessity of this evaluation is also evident in academic literature, which has to date mainly focused on the street days of the resistance and not on its legacy. The political movements of the ten-year period covered in this study show us that the general dynamics of Turkish politics in these years have, by and large, shaped how the socialist movements related to the legacy of Gezi. Generally speaking, especially after the Gezi uprising became a popular movement against the AKP government and its oppressive policies, Turkish politics have been framed with the AKP's strategy of intensifying oppressive methods against their opponents and keenly dividing the society in a familiar right-wing/popular conservative fashion. As a reaction to this, the mainstream opposition parties, in a different populist fashion, have designated social and political life as a duality between the one-party government and the rest, sometimes pushing anti-AKP political groups to merge into one general opposition with fascist, Islamist, secular, pro-Kurdish, and social democrat actors all together. This cadre of unlikely alliances resulted in considerable problems and obstacles in terms of bringing up and consolidating an alternative "third way" socialist bloc.

Nevertheless, it is evident that the Gezi movement, as an unprecedented social upheaval in Turkish history, is of critical importance for the country's socialist movements. Each socialist party we have elaborated upon in this chapter shares some common attitudes toward the resistance. Most see the Gezi uprising as a flashpoint, the culmination of significant individual movements that had their origins in the early 2010s, and the result of the pent-up social anger which had been simmering against AKP and its pro-capitalist ideology. But Gezi was also a milestone in the sense that different social groups that had either been inactive in street politics for years or that had never participated in any social protests finally came to recognise the strength of collective movements. Furthermore, these socialist movements were a natural part of a larger movement that was planning to consolidate and organize into a more defined leftist program.

The traditional socialist parties, which perceived an opportunity for real societal change at Gezi, at first aimed to articulate the demands of the uprising with a socialist program. Immediately after the street protests ended in the fall of 2013, either individual parties or their alliances acted to organize the different social groups under one banner to undermine the power of the AKP and simultaneously enlarge the scale and scope of the socialist movement as an independent and influential political force. Although the United June Movement (BHH) was the most popular of such alliances, the aforementioned tumultuous political arena, dominated by the division between the AKP and its opponents, led to some disagreements between the parties and smaller movements. It is apparent from the dissolution of certain alliances that the socialist movement was unable to overcome this division and offer a third/ socialist alternative. As a result, the progressive and emancipatory ideals that emerged in Gezi were then transferred to the electoral strategies of the CHP and HDP during Turkey's 2015 elections. Then, the BHH gradually lost its initial momentum over the successive election periods of 2017 and 2018, finally dissolving in 2018 due to internal political disputes.

After the two 2015 elections, the general strategy of the socialist movements shifted away from organizing the Gezi dynamics along purely socialist lines with longer-term political goals. Instead, the movements embraced the demands of the uprising, resisting AKP's discourse of denunciating Gezi as a "devilish plot" designed to halt the forward march of Turkey under the guiding hand of AKP leadership. While the AKP government's efforts to condemn the resistance continue today, the socialist parties openly reject this condemnation, declaring Gezi as a righteous people's movement, no matter how much AKP tries to demonize it. In the political turmoil after Gezi, however, the strategy of organizing the dynamics that emerged with the protests into a socialist cause became unrealistic in practice. Therefore, following the 2015 and 2018 elections, socialist parties started to re-establish their platforms without relying on the historical successes of the Gezi Resistance but relying instead on the ongoing progressive ideals that still exist within Turkish society, as the Gezi event itself undoubtedly proved. TİP remained outside of this general tendency, trying to keep a stronger rhetorical link with the Gezi Resistance. All other socialist parties today consider the resistance as a momentous people's movement that could not be organized into a stronger socialist bloc. Still, it is an event that continues to be a reminder of the possibility of a socialist alternative in Turkey one day coming to fruition. As AKP continues taking decisive measures to define the Gezi as a criminal act, the socialists' glorification of the uprising stands as an essential strategy to fight against the hopelessness of the masses. In fact, for the socialists, the legacy of Gezi today (re)affirms the assessments they made ten years earlier when the street resistance was at its peak. As such, all these different parties share a common position that the progressive and emancipatory ideals of the movement will not be swept aside, and the socialist struggle will be organized to fulfil that promise, in spite of the efforts of AKP to quash the movement.

Bibliography

Aytekin EA (2017) A "magic and poetic" moment of dissensus: Aesthetics and politics in the June 2013 (Gezi Park) protests in Turkey. *Space and Culture* 20(2): 191–208.

Baş E (2014) *Muhteşem Başlangıç: Türkiye'yi Sarsan Bir Ay. Komünist*, 1 (November): 27–47. Available (consulted April 8 2023) at: https://tip.org.tr/wp-content/uploads/2020/03/komunist_1.pdf.

Baş E (2021) *TİP ve gelecek: Sosyalizmin Mührünü Vurmak*. *Komünist*, 14 (July): 7–25. Available (consulted April 8 2023) at: https://tip.org.tr/wp-content/uploads/2022/05/Komunist_14_w.pdf.

BBC News Türkçe (2022) *Kılıçdaroğlu: Erdoğan Sokağa Çıkmamızı istiyor; Zorlayacak, Baskı Kuracak Ama Çıkmayacağız*. Available (consulted September 20 2022) at: https://www.bbc.com/turkce/haberler-dunya-59881472.

Birgün (2017) *HAZİRAN'dan 'HAYIR' kampanyası: 1 Milyon Mektup Elden Ele*. Available (consulted September 20 2022) at: https://www.birgun.net/haber/haziran-dan-hayir-kampanyasi-1-milyon-mektup-elden-ele-144771.

Birgün (2019) *Sol Parti Yola Çıktı: Umut, Coşku, Heyecanla*. Available (consulted September 20 2022) at: https://www.birgun.net/haber/sol-parti-yola-cikti-umut-cosku-heyecanla-281100.

Boratav K (2013) Olgunlaşmış bir sınıfsal başkaldırı: Gezi direnişi. In: Göztepe Ö (ed.) *Gezi Direnişi Üzerine Düşünceler*. Ankara: NotaBene Yayınları, 15–20.

Çulhaoğlu M (2014). *Haziran 2013'ten 'Ayrışmaya' ve Haziran Hareketine … Komünist*, 1 (November): 17–26. Available (consulted September 20 2022) at: https://tip.org.tr/wp-content/uploads/2020/03/komunist_1.pdf.

Cumhuriyet (2013) *CHP'de 'Gezi ruhu' Stratejisi*. Available (consulted September 20 2022) at: https://www.cumhuriyet.com.tr/haber/chpde-gezi-ruhu-stratejisi-435310.

Cumhuriyet (2014) *Hedefimiz Gezi'nin Sesi Olmak*. Available (consulted September 20 2022) at: https://www.cumhuriyet.com.tr/haber/hedefimiz-gezinin-sesi-olmak-165089.

Cumhuriyet (2015) *Birleşik Haziran Hareketi'nden Seçim Çağrısı*. Available (consulted September 20 2022) at: https://www.cumhuriyet.com.tr/haber/birlesik-haziran-hareketinden-secim-cagrisi-225565.

Cumhuriyet (2022) *Cumhurbaşkanı Erdoğan Gezi Eylemcilerine 'Sürtük' Dedi, Yandaş Medya Görmedi*. Available (consulted September 20 2022) at: https://www.cumhuriyet.com.tr/siyaset/cumhurbaskani-erdogan-gezi-eylemcilerine-surtuk-dedi-yandas-medya-gormedi-1942348.

Demokrathaber (2018) *Erkan Baş: HDP'nin Uzattığı Eli Havada Bırakmamak Devrimci Sorumluluktu*. Available (consulted September 20 2022) at: https://www.demokrathaber.org/erkan-bas-hdpnin-uzattigi-eli-havada-birakmamak-devrimci-sorumluluktu.

EMEP (2013) *The Resistance Needs to Grow*. Available (consulted September 20 2022) at: https://emep.org/en/the-resistance-needs-to-grow.

EMEP (2015) *EMEP's 7th Congress Calls on All Forces of Labour, Peace and Democracy*. Available (consulted September 20 2022) at: https://emep.org/en/emeps-7th-congress-calls-on-all-forces-of-labour-peace-and-democracy.

EMEP (2020) *Gezi'nin Birikimiyle Bağımsız ve Demokratik Türkiye Mücadelesine Devam.* Available (consulted September 20 2022) at: https://www.emep.org/gezinin-biri kimiyle-bagimsiz-ve-demokratik-turkiye-mucadelesine-devam.

Ertuğrul K (2022) Gezi insurgency as 'counter-conduct'. *Middle East Critique* 31(3): 221–240.

Farro AL and Demirhisar DG (2014) The Gezi Park movement: A Turkish experience of the twenty-first-century collective movements. *International Review of Sociology* 24(1): 176–189.

Gazete Duvar (2018) *Birleşik Haziran Hareketi'nin Başına Ne Geldi?* Available (consulted September 20 2022) at: https://www.gazeteduvar.com.tr/forum/2018/11/28/birlesik-haziran-hareketinin-basina-ne-geldi.

Gazete Duvar (2022) *EMEP Genel Başkanı Akdeniz: Çalışmalarda Üçüncü Seçeneği Örgütlüyoruz.* Available (consulted September 20 2022) at: https://www.gazetedu var.com.tr/emep-genel-baskani-akdeniz-calismalarda-ucuncu-secenegi-orgutluyo ruz-haber-1571926.

Güler A (2015) *Kolay Çare Solculuğu.* Available (consulted September 20 2022) at: https://haber.sol.org.tr/yazarlar/aydemir-guler/kolay-care-solculugu-106682.

Güler A (2016) *Haziran'a 2016'dan Bakmak. Gelenek,* 130. Available (consulted September 20 2022) at: https://gelenek.org/hazirana-2016dan-bakmak-0/.

Gültekin B (2014) *TKP Neden Bölündü? Birgün.* Available (consulted September 20 2022) at: https://www.birgun.net/haber/tkp-neden-bolundu-66287.

Gürcan EC and Peker E (2015) *Challenging Neoliberalism at Turkey's Gezi Park: From Private Discontent to Collective Class Action.* New York: Palgrave Macmillan.

Karahanoğulları Y and Türk D (2018) Otoriter devletçilik, neoliberalizm, Türkiye. *Mülkiye Dergisi* 42(3): 403–448.

Karakatsanis L (2016) Radicalised citizens vs. radicalised governments? Greece and Turkey in a comparative perspective from the December 2008 uprising to the 2013 Gezi Park protests. *Journal of Contemporary European Studies* 24(2): 255–279.

Karakayali S and Yaka Ö (2014) The spirit of Gezi: The recomposition of political subjectivities in Turkey. *New Formations* 83(83): 117–138.

Keyder Ç (2013) *Yeni Orta Sınıf, Bilim Akademisi,* 34. Available (consulted April 20 2023) at: https://bilimakademisi.org/yeni-orta-sinif-caglar-keyder/.

Komünist Parti (2014) *Komünist Parti Temmuz 2014 Siyasi Raporu. Gelenek,* 125. Available (consulted September 20 2022) at: https://gelenek.org/komunist-parti -temmuz-2014-siyasi-raporu/.

Komünist Parti (2015) *Komünist Parti Programı Sunuş Metni. Gelenek,* 126. Available (consulted September 20 2022) at: https://gelenek.org/komunist-parti-progr ami-sunus-metni/.

ÖDP (2013a) *ÖDP'den Direniş Üzerine Değerlendirme.* Available (consulted September 20 2022) at: https://www.ykp.org.cy/2013/07/odpden-direnis-uzerine-degerlendirme/.

ödp (2013b) *Direnişi Ülkenin Her Yanında Büyütelim!* Available (consulted September 20 2022) at: https://portal.odp.org.tr/direnisi-ulkenin-her-yaninda-buyutelim/.

Okuyan K (2013) *Haziran Direnişi'nden Devrim Teorisine ... Gelenek*, 121. Available (consulted September 20 2022) at: https://gelenek.org/haziran-direnisinden-devrim-teorisine/.

Okuyan K (2018) *Kemal Okuyan'la Haziran Direnişi Üzerine. tkp.org.tr*. Available (consulted September 20 2022) at: https://www.tkp.org.tr/uncategorized-tr/kemal-okuyanla-haziran-direnisi-uzerine/.

Özdemir E (2015) An assessment of the Gezi protests in Turkey in 2013: Political agency as an articulation practice. *Review of History and Political Science* 3(2): 51–58.

Ramazanogullari H (2022) After the protest: İstanbul park forums and people's engagement in political action. *Social Movement Studies* 21(4): 420–435.

Saraçoğlu C (2015) Haziran 2013 sonrası Türkiye'de ideolojiler alanının dönüşümü: Gezi Direnişi'ni anlamanın yöntemleri üzerine bir tartışma. *Praksis* 37: 299–321.

soL (2013a) *Selahattin Demirtaş: 'Gezi ile Aramıza Mesafe Koyduk'*. Available (consulted September 20 2022) at: https://haber.sol.org.tr/devlet-ve-siyaset/selahattin-demirtas-gezi-ile-aramiza-mesafe-koyduk-haberi-77251.

soL (2013b) *Çapulcular Gazdanadam Festivali'nde Buluşuyor*. Available (consulted September 20 2022) at: https://haber.sol.org.tr/kultur-sanat/capulcular-gazdanadam-festivalinde-bulusuyor-haberi-75712.

soL (2013c) *Sol Cephe Kuruldu*. Available (consulted September 20 2022) at: https://haber.sol.org.tr/soldakiler/sol-cephe-kuruldu-haberi-84209.

soL (2014a) *Soldan Ortak 'Mücadele' Deklarasyonu: Gericiliği ve Faşizmi Yeneceğiz*. Available (consulted September 20 2022) at: https://haber.sol.org.tr/soldakiler/soldan-ortak-mucadele-deklarasyonu-gericiligi-ve-fasizmi-yenecegiz-haberi-97596.

soL (2014b) *Birleşik Haziran Hareketi'nin Türkiye Meclisi'nde Sonuç Bildirgesi Açıklandı*. Available (consulted September 20 2022) at: https://haber.sol.org.tr/turkiye/birlesik-haziran-hareketinin-turkiye-meclisinde-sonuc-bildirgesi-aciklandi-104081.

soL (2022) *Akşener: 'Gezi Bir Duruş, Bir Direniştir'*. Available (consulted September 20 2022) at: https://haber.sol.org.tr/haber/aksener-gezi-bir-durus-bir-direnistir-333800.

Sözcü (2017) *Kılıçdaroğlu İlk Kez Açıkladı: Sokağa Çağırmadık Çünkü ...* Available (consulted September 20 2022) at: https://www.sozcu.com.tr/2017/gundem/kilicdaroglu-ilk-kez-acikladi-sokaga-cagirmadik-cunku-1832515/.

T24 (2017) *Halkın TKP'si Genel Başkanı Erkan Baş: Gezi'den Bu Yana Özlediğimiz Türkiye'ye Ulaşmak İçin Yürüyoruz*. Available (consulted September 20 2022) at: https://t24.com.tr/haber/halkin-tkpsi-genel-baskani-erkan-bas-geziden-bu-yana-ozledigimiz-turkiyeye-ulasmak-icin-yuruyoruz,411491.

tİp (2022) *Türkiye İşçi Partisi Devrim Programı*. Available (consulted September 20 2022) at: https://tip.org.tr/program/.

TKP (2013) *Haziran Direnişi İçin Eylül Tezleri. Gelenek*, 122. Available (consulted September 20 2022) at: https://gelenek.org/haziran-direnisi-icin-eylul-tezleri/.

Tuğal C (2013) "Resistance everywhere": The Gezi revolt in global perspective. *New Perspectives on Turkey* 49: 157–172.

Wacquant L (2014) Kentsel marjinallik ve devletin sağ eli: Loic Wacquant'la söyleşi. *Birikim* 298: 67–73.

Yalman G (2015) *CHP ve HDP Dışında Güçlü Bir Muhalefet Gerekiyor*. Available (consulted September 20 2022) at: https://sendikalmucadele.org/chp-ve-hdp-disinda-guclu-bir-muhalefet-gerekiyor/.

Yalman G (2019) *Kimlik Siyaseti, Otoriter Eğilimlerin İtici Gücü Oldu*. Available (consulted September 20 2022) at: https://www.birgun.net/haber/siyaset-bilimci-doc-dr-galip-yalman-kimlik-siyaseti-otoriter-egilimlerin-itici-gucu-oldu-261175.

Yaşlı F (2018) *16 Nisan'dan 24 Haziran'a Yeni Rejim*. Available (consulted September 20 2022) at: https://www.birgun.net/haber/16-nisan-dan-24-haziran-a-yeni-rejim-224238.

Yetkin M and Simsek A (2017) A theoretical analysis of the Gezi Resistance: Implications for political communication of new social movements. *Online Journal of Communication and Media Technologies* 7(2): 1–32.

Yörük E (2014) The long summer of Turkey: The Gezi uprising and its historical roots. *South Atlantic Quarterly* 113(2): 419–426.

Yücesan-Özdemir G (ed.) (2016) *The Road to Gezi: Resistance and Counter-publics in 21st Century Turkey*. Ottawa: Red Quill Books.

CHAPTER 10

From Gezi to the New Regime
How the AKP Continued Its Regime-Building after the Gezi Resistance

Fatih Yaşlı

The Justice and Development Party (Turkish: *Adalet ve Kalkınma Partisi*, AKP) was founded on August 14, 2001, by Recep Tayyip Erdoğan, and the party came to power under his leadership following the November 3, 2002 elections. At the time of writing, the AKP continues to rule Turkey, despite facing multiple domestic crises, including escalating economic problems. This chapter will assert that the AKP's fundamental characteristic is its never-ending plan to build a new regime, one that is markedly different from the preceding political order in the country. This chapter will demonstrate evidence as to how AKP is a "regime-building" party and will maintain that the past two decades in Turkey should be considered an ongoing "regime-building process." Further, the chapter will argue that the changes that relate to this process should not be viewed simply as a transition from the parliamentary regime to a presidential government system, but as a movement toward a religious-authoritarian regime in line with the AKP's political ambitions and the party's Islamist doctrines.

As this chapter also shows, however, Turkey's transformation under the AKP has been a gradual and de facto process in which the goal of a fundamental regime change was never openly acknowledged by the party. A significant portion of the electorate was tacitly or actively against such changes and the AKP's apparent regime-building process, and it is against this backdrop of dissent that the Gezi Resistance, the most expansive and most significant demonstration against the AKP government in 20 years, must be contextualized. This chapter will present Gezi as a direct reaction against the AKP's attempts to reshape the political direction of the country and will detail how the AKP dealt with the uprising, the most significant challenge it has thus far encountered during its regime-building process.

The first section of this chapter will present the early years of the AKP government using the construction of a novel regime as the central thesis. The period, starting from the AKP's 2002 election victory to the Gezi resistance in 2013 will be discussed both from the perspectives of the government and the rising social opposition it encountered. Discussions on the second period include the regime-building process as it continued after the Gezi resistance.

By focusing on crisis dynamics and political turmoil, the section will explain how the AKP accelerated regime-building after Gezi and ultimately completed the administrative dimension of the regime change, namely the transition from the parliamentary system to the presidential system of government. The third section will discuss the main characteristics of the "Erdoğan regime", a term used based on President Erdoğan's indisputable leadership within the party for the past 20 years, his desire to consolidate all power in his own hands, and the fact that the building process is based on the "cult of Erdoğan" that is so evident among his supporters. Yet, a related discussion will show that this regime cannot be analysed solely on the President's cult status and authoritarian nature. We need to add neoliberalism and religionization to the analysis to fully comprehend the AKP's regime-building strategies. The third section will also discuss the populist character of the regime, arguing that the AKP is an Islamic populist party and that its ongoing populism strategy is essential to the nature and success of the Erdoğan regime. The chapter will conclude with a look at the very recent political dynamics in Turkey.

1   The Start of AKP's Regime-Building and the Road to Gezi

The handful of people who came together on the evening of May 27, 2013 to stop the municipal office's demolition of İstanbul's Gezi Park could not have guessed that their resistance would turn into one of the most popular and long-lasting street protests in Turkey's history, and indeed one of the most significant protests the world has ever seen. Over just a few days, the Gezi movement spread from İstanbul to the capital, Ankara, and other major cities, including the AKP's provincial strongholds where thousands of people took to the streets and the ruling party was directly targeted by demonstrators.

This outpouring of dissent came after years of popular support for Erdogan and his party. The AKP came to power as a result of the financial and political crises at the end of the 1990s. The atmosphere of dovetailing crises at this time also corresponded with a crisis of hegemony for the establishment. The AKP's founders came from the National Vision (Turkish: *Milli Görüş*) movement of Turkish Islamism that rose to prominence during the 1990s. They took part in an internal power struggle with Necmettin Erbakan, the leader of the movement and its Virtue Party (Turkish: *Fazilet Partisi,* FP), but their attempt to claim leadership within that party misfired. Instead, they parted ways with the FP in 2000 and established the AKP in 2001, electing Recep Tayyip Erdoğan as their leader. In the November 3, 2002 elections, the AKP garnered enough votes to form a one-party government, however, Erdoğan could not be a parliamentary candidate because he was politically banned and was not eligible to be prime minister. Until the end of his political ban, Abdullah Gül, the second most powerful name in the party after Erdoğan at the time, filled the prime minister's seat.

In its first years, the AKP government, in line with Erdoğan's well-known statement, "We have now taken off the National Vision shirt," acted as a center-right party rather than an Islamist one. On the contrary, it declared its ideology as "conservative democracy," citing the Christian democrats in Europe as models for their organization. While adopting and expediting the neoliberal economic program initiated by the previous government and supported by the IMF, the AKP also took steps in the name of "democratization" by bringing Turkey's goal of full membership in the European Union to the fore. The government, which received the support of Turkey's capitalist class at home and in the USA and the EU, managed to keep loan interest and inflation rates low, mainly thanks to the generous cash flow that came with global economic expansion. As Turkey's economy grew, lower interest rates and the relative increase in purchasing power of the wage-earning masses brought popular support to the AKP.

The most substantial indicator of the AKP's growing influence was the result of the 2007 elections when the AKP increased its vote margin from 34.3% (in 2002) to 46.5%.[1] One month after the 2007 elections, Gül was elected President by the Parliament. His presidency was a significant victory since the AKP had struggled against "old" forces, especially some army members who did not want to see the AKP take control of the presidential mansion. Holding the presidential seat made the AKP's work easier because the previous president, Ahmet Necdet Sezer, was a representative of anti-AKP forces in the state. Sezer used his power to veto laws passed by the AKP government, claiming they were unconstitutional. The end of Sezer's presidency meant the end of a roadblock that had so far foiled the AKP's regime-building plans.

After coming to power again in 2007 with almost half of the electorate's votes and putting its second most powerful man in the presidential seat, the AKP began to build their new regime in earnest. It is important to note that this did not simply mean taking the necessary steps to realize the transition from the parliamentary to the presidential system: The regime change also entailed AKP's transition from being "the government" to being "the state," thus

---

1 The data on 2002 and 2007 general parliamentary elections as well as all other past parliamentary, local and presidential elections, which will be mentioned throughout this chapter, can be found at Turkey's Supreme Election Council website: https://www.ysk.gov.tr/en/past-elections/1852.

creating a de facto party-state. Furthermore, the founding and supreme principle of their envisioned regime was religion, although that was never officially declared. To this end, the government gradually started the religionization or Islamization of all public, political, and social spheres. Between 2007 and 2013, the AKP used its power to build a state-controlled regime and implemented a strategy to transform and seize all institutions, from the high judiciary to universities, from the media to the police.

Lacking sufficient resources to implement this strategy, the AKP formed a coalition with one of Turkey's most powerful religious sects, the Fethullah Gülen network. In the mid-1970s, the Gülenists began to organize within the state and achieved considerable influence and power, especially within the police and judiciary. The main strength of the network came from its activities in the field of education: For the children of low-income families, the Gülenists provided educational opportunities and facilities such as schools, private teaching institutions, dormitories, and student housing, making access to education easier and affordable. However, the same children were also obliged to pass through the network's religious program, and some became militants committed to the political goals of Gülen. When they finished their education and succeeded in getting a job in the state bureaucracy, they followed the instructions given to them according to their positions in the network's hierarchy. For this reason, it would be correct to say that the Gülenists organized a "parallel" hierarchy and became a functional state within the state.

The AKP's regime-building continued after the 2007 elections with large-scale police operations against anti-AKP forces, followed by punitive lawsuits being filed against dissenters. Liquidation operations were launched against those known or suspected of being anti-AKP, primarily in the army, and opposition groups such as academics, journalists, and writers who were publicly known as anti-AKP were threatened. The AKP's rhetoric to legitimize these operations and lawsuits was based on a "democratization" ideology. Despite this discourse, the party maintained political tutelage in Turkey and prevented the implementation of any real democratic tenets. The AKP's discourse primarily accused the Turkish Armed Forces of working to undermine the party, despite the forces' claim of support for the regime. For this reason, in the operations known as the Ergenekon trials and Operation Sledgehammer (Turkish: *Balyoz Operasyonu*), many officers or retired soldiers and civilians with similar worldviews were tried and arrested on accusations of forming a secret organization to overthrow the government, or plotting a coup. These detainees were imprisoned in Silivri, one of AKP's symbolic institutions and the prison where the "elites" of the old regime, such as officers, journalists, or military staff were confined.

Such judicial operations and lawsuits have three critical functions in the AKP's regime-building process, that is, in the transition from being simply a government to embodying the state. First, with the rhetoric of "democratization," the AKP was able to win the direct or indirect support of conservatives, liberals, Islamists, Kurdish political groups, and even some from the socialist left who have traditionally had problems with the Republican movement. Despite having different motives, these groups accepted the claim that the AKP was fighting against counter-guerrillas within the "deep state," and within tutelage forces themselves. These diverse political groups supported the AKP's so-called fight against these forces, albeit to varying degrees. Secondly, the liberal-conservative paradigm accused the 1923 Republic of being wrong in all aspects, further strengthening the Islamist hegemony by narrating the history of Turkey through a duality of pro-Westernization versus pro-tutelage elites, and the religious versus the secular masses. The AKP was able to disseminate this narrative through the media organs of the Gülenists. Thirdly, it was through these operations that opponents in key positions at state institutions were eliminated, and the control of various institutions was transferred to pro-AKP Gülenists, meaning the removal of a major obstacle to regime-building.

Just before the 2011 elections, the AKP held a referendum to "confront the September 12 coup," according to the party's rhetoric. The referendum was in line with its strategies of using the ballot box as a weapon, building politics on the friend-enemy duality, and strengthening the support of its electoral base. In this case, the constitutional article that supposedly prevented the prosecution of the September 12 coup plotters would be put to the vote, but this was only a facade to cover the real changes within the articles submitted. With the amendment's passing, the composition of the judiciary and the High Council of Judges and Prosecutors would change, and the pro-AKP Gülenists would seize control. A vote of "yes" in the referendum would make the execution of lawsuits against dissenters a straightforward matter, and the regime-building process would be accelerated.

The 2011 elections were held in a combative political atmosphere in which Turkish society was divided into supporters and opponents of the government. This was the time when the AKP reached the highest voter support in its history, namely, 49.8% of national votes. Afterward, the AKP started utilizing force instead of consent to maintain its hegemony. Predictably, social opposition against the AKP after the 2011 elections rose significantly. Before the next elections, TEKEL (a Turkish state-owned public company that once had the monopoly of manufacturing and distribution of tobacco and alcoholic beverages) workers, who were forced to work without social security after the privatization process, started a large-scale protest that would last for weeks and their tents lined the streets of Ankara. With the support of the general public, including artists and intellectuals, the workers' tent sites became a place of social resistance against the neoliberal policies of the AKP and the focal point of popular political discourse. Between 2011 and 2013, different segments of Turkish society took to the streets with different motives. For example, thousands of young people organized a mass march in İstanbul after allegations of fraud in university entrance exams. In the same year, thousands of people gathered in İstanbul to protest a legal regulation that would mean internet censorship. Members of the women's and LGBTQI+ movements organized mass demonstrations on March 8 and at pride parades that year. On October 29, 2012, on the anniversary of the foundation of the Republic, tens of thousands of people gathered in Ankara to voice their opposition to the AKP. Police intervened harshly against the crowd where social democrat and CHP chairman Kemal Kılıçdaroğlu was present, using pressurized water, pepper spray, and batons. Prior to these protests, police and judicial officials affiliated with Gülenists had launched a 2011 match-fixing operation against Fenerbahçe, one of the country's largest football clubs. This operation and the subsequent lawsuit quickly politicized Fenerbahçe supporters, leading them to organize protests targeting the Gülenists in stadiums and streets, and thus adding to the volatile nature of the movement. In short, before the Gezi protests began in 2013, there was visible polarization in society at large, and a wave of great anger against the AKP was rising in the streets. This anger came to a fever pitch in May 2013, at Gezi Park (see: Yücesan-Özdemir, 2016).

2 The Gezi Resistance and Its Aftermath

The Gezi Resistance did not have the typical hallmarks of a class movement; that is, millions of people all over Turkey did not take to the streets with economic demands; they were not the bearers of anger directed against Turkish capitalism, and labor organizations or socialist movements did not lead the protests. Instead, Gezi was primarily a reaction against the AKP government and its policies of Islamicising political, social, and public life. In general, the Gezi resistance was a protest against the authoritarian leanings of the new regime. Although both AKP and the Gülenists did not openly declare that their political agendas were based on Islamization policies, much of the public was aware of the party's underlying political agenda and they considered it to be government interference in their lifestyle. Those who reacted against AKP's political agenda were often urban white-collar workers, members of the women's movement, strong supporters of the Republic and/or the ideas of Atatürk, the non-Sunni Muslim Alevis – as they have been the target of Sunni Islamists for centuries – and Kurdish people represented under the Peoples' Democratic Party (Turkish: *Halkların Demokratik Partisi,* HDP). Socialist parties or organizations and various components of the trade union movement also stood with them.

Throughout the protest, Gezi was a spontaneous people's movement. No party, organization, or union could be called the leading force of the resistance. Taksim Solidarity, a body composed of representatives of different parties, associations, and non-governmental organizations, was the agreed-upon representative that would announce the masses' demands, namely, to end police violence and allow people to exercise their democratic rights. The demands expressed by the representatives of Taksim Solidarity in their meeting with then Deputy Prime Minister Bülent Arınç were as follows (Taksim Dayanışması, 2013):

- Gezi Park in Taksim should remain as a park and should not be turned into Artillery Barracks or any other official building; an official statement should be made that the project has been cancelled; attempts to demolish the Atatürk Cultural Center must stop.
- All those responsible for taking action against the protestors, especially the governors of İstanbul, Ankara, Hatay, and the police chiefs who prevented the people's use of the most fundamental democratic rights, such as resisting the demolition of the park, and those who gave the order to suppress the resistance with violence, who implemented this order, and who caused thousands of people to be injured and two of our citizens to die, should be discharged from their positions; the use of gas bombs and similar items should be prohibited.
- Our fellow citizens who were detained for participating in the resistance all over the country should be released immediately, and a statement should be made that no investigation will be opened against them.
- Bans on meetings, demonstrations, and obstructions should be ended in all our public squares and spaces in Turkey, especially in Taksim and Kızılay, which host May 1 protests; barriers to freedom of expression must be removed.

Following these demands to end AKP's authoritarian policies towards the Gezi Park movement, the Taksim Solidarity made further demands that directly confronted the regime's authoritarian characteristics and drew a broader framework supporting ecology, peace, women, LGBTQI, and the working class.

In the same declaration, Taksim Solidarity expressed the main reasons behind the public's disdain for the symbolic actions of the AKP regime that synthesized neoliberalism and Islamism (Taksim Dayanışması, 2013):

> We want to convey to the holders of power that the content of this rising reaction includes objections to the plunder of our ecological values, especially the construction of [İstanbul's] third bridge and the hydroelectric power plants, and the latest Nature and Biological Diversity Conservation Law Draft, the stance against the politics of war in our country and region and the demands for peace; in favour of the sensitivities of our Alevi citizens, the rightful demands of the victims of the urban transformation, the voice rising against the conservative male policies that control women's bodies, the demands of all workers (especially Turkish Airlines workers) against the usurpation of rights, the struggle against all sexual orientation and gender identity discrimination and against all obstacles to citizens' access to the right to education and health.

Representatives of Taksim Solidarity also met with Prime Minister Erdoğan after meeting with Arınç. The content of that meeting was made public much later by Cem Tüzün, a leading figure in Taksim Solidarity. Tüzün recounted (Terkoğlu, 2022):

> The Prime Minister arrived. He started to make a presentation with videos prepared by the police, complaining about the protesters in Gezi. The participants showed that they were uncomfortable with it. The Prime Minister was speaking in a scolding tone. I said, 'We did not come here to listen to the speeches we have been listening to for days; we came here to express our demands and find a solution. Six of our friends came; they were at the door. If they do not come in, I am leaving too', and I left. [...] Mahsun Kırmızıgül [Turkish singer, producer] came after me and calmed me down. They let us in again with six other people. Arzu Çerkezoğlu [leftist trade unionist] asked to speak after me. While she was talking, Erdoğan suddenly got angry. He said, 'Do not tell me about sociology; look how many votes I get and how many votes the parties you support get.' He stood up angrily. When he stood up, everyone stood up. At that time, Beyza Metin [a leading figure in Taksim Solidarity] said, 'You cannot talk to a woman like that; know your place.' Erdoğan thought that Arzu Çerkezoğlu said this. He turned to her in anger. 'You know your limits,' he said. It was like he was having a crisis. His words were jumbled. Sümeyye Erdoğan and his party members intervened and took him away.

This description of Erdoğan's anger reflected the AKP regime's general view of the Gezi movement. Throughout Turkey, the police intervened harshly against protestors and eight citizens lost their lives. Berkin Elvan, a 12-year-old boy, was killed by a gas canister launched by police, and a police bullet killed a worker named Ethem Sarısülük. A 19-year-old student, Ali İsmail Korkmaz, was also brutally beaten to death by government supporters in a dark street while fleeing police violence. The government preferred to close almost all doors of reconciliation for about a month, during which time they attempted to suppress the movement through violence. On June 15, police entered Gezi Park and dispersed the protesters by dismantling their tents. Despite brutal violence on the part of the police, the nationwide protests continued for about two more weeks, finally subsiding at the end of June.

The Gezi resistance failed to overthrow the AKP for many reasons; it was a people's movement that started and progressed spontaneously, lacked political leadership, a defined agenda, and any real prospect of power. Still, it became one of the critical events in the history of social struggles in Turkey, and it had reverberations around the world. It included millions of participants, had a nationwide impact, impressive duration, and international recognition and support. Its significance as a watershed moment in the country's history meant that, after the Gezi resistance, all political actors in Turkey started to reposition themselves and form new alliances or end old ones. Nevertheless, despite various crises, the AKP's regime-building process regained momentum. Some elements of the social opposition expected the protests to continue after the summer when workers and students returned to the big cities, but it did not happen. Even without the protests, however, stability did not return to the country and Turkish politics entered a new turbulent period in December 2013, when tensions between AKP and the Gülenists came to a head.

Signs of this new crisis began in November 2013 when the government was preparing a new draft law on private teaching institutions, one that targeted the Gülenists. Teaching institutions had historically been at the center of the organization and its plan to educate its cadre, and schools were financed by the donations of network members. Although negotiations were opened between the government and the Gülenists behind closed doors, the Gülenists were disappointed in the results. The network then decided to use its power in the judiciary and the police, which it directed against its rivals within the AKP in the past, against the ruling party. Between December 17 and 25, 2013, anti-government operations were undertaken as the Gülenists took on Erdoğan and the AKP over corruption. Propaganda was released but other more direct actions were carried out. On December 17, the children of some cabinet ministers were detained. The sons of the Interior Minister, the Economy Minister, and the Minister of Environment and Urbanization were accused of accepting bribes and being involved in corruption. The next day, prosecutors submitted documents they prepared calling for the detention of the ministers themselves, but the investigations were never carried out. On December 25, Gülenist prosecutors also issued a detention warrant for Prime Minister Erdoğan's son, Bilal Erdoğan. At that time, the newly appointed Minister of Interior placed government police officers around Erdoğan's house and ordered the officers to confront any Gülenists who may appear. With tensions rising between the two powerful factions, Turkey was experiencing an unprecedented state-level crisis.

The Gülenists took a risky step by detaining the children of ministers, however, the AKP blocked further legal actions by effectively stonewalling the judiciary and the police through pro-AKP appointees inside those offices. The government went on to dismiss the remaining Gülenist prosecutors and police officers, either relocating them or suspending some of them completely, thus repelling the Gülenists' attack through careful political resource management. However, video and audio recordings and documents publicized by the Gülenist network revealed the extent of the bribery and corruption surrounding the AKP. Upon those revelations, the government's hegemony crisis, which started with Gezi, deepened, dealing the regime-building process a second major blow.

Despite the deepening crisis, Erdoğan survived the Gülenist's anti-government operations and deepening hegemony crisis without resigning or being overthrown. The third round in the battle took place months later during municipal elections on March 30, 2014, when the opposition believed that Erdoğan's government would suffer a significant defeat and that it would be the beginning of the end for the regime. Instead, the AKP won 42.8% of the votes, 4.5 points more than the votes the party recorded in the previous municipal election. The CHP's main opposition also increased its vote share by 3.3%, coming in at 26% support overall. Unsurprisingly, the AKP presented their success as a victory against the December operations and started work immediately to secure the upcoming presidential election.

The AKP successfully sent Abdullah Gül to the Presidential Palace in 2007, but the election process was fraught with crises. The government held a constitutional referendum the same year, placing the president's election in the hands of the people instead of parliamentarians. The referendum result was a success for the AKP, and after Prime Minister Erdoğan ran for the presidency in 2014 and won, he often reminded the press that he was "the first president elected by the people." Based on the referendum, Erdoğan and the AKP created a narrative that the country had been founded for the second time by

Erdoğan, the first time being by the cultural icon Mustafa Kemal Atatürk. In 2018, Erdoğan said, "I believe the 26th Term Turkish Grand National Assembly is the second constituent assembly after the First Assembly" (TCCB, 2018) and in a speech in 2021, AKP founding member Latif Cem Baran said, "The leadership of the President has re-established Turkey. If you will excuse the expression, the President is the second Atatürk" (soL, 2021a). Moreover, Erdoğan also adopted the discourse that, unlike Atatürk and İnönü, the founders of the Republic, he was elected to the presidency directly by the vote of the people, making him the direct representative of the "national will." According to him, Turkey had been ruled by tutelary forces for a long time – i.e., free elections were held but the government was ruled by non-democratic actors – and now the true will of the nation was represented by the office of the president.

As an elected President, Erdoğan had to resign from his position as AKP chairman, since the President had to be "neutral" in Turkey's parliamentary system. Foreign Minister Ahmet Davutoğlu became both the party's chairman and the prime minister, and Erdoğan's new role as president became a critical one in terms of regime building. Despite the neutrality rule, he clarified his stance from the beginning, claiming that he "will not be neutral" (Evrensel, 2014a). In this way, Erdoğan openly transformed the presidency from a symbolic and impartial office into an executive office. The power within the executive apparatus had passed from the council of ministers and parliament to the president; in other words, Turkey had stepped into a de facto presidential system.

The large residential palace that Erdoğan built for himself symbolizes this de facto system. Erdoğan preferred to live in the palace he called "Külliye" instead of the Çankaya Mansion (Turkish: *Çankaya Köşkü*), where all the presidents of Turkey, including Abdullah Gül, had resided. It was not simply about a desire for show or luxury. Erdoğan intended to live in a building that would symbolize his legacy as the "second founder", whereas the Çankaya Mansion was historically associated with Atatürk. Moreover, Erdoğan draws links to the Ottoman past and has expressed his wish to be a kind of a "sultan," a desire common with other political actors of Turkish Islamism. Over time, he gradually transferred power from parliament to his residence at the palace.

With pressure from the Young Turks, the earliest opposition movement in the Ottoman Empire, the first constitution was proclaimed, and the first Parliament was formed in 1876. However, one of the favourite sultans of Turkish Islamism – and Erdoğan's idol – Abdulhamid II suspended the constitution, sent the Parliament on vacation by using the Ottoman-Russian war in 1878 as a justification, and ruled the country alone until the 1908 revolution. Afterwards, a constitutional and parliamentary regime was re-established in the country.

Following the defeat of the Ottoman Empire in World War I and the success of the War of Independence under the leadership of Mustafa Kemal, the Republic of Turkey was formed in 1923 under a parliamentary system. The phrase "sovereignty belongs to the nation unconditionally," used by Mustafa Kemal during the War of Independence, meant that the nation's sovereignty was taken from the sultan in İstanbul and given to the newly established Turkish Grand National Assembly in Ankara. After the results of the 2014 elections, sovereignty passed from parliament to the palace once again, and the source of the sovereignty – although not directly stated – became God. Similarly, the supreme principle of the regime built by AKP and Erdoğan is the religion of Islam, although it has never been officially declared, and the AKP's regime is based on the gradual Islamization of the political, public, and social spheres. Notably, Mustafa Kemal gave a secular collective identity to the country with specific terminology surrounding "the nation". Redefining that national identity would later become part of the AKP's Islamization strategies.

With Erdoğan's presidency and palace-rule, the AKP continued their regime-building, although the June 7, 2015 elections interrupted the process for a short period. The AKP finished the elections in first place but lost approximately 9% of voter support compared to the previous election and the number of deputies of the AKP in the Parliament decreased from 327 to 258, preventing the AKP from forming a one-party government. For their part, the CHP lost around 1% of its votes and three parliamentary seats compared to the previous election.

The lost votes in question were picked up by other parties after debates on the Kurdish question. The AKP government implemented a "solution process" in 2013 to address the Kurdish situation and Turkey's National Intelligence Organization (Turkish: *Milli İstihbarat Teşkilatı*, MIT) started direct talks with Abdullah Öcalan, the leader of the outlawed Kurdistan Workers' Party (Kurdish: *Partiya Karkerên Kurdistanê*, PKK), who had been imprisoned for many years. While the PKK was pulling its armed forces out of the borderlands, the HDP, as the legal party of the Kurdish political movement, found significant upward momentum under the leadership of its young and famous leader, Selahattin Demirtaş, who made gains over some of the leftist/socialist forces in the country. Demirtaş was presenting a rhetoric of "being from Turkey" which appealed not only to Kurds looking to fortify their identities in Turkey but also to some native Turks. This position was also echoed in mainstream media. It was also one of the main reasons behind the increasing support for HDP, which used the platform to lure more conservative voters. The party won 13.4% of the votes in 2013, the highest rate of votes Kurdish politicians had ever received. However, at the same time, opening the political sphere to Kurdish politics through the "solution process" brought negative reactions from hardline

Turkish nationalists, and a new nationalist wave arose in Turkish politics. This nationalistic fervour would benefit the traditional party of Turkish nationalism, the Nationalist Movement Party (Turkish: *Milliyetçi Hareket Partisi,* MHP), which would increase the number of parliamentary seats to 80, turning a 3.3% increase in votes into 27 new deputies. When the four parties all exceeded the 10% electoral threshold, the AKP could only continue on its way with a coalition government, another blow to their regime-building process. Erdoğan instead chose not to recognize the election results and called for a new election. The consequences of this choice would soon become apparent.

The bombing attack by ISIS on HDP's election rally in Diyarbakır on June 5, only two days before the election, was a harbinger of future chaos. Five people lost their lives and many more were injured by the bombing. Two days after the elections, Aytaç Baran, the President of the Science Service and Solidarity Research Association (Turkish: *İlim Hizmet Yardımlaşma ve Araştırma Derneği,* İHYA-DER), known for his closeness to the Free Cause Party (Turkish: *Hür Dava Partisi,* HÜDA-PAR), the legal wing of Turkey's Hezbollah, was killed in an armed attack in Diyarbakır. Although the PKK declared that it had nothing to do with the attack, Hezbollah militias took to the streets the next day and killed four PKK sympathizers. After the events, HDP Chairman Demirtaş made a prediction (Cumhuriyet, 2015):

> The country's President and Prime Minister are still silent. Someone has taken action to start a civil war in the country, but the Prime Minister is not there. Neither are the President or the ministers. The Minister of the Interior and the Minister of Justice do not say anything. [They will] let the country get into chaos, let a civil war break out, and then [they will say], "Look and appreciate the value of the AKP. The country was plunged into chaos and turmoil when the AKP was not the government."

Events were also unfolding in the capital, Ankara, dragging the country into a new political crisis. President Erdoğan appointed AKP Chairman Davutoğlu to form the government, but he was looking for grounds to lead the country into fresh elections. As a kind of "distraction tactic," the AKP organized "exploratory" talks with the CHP, but negotiations to form a real coalition never took place. On the contrary, the CHP offered to form a coalition government under the prime ministership of MHP Chairman Devlet Bahçeli, who won the elections as the third party, to establish a transitional government without the AKP, but Bahçeli rejected this offer. Later, this rejection revealed itself as the first step taken by the MHP to ally with the AKP.

It was clear that the "solution process" was coming to an end. The PKK withdrew its armed forces and decided on a ceasefire based on the advice of their leader, Öcalan, while the government was still doing nothing to fulfil its promises to solve the "Kurdish problem". Both sides knew that there was no real "peace" in this situation and that only a temporary ceasefire had been reached. Without firm agreements in place, clashes would surely resume. On July 15, 2015, the PKK declared that the "solution process" was over, saying that government promises were not fulfilled. Only five days after this statement, a bloody attack in the Suruç district of Urfa on the Syrian border shook the country. Members of the Socialist Youth Associations Federation (Turkish: *Sosyalist Gençlik Dernekleri Federasyonu,* SGDF), the youth organization of the Socialist Party of the Oppressed (Turkish: *Ezilenlerin Sosyalist Partisi,* ESP) known for its ties to Kurdish politics, gathered at the border to send toys for children in Kobanî, one of the symbols of the Kurds' resistance against ISIS in Northern Syria. Thirty-four people lost their lives in the July 20 attack there, and many others were injured in the suicide bombing organized by ISIS. On July 22, again in the Ceylanpınar district of Urfa, two police officers were shot dead. Although the PKK first claimed responsibility, they later claimed the violence was a result of provocation. The official end of the resolution process came on July 24, when the government embarked upon a new war against Kurdish factions.

The day before, news agencies reported that Erdoğan and US President Obama spoke on the phone and that long-standing negotiations between the US and Turkey were concluded, Turkey joined the anti-ISIS coalition and agreed to open a military base in İncirlik, Adana to coalition forces. In return, the US would allow Turkey to establish safe zones within 30 km of the Syrian border. On the day of the agreement, ISIS fired on Turkish Armed Forces (Turkish: *Türk Silahlı Kuvvetleri,* TSK) members and killed one for the first time in the Kilis district on the border. On July 24, the TSK launched air and ground attacks on PKK camps in the northern part of Iraq, at Qandil, and on ISIS positions in Syria. In İstanbul, houses allegedly belonging to the outlawed Revolutionary People's Liberation Party/Front (Turkish: *Devrimci Halk Kurtuluş Partisi-Cephesi,* DHKP-C) were raided. A multi-front war had begun, and it was a conflict that would soon prove to be part of the government's regime-building process.

During these skirmishes, Davutoğlu returned the task of forming the government to Erdoğan; however, Erdoğan refused to allow anyone to act as second in command. Thus, the decision was made to call a new election on November 1. The ongoing conflict intensified as the elections approached. PKK raided a police station in Dağlıca on September 7, killing 16 soldiers, and organized an attack in Iğdır on September 8, killing 13 police officers. Immediately after these attacks, crowds in the country's western regions took to the streets, targeting HDP buildings in various cities. The buildings were raided, stoned, and burned to the ground, but security forces did not intervene since the chaotic atmosphere served the regime-building plans of the government. The peak of this bloody process was the October 10 bombing in Ankara (Bianet, 2019).

The October 10 attack was the most violent terrorist attack in the history of Turkey. On that day, 103 people at a rally organized by social opposition forces in Ankara were killed by suicide bombers. Violence continued in the aftermath and fear gripped the nation. Security became the primary concern, and it seemed inevitable that this fear would translate into solid support for the ruling party at the polls. Between June 7 and November 1, a span of approximately five months, 862 people lost their lives in attacks, and the AKP got the desired result in the elections held on November 1. The AKP's votes rose from 40% to 49.5%, and the number of their deputies in parliament increased from 258 to 317. The AKP was able to form a government on its own and continue its regime building unchecked, which brought about further conflicts and crises.

After his election victory, Erdoğan asked Davutoğlu to form the government, but the power remained in Erdoğan's hands. Davutoğlu, a politician with an academic background and a man Erdoğan respected by calling him "hodja," was a figure who tended to expand his autonomy. When he tried to widen his influence within the party, he faced other cliques and the opposition of Erdoğan's son-in-law, Berat Albayrak. The opposition, "The Pelikan Group", so named after a file they prepared about Davutoğlu dubbed "the Pelikan file," yielded quick results. Erdoğan forced Davutoğlu to resign approximately six months after the elections. Binali Yıldırım, who is known to be more easily controlled, replaced Davutoğlu on May 24, 2016. Less than two months later, the coup attempt of July 15 would bring critical changes in Turkish politics.

Although more than six years have passed, details about the coup attempt on July 15, 2016, have remained cloudy in many aspects. It seems clear that Gülenist military officers and smaller groups collaborating with them were behind the coup attempt; however, the general opinion is that the AKP, which had advance warning of the coup, pushed the Gülenists to take early action and thus rendered their attempt futile. The AKP foiled the coup with the support of the MIT and anti-Gülen officers in the army and by calling the people to the streets to stand against the plotters. Questions such as what happened that night, what kind of talks and negotiations occurred, and who may have changed sides remain unanswered. Researchers and journalists in Turkey continue to share new findings about the July 15 coup attempt with the public (see, Terkoğlu, 2020). In the context of this study, what is of primary interest is that the coup attempt prompted the AKP to accelerate the construction of its regime. The AKP turned the crisis into an opportunity and took steps to give this ongoing construction process an official constitutional status.

On July 6, 2016, five days after the coup attempt, Erdoğan declared a state of emergency that they claimed would stay in place for three months. He stated the decision was "so that the terrorist organization that attempted a coup and all its parts can be brought down quickly" (AA, 2016). Instead, the state of emergency was extended seven times and remained in effect for two years. The AKP used the emergency declaration as a tool to suppress all opposition groups and build its regime. In particular, with the power to issue a Decree Law (Turkish: *Kanun Hükmünde Kararname,* KHK) granted by the state of emergency, large-scale purges were carried out within the state apparatus, and in this process, not only the Gülenists but also those from other anti-AKP circles lost their jobs. While the legislative apparatus was disabled through decrees, power was concentrated in the executive branch, headed by Erdoğan. The high judiciary refused to audit or repeal the emergency decrees and Erdoğan gained almost unlimited power which he used to change the structure of the state apparatus. In the state's bureaucracy, judiciary, police, and army, there was only one appointment criterion: loyalty to Erdoğan.

After being elected President, Erdoğan kept his promise to not remain neutral. He oversaw his party's election campaigns and said, "the parliamentary system is now in the waiting room" (Evrensel, 2015). However, he still had to be somewhat cautious about his non-neutral statements for a while due to the June 7 elections and the July 15 coup attempt. Fascist MHP's chairman Bahçeli came to his aid after the coup attempt by first pretending to criticize Erdoğan, saying that acting as an active party member-president was unconstitutional. Immediately after that, however, he called for a constitutional amendment to allow such impartial actions. According to Bahçeli, "the best would be for the President to give up forcing this and return to his legal and constitutional limits," but if this was not to happen, "the ways and methods had to be sought quickly so that the de facto situation could gain a legal dimension" (Cumhuriyet, 2016).

Since the AKP's rise to power, Erdoğan has seen the ballot box as the party's strength. The party mobilized its electoral base and established its hegemony through the ballot box. Between the referendums, local, general, and presidential elections, elections in Turkey were held almost every year under AKP rule. Just one year after the 2016 general elections, the AKP took the country into yet another election to consolidate its legitimacy after the coup attempt. What made this vote special was that the constitutional status of the regime change would be put to the people. Parliament passed the constitutional amendment in January 2017, and the referendum date was set for April 16.

The "presidential government system" gave the President almost unlimited power, abolishing traditional checks and balances and giving the executive/president almost complete control while leaving the legislature/parliament effectively powerless. The President was vested with the authority to rule the country by decrees that could only be nullified by law, but since the majority of parliamentary representatives were AKP deputies, nullification became practically impossible. The Supreme Court, namely the Constitutional Court of Turkey (Turkish: *Türkiye Cumhuriyeti Anayasa Mahkemesi,* AYM), was given the right to annul presidential decrees if they were unconstitutional; however, both the composition of AYM and the political pressure put on its members prevented them from taking action. Before the 2017 referendum date was set, the state of emergency was extended once again for three months, which included the date of the referendum. The AKP had already used state facilities in all elections to the fullest, and now the powers given to the government by the state of emergency would compound this advantage. Erdoğan organized many "yes" rallies for the referendum campaign while the opposition mounted no effective objection to its contents or having a referendum under a state of emergency. Nevertheless, the anti-AKP masses conducted an energetic referendum process and firmly believed that a "no" result could be obtained.

A dubious referendum was held on April 16, 2017, and the AKP narrowly won, based on unsealed votes that should not have been considered valid. In fact, it was shortly after the ballot boxes were opened that the AKP declared a fait accompli victory. People took to the streets to protest election fraud, but the opposition parties told their supporters to stay home, resulting in reduced participation in the demonstrations. Although CHP leader Kılıçdaroğlu said in a statement after the election that "we will not recognize the results of the referendum," no serious attempt was made to ignore the results, and the regime change gained constitutional status, even after a questionable election held under the state of emergency.

Leading up to the first election under the Turkish presidential government system, new alliances began to take shape. The MHP paved the way for their members' re-election by rejecting the coalition proposals made by the opposition after the June 7 elections. In the same period, it also intensified its support for the government in the name of "fighting terror." When the MHP supported Erdoğan's party-member presidency after the July 15 coup attempt, the AKP-MHP alliance became concrete. The MHP knew that the AKP needed a new ally as it parted ways with others, especially the Gülenists, and the alliance with the AKP gave MHP powers within the state apparatus that were outsized compared to their share of the vote. The MHP took advantage of staffing policies in the bureaucracy, judiciary, university, police, and army, enjoying the political and economic benefits of this new alliance. The AKP-MHP made their cooperation official in 2018 and dubbed it the "People's Alliance." After negotiating the deal, the MHP did not nominate a presidential candidate and instead supported Erdoğan. Meanwhile, the two opposition parties, namely the CHP and the İYİ Party – founded by those who had left the MHP under the leadership of Meral Akşener – allied with two other smaller parties, the Felicity Party (Turkish: *Saadet Partisi,* SP) and the Democrat Party (Turkish: *Demokrat Parti,* DP), forming the "Nation Alliance" on May 5, 2018. However, the Nation Alliance preferred to nominate their own candidates instead of a joint candidate. Turkey went to the polls again on June 24, 2018, to elect a party-member president. Although the opposition parties and anti-AKP groups were hopeful that the elections could at least see a second round, Erdoğan received 52.5% of the votes in the first round and was elected President for the second time, becoming the first president under the new presidential government system.

3   The Spirit of Erdoğan's Regime

Critical analyses of Erdoğan's regime tell us that authoritarianism is its primary characteristic (Benhabib, 2013; Esen and Gümüşçü, 2021; Yılmaz and Turner, 2019). Erdoğan has been the party's undisputed leader for 20 years and he has taken steps to concentrate state power in his own office. He has done the same in the state administration and attached all decision-making mechanisms to himself. It is now practically impossible for the party, parliament, or the state bureaucracy to make any decision that Erdoğan does not first approve. When ministers give public statements, they begin by saying, "by the order of our President." In addition, countless lawsuits have been filed against people accused of "insulting Erdoğan." The authoritarian nature of the regime is obvious, but it is necessary to look beyond those hallmarks of authoritarianism and examine the apparent aspects of neoliberalism and Islamism that stand out as two crucial characteristics shaping the party. These two elements are often ignored in analyses because liberal perspectives, which establish a linear relationship between the free-market economy and democracy, have typically ignored the neoliberal character of Erdoğan's regime. Similarly, while emphasizing the authoritarian side of the regime, the academic perspective that attributes a democratization mission to Islamism in Turkey ignores the religious ideology behind this authoritarianism, namely Islamism and the regime's Islamization policies. This perspective also does not offer a definition of political religionization in order to understand the regime.

In debating the Erdoğan regime in recent years, some scholars argued that its economic policies are not indicative of neoliberalism; rather, they interpret the policies as cronyism or clientelism in action (Esen and Gümüşçü, 2021; Kimya, 2019. While the AKP does not recognize the independence of the Central Bank, a required condition for neoliberalism, and the party intervenes directly or makes regulations that violate the autonomy of the country's supreme councils, some critical scholars contend that these policies are not indicative of the AKP's retreat from neoliberalism (Yalman, 2016). Critics correctly emphasize that neoliberalism has never been defined by anti-interventionist strategies. On the contrary, the state steers the economy in favour of capital and at the expense of labor, policies which the AKP government has adhered to for 20 years.

The AKP came to power in 2002 after a major crisis in Turkish capitalism and continued a neoliberal program, one originated by the IMF and the World Bank and initiated under the leadership of Kemal Derviş. One of the first moves of the AKP was to finalize the long-standing debate on privatization in Turkey, after which public assets, including Turkey's largest and most productive public companies, were quickly privatized. In this period, the total value of privatized public assets amounted to 70.4 billion dollars (AA, 2020). The private sector was also encouraged to venture into public services, and the state offered new investment opportunities to the capitalist class, especially in the areas of education and health. With the proliferation of private schools and hospitals, commodification and marketization accelerated and a dual picture emerged: While the upper-middle classes had the chance to access higher-quality education and health services by out-of-pocket payments, the lower classes, which made up a large part of society, had to be content with the services provided by the state, which were less adequate.

The neoliberal character of the Erdoğan regime manifests itself in its labor policies. Under AKP rule, subcontracted and insecure work became the norm, and informal employment was intentionally tolerated. More importantly, the trade union/labor movement was neutralized and began to experience the weakest and most powerless period in its history. While the regime was dismantling the labor movement, it also resorted to using police as enforcers, criminalizing the basic acts of being a union member, going on strike, and gathering in the street. In a side blow to labor, the regime also strengthened its AKP-affiliated unions and enabled workers to become members of some pro-government unions that made no economic demands of the regime. For example, the Confederation of Turkish Trade Unions (Turkish: *Türkiye İşçi*

Sendikaları Konfederasyonu, TÜRK-İŞ), which came to the table in the minimum wage negotiations in 2021, did not even negotiate for an increase above the "hunger line" wage limit they established (soL, 2021b). Ultimately, the wage increase was left entirely to Erdoğan's discretion, and Erdoğan presented a wage increase below the inflation rate to the workers as though it were a great magnanimous gesture (Birgün, 2022a).

Religionization was also used as a tool to construct a labor market that would conform to Erdoğan's wishes. Being thankful, obedient, showing unquestioning trust and not rebelling are presented as the primary conditions for being a good Muslim (see Durak, 2018). Those precepts were brought into the workplace by sects and religious networks as the AKP paved the way for a more substantial influence of religious foundations and associations. In recent years, social solidarity networks have been established to manage poverty using the resources and opportunities of municipalities. Turkey's already weak welfare state practices have also been replaced by programs of the so-called "charity state", and those social supports are accompanied by a religious discourse (see Çelik and Koray, 2015.

Until the end of 2022, conditions for workers had been the most severe in decades. The average net minimum wage in 2022 was the equivalent of $298 US per month and half of the working people were paid around or below the minimum wage (DİSK-AR, 2022). Furthermore, inflation and the cost of living are the highest in 20 years, while net profits for Turkish banks rose by more than 400% in the first nine months of 2022 (Reuters, 2022). In such an atmosphere, the absence of widespread strikes, rallies, and marches, the failure of class and labor movements, and the failure of the trade unions to grow their membership, all point to the AKP's success at coordinating a neoliberal labor market. The Turkish Industry and Business Association (Turkish: *Türk Sanayicileri ve İş İnsanları Derneği*, TÜSİAD), which represents the long-term interests of Turkey's biggest capitalist actors, continues to "warn" the government because it sees that the "accumulation regime" based on cheap labor costs is not sustainable in the long run, even though its members have seen enormous profits (TÜSİAD, 2022). But the Independent Industrialists and Businessmen Association (Turkish: *Müstakil Sanayici ve İşadamları Derneği,* MÜSİAD), which represents medium-sized capitalists who rely entirely on obtaining loans with low interests and employing cheap labor, supports the policies of the government (Cumhuriyet, 2021).

As mentioned, Islam is another supreme principle of the Erdoğan regime. Erdoğan and other AKP executives have never directly declared that they wanted to build an Islamic regime in Turkey, but they have always adhered to the goal of gradually religionised political, social, and public life, and have taken appropriate steps toward this goal. Erdoğan and the cadre who founded the AKP were brought up in the tradition of *National Vision*. The first political party of this tradition, the National Order Party (Turkish: *Milli Nizam Partisi*, MNP), was founded in 1969 but dissolved in the aftermath of the 1971 coup d'état, two years later. After returning to the multi-party, political stage, a new party emerged called the National Salvation Party (Turkish: *Milli Selamet Partisi*, MSP). This organization, which existed until the coup of September 12, 1980, took part in various coalition governments until it was shut down by the military government. When the country returned to multi-party life after the September 12 coup, National Visionists took their place in the political scene under the name Welfare Party (Turkish: *Refah Partisi*, RP). The National Vision network and its founding leader/ideologist, Erbakan, saw Atatürk's revolutions and the Republican regime based on the principle of secularism as the "enemy of religion." The abolition of the sultanate and the caliphate, changes to attire, the transition from Arabic letters to the Latin alphabet, secular education policies, the closure of religious organizations such as dervish lodges, zawiyas, madrasahs, civil law, and the rights granted to women were all considered contrary to the Sharia and were condemned by the party.

Erdoğan experienced the March 12, 1971, and September 12, 1980 coups as a youth, spending his formative years in turbulent political times. Erdoğan was one of the young, active members of the National Vision and one of Erbakan's best students until the day their paths diverged. Erdoğan, who assumed the duties of the İstanbul Provincial Youth Branch chair of the MSP before September 12, became the Beyoğlu district chair of the RP, which was founded in place of the MSP in 1984. The following year, he became the İstanbul provincial chairperson. After his election as Mayor of Beyoğlu in 1989, he continued his rapid rise by being elected the Mayor of İstanbul in 1994. By the late 1990s, Erdoğan had become Erbakan's natural rival within the party. Not long after, Erdoğan and his friends formed a group called "the New Reformists" (Turkish: *Yenilikçiler*) within the FP, which was established to replace the earlier RP, and raised a flag against Erbakan and his cadre. However, when it was understood that Erbakan's supporters would not surrender quickly, Erdoğan left the party and founded the AKP. The establishment of this new party corresponded with a significant political and economic crisis for Turkey, giving Erdoğan ample political fodder, and the AKP would go on to become the ruling party after the 2002 elections, only 15 months later.

Notably, it is at this point that Erdoğan and his cadres who founded the new party declared that they were no longer political Islamists. They called the party's ideology "conservative democracy" and called themselves "conservative democrats." "Democratization" and "confronting the coup plotters" were the central rhetoric of the party and their main strategy to retain power. Anti-AKP forces within the state apparatus were removed, and hegemony was established through this discourse as part of their regime-building process. Hegemony built on the promise of democratization was a powerful political tool and after they had secured the state apparatus by removing non-supporters, the AKP's plans for religionization were set in motion.

One of the critical institutions of the AKP's religionization policies was the existing Presidency of Religious Affairs (Turkish: *Diyanet İşleri Başkanlığı,* Diyanet). The mission of Diyanet, founded by Atatürk shortly after the proclamation of the Republic, was to teach the people the "correct" religion and develop an enlightened clergy. Diyanet was established as a part of the secularism policies of the Republic to keep religion under control and weaken the influence of competing religious organizations, sects, and communities. However, as the Turkish ruling class paved the way for religionization during the Cold War in the name of anti-communism, this institution gradually became a battleground between religious groups. Having strayed from its founding mission, Diyanet became one of the AKP's essential regime-building tools. Even in the most remote corners of the country, mosques and their state-appointed and employed imams played a major role in instilling the AKP ideology that places religiosity at the center of Turkish society. In the poorer neighbourhoods of major cities and provincial capitals, imams and muftis, who were the staff of Diyanet, became closely intertwined with AKP organizations. The close ties between religious leaders and the AKP were never more evident than when people were mobilized to the streets against the coup attempt on the night of July 15 by azan calls from tens of thousands of mosques all over Turkey.

The religionization policies of the Erdoğan regime can also be observed directly in educational institutions. Raising "generations owning their hatred and religion" (soL, 2012) is one of the main goals of the Erdoğan regime. To this end, the AKP worked with several foundations and made significant changes to the education system. Foundations such as The Youth and Education Service Foundation of Turkey (Turkish: *Türkiye Gençlik ve Eğitime Hizmet Vakfı,* TÜRGEV), which Erdoğan's son managed, and the Turkish Youth Foundation (Turkish: *Türkiye Gençlik Vakfı,* TÜGVA) have created religion-centered education, calling it an "alternative education" with dormitories, scholarships, and free teaching institutions and courses provided for some students. Vast amounts of money are transferred to these foundations from the state budget and AKP-ruled municipalities, enabling the institutions to operate throughout the country (see Cumhuriyet, 2022). In the same way, many sects and Islamic communities in Turkey continue to operate their networks of schools, private institutions, dormitories, and courses by taking advantage of the state's facilities. Children of low-income families especially are sent to the affiliated institutions of these foundations simply because there is no other affordable option.

One of the crucial steps taken in education for the religionization process is the execution of the system called "4+4+4". With this program, the former requirement for eight years of uninterrupted education was increased to 12 years. However, during this 12-year period, students could go to İmam-Hatip schools after the fourth grade, unlike the previous system in which İmam-Hatips were only for high school students. İmam-Hatip schools are vocational schools for the training of government employed imams. These schools have historically been one of the sources of political Islam in Turkey, and a significant part of the AKP cadre graduated from these schools. Today, the AKP appoints mostly İmam-Hatip graduates to critical bureaucratic posts. The increase in the number of İmam-Hatip schools and the number of students attending is seen as a guarantee of the regime's future support. In fact, according to the most recent changes, no more than 10% of students could enroll in higher quality schools after high school entrance exam, and the option for the rest has been to enroll mostly in İmam-Hatips or vocational high schools (Cumhuriyet, 2018). While the children of middle and upper-class families can choose private schools or attend high-quality public schools, the children of the lower classes are left with no choice other than to get a religious education.

The changed curriculum under the AKP is another concrete indicator of the party's religionization of education. Formerly a secular curriculum, the education system in Turkey has transformed to have more religion-based teachings after significant changes, such as longer class hours allotted for religious studies, the addition of religious courses in kindergarten under the umbrella of "values education", the removal of the theory of evolution from the classroom, a reduction in textbook chapters reserved for studying Atatürk and the Republic, along with an increase in the information about Ottoman history. Further, there has been an elimination of the term "laicism", the inclusion of religious hymns in music lessons, the suspension of classes during Friday prayers, the separation of male and female students' desks, and even gender-segregated classrooms in some schools. With these changes, religionization in education is where the overlooked religious nature of the Erdoğan regime can be observed most concretely.

Another social policy development that symbolizes the religious character of the regime comes in the area of alcohol sales and consumption. Historically, alcohol in Turkey was seen as a symbol of the Western and anti-Islamic lifestyle by political Islamists, and images of Mustafa Kemal's tables with alcoholic beverages on them were frequently vilified and used as an anti-propaganda tool against Mustafa Kemal by Islamists. The Erdoğan regime has run a campaign against alcohol use for many years and the Special Consumption Tax on alcohol has increased astronomically. Whereas the tax was 51 Turkish Liras per litre of alcohol in 2010, it was increased to 602 Turkish Liras as of May 27, 2022, meaning an increase of 1070% (Diken, 2022). Along with these tax increases, the Erdoğan regime also limited the sales hours of alcohol, conducted inspections and inflicted fines for small shops that sell alcohol, and brought in new regulations governing the opening hours of places with alcohol.

Taking all the evidence discussed in this chapter into consideration, we can state that the Erdoğan regime is built on a triad of authoritarianism, neoliberalism, and religionization. What holds these three pillars together is the populist power of the Erdoğan regime. In ideology and practice, AKP is a right-wing populist party and has built its regime ideologically and politically on populism. However, as mentioned above, particular emphasis should be put on the party's religionization policies and the differences in those policies from equivalent movements around the world. Characterizing the AKP as a "right-Islamic populist" party would be an accurate understanding of the Erdoğan regime. As a regime-building party, the AKP places religion at its core, establishes the legitimacy of the political and social arenas through the promotion of religion, and carries out its policies based on the friend-enemy distinction – a model that mirrors the divisive policies of religionization.

Elections are another lens through which one can understand the AKP's Islamic populism. With the AKP's strategy of using the ballot box as a political tool, it is unsurprising that Turkey has entered into a permanent election atmosphere, going through almost two elections annually, on average. As the standard-bearers of a populist regime, the AKP government gets its power and legitimacy from the ballot box, gets its mandate approved by the election results, and continues on its way by legitimizing even the most controversial policies with voter support. Elections not only allow the AKP to present itself as the representative of the people, but they also lend legitimacy to the party's democratic rhetoric. According to AKP, since "free elections" were held in the country, and the majority of the voters preferred AKP or Erdoğan, all claims of authoritarianism or dictatorship must be invalid.

Furthermore, the AKP's friend-enemy policies are crystallized at the ballot box. While populist regimes or parties declare themselves the sole representatives of the people, they also define enemies, the establishment, the status quo, the elites, the enemies of the state, and the enemies of religion. The AKP has painted itself as the sole representative of the people since its establishment; simultaneously, it has defined hard boundaries for political "friends" and "enemies" and established alliances accordingly.

In the first years of its rule, the AKP's friends were "democracy forces," and its enemies were mainly the "tutelage regime" and "tutelage forces." The party promoted a discourse of "democratization" in line with this dichotomy and it altered the state apparatus and legal system with various regulations. For example, the composition of the National Security Council was changed within the framework of the Harmonization Code of the EU, and the number of military members was reduced. Such major changes to state architecture were implemented through referendums during presidential elections in 2007, and by transforming the judiciary in 2010. During this time, the liberal intelligentsia assumed the task of ideologically carrying the democratization discourse. Here, the reckoning of Kemalism and the Republic was presented as a struggle against the center, state, and tutelage. Arguments were made on the dualities of center-periphery, state-society, tutelage-democracy, and the apparent public approval of the AKP's agenda, which was seen to promote the environment, the people, and democracy.

Later, the 2013 Gezi Resistance and the December 17–25 operations in 2013 resulted in changes to the AKP's friend-enemy policy. The party's old democratization paradigm was replaced with a security paradigm: Liberals were excluded from intellectual alliances, the coalition with the Gülenist network ended, and a fierce fight began with the Gülenists over the ownership of the state apparatus. The July 15, 2016 coup attempt was the key event of this fight. After that event, the AKP took the security discourse to the next level with the rhetoric of social control that was "a matter of survival." Liberals and the Gülenists were criminalized, and the new unofficial coalition partner became the fascist MHP. In the referendum on the presidential government system held after the coup attempt, and during the next general elections, a political strategy based on this friend-enemy distinction continued. Society was divided into two distinct parts, and those who did not vote for the ruling bloc were accused of being "terrorists, separatists, and traitors." According to the "matter of survival" discourse, Turkey is struggling for existence, and those outside the AKP-MHP bloc are hostile to the nation's survival. Erdoğan and MHP leader Bahçeli, in line with this discourse and friend-enemy policy, assert that the opposition is linked to, and even led by terrorist organizations. Although the names of alliances, friends, and enemies change, the central theme of the elections, namely the friend-enemy duality, remains unchanged for the AKP and it is an effective strategy in their regime-building process.

The AKP, as a populist regime, represents itself as the voice of the nation and Erdoğan as the "man of the nation." Even the word that the AKP uses to refer to a nation or people in Turkish, "*millet*," carries an ontological, mystical, and religious character beyond its lexical meaning. This particular word does not have a secular aspect (as in the Turkish word *"ulus"*), and it does not infer class in the same way that the left usually uses *"halk."* As opposed to other synonyms, the term millet has a religious connotation. For example, Erdoğan did not use the term "Turkish nation" until the recent detente with the MHP, when nationalism was added to Islamic populism but criticized by the MHP leader, who was not a partner at that time, saying, "Does the nation you are talking about not have a name?" Indeed, Erdoğan's millet does not refer to an ethnic affiliation or a nation. He lists all the ethnic groups living in Turkey – except non-Muslims – and says that they all form a single millet, without giving it a name. This definition sometimes directly refers to the "Muslim millet," highlighting Islam as a "super identity."

Moreover, according to Erdoğan's statements, millet refers to the sum of AKP supporters who vote for AKP. Thus, only by voting for AKP can one become a part of the collective identity called millet, and the political sphere is organized accordingly: As millet and its sole representative, the party that embodies the "national will," every action of the party and its leader is legitimate and proper. The political arena is opened only as a benevolent gesture to those not considered a member of millet, that is, to those not members of the AKP. They can only exist through the tolerance of millet, and the "national will" determines the limits of both their actions and their public discourse, according to the ruling party. At this point, it should be said that the "national will" for the government is manifested only through the votes given to the AKP and/or their coalition partners. Therefore, the other parties do not have the power to represent the "national will." In short, in AKP's terms, a member of millet is a Muslim and an AKP member; the arena where the national will is embodied in the AKP, and in the person of Erdoğan himself.

The "people vs. elites" dichotomy is one of the hallmarks of populist regimes. The AKP and its right-wing, Islamic, populist regime also internalize this distinction but, in a way, specific to Turkey. In this context, elites are differentiated based on their cultural identities rather than their class. In other words, elites do not necessarily have to be rich, and not every rich person is seen as an elite. The social segments which are labelled elites are those that are assumed to hold a cultural hegemony as the bearers of modernization and Westernism, i.e., "values alienated from millet." These elites may be military personnel, journalists, or businessmen. On the other hand, wealth is tied to the elite class when it can be used to rouse class anger among less wealthy conservative-religious people. The important thing for the Erdoğan regime is not that the elites are wealthy but that they have a political attitude that deserves to be called elite. The AKP makes exceptions for wealthy businessmen who are supposedly not alienated from the values of millet, who pray and fast. However, a Kemalist couple struggling to live on a teacher's salary can easily be included in the elite category.

The AKP's brand of Islamic populism fights capitalists, not capitalism, but is selective here, too, denigrating a small portion of capitalists, often associating them with "secularism." Although some new capitalist groups have been added to the traditional definition during AKP rule, the essential components of the bourgeoisie have not changed. The AKP pretends to fight with TÜSİAD, a group that represents traditional capital, but the main framework of the relations between the state and traditional capital remains unchanged. Erdoğan occasionally targets and implicitly threatens traditional capital, playing his role as "the man of the nation fighting with the magnates." Pro-AKP media emphasizes TÜSİAD's Westernism, secularism, distance from religion, international character, and the group's implied alienation from the values of millet; however, there is no change in taxation, fiscal, or employment policies. The AKP's economic policies continue in accordance with the general interests of Turkish capitalism and the party continues to act as a typical right-wing populist party, albeit with Islamic influences.

The AKP's Islamic populism also affects its foreign policy, as is apparent with the so-called anti-imperialism stance of the regime and its slogan, "the world is bigger than five." In his speeches in the international arena, Erdoğan constantly emphasizes the five permanent members of the United Nations Security Council (UNSC) and tries to display an anti-status quo position. The image of "Erdoğan as the voice of the oppressed" is a key propaganda point. Erdoğan insists that the fundamental structure of the UN should be changed, and that "oppressed nations" should be represented in the administration. The AKP's anti-imperialism rhetoric has always had religious motives, in line with its Islamic populism. To use the same example, Erdoğan especially criticizes the absence of a Muslim country among the five permanent members of the UNSC (Evrensel, 2014b) and makes similar statements about the European Union (EU). When tensions between Turkey and the EU increased, he claimed that if they did not accept Turkey, a Muslim country, it would confirm the EU as a "Christian Club" (Birgün, 2004). Such discussions arise primarily during election periods when new enemies are needed, and domestic polarization rhetoric must be accompanied by polarizing external groups.

An implicit "caliphate" claim accompanies the AKP's anti-imperialism discourse. The party presents itself as the protector of Muslims worldwide and Erdoğan as the leader of all Muslims. Islamic themes are consistently used to frame chronic political issues, such as Palestine, the Rohingya, and the problems of the Xinjiang autonomous region in East Turkestan. It is often stated that Turkey will not remain indifferent to the affairs of the Muslim world and will protect Islam against attacks, and these statements are presented to the public as indicators of a proactive foreign policy. Chronic problems outside the nation's borders are then translated into domestic politics when controversy erupts over funeral prayers in absentia, or demonstrations after Friday prayers, and religious protectionism is used in domestic policies to consolidate the electoral base. Therefore, AKP's anti-imperialism is pseudo-imperialism, or rhetorical anti-imperialism, which, following its Islamic populism, is based mainly on anti-Semitism and anti-Christianity. In practice, the AKP takes no action against imperialist dependency. In fact, protectionism policies mainly relate to internal matters, since they strengthen the friend-enemy duality in domestic politics, and thus are a useful tool for regime-building.

In summary, the Erdoğan regime, as an Islamic populist regime, thrives on positioning itself at the core of the "authentic" Turkish identity called millet, and that definition of identity carries religious connotations. This vision of the authentic national identity is embodied in the person of Erdoğan who claims to draw his power from the "national will," who claims to speak for the nation, and who has claimed the authority to make decisions on its behalf. Being against Erdoğan, therefore, means being against the national will and the imbued identity that is millet. This situation constitutes the source of legitimacy of the Erdoğan regime, in which democracy is reduced to elections, and all means and methods are used to win the elections so the party's perpetual regime-building can continue.

4 Conclusion

In his speech to his party's parliamentary group on December 20, 2021, Erdoğan talked about the Central Bank's interest rate cuts and said, "Nass is clear and obvious. Who else can say anything else?" (Birgün, 2022b). By *nass*, he was referring to religious provisions and pointing out that Islam prohibits charging interest on loans. As a political Islamist figure, the provisions of Islam were influential in Erdoğan's view of interest policies, but Erdoğan also claimed that he was an economist, that interest rates were the leading cause of high inflation, and that inflation would decrease if interest rates were lowered. The main factor determining Erdoğan's policy on interest rates was the structure of Turkish capitalism and the existing capitalist accumulation model. With the coup d'état of September 12, 1980, Turkish capitalism had switched to an export-based accumulation model, and the success of these exported products on international markets depended on the low value of the domestic currency and the reduction of labor costs.

With its neoliberal policies, the Erdoğan regime continued the export-based capital accumulation model for 20 years. The COVID-19 outbreak was seen as an opportunity to fortify this policy. It was predicted that one of the consequences of the pandemic would be a decrease in the global demand for Chinese goods, and it was assumed that Turkey could fill that void (Hürriyet, 2021). Erdoğan's "new economic model" in late 2021 was built on this assumption, requiring a radical reduction in the value of the domestic currency and wages. Indeed, with the successive interest rate cuts, the value of the Turkish lira fell rapidly, and correspondingly, the same decline occurred in real wages. The model was presented to the public with the claim that a decrease in interest rates would increase exports, an increase in exports would then accelerate the inflow of foreign currency into the country to close the export deficit, and the rate of inflation would fall as a result. However, in an economy heavily dependent on imports, primarily in the energy sector, the rise in foreign exchange rates increased all import costs, causing the inflation rate to increase radically. Consumer prices nearly quadrupled and increased by 78.6% in June 2022, after the new model was announced, compared to June 2021. Moreover, many economists argue that the official figures are misleading, and the actual inflation rate is more than 175% (Duvar English, 2022).

The secret of the AKP's 20-year rule is that, following the economic crisis of the 1990s and subsequent monetary expansion experienced around the world in the 2000s, the AKP was able to keep foreign currency prices, loan interests, and inflation rates low, thanks to the influx of money coming into Turkey, thus leading to economic growth. But as of 2013, as a result of the waning monetary flow entering Turkey, rates for exchange, interest, and inflation have started to rise again, and the purchasing power of the people began to erode. The "new economic program" announced at the end of 2021 brought economic shock and rapid impoverishment to large portions of Turkish society. While millions of people were living below the hunger and poverty lines, the profits of companies, holdings, and banks increased exponentially, and unequal income distribution became a much more profound problem.

This chapter has argued that Turkey has not only gone through a neoliberal and authoritarian transformation in the last two decades, but the AKP, a definitively political Islamist party, embarked on building a new regime in line with Islamist ideology. The historically significant Gezi Resistance emerged as a reaction of the masses against this process; however, when the protests subsided, and despite all kinds of political obstacles and difficulties, the AKP clung to power and continued its regime-building plans. Although, the political and social consequences of the economic policies pursued by the government have created instability for the AKP and Turkey entered the 2023 elections plagued by mass impoverishment, Erdoğan and AKP succeeded in renewing their power.

Following the outcomes of the elections on May 14, 2023, it becomes evident that the political landscape in Turkey has experienced a notable shift towards the right wing. This shift is discernible through the prominence of the Islamist faction within the right wing, which has made its presence felt in the composition of the parliament. Notably, the mechanism requiring a 50+1 percent majority for the presidential election has led to an interesting outcome wherein smaller parties have wielded an outsized influence within the Parliament. Both the AKP and MHP, the two prominent constituents of the existing government, and the CHP and İyi Party, the two principal opposition parties, have acted as conduits for carrying smaller right-wing parties into the parliamentary arena. Many of these minor parties represent distinct segments of Islamism, collectively forming a substantial portion of the National Vision's various factions, which, including the AKP, now command a majority presence in the Parliament. Despite the AKP's economic policies contributing to economic hardships, the persistence of a "functional" economy, albeit reliant on an "inflationary growth model," has emerged as a pivotal factor influencing the election's outcome. Additionally, the voters' preferences appear to have coalesced around a network of Islamism-based solidarity, intricately woven through governmental bodies, municipalities, foundations, sects, and communities. This network has effectively underpinned the AKP regime's ability to perpetuate itself, as underscored by its success in the recent elections.

Bibliography

AA (2016) *Cumhurbaşkanı Erdoğan: 3 Ay Süreyle Olağanüstü Hal İlan Edilmesi Kararlaştırıldı*. Available (consulted April 8 2023) at: https://www.aa.com.tr/tr/15-temmuz-darbe-girisimi/cumhurbaskani-erdogan-3-ay-sureyle-olaganustu-hal-ilan-edilmesi-kararlastirildi/612361.

AA (2020) *Özelleştirmede 70,4 Milyar Dolarlık Hasılat*. Available (consulted April 8 2023) at: https://www.aa.com.tr/tr/ekonomi/ozellestirmede-70-4-milyar-dolarlik-hasilat/2047572.

Benhabib S (2013) *Turkey's Authoritarian Turn. The New York Times*. Available (consulted April 20 2023) at: https://www.nytimes.com/2013/06/04/opinion/turkeys-authoritarian-turn.html.

Bianet (2019) *What Happened in Turkey between June 7 and November 1, 2015?* Available (consulted April 8 2023) at: https://bianet.org/english/politics/212210-what-happened-in-turkey-between-june-7-and-november-1-2015.

Birgün (2004) *AB Hıristiyan Kulübü mü?* Available (consulted April 8 2023) at: https://www.birgun.net/haber/ab-hiristiyan-kulubu-mu-22107.

Birgün (2022a) *Verilerle Asgari Ücret: Artış, Enflasyonun da Açlık Sınırının da Altında Kaldı!* Available (consulted April 8 2023) at: https://www.birgun.net/haber/verile rle-asgari-ucret-artis-enflasyonun-da-aclik-sinirinin-da-altinda-kaldi-394027.

Birgün (2022b) *Erdoğan, Vaadini Yine Erteledi.* Available (consulted April 8 2023) at: https://www.birgun.net/haber/erdogan-vaadini-yine-erteledi-403956.

Çelik A and Koray M (2015) *Himmet, Fıtrat, Piyasa AKP Döneminde Sosyal Politika.* İstanbul: İletişim Yayınları.

Cumhuriyet (2015) *Demirtaş: Bu Ülkede İç Savaş Çıkmasına İzin Vermeyeceğiz.* Available (consulted April 8 2023) at: https://www.cumhuriyet.com.tr/haber/demirtas-bu-ulk ede-ic-savas-cikmasina-izin-vermeyecegiz-295783.

Cumhuriyet (2016) *Bahçeli'den Başkanlık Sistemine Yeşil Işık.* Available (consulted April 8 2023) at: https://www.cumhuriyet.com.tr/haber/bahceliden-baskanlik-sistem ine-yesil-isik-613892.

Cumhuriyet (2018) *LGS Sonrası Tartışmalar Hızlandı: Yüz Binlerce Öğrenci Kendilerini İmam Hatip ya da Meslek Liselerinde mi Bulacak?* Available (consulted April 23 2023) at: https://www.cumhuriyet.com.tr/haber/lgs-sonrasi-tartismalar-hizlandi-yuz -binlerce-ogrenci-kendilerini-imam-hatip-ya-da-meslek-liselerinde-mi-bula cak-1011856.

Cumhuriyet (2021) *MÜSİAD Erdoğan'a Destek Verdi: 'Düşük Faiz Odaklı Politikamızın Destekçisiyiz'.* Available (consulted April 8 2023) at: https://www.cumhuri yet.com.tr/ekonomi/musiaddan-erdogana-destek-verdi-dusuk-faiz-odakli-politi kamizin-destekcisiyiz-1894061.

Cumhuriyet (2022) *TÜGVA ve TÜRGEV'e Hibe Adı Altında Dövizle Destek.* Available (consulted April 8 2023) at: https://www.cumhuriyet.com.tr/turkiye/tugva-ve-turg eve-hibe-adi-altinda-dovizle-destek-1975918.

Diken (2022) *Rakıda Şişenin Dörtte Üçünü Devlet İçiyor.* Available (consulted April 8 2023) at: https://www.diken.com.tr/rakida-sisenin-dortte-ucunu-devlet-iciyor/.

DİSK-AR (2022) *DİSK-AR Asgari Ücret Gerçeği 2023 Araştırması yayımlandı!* Available (consulted April 23 2023) at: https://arastirma.disk.org.tr/?p=9502.

Durak Y (2018) *Emeğin Tevekkülü.* İstanbul: İletişim Yayınları.

Duvar English (2022) *Turkey's Official Inflation Rate Hits 24 Year-High of 78.6 Percent.* Available (consulted April 23 2023) at: https://www.duvarenglish.com/turkeys-offic ial-inflation-rate-hits-24-year-high-of-786-percent-news-60991.

Esen B and Gümüşçü S (2021) Why did Turkish democracy collapse? A political economy account of AKP's authoritarianism. *Party Politics* 27(6): 1075–1091.

Evrensel (2014a) *Erdoğan: Saksı Seçmiyoruz, Tarafsız Olmayacağım* ... Available (consulted April 8 2023) at: https://www.evrensel.net/haber/87867/erdogan-saksi-sec miyoruz-tarafsiz-olmayacagim.

Evrensel (2014b) *Erdoğan'a Göre BM'nin Sorunu Müslüman olmamasıymış!* Available (consulted April 8 2023) at: https://www.evrensel.net/haber/98406/erdogana-gore-bmnin-sorunu-musluman-olmamasiymis.

Evrensel (2015) *Erdoğan: Parlamenter Sistem Artık Bekleme Odasına Girmiş Bulunuyor.* Available (consulted April 8 2023) at: https://www.evrensel.net/haber/109117/erdogan-parlamenter-sistem-artik-bekleme-odasina-girmis-bulunuyor.

Hürriyet (2021) *Erdoğan Ekonomide Yol Haritasını Anlattı: Çin de Böyle Büyüdü.* Available (consulted April 8 2023) at: https://www.hurriyet.com.tr/gundem/erdogan-ekonomide-yol-haritasini-anlatti-cin-de-boyle-buyudu-41952854.

Kimya F (2019) Political economy of corruption in Turkey: Declining petty corruption, rise of cronyism? *Turkish Studies* 20(3): 351–376.

Reuters (2022) *Turkish Bankers Fear Regulatory Burden will Reverse Profit Boom.* Available (consulted April 23 2023) at: https://www.reuters.com/business/finance/turkish-bankers-fear-regulatory-burden-will-reverse-profit-boom-2022-11-08/.

soL (2012) *AA Başbakanı mı Sansürledi?* Available (consulted April 8 2023) at: https://haber.sol.org.tr/medya/aa-basbakani-mi-sansurledi-haberi-51952.

soL (2021a) *AKP Kurucu Üyesi Baran: Erdoğan İkinci Atatürk'tür.* Available (consulted April 8 2023) at: https://haber.sol.org.tr/haber/akp-kurucu-uyesi-baran-erdogan-ikinci-ataturktur-305946.

soL (2021b) *Asgari Ücret Tartışmaları: 'Buradan Tek Çıkış Var.'* Available (consulted April 8 2023) at: https://haber.sol.org.tr/haber/soylesi-asgari-ucret-tartismalari-buradan-tek-cikis-var-320363.

Taksim Dayanışması (2013) *10.06.2013 Tarihli Duyuru: Türkiye Cumhuriyeti Hükümeti ve Kamuoyuna.* Available (consulted April 8 2023) at: https://www.taksimdayanisma.org/10-06-2003-tarihli-duyuru-turkiye-cumhuriyeti-hukumeti-ve-kamuoyuna.

TCCB (2018) *26. Dönem Türkiye Büyük Millet Meclisi, İkinci Kurucu Meclistir.* Available (consulted April 8 2023) at: https://www.tccb.gov.tr/haberler/410/92917/-26-donem-turkiye-buyuk-millet-meclisi-ikinci-kurucu-meclistir-.

Terkoğlu B (2020) *15 Temmuz'un Ertesi Günü Okunacak Yazı.* Available (consulted April 8 2023) at: https://www.cumhuriyet.com.tr/yazarlar/baris-terkoglu/15-temmuzun-ertesi-gunu-okunacak-yazi-1751785.

Terkoğlu B (2022) *Gezi Parkı'nı Savunan AKP Yöneticisi.* Available (consulted April 8 2023) at: https://www.cumhuriyet.com.tr/yazarlar/baris-terkoglu/gezi-parkini-savunan-akp-yoneticisi-1930557.

TÜSİAD (2022) *TÜSİAD Başkanı Kaslowski: "Enflasyona Üç Bacaklı Program Lazım".* Available (consulted April 8 2023) at: https://tusiad.org/tr/basin-bultenleri/item/10919-tusi-ad-baskani-kaslowski-enflasyona-uc-bacakli-program-lazim.

Yalman G (2016) Crises as driving forces of neoliberal "trasformismo": The contours of the Turkish political economy since the 2000s. In: *The Palgrave Handbook of Critical International Political Economy.* London: Palgrave Macmillan, 239–266.

Yılmaz Z and Turner BS (2019) Turkey's deepening authoritarianism and the fall of electoral democracy. *British Journal of Middle Eastern Studies* 46(5): 691–698.

Yücesan-Özdemir G (ed.) (2016) *The Road to Gezi: Resistance and Counter-publics in 21st Century Turkey*. Ottawa: Red Quill Books.

CHAPTER 11

Concluding Remarks
Ten Years of Contradictions and Possibilities

Ufuk Gürbüzdal and Ozan Siso

The previous decade is characterized by tremendous waves of popular rebellions as well as increasingly regressive and authoritarian turns in countries such as the United States, Russia, Hungary, Poland, Brazil and Turkey. Throughout the Gezi protests in Turkey, in particular, there were signs that a promising resistance against state repression could blossom into creative rebellion in myriad forms. Unlike its Southern European analogues, however, the movement did not consolidate into more institutionalized forms. To the contrary, not only did Gezi fail to precipitate a hegemonic project that could alter the political landscape in favor of progressive currents, but with its end, certain left alliances and organizations withered away and adherence to left parties considerably declined. To add insult to injury, the political centre of gravity has conspicuously shifted rightward with the mainstream left abandoning 'left' politics not only in words but also in deeds.

Consequently, the change in the power balance has since been twofold, with the subaltern forces further having dwindled and the incumbent party retrenched its dominance. The absence of an assertive popular opposition is felt most starkly through the relentlessly authoritarian manoeuvres of a power bloc, now represented by a president who infamously rules in both legislative and executive, if not also judicial, capacities by edicts in the form of statutory decrees issued from a lavish palace. In light of these predicaments, this book chapter concludes this edited volume by bringing together analyses from preceding chapters with a Marxist critique of the left ineptitude at transforming nascent collective energy in the wake of Gezi, which has impeded effective opposition against the further deterioration of perfunctory separation of powers in Turkey.

When we consider the Gezi uprising in an international context, we regard it as a complementary part of the worldwide consecutive uprisings that broke out between 2009 and 2015. The upheavals in Tunisia, Egypt, Yemen, Bahrain, Spain, Greece, the US and Brazil manifested themselves as other social incidents in recent global episodes of popular uprisings alongside Turkey's Gezi. Neoliberal waves of privatization, escalating authoritarianism and endless rounds of austerity policies had left billions breathless. Inevitably, the working masses had taken to the streets to breathe. For capitalism is condemned to continue producing large-scale crises of all sorts worldwide, such as economic crises and poverty, human rights violations and wars, and the ongoing and unending climate crisis; a free-market society does and will inevitably spark popular uprisings.

We took it upon ourselves to re-examine Gezi at its decennial in hopes that this edited volume could prove a modest step towards our goal of better understanding what took place in the past, and anticipating what may take place in the future, by examining Turkey's June 2013 uprising. In fact, we assumed putting together this edited volume to be our responsibility when it came to our attention that much of the previous scholarly work on the Gezi resistance had so far taken emotive approaches, either by romanticizing or tragicizing said events, while many others had limited their scope of analysis to threadbare discussions of discourse and representation. It is therefore the authors of this compendium most distinctively probe into the question of the people's methods of organizing in their evaluations of what followed the Gezi movement, as well as the transformations the Turkish state underwent.

The consensus of the contributors to this edited volume is that the Gezi resistance has already become and will remain a milestone in the political history of Turkey. Indeed, as Atılgan and Hayatsever highlight in Chapter 4, Gezi exceeded the historical political repertoire of the Turkish revolutionary movement by inspiring innovative and creative forms of political activism while still reflecting the movement's heritage. The Gezi Park protests demonstrated the potential of workers to build networks of solidarity and engage in direct democracy through the development of genuine political tools that reflected the masses' demands for democratic unity and participation, as it was the case with a number of other historic struggles, such as Yeni Çeltek resistance, the local government practice in Fatsa and the transformation of the 1st of May Neighborhood, all of which had previously revealed such potential. Ertuğrul and Topal conclude in Chapter 3 that the Gezi Park protests were marked by the use of direct democracy mechanisms like public park forums. The tents of the Taksim Commune exemplified the public desire for a solidaristic lifestyle, one that was not merely aspirational but was enacted *there and then*. In fact, as Arampatzi detailed in Chapter 6, the Gezi Park protests transcended the traditional, formal channels of political representation mediated by established political actors by embracing a horizontal and inclusive approach to politics.

It is indisputable that said methods of political activism that stood out Gezi will forever be ingrained in Turkish political history. In Chapter 3, Ertuğrul and Topal draw our attention to the fact that Gezi marked the nationwide incorporation of public park forums, informal solidarity networks and consumer cooperatives in Turkey along with a significant surge in the number of civil grassroots initiatives in such fields as alimentation, climate and ecology, which have since established themselves as familiar forms of grassroots politics in Turkey. In Chapter 8 authored by Pınar and Yeşilyurt, we are reminded of several other struggles that have taken place in the post-Gezi era, including the 2014 Greif strike in İstanbul, the Yatağan resistance of the same year, the metal workers' consecutive strikes in several Turkish cities throughout 2015 and the Flormar resistance in 2018. What sets apart these struggles most particularly from those preceding Gezi is the recourse of the former to political tactics and organizational means that materialized in Gezi, including occupation of workplaces and the establishment of democratic workers' councils.

While we give all due credit to the Gezi uprising in Turkey, we have to reiterate that Gezi, despite all its organizational novelties and sociopolitical potential, lacked a coherent and solid political platform of organization that merged diverse political forces, except for the short-lived initiative of the United June Movement (BHH), which unfortunately failed to retrench the values, the relationships and the forms of communication that emerged during the uprising. In Chapter 4, Atılgan and Hayatsever recount how socialist parties and revolutionary organizations that acted their part in the Gezi resistance fell short of directing the rioting masses, mostly due to participants of the resistance who were no longer willing to be mobilized by party intellectuals or politicized youth. It is our opinion that the relative ineffectiveness of socialist organizations in Gezi had an impact on the Turkish socialist movement in the years to follow. It highlighted existing organizational issues of left political entities and even resulted in some serious organizational splits, some of which are mentioned in Chapter 9 penned by Karaca and Balkılıç.

On the other hand, Savran points out in Chapter 2 that we need to take into account the youthful Gezi crowd's not only unwillingness but also resistance to constructing a reliable and persistent organization. According to Savran, the young people of Gezi were not only skeptical of socialist organizations that already existed, but they also tended to be reluctant to organize themselves as – and into – organized political entities. Savran stresses the importance of being organized in social uprisings like Gezi, since a non-representative "default leadership" will take the initiative if the rather organic core forces of mass movements are not properly organized.

We conclude from this edited volume that Gezi teaches us two important lessons about organization. First, organic agents of mass movements should be democratically organized to ensure representation of the people's real demands. Not every form of organization is necessarily anti-democratic.

Second, a meticulous reconsideration of the political practices and organizational structures of Turkey's existing socialist organizations may increase their political influence among the masses. Advancing a politics of *listening* instead of that of *telling*, transforming socialist organization buildings and bureaus into public forums and allowing people to form their own genuine political agenda rather than imposing a strict pre-designated political route may serve as starting points. After Turkey's 2023 elections, even the oppositional persuasiveness of opposing mainstream political parties, such as the Republican People's Party (CHP), has been in irreversible decline among the Turkish electorate opposed to the Justice and Development Party (AKP) government. While this may seem concerning at first glance, dissident people losing faith in the dull mechanisms of bourgeois liberal representative democracy may also give way to another wave of popular uprisings, thus opening up new paths for socialist politics.

When it comes to defining "the people," the authors propose different opinions that may further enrich relevant discussions. In Chapter 6, Arampatzi suggests that the popular uprisings in Athens, Madrid and İstanbul witnessed the construction of a "plural" political agency that encompasses "contradictory" groups in itself. In Arampatzi's view, the three left-populist parties – SYRIZA in Greece, Podemos in Spain and HDP in Turkey – owe their post-insurgency electoral success to their ability to constitute horizontal networks of mobilization with vertical party formations that align with the demands of this plural popular agency. In Chapter 5, Dolcerocca, Kazancı and Özçoban define Gezi as a rebellion by an emerging "new middle class," while Savran identifies Gezi with the struggles in working-class neighborhoods and the poor shanty towns beyond Taksim, including those of the Alevi minority in Turkey faced with the ever escalating Sunni stream of Islamic fundamentalism embraced by the AKP government.

For Dolcerocca, Kazancı and Özçoban, the propelling component of Gezi was apparently the new middle class, members of which, they claim, had witnessed a significant improvement of their life standards all the way to Gezi and even beyond until 2016 but rioted with political, libertarian and environmental concerns. We solemnly reject this hypothesis altogether and are obliged to draw our conclusion in accordance with Savran's analyses of the particularities of the class composition of the Gezi uprising. In Savran's view, despite the diverse composition of the assembled masses, the social constituents of the Gezi movement across the country were predominantly plebeian in essence. From İstanbul to Antakya, Savran argues, the dominant elements to the resistance were objectively the working class, the urban poor and the poorer sections of the traditional petty-bourgeoisie that, nevertheless, did not act in concert as one social class determined to gain the upper hand.

There is an academic tendency to refer to the working segments that engage in vocational fields of higher education, information technology and finance but are otherwise dispossessed of means of production and regardless compelled to sell their labor power as "the new middle class." Even so, members of this so-called new middle class had already begun to lose its relative economic advantage in Turkey well before the Gezi resistance. The number of unemployed Turkish citizens with undergraduate and graduate diplomas increased in Turkey from 2002 to 2009, as revelead in the study by Kaya Bahçe and Bahçe (2012: 172–174) among others. Over the same period, a significant increase was observed in the number of higher education graduates participating in physical or intellectual labor processes; around this time, in fact, more and more individuals with diplomas from higher education institutions engaged in manual labor to make their living.

As Boratav argues, Turkey's economy shrank after the 2001 economic crisis and reached the bottom of its potential. Accordingly, the growth momentum after 2001 was inevitable and, from 2001 to 2007, Turkey's economy grew by about 7% with the aid of an inflow of about 185 billion dollars into the country's economy between 2003 and 2007 (cited in Aydınonat, 2008: 18–21). However, as Arampatzi also mentions in Chapter 6, neither this growth, which was characterized by an influx of foreign capital and the swift privatization policies adopted by the earlier AKP governments, nor the neoliberal economic policies of the AKP prior to and following the 2008 global financial crisis have ever led to increased income levels and employment opportunities for Turkish society. In this context, whether we call it the precarized middle class or the impoverished proletariat, the educated masses who participated in the Gezi Park protests, particularly in Taksim, Beşiktaş and Kadıköy, had already begun to suffer socio-economically.

This phenomenon does not negate the argument that different social groups involved in the Gezi resistance acted in accordance with various sensitivities and different motivations, from social and cultural to economic ones. It is possible that individual freedoms, rather than economic sensitivities, served as the driving force behind the demonstrations that took place in İstanbul's relatively better-off neighborhoods. It is also more than likely that the LGBTQI+ movement, women's movements and sections of the youth that prefered a secular lifestyle engaged in the protests with their own social agendas, validating the multiple agency emphasis of Arampatzi. As Yaşlı further explains in Chapter 10, AKP has been driven by a desire to establish a new regime on the axis of Islamist ideology and has thus restricted the rights and freedoms of said social segments and those of several ethnic and religious minorities such as Kurds and Alevis. It is therefore quite natural for individual rights and freedoms to be at the top of the agenda for the participants of the uprising in a country where invasive state intervention to peoples' lifestyles is rampant and most fundamental civil liberties are abridged everyday.

The most intense and violent forms of struggle in June 2013 occurred in impoverished working-class neighborhoods, where the seizure of political rights and liberties was more densely accompanied by economic hardships. This is true notwithstanding the diversity and plurality of the participants. The Alevi minority of Turkey is the epitome of this, having lost its gains both politically and economically during the AKP era. The majority of the Alevi individuals who lost their lives in the Gezi protests were primarily residing on the marginalized outskirts of İstanbul and Hatay, regions where there is a significant presence of left-wing Alevi communities. In contrast, middle-income districts such as Taksim, Kadıköy and Beşiktaş in İstanbul witnessed no fatalities during the protests despite their longer duration and higher rates of participation. The young people murdered in Gezi resided in *suspected* peripheral slums, where the Turkish police has historically been more prone to commit excessive brutality, as Karakaya-Stump (2014) rightfully notes.

The myth of "middle class" in Turkey is on the verge of being shattered due to persistently high inflation and economic instability, particularly over the recent years. The challenges associated with meeting basic needs and accessing affordable housing have contributed to the convergence of economic issues faced by various segments of the labor force. As a result, the gap between the economic challenges experienced by different segments of wage labor has narrowed. The social and economic groups that were previously situated between the affluent capitalist class and the impoverished segments of the laboring class have almost diminished to none.

At this particular juncture of apparent political and economic leveling across diverse segments of the working class, which are traditionally deemed distinct from one another for their so-called political and/or economic differences, are not the circumstances riper than ever for establishing a bridge between Taksim and Gazi – or between Kadıköy and Antakya, for that matter – through a democratic organization that prioritizes labor? If an organized grassroots movement does not address the political void resulting from the recent elections, that void will be filled by ever-increasing rates of mental illnesses, crime and state violence – especially in its harsher illegal and extra-legal forms, as critically entreated by Dingiloğlu and Dölek in their contribution – coupled with dire conditions of the labor market.

In order to prevent the next generations of Turkey from being trapped in a vicious cycle of poverty, crime and violence in the shadow of neoliberal dismantlement of human rights and civic liberties, it is essential for the left-wing movement to urgently draw lessons from Gezi and take prompt action in organizing.

In light of all the aforesaid, this volume has been our attempt at critiquing our own shortcomings as left political subjects in the broader arena of class warfare and social struggle. Through such self-criticism, we are hoping that this volume will serve as an opportunity to recognize the beam in our eyes rather than merely the mote in powerholders'. As a matter of fact, we would be honored should this edited volume lend any help in better understanding, and shunning, the all-too-common organizational pitfalls of the left-wing movement in Turkey and elsewhere.

Bibliography

Aydınonat NE (2008) Korkut Boratav ile ekonomik kriz üzerine söyleşi. *Mülkiye Dergisi* 32(260): 8–23.

Karakaya-Stump A (2014) *Geziyi Alevîleştirmek*. Available (consulted September 4 2023) at: https://www.5harfliler.com/geziyi-alevilestirmek/.

Kaya Bahçe S and Bahçe S (2012) Observations on education and class in Turkey. *Mülkiye Dergisi* 36(274): 159–182.

Index

AKP   1, 6, 16, 22, 32, 38, 41, 55, 114, 134, 147, 162, 173, 199, 203, 217, 238, 243, 275
  AKP rule   17, 61, 127, 192, 199, 253, 256, 264
  presidential system   228, 239, 240, 248, 254
Alevis   24, 27, 33, 60, 76, 177, 244, 274, 276
ancien regime   33, 117
Ankara   4, 23, 25, 33, 105, 167, 194, 226, 239, 243, 252
Antakya   24
anti-AKP   115, 217, 221, 227, 241, 253, 259
anti-capitalist Muslims   21
Arab revolutions   18, 27, 31, 32
Arab Spring   96, 135
Arınç, Bülent   38, 245
Atatürk, Mustafa Kemal   189, 248, 249, 260
Atatürk Cultural Center (AKM)   189, 244
austerity   63, 134, 135, 141, 148, 150
authoritarianism   65, 67, 70, 96, 97, 99, 103, 124, 142, 150, 162, 173, 174, 175, 176, 190, 192, 194, 196, 217, 243, 255, 261

banking sector   133
BHH (The United June Movement)   221, 226, 228, 229, 230, 232
bombings   3, 149, 216, 250
Boratav, Korkut   34, 124, 193, 199, 214, 275
Brownshirts   161, 173, 175, 179

capital accumulation   62, 135, 166, 197, 201
capitalist class   200, 230, 240, 256, 276
çapulcu   49, 64, 74
Castells, Manuel   59, 60
Champs-Elysées   117
charity state   257
CHP   5, 17, 39, 44, 58, 63, 67, 171, 218, 224, 250, 255
civil initiatives   65
class
  class politics   124
  the class character of Gezi   31, 189, 192, 199, 214
  middle-class   32, 59, 125, 127, 181, 193, 214, 215

ruling class   38, 180
working class   2, 24, 32, 35, 44, 59, 90, 115, 124, 127, 165, 181, 192, 200
class struggle   75, 91, 94
climate-change   69, 117, 125
collective action   60, 84, 118, 131, 135, 190, 215
cooperatives   65, 69, 273
corruption   6, 47, 67, 174, 246

Davutoğlu, Ahmet   248, 250, 251, 252
Demirtaş, Selahattin   149, 219, 249, 250
democratization   16, 194, 241, 242, 255, 258, 262
Derviş, Kemal   256
Direnistanbul   63
DİSK   35, 52, 77, 196
Diyanet (Presidency of Religious Affairs)   259

economic crisis   6, 133, 266
Egypt   18, 29, 30, 31, 96
elections   4, 46, 57, 61, 62, 63, 64, 66, 68, 83, 84, 88, 123, 145, 146, 147, 149, 219, 220, 223, 225, 226, 227, 228, 229, 231, 233, 239, 240, 241, 242, 247, 249, 253, 261
elites   101, 122, 136, 174, 241, 263
EMEP   213, 221, 223, 225, 230
Engels, Friedrich   92, 163
environmental crisis   125
Erbakan, Necmettin   239, 258
Erdoğan, Recep Tayyip   4, 16, 38, 40, 57, 79, 115, 148, 174, 197, 245, 253, 264, 265
  Erdoğan's regime   20
  Erdoğan's rule   252
European Union (EU)   38, 45, 98, 133, 149, 240, 264

fascistization   173, 175
Fatsa   82
financial crisis   118, 131, 197
forums   25, 61, 65, 66, 224, 225, 226
French Revolution   29, 118

Gezi generation   43
Gezi Spirit   65, 220

Gezi Trial 2, 216
Gramsci, Antonio 21, 202
grassroots populism 135, 144, 150
Greece 29, 59, 98, 133, 139, 145, 271
Gül, Abdullah 38, 240, 247
Gülen network 241, 252
Gülen, Fethullah 174
Gülenists 161, 217, 242, 243, 246, 247, 254

Halkevi 83
Harvey, David 64, 135, 163
HDK (People's Democratic Congress) 147, 225
HDP 4, 50, 132, 145, 150, 170, 219, 221, 224, 244, 249
HÜDA-PAR 49

İmamoğlu, Ekrem 5, 66
Innovative Settlements Project 78
International Monetary Fund (IMF) 63, 138, 240
ISIS 48, 251
Islamic populism 261, 264
Islamism 16, 239, 245, 248, 255, 267
Islamist 58, 65, 79, 90, 101, 162, 170, 238, 242, 244, 261, 265, 266
Islamization 38, 249
Istanbul Canal 57, 58, 69
Istanbul City Council 58, 68
İYİ Party 171, 217, 255

Kemalism 16
    Kemalist 27, 142, 231, 264
KESK 35, 195
Keyder, Çağlar 32, 114, 125, 193, 214
Kılıçdaroğlu, Kemal 39, 218, 243
Kızılay Square 4, 105, 244
Kobanê 37, 47, 251
Kurdish movement 17, 36, 41, 46, 49, 50, 147, 166, 168, 219, 220, 225, 231

Lebowitz, Michael 93
the Left 16, 19, 22, 42, 43, 45, 53, 120, 123, 143, 144, 213
Left Party 213, 221
left-liberalism 16
LGBTI 7, 27, 177, 243
lumpen 179

Marx, Karl 82, 89n3, 163
Marxism 21
Marxist 15, 16, 92, 180, 190, 192, 214, 215, 221
May Day 3, 22
Metalworkers 51
MHP 49, 161, 250, 254, 262
military coup attempt 3, 4, 149, 161, 197, 204, 217, 228, 252, 259, 262
military coup of 12 September 85, 200, 219, 258
minimum wage 121, 205, 257
Mining Workers 80

Nation Alliance 6, 255
nationalism 131, 147, 250, 263
National Vision 239, 258, 267
NATO 45
neoliberal policies 97, 98, 101, 126, 174, 243, 266
neoliberalism 59, 65, 67, 91, 93, 94, 95, 96, 98, 99, 100, 102, 103, 114, 132, 133, 138, 142, 163, 166, 174, 191, 192, 202, 239, 245, 255, 256, 261
non-governmental organizations 7, 244

Öcalan, Abdullah 36, 50, 249
Occupy movement 18, 95, 101
ÖDP 213, 221, 228
Ottoman Empire 18, 79, 248

Paris 116
Paris Commune 28, 83, 85
parliamentary system 22, 228, 239
participatory democracy 68, 77
Peace Process 167
peasants 32, 40, 84, 97, 118
petty-bourgeoisie 35, 180
PKK 18, 36, 48, 166, 216, 219, 249, 251
Plaza del Sol 30
Podemos 102, 132, 145
police 40, 64, 161, 167, 173, 246
political subjectification 136
populism 132, 138
power bloc 100, 172, 197, 214, 271
privatization 38, 97, 127, 200, 242, 256
proletarianization 96, 191
proletariat 32, 53, 92, 123, 163, 180, 193
Puerta del Sol 136, 140

referendum   228, 247, 254
regime-building   238, 239, 259
the right to the city   58, 64, 68
right-wing   86, 101, 123, 144, 176, 232, 261
Rojava   48

self-organization   43, 46, 83
slums   86, 163, 167, 276
social media   113, 117, 146
socialists   17, 26, 39, 242
   socialist movement   42, 75, 87
   socialist organizations   4, 212, 220, 221, 229
   socialist parties   37, 44, 46, 213
solution process   37, 249, 251
Sönmez, Fikri   82, 85
Soylu, Süleyman   169
state of emergency   253, 254
students   3, 8, 22, 32, 76, 86, 105, 124, 146, 193, 246, 260
Syntagma Square   30, 102, 136, 138
Syria   24, 29, 47, 166
Syriza   102, 132, 144

Tahrir Square   31, 52
Taksim Solidarity   22, 35, 39, 43, 44, 61, 195, 214, 244
Taksim Square   2, 21, 41, 57, 58, 62, 65, 67, 78, 82, 136, 142, 189

Taş, Alper   42
Tekel Resistance   76, 215, 242
Third Wave of World Revolution   28
Third World   20
TİP   77, 83, 87, 88, 213, 221, 226, 228, 229, 230, 231
TKP   213, 221, 222, 224, 225, 226, 227, 229, 230
TMMOB   57, 64
TOKİ   62, 78
trade unions   8, 52, 80, 93, 114, 191, 195, 203, 244
Tunisia   28, 29, 31, 59, 96, 100, 271
TÜRK-İŞ   44, 257
TÜSİAD   38, 45, 257, 264

United Nations (UN)   66, 264
urban renewal   166
urban social movement   59
urban space   58, 64, 65, 66, 134, 135, 142, 150
USA   136, 143, 240

Watchmen   161, 168, 170, 172
Welfare Party (Refah Partisi)   62, 79, 258
white-collar   2, 97, 193, 194, 204, 243
women's organizations   7, 147, 243

Yellow Vests   113, 117, 121
Yeni Çeltek   80